SHAKESPEARE AND T

C000311205

Shakespeare and the Book Trade follows on from Lukas Erne's ground-breaking *Shakespeare as Literary Dramatist* to examine the publication, constitution, dissemination and reception of Shakespeare's printed plays and poems in his own time and to argue that their popularity in the book trade has been greatly underestimated. Erne uses evidence from Shakespeare's publishers and the printed works to show that in the final years of the sixteenth century and the early part of the seventeenth century, 'Shakespeare' became a name from which money could be made, a book trade commodity in which publishers had significant investments and an author who was bought, read, excerpted and collected on a surprising scale. Erne argues that Shakespeare, far from indifferent to his popularity in print, was an interested and complicit witness to his rise as a print-published author. Thanks to the book trade, Shakespeare's authorial ambition started to become bibliographic reality during his lifetime.

LUKAS ERNE is Professor of English at the University of Geneva. Holding degrees from the Universities of Lausanne, Oxford and Geneva, he has taught at the University of Neuchâtel and, as Visiting Professor, at Yale University. He has been the Fowler Hamilton Research Fellow at Christ Church, University of Oxford, and the recipient of research fellowships at the Folger Shakespeare Library and the Huntington Library. Erne is the author of *Shakespeare's Modern Collaborators* (2008), *Beyond 'The Spanish Tragedy': A Study of the Works of Thomas Kyd* (2001) and *Shakespeare as Literary Dramatist* (2003; 2nd edn, 2013), which was named 'book of the year' in *The Times Literary Supplement*, and is the editor, with Guillemette Bolens, of *Medieval and Early Modern Authorship* (2011), of *The First Quarto of Romeo and Juliet* (2007) and, with M. J. Kidnie, of *Textual Performances: The Modern Reproduction of Shakespeare's Drama* (2004). He gave the Lyell Lectures, on 'Shakespeare and the Book Trade', at the University of Oxford in spring 2012.

SHAKESPEARE AND THE BOOK TRADE

LUKAS ERNE

University of Geneva

CAMBRIDGE
UNIVERSITY PRESS

CAMBRIDGE
UNIVERSITY PRESS

University Printing House, Cambridge CB2 8BS, United Kingdom

Cambridge University Press is part of the University of Cambridge.

It furthers the University's mission by disseminating knowledge in the pursuit of
education, learning and research at the highest international levels of excellence.

www.cambridge.org
Information on this title: www.cambridge.org/9781316507582

First published 2013
First paperback edition 2015

Printed in the United States of America by Sheridan Books, Inc.

A catalogue record for this publication is available from the British Library

Library of Congress Cataloguing in Publication data
Erne, Lukas.
Shakespeare and the Book Trade / by Lukas Erne, University of Geneva.
pages cm
Includes bibliographical references and index.
ISBN 978-0-521-76566-4
1. Shakespeare, William, 1564–1616 – Criticism, Textual. 2. Shakespeare, William,
1564–1616 – Books and reading. 3. Shakespeare, William, 1564–1616 – Influence. 4. Book
industries and trade – England – History – 16th century. 5. Book industries and trade –
England – History – 17th century. 6. Literature publishing – England – History – 16th
century. 7. Literature publishing – England – History – 17th century. I. Title.
PR3071.E74 2013
822.3'3–dc23
2012039597

ISBN 978-0-521-76566-4 Hardback
ISBN 978-1-316-50758-2 Paperback

To
Katrin,
Rebecca, Raphael and Miriam

Contents

Figures

Tables

Acknowledgements

Substantial parts of this monograph were presented as the Lyell Lectures in Bibliography at the University of Oxford in April and May 2012. I wish to thank Dr Sarah Thomas, Bodley's Librarian, and the Board of Lyell Electors, for their invitation and generosity. From January to June of the same year, while on research leave from the University of Geneva, I had the good fortune to occupy the position of Fowler Hamilton Research Fellow at Christ Church, Oxford, which allowed me to complete the typescript of this monograph in ideal conditions. I am deeply grateful to the Dean, the Very Reverend Christopher Lewis, and Students of Christ Church.

The Swiss National Research Foundation (SNRF) has generously supported my research and enabled me to hire several post-doctoral research assistants who helped my work in various ways, notably by compiling data on which my monograph draws. I thank Tamsin Badcoe, Antoinina Bevan-Zlatar, Johanna Harris, Sarah Van der Laan and Louise Wilson for their precious assistance. The scholars who have been supportive of my SNRF research project in various ways include Jonathan Bate, Claude Bourqui, Patrick Cheney, Neil Forsyth, Jean-Philippe Jaccard, Michel Jeanneret, John Jowett, M. J. Kidnie, Sonia Massai, Anthony Mortimer, Paul Schubert, Ann Thompson, Margaret Tudeau-Clayton and Richard Waswo. My research project has also benefited from financial support granted by the Société académique, the Fondation Ernst et Lucie Schmidheiny and the Commission administrative, all of the University of Geneva.

I have presented various instalments of *Shakespeare and the Book Trade* as lectures at the University of Cambridge, the London Shakespeare Seminar, the University of St Andrews and the Shakespeare Institute of the University of Birmingham, at conferences at the University of Marburg and the Universities of Strasbourg and Mulhouse, and at the International Shakespeare Conference in Stratford-upon-Avon. I thank the generous hosts and organizers, in particular Anne Bandry, Jean-Jacques Chardin,

Michael Dobson, Ewan Fernie, Sonja Fielitz, Lorna Hutson, John Jowett, Sonia Massai, Subha Mukherji, Andrew Murphy and Ann Thompson.

While my research towards *Shakespeare and the Book Trade* was in progress, I had fruitful conversations about my work with many friends and esteemed colleagues from whose ideas and insights I have benefited, notably with Michael Alexander, Kate Bennett, Guillemette Bolens, Colin Burrow, Katherine Duncan-Jones, Alan Farmer, Zachary Lesser, Rhodri Lewis, Raphael Lyne, Ian Maclean, Gordon McMullan, Sonia Massai, David Matthews, Robert Miola, Stephen Orgel, Richard Proudfoot, Tore Rem, David Spurr, Tiffany Stern, Bart Van Es and Paul Werstine. Those who have kindly answered queries related to my work include Joseph Black, Hugh Cahill, Janet Clare, Carol Conlin, Giles Mandelbrote, Thirza Mulder, Helen Powell, Amanda Saville, Martin Spinelli and Germaine Warkentin. Peter Blayney answered several queries and generously shared with me some of his vast knowledge of the early modern London book trade. Alan Farmer and Lawrence Manley kindly gave me access to typescripts of as yet unpublished work. Patrick Cheney has provided encouragement, stimulation and feedback throughout the writing of this book, and he has read and incisively commented on the entire typescript, as has Neil Forsyth, a continuous source of inspiration and support ever since my undergraduate days at the University of Lausanne. My heartfelt thanks to them all.

At the University of Geneva, the Doctoral Workshop in Medieval and Early Modern English Studies has been a continuous source of intellectual stimulation and exchange, and provided a forum in which to present parts of my work. I owe thanks to several of my Ph.D. students, past and present, for assistance with my research at various stages: Julianna Bark, Emma Depledge, Susanna Gebhardt, John McGee, Oliver Morgan and Kareen Seidler.

An earlier and shorter version of Chapter 1 has appeared in *Shakespeare Survey* as 'Shakespeare's Popularity in Print' (2009), and the permission to reproduce the relevant portions of the article here is gratefully acknowledged. At Cambridge University Press, I thank my commissioning editor, Sarah Stanton, for her unfailing support and guidance. I also wish to acknowledge the incisive feedback I have received from Andrew Murphy and from the Press's anonymous reviewers, and I am grateful to Carol Fellingham Webb, Fleur Jones and Christina Sarigiannidou for seeing my typescript through the press.

Last and most, I wish to thank my wife and children for all their support, patience and love over the years: to Katrin, Rebecca, Raphael and Miriam this book is affectionately dedicated.

Abbreviations

bap.	baptized
BL	The British Library
d.	died
DEEP	*DEEP: Database of Early English Playbooks*, eds. Alan B. Farmer and Zachary Lesser (2007), http://deep.sas.upenn.edu
EEBO	*Early English Books Online*, http://eebo.chadwyck.com/
ELR	*English Literary Renaissance*
ESTC	*English Short-Title Catalogue*, http://estc.bl.uk/
F	folio
MRDE	*Medieval and Renaissance Drama in England*
MS	manuscript
NQ	*Notes and Queries*
O	octavo
ODNB	*The Oxford Dictionary of National Biography*, www.oxforddnb.com
OED	*The Oxford English Dictionary*, www.oed.com
PBSA	*Papers of the Bibliographical Society of America*
PRO	Public Record Office, London
Q	quarto
r	recto
RD	*Renaissance Drama*
RES	*Review of English Studies*
RORD	*Research Opportunities in Renaissance Drama*
SB	*Studies in Bibliography*
ShS	*Shakespeare Survey*
sig(s).	signature(s)
SQ	*Shakespeare Quarterly*

SS	*Shakespeare Studies*
STC	*A Short-Title Catalogue of Books Printed in England, Scotland and Ireland, and of English Books Printed Abroad, 1475–1640*. Compiled by A. W. Pollard, G. R. Redgrave, W. A. Jackson, F. S. Ferguson and Katharine F. Pantzer, 2nd edn, 3 vols. (London: Bibliographical Society, 1976–91)
TLS	*The Times Literary Supplement*
v	verso
Wing	*Short-Title Catalogue of Books Printed in England, Scotland, Ireland, Wales, and British America, and of English Books Printed in Other Countries, 1641–1700*. Compiled by Donald Wing, 2nd edn, 3 vols. (New York: Modern Language Association of America, 1972–98)

Introduction

Shakespeare and the Book Trade: argument and scope

Shakespeare was a man of the theatre who wrote plays for the stage, but he was also a dramatist and poet who wanted to be read and who witnessed his rise as print-published author. While the theatre made Shakespeare rich, the printing press ensured the survival of his works and made possible his posthumous rise to world-wide fame. During the years when he was active in London as a poet and dramatist, the English capital formed the centre of the country's book trade. An avid reader, who was personally acquainted with stationer and fellow-Stratfordian Richard Field, Shakespeare must have been acutely aware of the printing houses and bookshops in or near St Paul's Churchyard. His writings started to be published early on in his career and kept appearing for the rest of his life: between 1593 and 1616, no fewer than sixty-five editions of his plays and poems were published, on average one every four and a half months. Shakespeare thus came to occupy a significant place within the London book trade.

Shakespeare's bibliographic presence in the London of his own time has never been fully evaluated. The dominant scholarly paradigm used to place him firmly at the playhouse, where he acted, wrote play-scripts and was a shareholder. There is no doubt that Shakespeare was deeply involved in the theatre industry, yet this must not blind us to the fact that there were two cultural institutions which simultaneously put his plays into circulation: the public theatre and the printing press. Stanley Wells has written about Shakespeare's plays that 'It is in performance that [they] lived and had their being,'[1] but in fact, they also had a busy life elsewhere – in the book trade. While Shakespeare's place within the public theatre has been examined

---

[1] 'General Introduction', xxxviii.

I

in detail,[2] the place his publications occupy within the book trade remains underexamined. Scholars have indeed been interested in his plays in print, but their attention has been chiefly devoted to the make-up of the *texts* rather than to the constitution, dissemination and reception of his *books*. Now that book history has fully established itself as an academic discipline, a study which investigates in detail Shakespeare's presence within the textual culture of his own time seems a clear desideratum, all the more so as such studies exist for other early modern authors.[3]

Shakespeare and the Book Trade argues that Shakespeare's place within early modern textual culture made of him a surprisingly prominent man-in-print. I provide a corrective to the view that Shakespeare's early bibliographical reception in no way anticipates his eighteenth-century canonization. Rather, the printing, dissemination and reception of Shakespeare's texts in late sixteenth- and early seventeenth-century London already contains the seeds of the status he was to acquire posthumously. He had a commanding bibliographic presence among the dramatists of his time; quite a number of publishers had significant investments in Shakespeare; and early modern bibliophiles collected and read his quarto playbooks in ways which suggest they were valued from early on. In the course of the seventeenth century, Shakespeare in fact lost some of that appeal as a book trade commodity. If we imagine the history of his reputation as a linear rise from the seventeenth to the eighteenth to the nineteenth century, we will underestimate his bibliographic eminence in and shortly after his own lifetime.

Chapter 1, 'Quantifying Shakespeare's Presence in Print', assesses the comparative scope of Shakespeare's bibliographic presence in his own time. We have long known that approximately half of his plays were published during his lifetime, that some were reprinted early on and that thirty-six of them were gathered in the First Folio in 1623. Many 'Companions to

---

[2] See Gurr, *The Shakespearean Stage, 1574–1642*, now in its fourth edition, for the standard *summa*.

[3] See Loewenstein, *Ben Jonson and Possessive Authorship*; Dobranski, *Milton, Authorship and the Book Trade*; and Taylor and Lavagnino, eds., *Thomas Middleton and Early-Modern Textual Culture*. While no book-length study of Shakespeare and the book trade of his time exists, substantial work has been published on this topic in recent years. See, notably, Hooks, 'Book Trade' and 'Shakespeare at the White Greyhound'; Jowett, *Shakespeare and Text*, Chapter 3; Kastan, *Shakespeare and the Book*, chapter 1; Lesser and Stallybrass, 'The First Literary *Hamlet*'; Massai, *Shakespeare and the Rise of the Editor*, chapters 3 and 4, and 'Shakespeare, Text and Paratext'; Murphy, *Shakespeare in Print*, 15–41; and Stallybrass and Chartier, 'Reading and Authorship'. See also Straznicky, ed., *Shakespeare's Stationers*. Other publications with an important bearing on Shakespeare and the book trade include: Blayney, 'The Publication of Playbooks'; Cheney, *Shakespeare, National Poet-Playwright*; Farmer and Lesser, 'The Popularity of Playbooks Revisited', 'Structures of Popularity in the Early Modern Book Trade', and their forthcoming *Plays, Print, and Popularity in Shakespeare's England*; Massai and Berger's forthcoming *Paratext in English Printed Drama to the Restoration*; and Stern, '"On Each Wall and Corner Poast"'.

Shakespeare' contain a chapter on the early editions: 'Shakespeare Published', 'Shakespeare's Plays in Print', 'Shakespeare Writ Small: Early Single Editions of Shakespeare's Plays', 'Shakespeare in Print, 1593–1640', and so on.[4] The early chapters of David Scott Kastan's *Shakespeare and the Book* cover similar ground, and Andrew Murphy's *Shakespeare in Print* also devotes a chapter to 'The Early Quartos'.[5] What these chapters, useful though they are, do not examine in any detail is the comparative popularity of Shakespeare in print: With how much commercial success were his texts published, and how quickly and how often were they reprinted? Who were the successful literary authors in print in early modern England, and how does Shakespeare's bibliographic presence compare with theirs? How, specifically, do Shakespeare's playbooks compare in the frequency of their publication with those of his contemporaries, such as John Lyly, Robert Greene, Thomas Dekker, John Marston, Ben Jonson, Francis Beaumont, John Fletcher, Thomas Middleton, John Webster, Philip Massinger and John Ford? What does this comparison tell us about Shakespeare's textual prominence and his authorial status in early modern England? Are we right in assuming, with G. E. Bentley, that 'Jonson's general popularity was greater than Shakespeare's from the beginning of the century to 1690'?[6] This chapter concludes that, contrary to what has often been assumed, Shakespeare was a strikingly successful – in some ways the most successful – print author of fictional texts. *Pace* Bentley, the popularity of his playbooks clearly exceeded that of his contemporaries, including Jonson's.

My argument gains additional weight from the material studied in Chapter 2, which examines patterns and motives in title page misattributions. It provides a context for those quarto playbooks which were – or have been suspected of being – misattributed to Shakespeare by name or initials: *Locrine, Thomas Lord Cromwell, The London Prodigal, The Puritan, A Yorkshire Tragedy, 1, 2 The Troublesome Reign of John, King of England,* and *1 Sir John Oldcastle*. I ask what we know about early modern dramatic misattributions more generally, and how the Shakespeare misattributions relate to them. The answer which emerges is that patterns of misattribution, like those of reprint rates, suggest that Shakespeare was an exceptionally coveted book trade commodity among the dramatists of his own time and that his name had become a label with which people thought money could

[4] Maguire, 'Shakespeare Published'; McDonald, 'Shakespeare's Plays in Print'; Berger, 'Shakespeare Writ Small'; and Berger and Lander, 'Shakespeare in Print'.
[5] Kastan, *Shakespeare and the Book*, 14–49; Murphy, *Shakespeare in Print*, 15–35.
[6] *Shakespeare and Jonson*, 1.138.

be made. This is corroborated by the poetic miscellany *The Passionate
Pilgrim* which constitutes a particularly instructive case of Shakespeare
misattribution insofar as the deliberate nature of the misattribution and
Shakespeare's displeasure with it can both be documented.

Chapter 3 approaches Shakespeare's quarto playbooks from the angle of
their bibliographic and paratextual makeup. Most people today read
Shakespeare's plays in modern rather than in early modern editions.
Yet the early editions incorporate cultural and bibliographical meanings
which it is important to recover if we want to arrive at a better sense of
Shakespeare's early modern textual presence. The chapter explores what we
can learn about Shakespeare's printed texts if we examine them alongside
other printed texts, in particular generically related ones. I investigate paratextual features such as authorial ascriptions, Latin title page mottoes,
dedications, prefatory epistles, commendatory poems, lists of dramatis
personae, arguments, sententiae markers and act and scene division, and
bibliographic features such as format, typeface and paper, to examine
how Shakespeare's playbooks compare with those by his contemporaries.
Shakespeare's name started appearing on title pages in 1598 with a suddenness and frequency unrivalled by fellow dramatists. A number of his
playbooks are said to have been 'Newly corrected' according to the title
page, suggesting to potential customers that particular care has been taken
to provide an accurate text. Yet Shakespeare's quarto playbooks are generally governed by a scarcity of paratexts such as dedications, prefatory
epistles and commendatory poems. The chapter argues that their paratextual makeup conforms to the dominant generic conventions of the
time, from which the playbooks of Jonson and, to a lesser extent,
Marston and Chapman were breaking away, contrary to Shakespeare's
which reflect a more unpossessive authorship. Whereas the playbooks of
Jonson and Co. show the desire to create an elite, high-culture drama,
Shakespeare's – in keeping with the popular outdoor theatres for which he
wrote most of his plays – do not.

Chapter 4, 'Shakespeare's Publishers', turns to the people who decided to
invest considerable sums of money in texts written by Shakespeare. After
surveying and evaluating the sources that provide access to information
about who published and who owned the rights in his texts, I ask what light
is shed on his publishers if we look at their Shakespeare publications in the
context of their overall outputs. The chapter analyses strategies pursued by
late Elizabethan and early Jacobean publishers, and how their Shakespeare
publications were part of these strategies. It demonstrates that Shakespeare's
poems and plays – far from being the stop-gap trivia for which they have

sometimes been mistaken – figured prominently in the professional strat-
egies of a number of early modern stationers, notably Cuthbert Burby, John
Busby, Nathaniel Butter, John Harrison, William Jaggard, Matthew Law,
William Leake, Nicholas Ling, Thomas Millington, Thomas Pavier,
Robert Raworth, Thomas Thorpe and Andrew Wise. The results, as
I show, were mixed: several publishers made impressive profits from their
Shakespeare publications, but one of them risked his livelihood because
of Shakespeare – and lost it.

Chapter 5, 'The Reception of Printed Shakespeare', examines the various
forms Shakespeare's early bibliographic reception took. It has often been
asserted that early modern quarto playbooks constituted mere ephemera,
swiftly read and discarded, unworthy of inclusion in libraries. I argue that
the truth is more complex and that many considered Shakespeare's playbooks worth preserving, recording their ownership, integrating them into
collections, cataloguing them, having them bound at considerable expense,
subjecting them to careful reading, providing them with annotations, and
excerpting and adapting them in commonplace books and florilegia. The
various forms of Shakespeare's early bibliographic reception provide
evidence, I argue, of his authorial standing and the cultural status of his
quarto playbooks. Clearly, his books were for many rather more than the
'riffe-raffe' to which Sir Thomas Bodley tried to reduce them.

Throughout *Shakespeare and the Book Trade*, my emphasis is on synthesis
rather than case study. It is possible to focus on singularity, to start with
specific Shakespearean publications, misattributions, publishers, paratextual features or collectors, without worrying about the great mass of others.
Case studies offer greater scope for detail and elaboration, and they come
with the tempting promise that the one is representative of the many. Such
case studies have been undertaken, some with great success, and many of
them are referred to in my five chapters. My methodology has been a
different one. Research for each of my chapters has begun with the attempt
to gain an overall picture. For Chapter 1, this meant compiling a series of
tables, including the publication record for each early modern professional
playwright with at least a minimal corpus of playbooks. For Chapter 2,
the starting point consisted of all playbooks from 1584 to 1660 that may be
suspected of having been published with an authorial misattribution.
Preliminary research towards Chapter 3 went into establishing all paratextual and bibliographic features of professional playbooks published
between 1584 and 1622 and in compiling a database which recorded the
presence or absence of each of these features in each professional playbook
of this period. Work towards Chapter 4 began with the identification of

each person who was involved – as owner of the rights in a text or as its actual publisher – in a Shakespeare publication between 1593 and 1622, and with the compilation of databases with the bibliographic output of each of these publishers. Chapter 5, finally, is based on a comprehensive corpus which details instances of the bibliographic reception (ownership, collecting, cataloguing, book-binding, reading and commonplacing) of early Shakespeare books. In the actual writing of this study, much of the gathered data has of course been shed and the rest synthesized into discursive chapters in which I foreground some things and pass quickly over others. Nonetheless, I believe that a fuller and more accurate picture emerges from this study of Shakespeare's place in the early modern book trade than would have if my starting points had been more selective.

The temporal focus of *Shakespeare and the Book Trade* is 'Shakespeare's own time', an expression which I use with some flexibility. In Chapter 1, I compare Shakespeare's bibliographic presence as a dramatist with those of his contemporaries in a variety of time windows: the periods up to 1616 (Shakespeare's own time in *stricto sensu*), 1622 (the period before the First Folio), 1642 (up to the closing of the theatres) and 1660 (up to the Restoration). In Chapter 2, it has seemed useful to compare the misattribution of playbooks to Shakespeare in the period up to 1622 with later misattributions in the period up to 1660. In Chapters 3, 4 and 5, I focus on the period up to 1622 but occasionally refer to later material. While I thus occasionally venture beyond 1616 or 1622, my focus is always on the time before, on Shakespeare's lifetime and the years immediately following it. This is the chief reason why this study does not foreground the 1623 First Folio edition of Shakespeare's plays, nor any of the subsequent Shakespeare folios. Published seven years after Shakespeare's death by a conglomerate of stationers in collaboration with Shakespeare's former colleagues, John Heminge and Henry Condell, the First Folio inaugurates a new time as far as Shakespeare's place in the book trade is concerned, a time which is distinctly posthumous to Shakespeare rather than contemporaneous with him. It is true that Shakespeare may well have anticipated the publication of his collected works,[7] but, as far as his status in the book trade is concerned, what is important is that the collection did not materialize until 1623. The making of the First Folio and the history of its dissemination and reception have been examined in exhaustive detail elsewhere, an additional reason

---

[7] See Erne, *Shakespeare as Literary Dramatist*, 112–13 (136–7). The parenthetical page numbers refer to the second edition.

why it makes sense to focus on the comparatively uncharted territory of Shakespeare's pre-Folio publications.[8]

At the heart of much of *Shakespeare and the Book Trade*, then, are the publication, constitution, dissemination and reception of Shakespeare's quarto-playbooks published from 1594 to 1622, along with his poetry books. The term 'quarto playbooks', even though it may sound like a technical term devised by modern bibliographers, is in fact an early modern word, used, for instance, by William Prynne in the address 'To the Christian Reader' prefacing his *Histrio-Mastix*.[9] It encapsulates genre (play), medium (book) and format (quarto) to designate a product with a distinct cultural valence that differs from both the prestigious folio and the smaller-format poetry book. *Shakespeare and the Book Trade* examines how this cultural valence interacts with the publication, constitution, dissemination and reception of Shakespeare's playbooks.

Shakespeare and the Book Trade and *Shakespeare as Literary Dramatist*

Recent work on Shakespeare and print culture has seen Shakespearean authorship as an effect of the book trade rather than a creation to which Shakespeare and the book trade simultaneously contributed.[10] *Shakespeare and the Book Trade* is the first study that presents a comprehensive case for seeing the presence of Shakespeare in, and use of him by, the book trade as consistent with the terms of his own literary art in plays and poems alike. A related concern of this study is to contribute to a historically accurate assessment of Shakespeare's early authorial status. From the 1970s to the 1990s, during the heyday of so-called performance criticism, a number of critics claimed that a readerly engagement with Shakespeare was anachronistic, a modern perversion that fails to do justice to how he functioned in his own time. Since the turn of the new century, however, the pendulum has begun to swing back, restoring a sense of how Shakespeare perceived his own authorial status and how he composed his texts for more than the fleeting theatrical moment. This has led Catherine Belsey to diagnose a 'quiet revolution in Shakespeare studies' to which this project wishes to contribute.[11]

---

[8] See West, *The Shakespeare First Folio: Volume I* and *Volume II*; Rasmussen and West, *The Shakespeare First Folios*; and Blayney, *The First Folio of Shakespeare* and the 'Introduction' to *The Norton Facsimile*.

[9] *Histrio-Mastix. The Players Scourge, or, Actors Tragedie* (London, 1633), sig. **6v.

[10] See, for instance, Kastan, *Shakespeare and the Book*; and Lesser and Stallybrass, 'The First Literary Hamlet'.

[11] Review of *Shakespeare National Poet-Playwright*.

Specifically, *Shakespeare and the Book Trade* constitutes an extension of my earlier study, *Shakespeare as Literary Dramatist*, published in 2003, of which a second edition, with a substantial new Preface, is being published at the same time as *Shakespeare and the Book Trade*, thereby marking the close relationship between the two monographs. While *Shakespeare as Literary Dramatist* argues that Shakespeare had the ambition of becoming a successful 'literary dramatist', *Shakespeare and the Book Trade* demonstrates that the ambition was fulfilled.[12] *Shakespeare as Literary Dramatist* examines Shakespeare's standing from the angle of the man himself, his attitude to publication and to the dramatic texts he wrote, and examines what his texts reveal about the reception he anticipated. *Shakespeare and the Book Trade* foregrounds the agency of the printing press, focusing on what the book trade did to earn his writings a readerly reception. It is worth distinguishing between the two perspectives: Shakespeare's agency largely ended at the moment when his manuscripts were sold to stationers, which is when the book trade took over.[13] In that sense, this second book continues the account of Shakespearean authorship where the first one leaves off. The two perspectives are thus complementary and together show how Shakespeare's texts took on the permanent shape which led to his canonization.

The two books aim to overturn a view that has long been prominent, according to which Shakespeare had no success, and had no ambition to be successful, as a dramatist in print: he was uninterested in, perhaps opposed to publication. Some plays found their way into print, but playbooks were read and discarded, inconsequential as bibliographic presences, and the only printed playbooks that mattered and were successful were Jonson's. So the myth goes. *Shakespeare as Literary Dramatist* argues against the first half of this myth. *Shakespeare and the Book Trade* aims to overturn the second half. Without the first half, we might go on thinking of Shakespeare as someone who became an important literary dramatist early on but only through the agency of the book trade. 'Shakespeare' was successful, but in spite of Shakespeare, not because of him. Without the second half, we might go on thinking of Shakespeare as someone who *wanted* to be a literary dramatist, and adjusted his writings accordingly, but did so to no great effect. One half without the other would imply ambition without success,

---

[12] I revisit the meaning of the label 'literary dramatist' in the Preface to the second edition of *Shakespeare as Literary Dramatist*, 2–4.

[13] As I point out in *Shakespeare as Literary Dramatist*, there is no reason to believe that Shakespeare supervised the printing of either his plays or his poems (see 96–7 (120–1)). In general, it was very unusual in the early modern period for authors to assist in reading the proofs. See also Johns, *The Nature of the Book*, 102–3.

or success without ambition. Together, the two monographs suggest that Shakespeare wanted to be published, bought, read and preserved, and that indeed he was all those things. *Shakespeare and the Book Trade* demonstrates that Shakespeare's authorial ambition started becoming bibliographic reality during his lifetime.

The two studies also differ in their respective emphasis on texts and books. Shakespeare wrote his texts; the book trade produced his books. A focus on the book leads me to the conclusion in the present monograph that his literary drama is partly a book trade effect; an examination of the plays' texts leads me to the conclusion in *Shakespeare as Literary Dramatist* that Shakespeare's literary drama was also occasioned by Shakespeare himself. That the conjunction of the two perspectives is important is illustrated by a recent article by Zachary Lesser and Peter Stallybrass. They incisively demonstrate that the first quarto of *Hamlet* (1603), although traditionally labelled a 'bad quarto', is in fact a key participant in the construction of literary drama given its use of commonplace markers. In that sense, Q1, as their title has it, is 'The First Literary *Hamlet*'.[14] They write: 'while Lukas Erne treats Q1 (and the other so-called bad quartos) subtly and compellingly . . . , the first quarto of *Hamlet* nonetheless remains the unliterary acting version that, as a foil, sets off the literariness of *Hamlet* to be discerned in Q2'.[15] Referring to the emergence of literary drama in Shakespeare's own lifetime, they add:

We disagree with Erne about both the origin of this literary value and its nature. For Erne, literary drama originates in the author himself, from 'what an emergent dramatic author wrote for readers in an attempt to raise the literary respectability of playtexts.' We argue that literary drama as it was created through printed commonplace markers emerged primarily through the activity of readers, not authors, beginning with the circle of John Bodenham and widening to include a host of other readers, including the London stationers who published these playbooks.[16]

This creates a dichotomy where none exists, and it does so precisely because it does not distinguish between Q1 *Hamlet* as a book and as a text. While their article persuades me that the book of Q1 *Hamlet* has considerable 'literary value', the text of Q1 does not but is important for something else, namely its theatrical proximity. As Lesser and Stallybrass admit, Q1 'testifies in some way to a version of the play as produced on the early modern stage'.[17] Its textual theatricality contrasts with the textual literariness of Q2 (which is almost twice as long as the text of Q1), allowing

---

[14] 'The First Literary *Hamlet*'.   [15] 'The First Literary *Hamlet*', 372.
[16] 'The First Literary *Hamlet*', 414.   [17] 'The First Literary *Hamlet*', 379.

us to glimpse in the gap between the two texts Shakespeare's intentions for the two media in which his plays were disseminated. In other words, literary value can inhere in (the book trade's) books as well as in (the author's) texts. If we locate it exclusively in the former, we miss one half of the total picture. If we focus exclusively on the book, we cannot hope to recover the origins of the text.

Shakespeare and the Book Trade completes a diptych of monographs which, as a whole, might be entitled 'Readerly Shakespeare'. Either part of the diptych falls into a series of smaller arguments, each of which readers will or will not agree with, but ultimately, I believe, my work on 'Readerly Shakespeare' asks us to choose between two conceptions of Shakespeare. One sees in Shakespeare a 'man of the theatre' so bound up in the collective ethos of his company that he is indifferent to any other form of publication for his plays than that offered by the stage. His play texts may be longer than those of his contemporaries, and several of his plays may survive in variant forms of very different length, but even his longest texts reflect an exclusively theatrical teleology. Many of his plays found their way into print, but they did so despite Shakespeare and his company, not because of them. The success he was having as a dramatist in print did not affect his theatrical writing. Quarto-playbooks were ephemera, and to the extent that Shakespeare had a name in print, this was the result of his poems, not his plays.

According to the other conception, Shakespeare was profoundly invested in the world of the theatre as actor, in-house playwright and shareholder, but recognized that the printing press offered an additional outlet for his plays that was compatible with his corporate theatrical interests and gave him desirable visibility as a dramatic poet and author. He anticipated a readership for his plays, and, being in an economically privileged position as company (and later playhouse) shareholder, he could afford to write longer play texts than he knew would be performed, in the knowledge that the full texts would be published and read. His quarto playbooks contributed to the genre's rise of social status and started being read, annotated, common-placed, collected and catalogued in his own time. He witnessed and was not indifferent towards his rise to popularity in the book trade, which clearly exceeded that of other dramatists, as he must have noticed. He had no desire for a display of possessive authorship *à la* Jonson and happily entrusted the publication and paratextual makeup of his playbooks to the stationers, but he had enough of a 'bibliographic ego' to intervene when, as on the title page of *The Passionate Pilgrim*, his name was taken in vain.

Offering a choice between these two views of Shakespeare may be reductive, but I do contend that their different components are related.

For instance, if playbooks were being published as literary drama during his career, it is more difficult to believe in his indifference to his published plays than if playbooks were mere ephemera. Jointly, *Shakespeare as Literary Dramatist* and *Shakespeare and the Book Trade* demonstrate the causal relationship between the various parts of the second conception of Shakespeare I have sketched above, and argue that it offers a more plausible account of Shakespearean authorship than the first.

Shakespeare in print, 1593–1660

The following chapters deal with different aspects of the early history of Shakespeare and the book trade, so I wish to provide a brief introduction here to the publication history of Shakespeare's plays and poems in the late sixteenth and early seventeenth century. Of the thirty-nine plays he wrote alone or in collaboration that appeared in print in the early modern period (the thirty-six First Folio plays, *Edward III*, *Pericles* and *The Two Noble Kinsmen*), eighteen were published during his lifetime in quarto (and in one case, *Richard Duke of York*, in octavo): *Titus Andronicus* (1594); *The First Part of the Contention*, a version of *2 Henry VI* (1594); *Richard Duke of York*, a version of *3 Henry VI* (1595); *Edward III* (1596); *Romeo and Juliet* (1597); *Richard II* (1597); *Richard III* (1597); *Love's Labour's Lost* (1597); *1 Henry IV* (1598); *2 Henry IV* (1600); *Henry V* (1600); *The Merchant of Venice* (1600); *A Midsummer Night's Dream* (1600); *Much Ado about Nothing* (1600); *The Merry Wives of Windsor* (1602); *Hamlet* (1603); *King Lear* (1608); *Pericles* (1609); and *Troilus and Cressida* (1609).[18]

One play, *Othello* (1622), appeared between Shakespeare's death and the First Folio (1623), in which another eighteen plays were first published: *All's Well That Ends Well*, *Antony and Cleopatra*, *As You Like It*, *The Comedy of Errors*, *Coriolanus*, *Cymbeline*, *1 Henry VI*, *Henry VIII*, *Julius Caesar*, *King John*, *Macbeth*, *Measure for Measure*, *The Taming of the Shrew*, *The Tempest*, *Timon of Athens*, *Twelfth Night*, *The Two Gentlemen of Verona* and *A*

---

[18] For the 1597 date for *Love's Labour's Lost*, see below, p. 13. *Edward III*, probably a collaborative play, has now entered the Shakespeare canon and is included in most volumes or series of Shakespeare's complete works, including the New Cambridge Shakespeare, the second edition of *The Riverside Shakespeare* (1997, ed. Evans), the second edition of the Oxford *Complete Works* (2005, gen. eds. Wells and Taylor), and the second edition of *The Norton Shakespeare* (2008, gen. ed. Greenblatt). Note that several other plays I list here as Shakespeare's are likely to have been written in co-authorship: *Titus Andronicus* (with George Peele), *Pericles* (with George Wilkins), *The Two Noble Kinsmen* (with John Fletcher) and perhaps *1 Contention* and *Richard Duke of York*. See Vickers, *Shakespeare, Co-Author*. and Jackson, 'Collaboration'. For the question of why comparatively few Shakespeare plays first reached print between 1603 and 1623, see Erne, *Shakespeare as Literary Dramatist*, chapter 4.

Winter's Tale. One play, *The Taming of the Shrew*, appeared in quarto format in 1631 in a text reprinted from the First Folio. Finally, *The Two Noble Kinsmen*, written in collaboration with John Fletcher, was first published as a quarto in 1634.

Many of Shakespeare's plays went through several editions. The top sellers were three history plays: *1 Henry IV*, *Richard III* and *Richard II*: *1 Henry IV* went through six editions by 1616 and nine by 1660; *Richard III* through five by 1616 and eight by 1660; and *Richard II* five by 1616 and six by 1660. Other successful plays were *Romeo and Juliet*, *Hamlet* and *Pericles*, with four, four and five reprints respectively, including two per play during Shakespeare's lifetime. Of the Shakespeare plays published up to 1616, only three did not receive a quarto reprint: *2 Henry IV*, *Much Ado about Nothing* and *Troilus and Cressida*. Despite the failure of *2 Henry IV* to reach a second edition, Shakespeare's history plays were easily the most popular of the three genres into which the First Folio divided Shakespeare's plays, with twenty-five editions during Shakespeare's lifetime, as opposed to ten for the comedies and tragedies respectively.

As for Shakespeare's poetry, *Venus and Adonis* was published in 1593 and *The Rape of Lucrece* in the following year, both in quarto format, although from 1595, their later reprints were in octavo.[19] *The Passionate Pilgrim* first appeared towards the end of the century, probably in 1599, in octavo.[20] It was attributed to Shakespeare on the title page but is in fact a miscellany with twenty poems by various hands, with versions of Shakespeare's Sonnets 138 and 144 and three poems from *Love's Labour's Lost*. In 1601, 'The Phoenix and the Turtle' was included in the quarto edition of Robert Chester's *Love's Martyr*, and a quarto edition of Shakespeare's *Sonnets*, including 'A Lover's Complaint', appeared in 1609. In 1640, finally, an edition of Shakespeare's *Poems* brought together most of his sonnets (in rearranged form), 'A Lover's Complaint', 'The Phoenix and the Turtle' and the poems of the enlarged 1612 edition of *The Passionate Pilgrim*.[21]

The popularity of *Venus and Adonis* has often been acknowledged. It went through ten editions before the end of Shakespeare's life and six more by 1636 (including one, dated 1627, published in Edinburgh, the first

---

[19] For this change of format, see below, pp. 147–8.

[20] The earliest edition of *The Passionate Pilgrim* is extant in a single copy of which the title page is lost. For *The Passionate Pilgrim*, see Duncan-Jones and Woudhuysen, eds., *Shakespeare's Poems*, 82–91; Burrow, ed., *Complete Sonnets and Poems*, 74–82; and Rollins, ed., *The Poems*. See also Cheney, *Shakespeare, National Poet-Playwright*, 151–71; and Bednarz, '*The Passionate Pilgrim* and "The Phoenix and Turtle"', and 'Canonizing Shakespeare'.

[21] The 1640 edition of Shakespeare's *Poems* omits Sonnets 18, 19, 43, 56, 75 and 76 for reasons which are unknown (see Schoenfeldt, *The Cambridge Introduction to Shakespeare's Poetry*, 134).

Shakespeare edition to appear outside London), making it Shakespeare's most successful publication in the early modern period.[22] Sasha Roberts has demonstrated its success with early readers, and *The Shakspere Allusion-Book* documents a wealth of early references to and quotations from it.[23] *The Rape of Lucrece* was also popular: it was printed six times in the course of Shakespeare's life and received three more editions by 1655. The other print publications of 'Shakespeare the poet' were less successful than the narrative poems. His *Sonnets* proved strangely unpopular in print, although it should be acknowledged that some of the sonnets also circulated in manuscript.[24] They were not reprinted until 1640. With three editions in Shakespeare's lifetime, *The Passionate Pilgrim* was reasonably successful, yet without approaching the popularity of the narrative poems or the most popular plays. The picture that emerges of the early popularity of Shakespeare's poetry is thus rather complex: two very popular narrative poems, a reasonably successful collection and a volume of sonnets which was not reprinted for more than thirty years.[25]

Table 1 provides a chronological list of all Shakespeare publications from 1593 to 1660. A few explanations are necessary. For easier visibility, I distinguish the poems (using background shading) from the playbooks. A question mark in the left-hand column indicates that the date of publication is conjectural since the title page contains no or an erroneous date.[26] Not a single copy of the 1597 edition of *Love's Labour's Lost* is extant (whence the square brackets), but given the reference on the title page of the second edition of 1598 to an earlier edition and the reference to a copy of the 1597 edition in an early catalogue of playbooks, there can be no reasonable doubt that it existed.[27] Since the 1598 edition is the earliest one with an extant text, textual scholars refer it as 'Q1', but from my book-historical perspective, that would be misleading: the 1597 edition is the earliest of which we have

---

[22] *Venus and Adonis* is also the first Shakespeare publication known to have been sold outside London: it appears in a 1616 inventory of a bookseller's shop at York (see Barnard and Bell, *The Early-Seventeenth-Century York Book Trade*, 87).

[23] See Roberts, *Reading Shakespeare's Poems in Early Modern England*; and Ingleby, ed., *The Shakspere Allusion-Book*.

[24] See Marotti, 'Shakespeare's Sonnets as Literary Property', and Taylor, 'Some Manuscripts of Shakespeare's Sonnets'.

[25] See also Badcoe and Erne, 'The Popularity of Poetry Books in Print, 1583–1622', and Erne, 'Print and Manuscript'.

[26] For the conjecturally dated *Venus and Adonis* editions, see below, pp. 150–4. For the 1599? edition of *The Passionate Pilgrim*, see below, p. 84. For the 1623? edition of *Romeo and Juliet* and the 1625? edition of *Hamlet*, see Hailey, 'The Dating Game'.

[27] See Freeman and Grinke, 'Four New Shakespeare Quartos?'. For the other quarto editions mentioned by Freeman and Grinke, see below, p. 207.

Table 1 *A chronological list of Shakespeare publications, 1593–1660*

Year of publication	Title	Edition	Format	Anonymous
1593	*Venus and Adonis*	1	4°	
1594	*1 Contention*	1	4°	x
1594	*Titus Andronicus*	1	4°	x
1594	*The Rape of Lucrece*	1	4°	
1594	*Venus and Adonis*	2	4°	
1595	*Richard Duke of York*	1	8°	x
1595?	*Venus and Adonis*	3	8°	
1596	*Edward III*	1	4°	x
1596	*Venus and Adonis*	4	8°	
[1597]	*Love's Labour's Lost*	1	[4°]	?
1597	*Richard II*	1	4°	x
1597	*Richard III*	1	4°	x
1597	*Romeo and Juliet*	1	4°	x
1598?	*1 Henry IV*	1	4°	?
1598	*1 Henry IV*	2	4°	x
1598	*Love's Labour's Lost*	2	4°	
1598	*Richard II*	2	4°	
1598	*Richard II*	3	4°	
1598	*Richard III*	2	4°	
1598	*The Rape of Lucrece*	2	8°	
1599	*Edward III*	2	4°	x
1599	*1 Henry IV*	3	4°	
1599?	*The Passionate Pilgrim*	1	8°	
1599	*The Passionate Pilgrim*	2	8°	
1599	*Romeo and Juliet*	2	4°	x
1599	*Venus and Adonis*	5	8°	
1599	*Venus and Adonis*	6	8°	
1600	*1 Contention*	2	4°	x
1600	*2 Henry IV*	1	4°	
1600	*Henry V*	1	4°	x
1600	*The Merchant of Venice*	1	4°	
1600	*A Midsummer Night's Dream*	1	4°	
1600	*Much Ado about Nothing*	1	4°	
1600	*The Rape of Lucrece*	3	8°	
1600	*The Rape of Lucrece*	4	8°	
1600	*Richard Duke of York*	2	4°	x
1600	*Titus Andronicus*	2	4°	x
1602	*Henry V*	2	4°	x
1602	*The Merry Wives of Windsor*	1	4°	
1602	*Richard III*	3	4°	

Table 1 (*cont.*)

Year of publication	Title	Edition	Format	Anonymous
1602?	*Venus and Adonis*	7	8°	
1603	*Hamlet*	1	4°	
1604	*1 Henry IV*	4	4°	
1604/5	*Hamlet*	2	4°	
1605	*Richard III*	4	4°	
1607	*The Rape of Lucrece*	5	8°	
1607/8? ('1602')	*Venus and Adonis*	8	8°	
1608	*1 Henry IV*	5	4°	
1608	*King Lear*	1	4°	
1608	*Richard II*	4	4°	
1608/9? ('1602')	*Venus and Adonis*	9	8°	
1609	*Pericles*	1	4°	
1609	*Pericles*	2	4°	
1609	*Romeo and Juliet*	3	4°	x
1609	*Sonnets*	1	4°	
1609	*Troilus and Cressida*	1	4°	
1610? ('1602')	*Venus and Adonis*	10	8°	
1611	*Hamlet*	3	4°	
1611	*Pericles*	3	4°	
1611	*Titus Andronicus*	3	4°	x
1612	*The Passionate Pilgrim*	3	8°	
1612	*Richard III*	5	4°	
1613	*1 Henry IV*	6	4°	
1615	*Richard II*	5	4°	
1616	*The Rape of Lucrece*	6	8°	
1617	*Venus and Adonis*	11	8°	
1619 ('1608')	*Henry V*	3	4°	x
1619 ('1608')	*King Lear*	2	4°	
1619 ('1600')	*The Merchant of Venice*	2	4°	
1619	*The Merry Wives of Windsor*	2	4°	
1619 ('1600')	*A Midsummer Night's Dream*	2	4°	
1619	*Pericles*	4	4°	
1619	*The Whole Contention*	1	4°	
1620	*Venus and Adonis*	12	8°	
1622	*1 Henry IV*	7	4°	
1622	*Othello*	1	4°	
1622	*Richard III*	6	4°	
1623	*Comedies, Histories, & Tragedies*	1	2°	
1623?	*Romeo and Juliet*	4	4°	
1624	*The Rape of Lucrece*	7	8°	
1625?	*Hamlet*	4	4°	

Table 1 *(cont.)*

Year of publication	Title	Edition	Format	Anonymous
1627	*Venus and Adonis*	13	8°	
1629	*Richard III*	7	4°	
1630	*The Merry Wives of Windsor*	3	4°	
1630	*Othello*	2	4°	
1630	*Pericles*	5	4°	
1630	*Venus and Adonis*	14	8°	
1630–6?	*Venus and Adonis*	15	8°	
1631	*Love's Labour's Lost*	3	4°	
1631	*The Taming of the Shrew*	1	4°	
1632	*Comedies, Histories, & Tragedies*	2	2°	
1632	*1 Henry IV*	8	4°	
1632	*The Rape of Lucrece*	8	8°	
1634	*The Two Noble Kinsmen*	1	4°	
1634	*Richard II*	6	4°	
1634	*Richard III*	8	4°	
1635	*Pericles*	6	4°	
1636	*Venus and Adonis*	16	8°	
1637	*Hamlet*	5	4°	
1637	*The Merchant of Venice*	3	4°	
1637	*Romeo and Juliet*	5	4°	
1639	*1 Henry IV*	9	4°	
1640	*Poems*	1	8°	
1655	*King Lear*	3	4°	
1655	*Othello*	3	4°	
1655	*The Rape of Lucrece*	9	8°	

knowledge (and so I refer to it as 'Q1' below), whereas the 1598 edition is the second (whence 'Q2' below). Similarly, of the first edition of *1 Henry IV*, only a fragment of a single copy is extant, which is why that edition is sometimes referred to as 'Q0'. I refer to it as 'Q1' and to the later edition of 1598 as 'Q2'. In 1619, *The Whole Contention* contained texts of *1 Contention* and *Richard Duke of York*, but it is a single publication, with one title for both texts, and so it makes sense from a book-historical angle to treat it as the first edition of *The Whole Contention*, not as the third editions of *1 Contention* and *Richard Duke of York*. On the other hand, the 1619 *Whole Contention* and *Pericles*, even though printed with continuous signatures, were clearly issued separately, which is why I consider them as two publications, not one.[28] As for Shakespeare's 67-line 'The Phoenix and the Turtle', it appeared in a book – *Love's Martyr* – of some two hundred pages, of which the poem occupies three. Given that *Love's Martyr* (attributed to Chester on the title page) is in no conceivable sense a Shakespeare book, I do not include it in the present table.

A few plays have been associated with Shakespeare which, however, I do not include in my account of his presence in the book trade. *Sir Thomas More*, to which Shakespeare may well have contributed a scene and a soliloquy, is a manuscript play which was not printed until 1844.[29] *The Taming of a Shrew*, published in 1594 and reprinted in 1596 and 1607, has been considered by some a version of Shakespeare's *The Taming of the Shrew*, but there seems to be a growing consensus that *A Shrew* is a play of independent origin, not by Shakespeare.[30] It has been argued that Shakespeare had a hand in the anonymously published *Arden of Faversham*, but the attribution has not been generally endorsed, and the play is absent from all standard editions of Shakespeare's complete works.[31] A play called 'Love's Labour Won' is mentioned among Shakespeare's plays in 1598 and is referred to as a published play in a bookseller's account book in 1603, but it seems more likely that it was an alternative title of a known play than that a separate Shakespeare play of this name existed, was published, but is now lost.[32] – Disagree (one can hope)

As we see in the right-hand column of Table 1, at least eighteen and perhaps as many as twenty of Shakespeare's playbooks originally appeared anonymously, though only four did so after the turn of the century, a topic to which I return in Chapter 1. All in all, the number of Shakespeare books published before the Restoration is 106: 76 playbooks (including the two Folios) and 30 poetry books. Only three of them appeared after 1640 when, with the closing of the theatres, the English Civil War and the Interregnum, the publication of Shakespeare came to a standstill, only briefly interrupted

---

[28] In none of the bound volumes of the Pavier Quartos whose order is on record did *Pericles* follow immediately after *The Whole Contention* (see Pollard, *Shakespeare Folios and Quartos*, 81–104). The 1635 edition of *Pericles* was printed on large-size paper which was divided into two halves. Contrary to regular quartos, the book's chain lines are thus vertical, not horizontal. This format is variously described as 'octavo-in-fours', 'quarto-form octavo' or 'large-paper quarto'. See also Tanselle, 'The Concept of Format'.

[29] The play *Cardenio*, on which Shakespeare may have collaborated with John Fletcher, is lost, although it is possible that Lewis Theobald's *Double Falsehood* is based on it (see Stern, '"The Forgery of Some Modern Author"?'; Carnegie and Taylor, eds., *The Quest for Cardenio*; and Hammond, ed., *Double Falsehood*).

[30] See Miller, ed., *Taming of a Shrew*.

[31] See Jackson, 'Shakespeare and the Quarrel Scene in *Arden of Faversham*'.

[32] See Erne, *Shakespeare as Literary Dramatist*, 82 (106).

in the mid-1650s. During Shakespeare's lifetime, forty-five playbook editions appeared (with twelve more by 1622) and twenty editions of his poems (two more by 1622). It has been argued that in Shakespeare's own time, 'The "authorial" Shakespeare was above all Shakespeare the poet, not Shakespeare the dramatist,'[33] a view the present study does not confirm. Francis Meres, in 1598, compares Shakespeare not only to Ovid but also to Plautus and Seneca; John Weever, in his *c.* 1595 poem 'Ad Gulielmum Shakespeare', refers not only to *Venus and Adonis* and *The Rape of Lucrece* but also to *Romeo and Juliet* and *Richard III*; the *Parnassus* plays (*c.* 1598–1601) parody both *Venus and Adonis* and *Romeo and Juliet*; around the turn of the century, Gabriel Harvey names not only 'Shakespeare's Venus and Adonis' and 'Lucrece' but also 'his tragedy of Hamlet'; Richard Barnfield, in 1598, associates Shakespeare with his narrative poems, but Anthony Scoloker, in 1604, refers to 'Friendly Shakespeare's Tragedies' and John Davies of Hereford, in 1611, calls him 'our English Terence'.[34] As Table 1 shows, plays constitute almost 60 per cent of the editions of this period which identify Shakespeare as the writer, on the title page or – as is the case with *Venus and Adonis* and *The Rape of Lucrece* – in the dedicatory epistle. The evidence suggests that Shakespeare, as Patrick Cheney has argued, was a poet-playwright, whose presence in print precisely combined the two genres.[35]

Another observation which emerges from the chronological table is that Shakespeare's arrival in the book trade was sudden and massive. If we divide the publication history into slices of ten years, by far the greatest number of editions were published from 1593 to 1602 (forty-one, including twenty-eight playbooks), with about half as many from 1603 to 1612 (twenty-one, including fifteen playbooks) and even fewer subsequently, 1613–22 (fifteen, including twelve playbooks), 1623–32 (sixteen, including eleven playbooks) and 1633–42 (ten, including eight playbooks). The number of Shakespeare publications peaked early and then steadily declined over the next decades. The view that Shakespeare was not discovered by the book trade until after his death and that the rise of his reputation was gradual and posthumous is thus precisely wrong.

In addition to the titles listed in Table 1, ten playbook editions published between 1595 and 1622 and one poem of 1612 (the *Funeral Elegy for Master William Peter*) were attributed to Shakespeare, or may have hinted at his

[33] Stallybrass and Chartier, 'Reading and Authorship', 39.
[34] See Ingleby, ed., *The Shakspere Allusion-Book*, 1.24, 46–8, 51, 56, 67–9, 133, 219.
[35] See *Shakespeare, National Poet-Playwright*.

authorship by means of his initials, 'W. S.' or 'W. Sh.', even though the modern scholarly consensus is that Shakespeare did not author them. These publications will be at the heart of Chapter 2, and a separate table in that chapter (see p. 57) lists the titles and publication dates of the misascribed playbooks.

Shakespeare and the book trade's 'Shakespeare'

The book trade of the late sixteenth and early seventeenth century was centred on London, where about 85 per cent of the books published in Britain were produced.[36] The heart of the London book trade was in and around St Paul's Churchyard, which has been described as 'the Elizabethan equivalent of a modern shopping mall, albeit with an emphasis upon books rather than shoes'.[37] The principal actors in the book trade on which my study focuses are publishers, printers and booksellers, along with authors (Thomas Nashe called St Paul's Churchyard the 'Exchange of All Authors') and book-buyers.[38] My study as a whole (and Chapter 4 in particular) stresses the importance of publishers, and it does so in the context of an author, Shakespeare, whom I see as complicit with – albeit not directly involved in – his dissemination by the book trade.[39] Chapter 3 highlights

[36] Alain Veylit has pointed out that 'For the STC period (1475–1640), London publishers account for about 29,200 titles out of a total of a little under 35,000. The other "centers" of publication in Britain are far behind: Oxford contributes 850, Edinburgh about 875, Cambridge 570, and Dublin 231 titles to the STC' ('Some Statistics on the Number of Surviving Printed Titles'). For the early modern London book trade, see *The Records of the Stationers' Company 1554–1920*; Myers, *The Stationers' Company Archive 1554–1984*; Arber, ed., *A Transcript of the Registers of the Company of Stationers 1554–1640*; Greg, *A Companion to Arber*; Blagden, *The Stationers' Company*; Plant, *The English Book Trade*; Barnard and McKenzie, eds., *The Cambridge History of the Book in Britain, Volume IV*; Myers and Harris, eds., *The Stationers' Company and the Book Trade*; and Feather, *A History of British Publishing*. Blayney is working on a comprehensive history of the Stationers' Company from 1501 to 1616 of which the first volume, covering the period up to the royal charter in 1557, is forthcoming from Cambridge University Press.

[37] Weiss, 'Casting Compositors, Foul Cases, and Skeletons', 195. For an expert reconstruction, see Blayney, *The Bookshops in Paul's Cross Churchyard*. Michael Saenger observes that 'At no other time . . . was the culture of books so focused; the earlier scriptorium system had been diffuse and, by the eighteenth century, modern printing would expand to the point where no one churchyard could possible operate as a center. This unique temporally specific, and contingent set of conditions allows us to understand Elizabethan publishing and printing as a thriving, coherent, collaborative (and also competitive) microculture' (*The Commodification of Textual Engagements in the English Renaissance*, 10). For the different areas of the London book trade, see also Johns, *The Nature of the Book*, 66.

[38] Nashe, *Works*, 1.278.

[39] For the relationship Shakespeare and his company entertained with London stationers, see also Erne, *Shakespeare as Literary Dramatist*, 87–9 (111–13). Concerning the relationship between authors and stationers more generally, I agree with Weiss that 'the acquisition of texts is one of the most fascinating issues of printed publication' in the late sixteenth and early seventeenth century, although, regrettably, 'the historical record is nearly blank' ('Casting Compositors, Foul Cases, and Skeletons', 199).

the makeup of the books the printers produced (as instructed by the publishers);[40] Chapter 4 repeatedly addresses the importance of booksellers; and Chapter 5 moves the focus to those who bought, owned and read plays and poems by Shakespeare. The book trade as studied in this monograph thus consists of an economic, literary and bibliographic web of relationships and transactions in late sixteenth- and early seventeenth-century London at the heart of which I place Shakespeare's playbooks and poetry books.

The London book trade was regulated by the Stationers' Company, which had received its royal charter in 1557 and in effect exerted a monopoly over the production of books. No authorial copyright existed in the early modern period, and Shakespeare and his fellow dramatists and poets had ultimately no control over the publication of their works (although they could try to influence it by offering manuscripts to stationers, or withholding them from them). The Stationers' Company conferred publishing rights on their members provided a text had been licensed by a warden of the Company and approved by the ecclesiastic authorities (the Bishop of London, the Archbishop of Canterbury or one of their subordinates).[41] Once these rights had been obtained, publication could proceed independently of the will (or even knowledge) of the author.

The number of London printing houses did not exceed two dozen, with a total of about fifty presses.[42] In the mid-sixteenth century, the average yearly output was fewer than 150 titles, but it rose to more than 250 by the turn of the century and over 400 by the 1620s.[43] If we divide the book trade's output into different subject areas, then religion figures most prominently throughout the early modern period, but literature rises from only 13 per cent of all publications before 1560 to about 25 per cent by the end of the century, reflecting a growth in leisure reading of secular texts.[44] The fraction of the book trade's output accounted for by playbooks was by no means negligible and in some years exceeded 6 per cent of the total number of speculative titles.[45] What is more, playbooks generally sold well and, on average, received

---

[40] For more about the relationship between publishers and printers, see below, pp. 135–6.

[41] For press control in the early modern period, see Clegg, *Press Censorship in Elizabethan England, Press Censorship in Jacobean England,* and *Press Censorship in Caroline England,* and (for drama) Clare, *Art Made Tongue-Tied by Authority.*

[42] See Blayney, 'The Publication of Playbooks', 420. For the number of presses, see H. S. Bennett: 'In May 1583 there were twenty-three printers at work: C. Barker and J. Wolfe each had five presses; J. Day and H. Denham each had four. Four other printers each had three, seven others had two, and eight others had one apiece, making a total of fifty-two presses in all' (*English Books and Readers,* 270).

[43] See Barnard and Bell, 'Statistical Tables'.   [44] See Bennett, *English Books and Readers,* 247–8.

[45] Farmer and Lesser, 'The Popularity of Playbooks Revisited', 16.

more reprints than other books,[46] although <u>no dramatist's playbooks, as we will see, sold as well as Shakespeare's.</u>

What, then, did Shakespeare's printed books mean to him? He clearly sought publication for his narrative poems, dedicating them to Henry Wriothesley, the Earl of Southampton, but the traditional answer to this question as far as his plays are concerned is 'not much' or even 'nothing'. In 1998, an influential biographer commented on Shakespeare's attitude towards his plays in performance and print by writing that 'A play's performance was its virtual publication … Throughout his life, he had little to gain from seeing his name in a London bookshop.'[47] Three years later, a scholar explained Shakespeare's 'indifference to the publication of his plays' as follows: 'Literally his investment was elsewhere: in the lucrative partnership of the acting company.'[48] As long as the myth of Shakespeare's indifference to the publication of his plays was safely in place, there was little reason to assume that he cared about them once they were in print. I explain in *Shakespeare as Literary Dramatist* why I think this view is wrong, and I briefly return to the question here in light of recent research which adds to the case I presented in 2003.

To believe in a diametrical opposition between Shakespeare's interest in the playhouse and indifference to the printing house is to 'underestimate', as Tiffany Stern has rightly stressed, 'the extent to which they shared interests'.[49] Stern was preceded by Peter Blayney who, as early as 1997, had argued that the publication of playbooks served the companies as publicity for plays performed in the theatres, which suggests that playhouse and book trade publications are to be seen as synergetic rather than in opposition to each other.[50] Stern's research corroborates Blayney's, leading her to argue that playbooks 'seem regularly to have been marketed and sold in the theater precincts, probably because a playbook, read in the playhouse in which it was first performed, or for which its playwright was now writing, worked well as a marketing ploy'.[51] Not only did Shakespeare and his fellows have reason to be supportive of the publication of playbooks, but their dissemination, Stern's findings suggest, happened in the vicinity of the theatre, or even in the theatres themselves: 'playhouse sale of playbooks seems highly

---

[46] See Farmer and Lesser, 'The Popularity of Playbooks Revisited'.

[47] Honan, *Shakespeare*, 114–15.   [48] Kastan, *Shakespeare and the Book*, 16.

[49] '"On Each Wall and Corner Poast"', 64. The fanciful suggestion of William Blades and Captain W. Jaggard that Shakespeare had once been a printer need not detain us (see Blades, *Shakspere and Typography*, and Jaggard, *Shakespeare Once a Printer and a Bookman*).

[50] See Blayney, 'The Publication of Playbooks'; and Peters, *Theatre of the Book 1480–1880*.

[51] 'Watching as Reading', 139.

likely'.[52] The printed plays, in other words, were firmly embedded in the world of the playhouse.[53]

Stern shows that an important tie between playhouse and printing house came through the printers of playbills, who 'had a particularly strong connection with the playhouse'.[54] Her demonstration of the importance of playbills belies any antagonism between playhouse and printing house. It suggests instead that, in a sense, a company took a play to the printing house even before it reached the stage: 'Performances were "published" or publicized by having their title and other details hung over London in printed texts; every play ever put on was first met in printed form whether or not a passer-by could read it. Plays readied for performance already belonged to the world of the printing-house – every play was a little bit printed.'[55]

Stern believes that Shakespeare may well have composed the title pages and playbills himself:

> Why should the playbill/title-page for *The Merchant of Venice*, say, not actually be composed as a playbill by the performing company? And if by the company, then why not by its resident wordsmith/businessman/playwright? Why should the promotion of the play not be as 'authentic' as the rest of its text? That is, why should the playbill-title-page not be by Shakespeare?[56]

Stern's research thus corroborates my argument that it was perfectly compatible for Shakespeare to be a man of the theatre strongly implicated in his company and a man of books who was far from indifferent to the publication of his plays in the book trade.

More plausible than a Shakespeare mindful only of the theatre, removed from the book trade, indifferent to his plays in print, is the Shakespeare argued for by James Shapiro:

There's no way that Shakespeare could have bought or borrowed even a fraction of the books that went into the making of his plays. Besides his main sources for his British histories and Roman tragedies, which he probably owned – Holinshed's *Chronicles* and Plutarch's *Lives* – he drew on hundreds of other works. From what we know of Shakespeare's insatiable appetite for books, no patron's collection – assuming that Shakespeare had access to one or more – could have accommodated his curiosity and range. London's bookshops were by necessity Shakespeare's working libraries, and he must have spent a good many hours browsing there ... , either jotting down ideas in a commonplace book or storing them away in his

---

[52] 'Watching as Reading', 141.
[53] For a wide-ranging study of economic motives in writing for the page and the stage around the turn of the seventeenth century, see Baker, *On Demand*.
[54] "On Each Wall and Corner Poast", 63.   [55] "On Each Wall and Corner Poast", 64–5.
[56] "On Each Wall and Corner Poast", 86.

prodigious actor's memory. Between his responsibilities vetting potential plays for the Chamberlain's Men's repertory and his time spent paging through recently published books, it's hard to imagine anyone in London more alert to the latest literary trends.[57]

Not only was Shakespeare important to the book trade, but the book trade was also important to Shakespeare. He was one of its keenest observers, collaborated with it, drew on it and responded to it.[58] As Adam Hooks has put it, he 'inhabited the world of print as immediately and enduringly as he did the theatre'.[59] And one of the things Shakespeare must have observed with acute interest in the closing years of the sixteenth century is the remarkable rise in prominence of one William Shakespeare.

   This rise took the form not only of the publication of his plays and poems and the recurrent appearance of his name on title pages but also of texts which mention Shakespeare. His appearance in Meres's *Palladis Tamia* is a case in point and illustrates Shakespeare's acute awareness of the literary eminence to which he was being promoted. Meres's famous 'Comparative Discourse' of ancient and English writers – 'the first "evaluative survey" of Elizabethan literature' – praises Shakespeare several times and positions him near the top of the English literary canon alongside Sidney, Spenser, Daniel, Drayton and Warner.[60] MacDonald P. Jackson has shown that 'It seems highly probable that [Shakespeare] read attentively Francis Meres's remarks about him and his fellow writers . . ., and that Meres's glib critical survey helped provoke the Rival Poet sonnets.'[61] Jackson argues that 'Statistical studies of Shakespeare's rare-word vocabulary have, in recent years, come close to solving the problem of dating', and that for the Rival Poet group the evidence has been 'converging on 1598–1600'.[62] His rare-word analysis shows that Meres's 'Comparative Discourse' contains a number of words which Shakespeare first used after its publication in 1598 and several passages to which Shakespeare's Rival Poet group seems indebted. Jackson's work suggests that, far from being indifferent to seeing his name in print and his reputation as an author on the rise, Shakespeare gave Meres's tribute his

[57] *A Year in the Life of William Shakespeare*, 190–1.
[58] For the books Shakespeare read, see Baldwin, *Shakespeare's Small Latine and Lesse Greeke*, 1.494–531; Bullough, ed., *Narrative and Dramatic Sources of Shakespeare*; Miola, *Shakespeare's Reading*; Barkan, 'What Did Shakespeare Read?'; and Gillespie, *Shakespeare's Books*.
[59] 'Book Trade', 128.
[60] Jackson, 'Francis Meres and the Cultural Contexts of Shakespeare's Rival Poet Sonnets', 233. See also Erne, *Shakespeare as Literary Dramatist*, 64–8 (89–93).
[61] 'Shakespeare's Sonnet CXI and John Davies of Hereford's *Microcosmos* (1603)', 1.
[62] 'Francis Meres and the Cultural Contexts of Shakespeare's Rival Poet Sonnets', 225.

closest attention.[63] The stationers, to whom Shakespeare and his fellows released many of his play texts, turned Shakespeare into a remarkably successful author in print, and we have every reason to believe that he was keenly aware of, and affected by, this development. Douglas Bruster's rhetorical question seems to the point: 'when Shakespeare frequented London's bookshops (as he must have, for his literary resources), are we to think that he did not look for his own books, picking them up and thumbing through their pages?'[64]

Suggestive evidence that Shakespeare cared not only about the theatre but about both theatrical and bibliographical culture as well as their conjunction can also be found in the fiction of Shakespeare's plays, as demonstrated in Patrick Cheney's *Shakespeare, National Poet-Playwright* (2004) and *Shakespeare's Literary Authorship* (2008), and in Charlotte Scott's *Shakespeare and the Idea of the Book* (2007). Cheney's studies suggest that Shakespeare recurrently fictionalized his predicament as an author, while Scott demonstrates Shakespeare's interest in books in the fiction of his plays. Cheney's and Scott's readings restore a dimension to Shakespeare's writings which earlier critics had neglected. Significantly, when an eminent scholar registered Shakespeare's preoccupation with the scripted and printed page, as Jonas Barish did in 1991, he considered it a 'paradox' that Shakespeare, 'so notoriously indifferent to the printing of his plays', should, in his plays, be 'so endlessly and inventively preoccupied with written communication of all kinds'.[65] Barish's paradox is more apparent than real: once we dismantle the time-honoured myth of a Shakespeare warbling 'his native woodnotes wild', growing 'immortal in his own despight',[66] indifferent to publication, literary fame and posterity, we are able to see that there is no contradiction between Shakespeare's fictionalization of texts and books on the one hand and his interest in the publication and readerly reception of his writings on the other. Not only was the book trade interested in Shakespeare, but Shakespeare, we can be confident, was also interested in the 'Shakespeare' the book trade produced.

---

[63] Note that in 'Shakespeare's Sonnet CXI and John Davies of Hereford's *Microcosmos* (1603)', Jackson builds on his earlier article to argue that Shakespeare took a close interest in Davies's comments on him in *Microcosmos* and drew on them in Sonnet 111. Henry Woudhuysen similarly believes that 'Shakespeare must have been aware that his plays had reached print' and that 'this may have influenced the ways in which he wrote' ('The Foundations of Shakespeare's Text', 92, 99).

[64] Bruster, 'Shakespeare the Stationer'.   [65] '"Soft, Here Follows Prose"', 34.

[66] I quote from John Milton's 'L'Allegro', line 134, in Carey, ed., *John Milton*; and Pope, 'The First Epistle of the Second Book of Horace, Imitated', in Butt, ed., *Imitations of Horace*, 199.

CHAPTER I

Quantifying Shakespeare's presence in print

Shakespeare in numbers

This chapter examines the extent of Shakespeare's presence as 'a man in print' compared with contemporary writers, in particular contemporary playwrights, and asks what we can infer from this presence about his early authorial status. Significant portions of this chapter are unashamedly numerical, statistical, quantitative and economic. As Michael Suarez has put it, 'we cannot think very far about the transmission of texts before we bump into matters of money because, invariably, money matters. Books are business.'[1] To some, it may seem an aberration to apply numbers to the study of literature, but if we want to understand what Shakespeare meant to the book trade, then this is precisely what we must do. In this and subsequent chapters, I look at the early history of Shakespeare in print from the angle of commerce. 'For stationers', as Adam Hooks rightly points out, 'Shakespeare's works were not great books; they were good business.'[2] Quantitative analysis is a way of trying to understand what made them good business.

Given my focus in this chapter, it may be useful to reflect on the merits and limitations of such quantitative analysis. Bibliometrics is not always a precise tool, whether in assessing the popularity of early modern playwrights or the publication productivity of modern academics. While its quantifications measure certain things, they are blind to others. A simple count of academic publications says little or nothing about their quality and importance. Similarly, a count of early modern playbook editions reflects how often a publisher decided to invest in certain texts by certain authors, which may serve as an indicator of popularity, but it reveals nothing about other features of the dissemination of playbooks in print that would help us refine our analysis. We know little about the social and geographic distribution of playbook buyers.

---

[1] 'Historiographical Problems and Possibilities in Book History and National Histories of the Book', 164.
[2] 'Book Trade', 127.

Adam Hooks

We have only very limited awareness of the multiple circumstances over and above the sale of playbooks that led to or prevented new editions. We have similarly limited knowledge of the production costs and prices of playbooks, and of how differences in prices may have impacted sales. Uncertainties about the authorship of plays further complicate the assessment of the popularity of playwrights' output, as does the loss of entire editions.

We also know all too little about print runs.[3] A new edition means a new setting of type, but information about how many copies were printed is usually not available. In order to recoup the initial investment, a publisher would have commissioned at least a few hundred copies of an edition, but if he anticipated large sales, he could also opt for well over a thousand. In the period from 1586 to 1637, a decree limited the number of copies of ordinary books to 1,500, but, as Philip Gaskell has shown, 'the masters ignored the decree and printed larger editions whenever it suited them to do so'.[4] The best we can go by, then, is informed guesswork and the occasional scrap of evidence. Peter Blayney believes that a publisher would typically have ordered about 800 copies for a first edition and more for a second if the first sold out quickly but perhaps no more, or even fewer, if it did not.[5] From the records of a lawsuit, we gather that Thomas Walkley (the publisher of Q1 *Othello*) ordered 1,500 copies for the second edition of Beaumont and Fletcher's *Philaster* (1622) after the first one, of 1620, had sold out.[6] In the absence of fuller documentation, we cannot know with any certainty whether these figures are typical or not. While we can count editions, we thus have no way of recovering how many copies of most of these editions were produced.[7] Yet our ignorance does not invalidate the results presented below: there is every reason to suppose that what fluctuations there were affected all dramatists and that, in the absence of more precise data, the number of editions can still provide important information about popularity and success in the book trade.

While one source of reservations about quantitative analysis is the limitations of our knowledge, another arises from the interpretation of the data. Digested into statistics and tables, numbers can be made to yield manifold results, some more tendentious than others. 'Lies, damned lies,

---

[3] Concerning print runs, see also below, p. 143.

[4] *A New Introduction to Bibliography*, 162; see also Greg, *A Companion to Arber*, 43, 94–5; and Arber, *Transcript*, II.43, II.883 and v.liii.

[5] See 'The Publication of Playbooks', 412.   [6] See Blayney, 'The Publication of Playbooks', 422.

[7] For the limitations of our knowledge about the economics of the London book trade, see McKenzie, 'Printing and Publishing 1557–1700'; and St Clair, *The Reading Nation in the Romantic Period*, 9. See also McKenzie's seminal essay 'Printers of the Mind'.

and statistics', as Benjamin Disraeli reportedly said.[8] Even if a bibliometric analyst can be trusted not to produce results that are wilfully tendentious, data do not speak for themselves but need to be interpreted. Readers in literary studies are well equipped to judge the credentials of the interpretation of a text, but they may more easily feel out of their depth in the interpretation of statistics.

Given the limitations and pitfalls of quantitative analysis in the study of literature, my stance is not to avoid it but to try to proceed with the necessary circumspection and methodological awareness. It would be naïve to claim that the conclusions at which my analysis arrives are purely objective. They inevitably depend on the principles of classification I adopt, on the questions I ask and on the avenues these questions lead me to explore. With Pierre Bourdieu, I readily admit that 'Statistical analysis . . . often applies to *preconstructed* population principles of classification that are themselves preconstructed.'[9] Yet by striving for maximal transparency in the establishment of the corpus of data, my aim is not only to allow the verification of my statistics but also to enable others to ask different questions, pursue other avenues and refine earlier conclusions. As Robert Darnton has pointed out, bibliometric statistics, 'however flawed or distorted', provide 'something comparable to the early maps of the New World', whose general contours are, more often than not, largely accurate, despite the fact that they failed to record the details of the actual landscape.[10]

Shakespeare and contemporaries in print

As I turn to Shakespeare's place as a man in print amidst his contemporaries, it may be useful to start by taking a snapshot of the presence of Shakespeare's writings in the London book trade in a single year: 1600. It is true that this is an extraordinary year for Shakespeare, with more publications than in any other year during his life, yet the year's total book production, with approximately 260 titles produced and published in London, is also of unprecedented scope.[11] The subject matter to which the greatest part of these titles was devoted is religion, which accounted for

---

[8] See Shapiro and Epstein, *The Yale Book of Quotations*, 208, arguing that considerable evidence suggests that the phrase does indeed go back to Disraeli.

[9] *The Field of Cultural Production*, 180.　　[10] 'Book Production in British India, 1850–1900', 240.

[11] Mark Bland writes that 'the Short-Title Catalogue lists 342 books published either during 1600 or in a few cases approximately dated to that year'. After deducting variant imprints and items printed outside London, he arrives at '262 items . . . printed in London' ('The London Book-Trade in 1600', 457). John Barnard and Maureen Bell's statistical tables mention 298 items produced in London in

more than a third of the total output.[12] A fair number of other books dealt with historical and political subjects (about 10 per cent each) and a smaller number (around 5 per cent) with science or what we might call sociological subjects (such as commerce, education, good conduct and tobacco pamphlets). A handful of books concerned the arts (music and the fine arts) and sports. Finally, quite a considerable segment of the year's book production, approximately 30 per cent of the titles published, was devoted to what we now call 'literature', a category under which a surprising range of texts appeared, including translations from Latin (Ovid's *Heroides*, translated by George Turberville) and from vernacular languages (e.g. Edward Fairfax's rendering of Tasso's *Jerusalem Delivered*), romances (the anonymous *Heroicall Adventures of the Knight of the Sea*), plays (Dekker's *Shoemaker's Holiday*), prose fiction (Thomas Deloney's *The Gentle Craft*), collections of tales (Robert Armin's *Fool upon Fool*), lengthy narrative poems (*The Legend of Humphrey Duke of Glocester*, by Christopher Middleton), verse satires (*Pasquil's Mad-Cap*, by Nicholas Breton), allegorical poems (Cyril Tourneur's *The Transformed Metamorphosis*), epyllia (Marlowe's *Hero and Leander*), elegies (*An Italian's Dead Body, Stuck with English Flowers*, by Joseph Hall and others), religious poetry (Robert Southwell's *Saint Peter's Complaint*), epigrams (Thomas Rowlands's *The Letting of Humour's Blood in the Head-Vein*), poetic miscellanies (*The Paradise of Dainty Devices*), anthologies (*England's Parnassus, or the Choicest Flowers of Our Modern Poets*), single-sheet verse ('As Pleasant a Ditty as Your Heart Can Wish') and ballads (Thomas Deloney's 'Most Pleasant Ballad of Patient Grissell').[13]

1600 ('Appendix 1', 782). As Blayney has shown, the figures in Barnard and Bell's tables need to be used with circumspection and, if read in terms of book trade productivity, tend to exaggerate the number of different titles that were actually produced (see 'STC Publication Statistics').

[12] In '"People of the Book"', Kari Konkola compares the number of editions of religious titles with that of literary works and documents the greater frequency of the former. Konkola also compares the number of editions of 'the leading religious writer of the time, William Perkins' with those of Shakespeare and shows that 'judged by known editions, Perkins steadily outsold Shakespeare by almost two to one' (25–6).

[13] For the approximate percentages in the preceding division of subjects, see Klotz, 'A Subject Analysis of English Imprints for Every Tenth Year from 1480 to 1640'. H. S. Bennett divides up the book production in similar fashion: 'Religion', 'Law', 'Education', 'Medicine', 'Information', 'Arithmetic, astronomy and popular science', 'Geography', 'History', 'News' and 'Literature' (*English Books and Readers*, 112–258). David Gants's *Early English Booktrade Database*, in 'A Discussion of Project Methods', proposes the following subject division: '1. Information, including works on language, business training and skills, education, husbandry, popular science and medicine. 2. Ephemera, including ballads, almanacs, catalogues and news pamphlets. 3. History, both popular and scholarly. 4. Law & Politics, including law books and non-religious polemics. 5. Literature, including *belles lettres* and popular, classical and travel works. 6. Official Documents, including forms, and proclamations. 7. Religion, including sermons, bibles, prayer books, instruction and commentary along with controversial and devotional works.'

Shakespeare made a remarkable contribution to the year's output: the first editions, all in quarto, of *Henry V, Much Ado about Nothing, 2 Henry IV, A Midsummer Night's Dream* and *The Merchant of Venice*; the second editions, also in quarto, of *Titus Andronicus, 1 Contention* and *Richard Duke of York*; and the fourth and fifth editions (the second and third in octavo) of *The Rape of Lucrece.* In other words, no fewer than ten books published in 1600 were by Shakespeare. Moreover, two commonplace books (*England's Parnassus* and *Belvedere, or the Garden of the Muses*) and a poetical anthology (*England's Helicon*) were published the same year with excerpts from Shakespeare's writings.[14] If we add these to Shakespeare's plays and poem published in 1600, we arrive at a total of thirteen books – 5 per cent of the year's output – which contain writings by Shakespeare. It seems fair to say that Shakespeare had a remarkable presence in the London book trade at the turn of the seventeenth century.

I have mentioned above that *Venus and Adonis* received more editions than any other of Shakespeare's writings, but it is not commonly observed that Shakespeare's narrative poem was in fact one of the literary bestsellers of its time, with eleven printings in twenty-five years and sixteen in half a century.[15] Let me provide the figures for other commercially successful poems or collections of poems, indicating parenthetically the original year of publication and the number of editions within twenty-five and fifty years respectively: *Songes and Sonettes*, by Henry Howard, the Earl of Surrey, Sir Thomas Wyatt and others, better known as *Tottel's Miscellany* (1557, 7 / 9), Spenser's *Shepheardes Calender* (1579, 5 / 7) and *Faerie Queene* (1590, 4 / 4),[16] Sidney's *Astrophil and Stella* (1591, 3 / 3), Samuel Daniel's *Delia* (1592, 6 / 7) and Marlowe's *Hero and Leander* (1598, 8 /10).[17] Compared to other epyllia, the popularity of Shakespeare's poem emerges with particular clarity: Thomas Lodge's *Glaucus* (1589), Marston's *Metamorphosis of Pigmalion* (1598), John Weever's *Faunus and Melliflora* (1600) and Beaumont's *Salmacis and Hermaphroditus* (1602), based on Ovid's *Metamorphosis*, all

---

[14] See below, pp. 228–9.

[15] Concerning *Venus and Adonis*, Katherine Duncan-Jones and Henry Woudhuysen have pointed out that 'The 16 separate editions between 1593 and 1636 survive in only 22 more or less complete copies and 3 fragments' (*Shakespeare's Poems*, 514). Harry Farr was thus right in pointing out that additional editions of the poem may well have been lost: 'No one would be rash enough to assert that the copies now extant represent all the editions which were published. *Venus and Adonis* was one of the most popular books of its time, and its very popularity makes it all the more likely that there were editions of which not a single copy has come down to us' ('Notes on Shakespeare's Printers and Publishers', 235).

[16] A simple number cannot do justice to *The Faerie Queene*'s complex publication history: see Johnson, *A Critical Bibliography of the Works of Edmund Spenser Printed before 1700*.

[17] For early modern lyric poetry and print, see Marotti, *Manuscript, Print, and the English Renaissance Lyric*, 209–90.

failed to be reprinted. *Venus and Adonis* also went through more editions than important literary translations, such as Arthur Golding's rendering of Ovid's *Metamorphoses* (1565, 5 / 8). Even the two most successful quarto playbooks of the early modern period, the anonymous *Mucedorus* (1598, 10 / 15) and Thomas Kyd's *Spanish Tragedy* (1592, 8 / 11), received fewer printings than Shakespeare's narrative poem,[18] and so did popular romances such as Greene's *Pandosto* (1588, 6 / 12) and Sidney's *Arcadia* (1590, 6 / 10), or Deloney's prose fiction *Jack of Newberry* (1597?, 8? / 12?).[19] As far as I am aware, the only literary titles in English first published in Elizabethan or Jacobean London of which there were more editions than of *Venus and Adonis* are John Lyly's prose romances, *Euphues, the Anatomy of Wit* (1578) and *Euphues and His England* (1580).[20] *Euphues and His England* went through twelve editions within a quarter-century and eighteen editions within a half-century, and *Euphues, the Anatomy of Wit* was even marginally more popular, with fifteen and nineteen editions in the same periods. Thus if the popularity of *Venus and Adonis* is considered alongside other literary titles of the late sixteenth and early seventeenth century, it emerges that its success was massive.[21]

If we now examine Shakespeare's published output as a whole, it may be instructive to compare it with that of Robert Greene, whom Steve Mentz has called 'The most successful Elizabethan print author'.[22] Greene is sometimes considered England's first professional writer, with an output which spans various genres, including romances, plays, moral dialogues and pamphlets (among them the notorious coney-catching pamphlets). His earliest publication was the romance *Mamilia*, published in 1583, exactly a

---

[18] These totals include the recently discovered *c.* 1615–18 edition of *Mucedorus* (see Proudfoot, '"Modernizing" the Printed Play-Text in Jacobean London') and the first, lost edition of *The Spanish Tragedy* (see Erne, *Beyond 'The Spanish Tragedy'*, 59).

[19] The earliest editions of *Jack of Newberry* appear to have been read out of existence. It was entered in 1597 and the first extant edition, dated 1619, is in fact the eighth, according to the title page. Mish suggests that prior to the 1590s, more prose fiction was published than drama, and in the 1590s the output for the two genres was more or less identical, whereas after the turn of the century, the frequency of drama editions was superior to that of prose fiction by a factor of almost two to one ('Comparative Popularity of Early Fiction and Drama').

[20] For a recent edition of these prose romances, see Lyly, *'Euphues'*.

[21] The main sources for the figures in this paragraph are the *STC* and Wing, but I have also consulted Esdaile, *A List of English Tales and Prose Romances Printed before 1740*, and O'Dell, *A Chronological List of Prose Fiction in English Printed in England and Other Countries, 1475–1640*. The *STC* and Wing are the more reliable sources as Esdaile and O'Dell occasionally mistake reissues or variants for new editions.

[22] *Romance for Sale in Early Modern England*, 8. For other important recent work on Greene, see Newcomb, *Reading Popular Romance in Early Modern England*; and Melnikoff and Gieskes, eds., *Writing Robert Greene*.

decade before Shakespeare's first text reached print. By the year of his death, 1592, prolific Greene had thirty-one titles in print, and another nine followed posthumously, including all the plays now attributed to him – see Table 2.[23]

Table 2 *Robert Greene, publications by title, 1583–1650*

Title	Dates of editions	Reprints within ten years	Reprints within twenty-five years	Editions to 1650
Mamilia, Part One	1583	0	0	1
Mamilia, Part Two	1583, 1593	1	1	2
The myrrour of modestie	1584 (8°)	0	0	1
Arbasto, the anatomie of fortune	1584, 1589, 1594, 1617, 1626	2	2	5
Gwydonius. The carde of fancie	1584, 1587, 1593, 1608	2	3	4
Morando, the tritameron of loue (Part One)	1584	0	0	1
Planetomachia	1585	0	0	1
Oration or funerall sermon uttered at Rome (translation)	1585 (8°)	0	0	1
Morando, the tritameron of loue (Parts One and Two)	1587	0	0	1
Penelopes web	1587, 1601	0	1	2
Euphues his censure to Philautus	1587, 1634	0	0	2
Perimedes the blacke-smith	1588	0	0	1
Pandosto the triumph of time (from 1635: *Dorastus and Fawnia*)	1588, 1592, 1595, 1600, 1607, 1609, 1614, 1619, 1629, 1632, 1635, 1636, 1640, 1648	2	5	14
Ciceronis amor. Tullies loue.	1589, 1597, 1601, 1605, 1609, 1611, 1616, 1628, 1639	1	5	9
The Spanish masquerado	1589, 1589	1	1	2

[23] The main source for the compilation of the Greene corpus in Table 2 is Melnikoff and Gieskes, eds., *Writing Robert Greene*, which has been checked against and complemented by data in the *STC*, the *ESTC* and *DEEP*. Note that Melnikoff and Gieskes attribute *Selimus* to Greene, whereas *DEEP* considers the play's authorship uncertain. The *ESTC* suggests that *The Defence of Conny-catching* (1592, reprinted the same year), assigned to 'Cuthbert Cunny-Catcher' on the title page, is by Greene, whereas Melnikoff and Gieskes do not endorse Greene's authorship. Melnikoff and Gieskes and *DEEP* state that Greene's authorship of *George a Greene, the Pinner of Wakefield* is uncertain. In 1651–60 (and thus not included in Table 2), editions appeared of *Pandosto* (1655, 1660), *Menaphon* (1657) and *Friar Bacon and Friar Bungay* (1655).

Table 2 (*cont.*)

Title	Dates of editions	Reprints within ten years	Reprints within twenty-five years	Editions to 1650
Menaphon (from 1610: *Greenes arcadia*)	1589, 1599, 1605, 1610, 1616	1	3	5
Greenes mourning garment	1590, 1616	0	0	2
Greenes neuer too late (Parts One and Two)	1590, 1599, 1600, 1602, 1607, 1611, 1616, 1631	2	5	8
The Royal Exchange (translation)	1590	0	0	1
A notable discouery of coosenage	1591, 1591, 1591, 1592	3	3	4
The second part of conny-catching	1591, 1592	1	1	2
A maidens dreame. Vpon the death of Sir Christopher Hatton	1591	0	0	1
Greenes farewell to folly	1591, 1617	0	0	2
A quip for an vpstart courtier	1592, 1592, 1592, 1592, 1592, 1592, 1606, 1620, 1622, 1635	5	6	10
The third and last part of conny-catching	1592, 1592	1	1	2
The repentance of Robert Greene	1592	0	0	1
Greenes groats-worth of witte	1592, 1596, 1617, 1621, 1629, 1637	1	2	6
Greenes vision: written at the instant of his death	1592	0	0	1
A disputation betweene a hee conny-catcher and a shee conny-catcher	1592, 1615, 1617, 1621, 1637	0	2	5
The blacke bookes messenger	1592	0	0	1
Philomela. The Lady Fitzwaters nightingale	1592, 1615, 1631	0	1	3
The historie of Orlando Furioso	1594, 1599	1	1	2
The honorable historie of frier Bacon, and frier Bongay	1594, 1630	0	0	2
A looking glasse for London and England (with Thomas Lodge)	1594, 1598, 1602, 1605?, 1617	2	4	5
Selimus	1594	0	0	1
The Scottish historie of Iames the fourth	1598	0	0	1
Alphonsus, King of Aragon	1599	0	0	1
Greenes Orpharion	1599	0	0	1
George a Greene, the Pinner of Wakefield	1599	0	0	1
Alcida Greenes metamorphosis	1617	0	0	1
Total (40 titles)		26	47	116
Average		0.65	1.18	2.90

It is true that Greene was a widely published author, but how does his bibliographic presence compare with that of Shakespeare (Table 3)? Greene had forty book titles to his credit, as compared with twenty-nine for Shakespeare, but one of these twenty-nine titles is the Folio collection with its thirty-six plays, of which half were not published as separate titles. Greene's texts, by contrast, received no collected edition but were published individually (with the exception of the two parts of *Morando, the Tritameron of Love*

Table 3 *William Shakespeare, publications by title, 1593–1660*

Title	Dates of editions	Reprints within ten years	Reprints within twenty-five years	Editions to 1660
Venus and Adonis	1593, 1594, 1595? (8°), 1596 (8°), 1599 (8°), 1599 (8°), 1602? (8°), '1602' [c. 1607/8] (8°), '1602' [c. 1608/9] (8°), '1602' [c. 1610] (8°), 1617 (8°), 1620 (8°), 1627 (8°), 1630 (8°), 1630–6? (8°), 1636 (8°)	6	10	16
The Rape of Lucrece	1594, 1598 (8°), 1600 (8°), 1600 (8°), 1607 (8°), 1616 (8°), 1624 (8°), 1632 (8°), 1655 (8°)	3	5	9
Titus Andronicus (with Peele)	1594, 1600, 1611	1	2	3
1 Contention (2 Henry VI)	1594, 1600	1	1	2
Richard Duke of York (3 Henry VI)	1595 (8°), 1600	1	1	2
Edward III	1596, 1599	1	1	2
Richard II	1597, 1598, 1598, 1608, 1615, 1634	2	4	6
Richard III	1597, 1598, 1602, 1605, 1612, 1622, 1629, 1634	3	5	8
Romeo and Juliet	1597, 1599, 1609, 1623?, 1637	1	2	5
Love's Labour's Lost	[1597], 1598, 1631	1	1	3
1 Henry IV	[1598], 1598, 1599, 1604, 1608, 1613, 1622, 1632, 1639	4	6	9
The Passionate Pilgrim	1599? (8°), 1599 (8°), 1612 (8°)	1	2	3
Henry V	1600, 1602, '1608' [i.e. 1619]	1	2	3
2 Henry IV	1600	0	0	1

Table 3 (*cont.*)

Title	Dates of editions	Reprints within ten years	Reprints within twenty-five years	Editions to 1660
Much Ado about Nothing	1600	0	0	1
A Midsummer Night's Dream	1600, '1600' [i.e. 1619]	0	1	2
The Merchant of Venice	1600, '1600' [i.e. 1619], 1637	0	1	3
The Merry Wives of Windsor	1602, 1619, 1630	0	1	3
Hamlet	1603, 1604, 1611, 1625?, 1637	2	3	5
King Lear	1608, '1608' [i.e. 1619], 1655	0	1	3
Sonnets	1609	0	0	1
Troilus and Cressida	1609	0	0	1
Pericles (with Wilkins)	1609, 1609, 1611, 1619, 1630, 1635	3	4	6
The Whole Contention	1619	0	0	1
Othello	1622, 1630, 1655	1	1	3
Comedies, Histories, and Tragedies	1623 (2°), 1632 (2°)	1	1	2
The Taming of the Shrew	1631	0	0	1
The Two Noble Kinsmen (with Fletcher)	1634	0	0	1
Poems	1640 (8°)	0	0	1
Total (29 titles)		33	55	106
Average		1.14	1.90	3.66

and the two parts of *Greene's Never Too Late*, of which joint quarto editions were published). Some of Greene's works had considerable success: within twenty-five years of publication, *Pandosto*, *Ciceronis Amor* and *Greene's Never Too Late* went through six editions and *A Quip for an Upstart Courtier* through seven. Quite a few other titles, however, were never reprinted. Overall, if we examine the 68-year period from 1583 to 1650, Greene's forty titles received a total of 116 editions, an average of not quite three editions (i.e. not quite two reprints) per title. During the equivalent 68-year period from 1593 to 1660, Shakespeare's twenty-nine titles went through 105 editions (including the two Folio collections of 1623 and 1632), an average of more than 3.6 editions per title (or 2.6 reprints). If we compare Greene's and Shakespeare's titles in the ten and twenty-five years following their initial publication, Greene's popularity in print is again inferior to Shakespeare's: Greene's average number of reprints is 0.65 (ten years) and 1.18 (twenty-five years), Shakespeare's 1.14 (ten years) and 1.90 (twenty-five years). <u>Greene and Shakespeare are genuine rivals</u> <u>as successful print authors, which seems ironic given that what literary history</u> <u>best remembers about Greene is the attack on Shakespeare in *Greene's*</u> <u>*Groatsworth of Wit.*</u>[24] However, if, as I suggest below, reprint rates are a reliable indicator, Shakespeare was arguably a more successful print author than Greene.[25]

The number of early playbook editions: Shakespeare compared

How then does the bibliographic presence of Shakespeare, the dramatist, compare with that of his contemporary playwrights? The question of the popularity of playbooks has received sustained scholarly attention, most notably by Alan Farmer, Zachary Lesser and Peter Blayney.[26] Yet despite the fact that their debate came to a head in the journal *Shakespeare Quarterly*, in three articles published in 2005, their work, including Blayney's seminal 1997 article on 'The Publication of Playbooks', shows little interest in the specific case of Shakespeare. Indeed, a reader could easily come away from reading Blayney's 1997 article thinking that Shakespeare playbooks were not particularly popular. Blayney compiles a bestseller list with eleven plays of which only three are by Shakespeare, and none of them appears at the top of the list. Blayney adds that if he had included 'closet and academic plays', this 'would have pushed Shakespeare firmly out of the top five', adding that 'Shakespeare's best-selling work, *Venus and Adonis*, out-sold his best-selling play by four editions'.[27] None of this is wrong, but the effect of Blayney's influential essay, to the extent that it focuses on dramatic

[24] See Carroll, ed., *Greene's Groatsworth of Wit*. For the question of the text's authorship, see Jowett, 'Johannes Factotum'. For a provocative take on the relationship between Shakespeare and Greene and the argument that Shakespeare created a 'proximity between Greene and Falstaff', see Greenblatt, *Will in the World*, 216–20 (the quotation is from p. 218).

[25] In the context of this study of Shakespeare and the book trade, I consciously restrict my analysis to the popularity of literary authors in print. Literature, in particular poetry, also circulated in manuscript, of course, and the lyric poems of someone like John Donne were widely disseminated in the late sixteenth and early seventeenth century, even though they did not appear as a printed collection until after his death in 1631. See Beal, 'John Donne and the Circulation of Manuscripts'.

[26] See Farmer and Lesser, 'The Popularity of Playbooks Revisited' and 'Structures of Popularity in the Early Modern Book Trade'; and Blayney, 'The Publication of Playbooks' and 'The Alleged Popularity of Playbooks'.

[27] 'The Publication of Playbooks', 388. The bestselling plays in Blayney's list are the anonymous *Mucedorus* (1598), Marlowe's *Doctor Faustus* (1604) and Kyd's *Spanish Tragedy* (1592), with nine, eight and seven editions respectively in twenty-five years, and two closet and academic plays, Samuel Daniel's *Cleopatra* (1594), included in collections of Daniel's verse, with eight editions, and Thomas Randolph's *Aristippus* and *The Conceited Pedlar* (1630) with seven.

authors, is to suggest that Shakespeare's playbooks were relatively unpopular.[28]

My aim here is not to make a contribution to the debate over whether playbooks constituted a significant share of the book trade in early modern England.[29] Rather, my chief objective is to arrive at a better sense of Shakespeare's authorial presence in print, with which I hope to contribute to a re-evaluation of Shakespeare's authorial standing in his own time, in which a variety of scholars have recently participated, including Richard Dutton, James Bednarz, Brian Vickers, Patrick Cheney, Henry Woodhuysen, Jeffrey Knapp and MacDonald P. Jackson.[30]

The point is sometimes made that Shakespeare, from early on, outshone his contemporaries not only as a playwright writing for the stage but also as a dramatist in print. John Jowett, for instance, states that 'By 1600 Shakespeare had become the most regularly published dramatist.'[31] Other critics, however, seem more inclined to stress the radical difference between Shakespeare's authorial standing in the eighteenth century and that before. John Pitcher writes that 'The modern dispute about who the seventeenth century regarded as its pre-eminent dramatist – Shakespeare or Jonson or Beaumont and Fletcher – is not yet concluded, because literary historians are properly concerned not to project back into this earlier period the reputation Shakespeare subsequently enjoyed.'[32] We might be tempted, Pitcher seems to be saying, to consider Shakespeare the seventeenth century's pre-eminent dramatist because of the eminence he later came to acquire, but we should beware of jumping to such a conclusion without good evidence. Others have even categorically contested that Shakespeare was the most popular dramatist during his active life and the decades immediately following it. Gerald Eades Bentley devoted a two-volume study to answering the question of Shakespeare's and Jonson's relative popularity, concluding that 'throughout the [seventeenth] century until

---

[28] Farmer and Lesser note that Shakespeare was 'England's first best-selling playwright', adding that 'the success of the printed editions of his plays . . . helped to establish the playbook market itself' ('The Popularity of Playbooks Revisited', 11).

[29] I argued in 2003 that 'printed playbooks became a conspicuous presence in St Paul's Churchyard' (*Shakespeare as Literary Dramatist*, 16 (41)) in Shakespeare's time, a view for which I find confirmation in the work by Farmer and Lesser.

[30] See Dutton, 'The Birth of the Author' (in *Licensing, Censorship and Authorship*, pp. 90–113); Bednarz, *Shakespeare and the Poets' War*; Vickers, *Shakespeare, Co-Author*; Cheney, *Shakespeare, National Poet-Playwright*; Woodhuysen, 'The Foundations of Shakespeare's Text'; Knapp, 'What Is a Co-Author'; and Jackson, 'Francis Meres and the Cultural Contexts of Shakespeare's Rival Poet Sonnets' and 'Shakespeare's Sonnet CXI and John Davies of Hereford's *Microcosmos* (1603)'. See also Meek, Rickard, and Wilson, eds., *Shakespeare's Book*, and Cheney, ed., 'Forum'.

[31] *Shakespeare and Text*, 8.   [32] 'Literature, the Playhouse, and the Public', 373.

the last decade Jonson was more popular in England than Shakespeare', adding that 'Clearly, Jonson, and not Shakespeare, was the dramatist of the seventeenth century' and that 'Jonson's general popularity was greater than Shakespeare's from the beginning of the century to 1690.'[33] The instances of Jowett, Pitcher and Bentley suggest that no scholarly consensus has emerged so far, and a closer investigation may therefore seem desirable.

A fairly straightforward way of examining the bibliographic presence of Shakespeare, the dramatist, compared with that of his contemporaries is to count the number of editions in which their playbooks appeared. Yet as soon as one starts undertaking such a count, various methodological questions arise: What kinds of plays should be included or excluded? How about closet drama or university drama or drama translated from other languages? What about plays which were written in co-authorship, such as *Titus Andronicus*? And what about collections containing several plays, such as the Shakespeare First Folio, which contains thirty-six plays, the Jonson First Folio, with nine professional plays, or the 1590 octavo edition of the two parts of *Tamburlaine*? The first figures I present here include all plays written in sole or co-authorship (so *The Two Noble Kinsmen* is counted not only as one of Shakespeare's but also as one of Fletcher's plays); in addition, I concentrate in the first stage on play*books* rather than play *texts*, meaning the number of times a publisher invested in a playwright, be it in the form of a collection or a single play. Finally, I focus throughout the rest of this chapter on what Farmer and Lesser call 'professional plays', plays, that is, that were written for adult or boys' companies performing them in front of paying audiences.[34]

The result of this first count is that for the whole period from the beginning of the publication of professional plays to 1642, when public performances ceased, Shakespeare, with seventy-four editions of playbooks, out-publishes all his contemporaries by more than 50 per cent. The second most published playwright is not Jonson, who has only twenty-two editions of playbooks to his credit by 1642, or Middleton, whose total is twenty-six, or Beaumont or Fletcher, for whom I count twenty-six and thirty-four editions respectively, but Heywood, with forty-nine editions, which is fifteen more than Fletcher, and more than twenty editions ahead of everyone else.

Figure 1.1 shows the number of editions of playbooks, per dramatist, for the period up to 1642, and includes all playwrights with at least fifteen playbook editions to their credit. Even though public performances stopped

[33] *Shakespeare and Jonson*, 1.133, 139, 138.
[34] 'The Popularity of Playbooks Revisited', 6, in particular note 24.

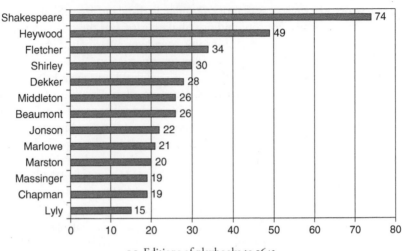

1.1 Editions of playbooks to 1642

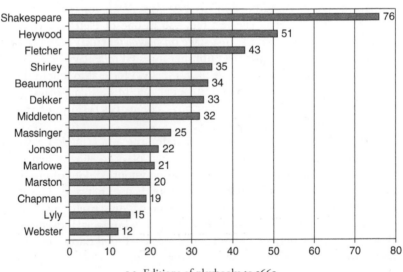

1.2 Editions of playbooks to 1660

in 1642, the publication of playbooks did not, so 1642 may seem an arbitrary end point and 1660 a valid alternative, all the more so as this may do better justice to playwrights who, unlike Shakespeare, were still active during the Caroline period. In Figure 1.2, with the period extended to 1660, Shakespeare still comes first with seventy-six editions. Only two of

Shakespeare's plays were reprinted between 1642 and 1660, *King Lear* and *Othello*, both in 1655. Yet Shakespeare's number of playbooks up to 1660 is still almost one and a half times that of Heywood, almost twice that of Fletcher and twice or more that of everyone else. Shakespeare exceeds Jonson's number of playbooks by a factor of more than three. Heywood's prominence in print is easily overlooked. For instance, Kastan, in *Shakespeare and the Book*, writes that 'in his own age more editions of [Shakespeare's] plays circulated than of any other contemporary playwright', adding that 'Eventually the prolific Beaumont and Fletcher would close the gap.'[35] According to my count, Beaumont and Fletcher never came close to rivalling Shakespeare, and the playwright who came closest to doing so was Heywood.

This may be the moment to address the objection that lost editions falsify these statistics. It might be argued that Shakespeare, from the eighteenth century, had a status which ensured the survival of a greater number of copies of his playbooks then still extant than of his contemporaries' and may have prevented the disappearance of entire Shakespeare editions, while editions of plays by his contemporaries perished. It is true that a certain number of editions have disappeared, for instance the first edition of Shakespeare's *Love's Labour's Lost* (1597) and of Kyd's *Spanish Tragedy* (1592).[36] Also, the first edition of *1 Henry IV* (1598) survives in no more than a fragment of a single copy, and a previously lost edition of *Mucedorus* (*c.* 1615–18) was discovered earlier this century by Richard Proudfoot.[37] Yet we can be confident that their number has no significant impact on the analysis presented here. Based on the rate of entries in the Stationers' Register of titles that may have been professional playbooks but for which no corresponding printed text is extant, Farmer and Lesser have argued for 'an upper limit of forty-six lost first editions' in the period from 1576–1640, meaning less than one playbook per year, although they believe that the most likely number of lost editions is significantly lower (twenty or fewer).[38] They also analyse the most likely number of lost reprints and arrive at an even lower total ('between one and fifteen').[39] Even if we assume, for the sake of argument, that a number of editions close to Farmer and Lesser's 'upper limit' were lost and that, with the exception of the 1597 *Love's Labour's Lost*, these editions were not by Shakespeare, the resulting total of approximately one lost edition per year would constitute no challenge to my argument for

[35] *Shakespeare and the Book*, 21. Kastan adds that Beaumont and Fletcher 'never actually surpassed Shakespeare' (21).

[36] See above, pp. 13, 30.   [37] See '"Modernizing" the Printed Play-Text in Jacobean London'.

[38] 'The Popularity of Playbooks Revisited', 29.   [39] 'The Popularity of Playbooks Revisited', 30.

Shakespeare's superior popularity as a dramatist in print. Clearly, even though ballads, almanacs and other ephemeral titles typically disappeared, playbook editions, with few exceptions, did not (see below, pp. 192–3).

A few words of caution before I proceed: reduced into simple figures and tables, my statistics look more straightforward than they are, and this for more than one reason. First of all, collaborative plays are so common that they cannot be ignored, yet their inclusion inevitably distorts the evidence. *Eastward Hoe*, for example, a collaborative play by Jonson, Marston and Chapman, received three editions, all dated 1605. In my count, the play appears under all three playwrights, adding three editions to their totals, even though each of them wrote no more than a part of the play. My figures for playwrights who often wrote collaboratively thus exaggerate the amount of their dramatic writing that was available in print. Shakespeare, even though he collaborated on a number of plays, did so much less than many of his contemporaries, so what this means for my figures is that Shakespeare's superiority in terms of the bibliographic presence of his dramatic writings may have been even greater than my tables suggest.

A further problem is that the authorship of many collaborative plays is a matter of ongoing scholarly discussion and may never be known with certainty. *The Spanish Gypsy*, for instance, was ascribed to Middleton and William Rowley on the title page of the first quarto (1653), but a number of scholars, including David J. Lake, argue that it was written by Dekker and Ford, whereas Gary Taylor, in *Thomas Middleton: the Collected Works*, contends that all four contributed to the play.[40] In a situation like this, I adhere to the argument I find most convincing – meaning that presented in the Middleton *Collected Works* in the case of *The Spanish Gypsy* – but it is clear that the authorship of many early modern plays, and in particular of collaborative plays, will remain a matter of debate and that, therefore, figures such as those presented here cannot be considered definitive. In order to document as transparently as possible how I arrive at the figures in this chapter, and to acknowledge the assumptions on which they rely, I provide in Appendix A the corpus of the nineteen best-published early modern dramatists, mentioning all their editions that reached print up to 1660.[41]

The preceding statistics give us a sense of the number of editions of dramatic writings by Shakespeare and his contemporaries that were

---

[40] See Lake, *The Canon of Thomas Middleton's Plays*, 215–30, and Taylor and Lavagnino, gen. eds., *Thomas Middleton and Early Modern Textual Culture*, 433–7.

[41] For the sources on which I have drawn in compiling the corpus of the various playwrights, see Appendix A.

published in the early modern period, but they fail to distinguish between simple quarto playbooks and collections, including large Folio collections, and therefore do not assess how many play *texts* and editions thereof were available in print. Clearly, the totals of dramatists whose plays were published in large collections (such as Shakespeare, Jonson and Fletcher) are affected if we take into account the individual plays these collections included rather than only the collection as a whole. Whereas the statistics for playbooks inform us of the number of commercial ventures publishers undertook, the figures for play texts are more apt to convey the availability in print of the full breadth of the playwrights' dramatic output.

Such an examination documents with even greater clarity Shakespeare's predominance as a published playwright in early modern England, as Figure 1.3 makes clear. In the period up to 1642, the texts of the thirty-nine plays Shakespeare wrote or to which he contributed a significant portion – meaning the thirty-six plays in the First Folio plus *Edward III*, *Pericles* and *The Two Noble Kinsmen* – appeared in a total of 145 editions, almost 90 more than Heywood, with 55. Owing to the nine plays in the 1616 Folio, Jonson comes third, but remains more than a hundred play-text editions behind Shakespeare. (Playwrights with fewer than fifteen editions are again not recorded.) If the period is extended to 1660 (Figure 1.4), Fletcher, thanks to the Folio of 1647, overtakes Heywood and comes somewhat closer to Shakespeare, but with 147 editions of play texts as

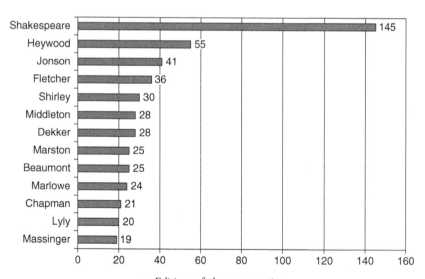

1.3 Editions of play texts to 1642

— Including folios as individual playbooks (so 36 for Shakes)

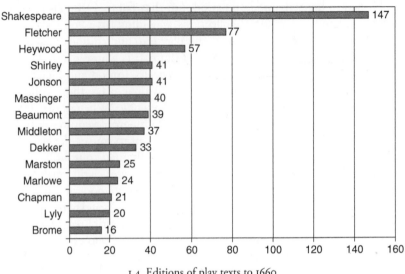

1.4 Editions of play texts to 1660

opposed to Fletcher's 77, Shakespeare still out-publishes Fletcher by a factor of almost two to one, with the number of Heywood's editions being approximately 40 per cent and Shirley's, Jonson's, Massinger's and Beaumont's fewer than 30 per cent of Shakespeare's.

My analysis has so far focused on the period up to 1642 or 1660, but it seems important to examine also the number of publications during Shakespeare's lifetime. If we consider the period from 1584, when Lyly's and Peele's earliest playbooks were published, to the year of Shakespeare's death, then, as shown in Figure 1.5, Shakespeare again comes out top with forty-five editions, Heywood follows behind with about half that number and Marston, third with eighteen, is followed by Dekker, Jonson, Middleton, Marlowe, Lyly and Chapman, whose number of editions constitutes approximately one-third of Shakespeare's.

The advantage of looking at playbook publication from this angle is that it can provide us with a sense of how Shakespeare's exact contemporary playwrights and Shakespeare himself may have experienced the success of their plays in printed form. During the time of his active career, not only was Shakespeare the most published playwright, but his bibliographic presence compared with that of his contemporaries was massive. No two playwrights together saw as many editions of their plays reach print as Shakespeare did alone. Nor did Shakespeare have to wait until the end of

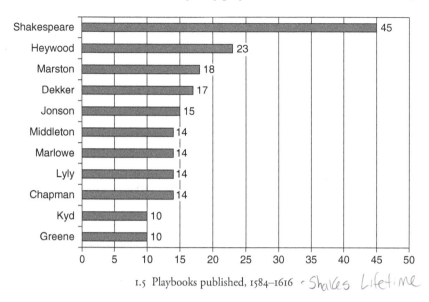

1.5 Playbooks published, 1584–1616 ‹ Shakes Lifetime

his career to become the best-published playwright: until 1597, this distinction had gone to Lyly, who was in print with twelve playbook editions, but by the end of 1598, Shakespeare's total had risen to fourteen, Lyly's only to thirteen. By the end of 1600, Shakespeare had taken a commanding lead with twenty-five editions (Figure 1.6), which he had further consolidated by the end of the year in which Queen Elizabeth died (Figure 1.7).

It is true that many of Shakespeare's early playbooks were published without authorship attribution. In the 1590s, the majority of playbooks were published anonymously, although ascriptions were becoming increasingly common towards the turn of the century, and, as early as the first decade of the seventeenth century, the majority of playbooks mentioned the author on the cover.[42] Shakespeare's plays participated in this trend, and his number of title page mentions soon surpassed that of his contemporaries.[43] His name first appears on a title page in 1598, in the second and third quartos of *Richard II*, the second quarto of *Richard III* and the first extant (though in fact the second) edition of *Love's Labour's Lost*. With four title page ascriptions, Shakespeare catches up at once with Greene, who also has

---

[42] See the chapter devoted to 'The Legitimation of Printed Playbooks in Shakespeare's Time' in Erne, *Shakespeare as Literary Dramatist*, 31–55 (55–79).

[43] I address the question of the *relative* frequency of playbooks with authorship attributions below, p. 95.

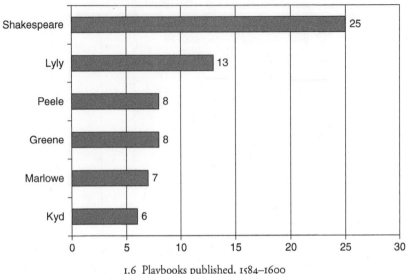

1.6 Playbooks published, 1584–1600

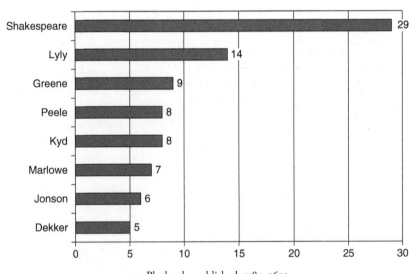

1.7 Playbooks published, 1584–1603

four editions of playbooks with his name on the title page by 1598. Shakespeare takes the lead the following year, with a fifth attribution on the title page of *1 Henry IV*, and outdistances Greene and everyone else in 1600, by the end of which Shakespeare's name figures on the title pages of

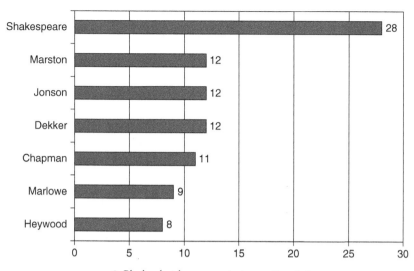

1.8 Playbook title page ascriptions, 1584–1616

no fewer than nine playbook editions. By the end of Shakespeare's life (see Figure 1.8), the number of his title page mentions totals twenty-eight (including the apocryphal *London Prodigal* of 1605 and *A Yorkshire Tragedy* of 1608), far ahead of Marston, Jonson and Dekker with twelve and Chapman with eleven.[44] Shakespeare's advance over his contemporaries is thus no less impressive than in the earlier figures. <u>Clearly, it was not only Shakespeare that sold, but also Shakespeare's name.</u>

Another way of measuring the bibliographic presence of Shakespeare's playbooks in his own time is to determine what fraction of the total output of professional plays they constituted. Appendix B provides access to the yearly number of 'Printed playbooks of professional plays, including reprints, 1583–1622', the forty-year period leading up to the publication of the Shakespeare First Folio, which allows us to extract several revealing figures. In the period from 1594, when the first Shakespeare playbook reached print, to 1616, the year of Shakespeare's death, 263 editions of professional plays were published, of which 45 were by Shakespeare, just over 17 per cent, or more than one in six. In the 'Jacobean' years, 1603–16, the fraction is lower: 17 of 161 playbook editions are Shakespeare's, which is

---

[44] The totals include the abbreviated 'Ch. Marl.' or 'Ch. Mar.' on the title pages of *Doctor Faustus*, but not simple initials, such as 'B. I.' on the title pages of Jonson's *Every Man Out of His Humour* (three editions in 1600), or 'W. S.' in *Locrine* (1595), *Thomas Lord Cromwell* (1602 and 1613) and *The Puritan* (1607), nor 'W. Sh.' in the second quarto of *1, 2 The Troublesome Reign of John, King of England* (1612).

still more than 10 per cent. Most remarkably, in the nine-year 'Elizabethan' period, 1594–1602,[45] the total number of playbook editions is 102, including 28 by Shakespeare. In other words, in the period in which Shakespeare wrote plays for the Lord Chamberlain's Men, an astounding 27 per cent of the editions of professional plays were Shakespeare's, more than one in four. Shakespeare had a commanding presence among the playwrights in print.

It may be objected that Shakespeare's bibliographic presence exceeds that of his contemporaries simply because he wrote more plays than they did. This is correct, but only up to a point. If Marlowe's career was short-lived and his dramatic oeuvre small, then it is hardly surprising that the number of editions of his playbooks did not rival Shakespeare's. Yet other playwrights, like Shirley or Fletcher, had a dramatic output which rivalled or surpassed Shakespeare's. Heywood, it may be useful to remember, claimed that he had 'either an entire hand, or at the least a maine finger' in the writing of 220 plays.[46] A large dramatic output did not automatically translate into a large bibliographic presence. Shakespeare in fact wrote no more than a small fraction of the plays written for the public stage and advertised in playbills. Roslyn L. Knutson believes that, in Shakespeare's time, a company had about fifteen new plays per year.[47] Two or more companies were usually active, and Shakespeare usually wrote about two plays per year for one of these companies. In other words, a very small fraction of the plays performed in the playhouses were Shakespeare's, yet his playbooks account for more than a sixth of the playbook editions published between 1594 and 1616 and more than a quarter of those published between 1594 and 1602. Quite clearly, Shakespeare, in many ways, was not just one playwright among many, providing scripts for an entertainment industry, but an exceptionally successful dramatist who had his plays printed and reprinted like no one else.

Reprint rates and the popularity of Shakespeare's playbooks

The preceding figures give us a sense of the total number of editions in which the plays appeared, but they tell us little about how well Shakespeare's or other dramatists' plays sold once they were in print. The total number of editions conveys how often stationers decided to invest in

---

[45] Queen Elizabeth died in March 1603, so I consider that year as Jacobean for the sake of the present count.
[46] *The English Traveller* (1633), sig. A3r.   [47] See 'Shakespeare's Repertory'.

plays by certain authors, but if we are interested in knowing whether these investments proved worthwhile, then – as Farmer and Lesser have insisted – we need to focus on reprint rates.[48] A reprint means that an edition had sold out, or was on the point of selling out, and that the publisher anticipated enough of a demand for a second edition to pay for its production. Since expenses for a reprint were considerably lower than for a first edition (see below, p. 143), reprints tended to be more profitable than first editions. Of course, on a purely textual level, reprints are often less interesting than so-called substantive editions, insofar as they simply copy the text of an earlier edition. E. K. Chambers's view may be representative of how little value was long attached to reprints: 'several of the plays had been reprinted from time to time', Chambers wrote, adding that 'there is not much to be said about – *ha!* the reprints'.[49] More recently, however, Sonia Massai has warned us against underestimating the textual importance of reprints, showing that many of them contain local, but important, editorial interventions.[50] Independently of the question of the textual importance of reprints, bibliographically they are crucial witnesses to a book's popularity.[51]

Blayney led the way in establishing the importance of reprints. He counted the professional plays published between 1583 and 1642 and their reprints, showing that 'Fewer than 21 percent of the plays published in the sixty years under discussion reached a second edition inside nine years.'[52] This allows for an instructive comparison: thirteen of Shakespeare's twenty-two plays published separately in quarto or octavo format – namely, the nineteen published during Shakespeare's lifetime plus *Othello* (1622), *The Taming of the Shrew* (1631) and *The Two Noble Kinsmen* (1634) – received at least a second edition inside nine years, that is almost 60 per cent, as opposed to the 20 per cent for all professional plays, meaning almost three times as many. Since comparatively few plays first published during the Caroline period reached a second edition – what Farmer and Lesser call

---

[48] See 'The Popularity of Playbooks Revisited', 5: 'The criterion that brings us closest to consumer demand is the rate of reprinting of playbooks, since a publisher's decision to reprint can usually be assumed to indicate both that the previous edition had sold out (or was about to sell out) and that the publisher anticipated continued demand for the book. By comparing playbook reprint rates . . . , we can learn a great deal about the popularity of playbooks with book-buyers.' See also Farmer and Lesser, 'Structures of Popularity in the Early Modern Book Trade', 208: 'Why do reprint rates matter? Because they provide the best available criterion for answering such questions as: How eager were customers to buy the playbooks that were for sale in bookshops? Was a playbook a good publishing investment? Did playbooks reliably turn a profit?'
[49] *William Shakespeare*, 1.133.   [50] See *Shakespeare and the Rise of the Editor*.
[51] For the meaning of 'reprint' in the context of this chapter, see Appendix A. For 'second-plus editions', see Farmer and Lesser, 'The Popularity of Playbooks Revisited', 7.
[52] 'The Publication of Playbooks', 389.

'The Caroline Paradox'[53] – it may be more pertinent to focus on an earlier, shorter period. Blayney writes that 'Of the 96 plays first published in 1583–1602, only 46 (just under 48 percent) were reprinted inside twenty-five years. The percentage is slightly higher for the plays of 1603–1622 (58 out of 115, or just over 50 percent).'[54] If we add up Blayney's figures, then 104 of the 211 plays published between 1583 and 1622, or not quite 50 per cent, reached a second edition within twenty-five years. As for Shakespeare, twenty of his plays were first published during the same years and only three of them, *The Second Part of Henry IV*, *Much Ado about Nothing* and *Troilus and Cressida*, did not receive a second edition within twenty-five years, so the rate of plays that reached at least one reprint within a quarter-century is an astounding 85 per cent, as opposed to the not-quite 50 per cent for playbooks in general. Of the seventeen Shakespeare plays that were reprinted at least once, seven received two editions, four went through three editions, three through four, *Richard II* through five, *Richard III* through six and *1 Henry IV* through seven editions. On average, the twenty Shakespeare plays published between 1594 and 1622 received 2.95 editions (fifty-nine editions for the twenty plays), or almost three editions per play, within twenty-five years of original publication. If we consider *The Whole Contention* as a separate playbook rather than as a reprint of *1 Contention* and *Richard Duke of York*, and if we add *The Taming of the Shrew* (1631) and *The Two Noble Kinsmen* (1634), which received no reprints, and the 1623 Folio (reprinted in 1632), then the average number of editions drops slightly but remains high at 2.6.[55]

This frequency of reprints and the scarcity of Shakespeare playbooks that did not reach a second edition are even more remarkable if we now look at some of Shakespeare's contemporaries. Only three of Lyly's nine playbooks published between 1584 and 1632 received at least a second edition, one of them going through three and one through four editions within twenty-five years. Five of George Peele's plays reached print between 1584 and 1599, of

---

[53] 'The Popularity of Playbooks Revisited', 27–8. See also Farmer and Lesser, 'Canons and Classics'.
[54] 'The Publication of Playbooks', 387.
[55] Like Blayney and Farmer and Lesser before me, I do not distinguish between variant texts such as Shakespeare's 'good' (better: 'long') and 'bad' (better: 'short') quartos in calculating reprint rates. It is true that publishers tried to capitalize on enlarged editions as suggested by playbooks which, correctly or incorrectly, announce better and longer play texts, and it is possible that the promise of an enlarged edition helped sales. Nonetheless, most early modern book-buyers – less interested in textual scholarship than are modern academics – likely did not distinguish between variant texts of the same play. Significantly, none of the book collectors I discuss in Chapter 5 had long and short quartos of *Romeo and Juliet* or *Hamlet*, although many had one or the other. Although I consider the differences between the long and short quartos crucial witnesses for the origins of Shakespeare's plays (see *Shakespeare as Literary Dramatist*), I believe they are of minor importance for the evaluation of the plays' early popularity.

which only *Edward I* reached a second edition. The only play to which Peele contributed which was more successful is the mostly Shakespearean *Titus Andronicus*, of which Peele seems to have written Act 1 and two or three additional scenes,[56] which went through three editions within twenty-five years. Greene contributed to a commercial hit, *A Looking Glass for London and England*, co-authored with Lodge, which went through five editions within twenty-five years. Yet of the five plays Greene seems to have written in sole authorship, only one received a second edition.

As for Shakespeare's later contemporaries, twenty-three of Heywood's playbooks appeared between 1599 and 1656, of which fifteen, or more than 65 per cent, failed to reach a second edition within twenty-five years. Some of Heywood's early plays were genuinely popular, yet without rivalling the popularity of Shakespeare's playbooks: in Shakespeare's lifetime, ten of Heywood's plays appeared in print, of which two received a single reprint, one two, one three, two four and one even five editions within twenty-five years, with the remaining three failing to receive a second edition.

While Heywood's popularity as a print-published dramatist, judging by the number of reprints, was clearly inferior to that of Shakespeare, it was distinctly superior to that of many others. Fourteen of Chapman's playbooks found their way into print between 1598 and 1639, and only two of them received at least a second edition within twenty-five years. *The Conspiracy and Tragedy of Charles Duke of Byron* was reprinted seventeen years after the first edition, and only the collaborative *Eastward Hoe* had considerable commercial success, with three editions. Similarly, twenty-one of Dekker's plays were published between 1600 and 1658, of which sixteen, or 76 per cent, were never reprinted, while three plays received a second and two a fourth edition within twenty-five years. As for Marston's twelve playbooks published between 1601 and 1633, three of them went through three editions and two of them through two, but as many as seven plays were not reprinted within a quarter-century of original publication. Middleton, now considered one of the greatest Renaissance dramatists since the Oxford *Collected Works* have established the full scope of his dramatic oeuvre, was no more popular in print judging by the rate of reprints. Twenty of his playbooks appeared between 1604 and 1657, of which six received a second edition and only two a third within twenty-five years, whereas twelve remained without a reprint inside twenty-five years. Of William Rowley's ten (mostly collaborative) playbooks which

---

[56] See Vickers, *Shakespeare, Co-Author*, 148–243.

This Section has good comparisons

appeared between 1607 and 1660, seven remained without reprint and three reached a second but none a third edition.

As for Jonson, eleven quarto playbooks were published between 1600 and 1620, of which eight failed to receive a reprint within twenty-five years, and the three that were reprinted include the collaborative *Eastward Hoe*. Jonson's First Folio reached a second edition after twenty-four years, but the Second Folio of 1641, which partly built on the abortive 1631 Folio, failed to receive a second edition within twenty-five years, as did *The New Inn*, published in octavo in 1631.

Of Shakespeare's Jacobean and Caroline successors, seventeen of Massinger's playbooks were published prior to 1660, of which only five reached a second edition and none a third within a quarter-century.[57] Eight plays, or play collections, by Richard Brome were published prior to 1660, and only two of them reached a second edition within twenty-five years. Finally, eleven of Ford's plays were published in quarto between 1629 and 1660, and only one of them received a reprint, while thirty playbooks by Shirley were published between 1629 and 1657, of which twenty-six remained without reprint inside a quarter-century.

What all of the dramatists I have just mentioned have in common is that the majority, and often the vast majority, of their playbooks failed to reach a second edition within twenty-five years.[58] In fact, apart from Shakespeare, there appear to be only four exceptions to this rule: Marlowe, Webster, Beaumont and Fletcher. Seven of Marlowe's plays reached print between 1590 and 1633. Three of them were not reprinted within twenty-five years, but the others were, going through four editions (the *Tamburlaine* plays and *Edward II*) or even eight editions (*Doctor Faustus*) within twenty-five years of original publication.[59] As for Webster, seven playbooks reached print before 1660, of which four received at least a second edition (including *The Duchess of Malfi* and *The White Devil*). Of the eight plays Beaumont wrote alone or in co-authorship that were published in quarto between 1607 and

[57] In addition, the 1647 'Beaumont and Fletcher' Folio (reprinted, with additions, in 1679) contains so many plays to which Massinger contributed that it deserves to be considered not only as a Beaumont and a Fletcher but also as a Massinger playbook.

[58] The playbooks of Shakespeare's contemporaries and successors were distinctly less popular than Shakespeare's own, but it is important to remember that their general reprint rate, as Farmer and Lesser have shown, was nonetheless quite high compared with the book trade norm (see 'The Popularity of Playbooks Revisited').

[59] Note that the *Tamburlaine* plays appeared as a two-play collection in 1590, which was reprinted twice in 1593 and 1597, before the plays were published separately in 1605 (*Part I*) and 1606 (*Part II*). Since I am counting playbooks and distinguish collections from single plays, the 1605 and 1606 editions do not qualify as reprints.

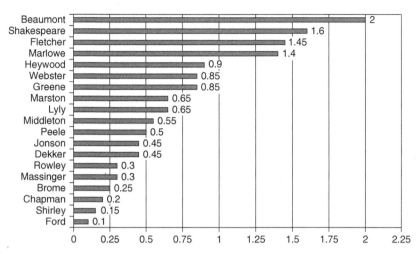

1.9 Average number of reprints within twenty-five years of a playbook's original
publication (1)

1621, only two received not a single reprint within a quarter of a century,
while three received as many as four reprints. As for Fletcher, fourteen of his
plays were published in quarto format between 1610 and 1640. Of these,
four were not reprinted within twenty-five years, but four received a second,
two a third, one a fourth and three even a fifth edition within the same
period.

To sum up, if we calculate the average number of reprints per play, by
author (Figure 1.9), then Beaumont heads the list, with exactly two reprints,
followed by Shakespeare (1.6), Fletcher (1.45) and Marlowe (1.4).[60] Since
the number of first editions of playbooks is small in the cases of Marlowe
(eight) and Beaumont (nine), their averages may not be very representative.
For Marlowe, for instance, the average greatly depends on *Doctor Faustus*,
with its eight editions. If we calculate the average number of reprints of
Marlowe and Shakespeare without taking into consideration their most
popular play, *Faustus* for Marlowe, *1 Henry IV* for Shakespeare, then the
average rate of reprints drops sharply, from 1.4 to 0.85, in the case of
Marlowe, but only slightly, from 1.6 to 1.4, in that of Shakespeare. The
representative sample may thus be the one which confines itself to those

60 These figures reflect the average number of reprints per play*book*, not play *text*. In other words, a
reprint of *Othello* in the 1623 First Folio does not count as a reprint of the 1622 quarto.

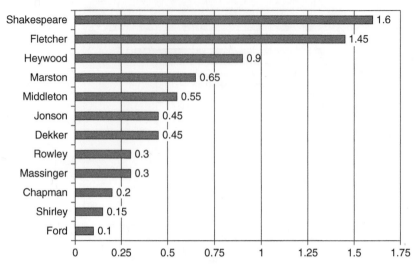

1.10 Average number of reprints within twenty-five years of a playbook's original publication (2) – *Corpus of at least 10 printed plays*

playwrights with a solid corpus of at least ten different plays (Figure 1.10). The noteworthy point about Figure 1.10 is not so much that Shakespeare, followed by Fletcher, heads the list, but that Shakespeare's reprint rate is massively superior to the playwrights in the lower half of the figure, starting with Jonson and Dekker. The average number of reprints of a Shakespeare playbook is eight times that of a Chapman and almost four times that of a Jonson playbook.

If we calculate the average number of reprints within ten years of original publication, the popularity of Shakespeare's printed plays emerges with even greater clarity (Figure 1.11). With almost one reprint per play on average, Shakespeare is ahead of everyone else by about a third or more. Lyly, much in vogue for a limited time, comes second, level with Marlowe. Beaumont and Fletcher figure considerably lower in Figure 1.11 (reprints within ten years) than in Figure 1.9 (reprints within twenty-five years), suggesting that their popularity in print grew steadily and took some time to establish itself. If we again restrict the sample to the playwrights with a representative corpus of at least ten different playbooks (see Figure 1.12), then the difference between Shakespeare and the others is even starker. Shakespeare's average number of reprints again exceeds Jonson's by a factor of almost four to one and even Fletcher's by more than two to one.

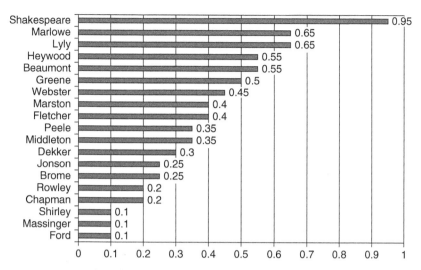

1.11 Average number of reprints within ten years of a playbook's original publication (1)

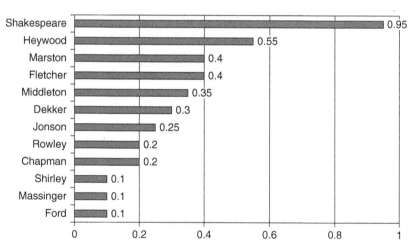

1.12 Average number of reprints within ten years of a playbook's original publication (2)

Corpus of @ least 10

Conclusion

With these figures in mind, we may now wish to return to the question of Jonson's and Shakespeare's comparative popularity. We remember that Bentley, in his two-volume study, argued that 'Jonson's general popularity was greater than Shakespeare's from the beginning of the century to 1690.'[61] Yet the number of editions of Shakespeare playbooks up to 1660 is 76 as compared with 22 for Jonson, and the number of editions of play texts for the same period is 147 for Shakespeare and only 41 for Jonson. In addition, and perhaps most eloquently as a comment on popularity, Shakespeare's reprint rate, within both ten and twenty-five years, is almost four times that of Jonson. The dominent sense in which I have been using the term 'popularity' is the fact of being read by many people (cf. *OED* n.3), as reflected by the number of editions. There are limits to our knowledge (as acknowledged above, pp. 25–7) that complicate the measurement of popularity by means of quantitative analysis, but what underlies my methodology is the belief that the extant editions provide the best evidence we have of the breadth of bibliographic dissemination. It is true that there are other ways of judging the popularity of playwrights than the scope of their bibliographic presence. Bentley arrived at his very different conclusions by counting not editions but allusions to and quotations from the playwrights and their plays. What this suggests is that while Jonson may have been the writers' writer, who was frequently drawn upon and pointed to, Shakespeare was the readers' writer, whose popularity called for a steady supply of new editions. Shakespeare thus appears to have been popular in more than one sense, not only widely read but also enjoyed by a more general, less specialized and elite readership (cf. *OED* adj.4) than Jonson, who pleased not the million.[62]

Another conclusion to be drawn from this chapter is that insofar as Shakespeare's popularity in the seventeenth century is concerned, it is important to distinguish between the first and the second half of the century. If we focus on the second half, it appears, as Paulina Kewes has argued, that Shakespeare's later pre-eminence was still very much in

---

[61] *Shakespeare and Jonson*, 1.138.

[62] Note, though, that a facile dichotomy between a 'popular' Shakespeare and an 'elitist' Jonson in the book trade would be undermined by the fact that when they were published in expensive folios (whose price must have put them out of reach for most people), Shakespeare's took only nine years to reach a second edition, whereas Jonson's took twenty-four. For the complexity of the term 'popular' in relation to Shakespeare, printed playbooks and early modern print culture more generally, see Henderson, 'From Popular Entertainment to Literature', 17–23; Farmer and Lesser, *Plays, Print, and Popularity in Shakespeare's England*; and Kesson and Smith, eds., *The Elizabethan Top Ten*.

doubt.[63] Yet if we focus on Shakespeare's own time and the early seventeenth century, then it emerges that Shakespeare was considerably more popular, judging by how often his plays were printed, than his contemporaries. What this implies is that the question of whether playbooks were popular or not may have depended importantly on the identity of the playwrights: whereas the publication of the playbooks of some of Shakespeare's contemporaries seems to have constituted mostly unprofitable commercial ventures, that of Shakespeare's playbooks was mostly profitable, in fact several times more profitable, on average, than that of Jonson, Chapman and other contemporaries and successors.

I would argue, then, that our thinking about Shakespeare's status from his own time to the eighteenth century has been too linear, too much anchored in the belief that the reputation he came to acquire in the eighteenth century is diametrically opposed to his lack of cachet in the early seventeenth century. In *The Making of the National Poet*, Michael Dobson announces at the outset that his aim is to describe how the 'extraordinary change in Shakespeare's status came about', and Gary Taylor, in *Reinventing Shakespeare*, is similarly interested in tracing the evolution in the reception of Shakespeare from a moment of relative insignificance to a moment of perceived greatness: 'When did people decide that Shakespeare was the greatest English dramatist? The greatest English poet?'[64] What this does not take into account is that for the English book-buying public, Shakespeare was already the greatest English dramatist in the late sixteenth and early seventeenth century, although he lost that position in the course of the century. To a surprising extent, Shakespeare's popularity as a printed dramatist in his own time anticipated his authorial pre-eminence in later centuries.

---

[63] 'Between the "Triumvirate of wit" and the Bard'. See also Taylor's comments on the general 'failure to remember much of Shakespeare' by 1660 (*Reinventing Shakespeare*, 10).

[64] Dobson, *The Making of the National Poet*, 2; and Taylor, *Reinventing Shakespeare*, 5.

CHAPTER 2

Shakespeare, publication and authorial misattribution

In the early 1590s, most plays were still published anonymously, yet after the turn of the century, authorial ascriptions became a standard feature of playbook title pages. The name of the dramatic author was increasingly counted on to authorize and sell playbooks. What this commercial mechanism led to is the occasional practice of title page misattribution. Perhaps most famously, *The Passionate Pilgrim*, first published in late 1598 or 1599, attributes to Shakespeare a collection of twenty poems of which only five (poems 1, 2, 3, 5 and 16) are now generally recognized to be by him. There is awareness among scholars of early modern drama that not all playbooks ascribed to Shakespeare in his own time are now believed to have been written by him, but the remarkable conjunction of the following two facts does not seem to have been noticed. Firstly, the number of editions whose title pages wrongly ascribe a play to Shakespeare, or hint at Shakespeare's authorship by means of his initials, is remarkably high: there are perhaps as many as ten between 1595 and 1622, of seven different plays. Secondly, no other dramatist had any playbooks misattributed to him during the same period. We might be tempted to think that if we are aware of misattributions to Shakespeare rather than to his contemporaries, this may be simply because the focus of posterity has chiefly been on Shakespeare. But this is not so. As we will see more fully below, it is only from the mid-1630s that several other dramatists started having plays misattributed to them, including Chapman, Beaumont and Fletcher. In the fifty-year period from 1584 (when the first plays by Lyly and Peele reached print) to 1633, no professional play has been identified as being wrongly attributed to anyone other than Shakespeare. During his lifetime and in the years following it, pseudepigraphy appears to have been a Shakespearean prerogative.

Table 4 lists in chronological order the misattributed playbook editions. In four of the ten editions, the misattribution takes the indirect form of

Table 4 *Authorial misattribution in playbooks, 1584–1633*

Date	Title	Title page attribution	Author(s)
1595	*Locrine*	W. S.	Anonymous
1602	*Thomas Lord Cromwell*	W. S.	Anonymous
1605	*The London Prodigal*	William Shakespeare	Anonymous
1607	*The Puritan (Widow)*	W. S.	Thomas Middleton
1608	*A Yorkshire Tragedy*	W. Shakspeare	Thomas Middleton
1611	*1, 2 The Troublesome Reign of John, King of England*	W. Sh.	Anonymous (George Peele?)
1613	*Thomas Lord Cromwell*	W. S.	Anonymous
1619	*A Yorkshire Tragedy*	W. SHAKESPEARE	Thomas Middleton
1619 ('1600')	*1 Sir John Oldcastle*	William Shakespeare	Robert Wilson, Michael Drayton, Anthony Munday and Richard Hathaway
1622	*1, 2 The Troublesome Reign of John, King of England*	W. Shakespeare	Anonymous (George Peele)

Shakespeare's initials rather than his full name, and in one case, the 1595 edition of *Locrine*, it is conceivable that the initials do not point to him. After all, even though *Venus and Adonis* and *The Rape of Lucrece* were a great success in the mid-1590s, the first appearance of Shakespeare's name on a title page did not occur until 1598. Howsoever that be, the number of playbooks misattributed to Shakespeare and the absence of misattributions to other dramatists in the same period appears to corroborate what Chapter 1 has suggested, namely that Shakespeare was by no slight margin the most popular playwright in print in his own time.

I will return below to the playbooks misattributed to Shakespeare and other dramatists, but before I do so, these misattributions require some contextualization for their meanings to emerge as fully as possible.

Pseudepigraphy: the meanings of authorial misattributions

The practice of authorial misattribution has a long history. Biblical and patristic scholars have a term to designate the ascription of false names of authors to works: 'pseudepigraphy' – from the Greek ψευδής, *pseudēs*, 'false' and ἐπιγραφή, *epigraphē*, 'inscription'. The stronger the nexus between authority and authorship, the more was at stake in pseudepigraphy: to the extent that the authority of a text crucially depended on the authority of its author, authorial misascription was an essential tool in the adjudication of meaning and power. It is unsurprising, then, that religious texts were long misattributed to biblical figures and Church Fathers.[1] Jerome, for instance, accused Rufinus, one of his opponents, of false attributions to lend greater authority to his arguments in controversy.[2] As a result, studies of pseude-pigraphy remained of crucial importance in religious controversy until the Reformation. Robert Cooke (1550–1615), a vicar from Leeds, prepared an extensive catalogue of pseudepigrapha, called *Censura* (1614), and Thomas James (1573?–1629), the first librarian of the Bodleian Library, compiled a list of almost two hundred theological treatises, titled 'Bastardie of the False Fathers', which had been falsely attributed.[3] False attributions and their detection thus long played a major role in religious controversy.

What distinguishes this pseudepigraphic practice most fundamentally from that practised in the London book trade in the late sixteenth and early seventeenth century is its motivation. In religious controversy, the name of the author to whom a text is falsely attributed was often counted on to lend authority to one's arguments and thus to persuade. By contrast, within the early modern London book trade, false authorship ascriptions on title pages of literary titles usually functioned as an advertisement strategy and were moti-vated by the desire to maximize sales. This neat distinction breaks down in a case like that of Chaucer, whose sixteenth-century publishers Lollardized him by misattributing to him various anti-clerical works, thereby enlisting the most prestigious English author in the cause of the Reformation and simulta-neously swelling the scope and increasing the marketability of his works.[4] Whether in the case of religious controversy, early modern playbooks or sixteenth-century works of Chaucer, it seems fair to say that pseudepigraphy serves the increase of what, following Pierre Bourdieu, we can call capital: symbolic capital, economic capital or a combination of the two.[5]

Pseudepigraphy appropriates the meanings and authority of a name other than that of the text's actual writer, something it shares with the practice of

[1] See North, *The Anonymous Renaissance*, 15.
[2] See Taylor and Mosher, *The Bibliographical History of Anonyma and Pseudonyma*, 40.
[3] James's list was published in *A Treatise of the Corruption of Scripture, Councels, and Fathers, by the Prelats, Pastors, and Pillars of the Church of Rome, for Maintenance of Popery and Irreligion* (1611). See Taylor and Mosher, *The Bibliographical History of Anonyma and Pseudonyma*, 50–6.
[4] See Simpson, *Reform and Cultural Revolution*, 40–2; Miskimin, *The Renaissance Chaucer*, 255–7; Swart, 'Chaucer and the English Reformation'; Pask, *The Emergence of the English Author*, 14–29; and Gillespie, *Print Culture and the Medieval Author*, 187–206.
[5] See *The Rules of Art*.

forgery. Forgery, like pseudepigraphy, can serve to increase a work's prestige (e.g. William Henry Ireland's Shakespeare forgery *Vortigern*) or its market-ability (e.g. the sixteenth-century printmakers who signed their prints 'AD', for 'Albrecht Dürer'). What distinguishes the two practices, however, is that in forgery, the agent responsible for the misattribution is the text's writer (who passes it off as someone else's), whereas in pseudepigraphy, it is not. The appropriation of someone else's text further relates pseudepigraphy to plagiarism, but whereas plagiarism designates a writer's misappropriation to himself of a text written by someone other, pseudepigraphy refers to erroneous authorial labelling of original texts.

Forgery and plagiarism are thus perpetrated by writers (or artists), whereas the kind of pseudepigraphy in which I am interested here is a book trade effect whose specific context is the regulations and practices of the Stationers' Company. In the late sixteenth and early seventeenth century, printers had the freedom to name or not to name the author. At the end of the reign of Henry VIII, in 1546, a royal proclamation had in fact ordered that 'every book should bear the author's and the printer's name, and exact date of printing'.[6] Yet its effect appears to have been short-lived, and when the Stationers' Company received its royal charter of incorpo-ration in 1557, no such obligation existed.[7] Not only could a publisher own the right in a text once he had it licensed – in the absence of any formal authorial copyright regulations prior to 1710 – but he could also decide whether the title page would name the author or not.

Although authorial title page naming was not a legal requirement, it obviously could have its benefits. Many textual genres, including most non-literary genres, were traditionally expected to be assigned to authors, whereas others, like playbooks, could be if mention of the name was thought to serve business needs. A play could be 'authoriz'd by the Authors name' (sig. A2r), as Richard Brome put it in a commendatory poem prefaced to Beaumont and Fletcher's *Monsieur Thomas* (1639). Within an economy of textual attribu-tions, the name of the author, as Mark Rose has put it, can become 'a kind of brand name, a recognizable sign that the cultural commodity will be of a certain kind and quality'.[8] The proliferation of Shakespeare's name on title pages from 1598 suggests that it did acquire such marketable recognition value. Shakespeare's Juliet asks, 'What's in a name?', and stationers seem to have realized that one thing that is in it is money, and that a name to make money with was 'Shakespeare'.

[6] McKenzie, 'Stationers' Company Liber A', 39.   [7] See Griffin, 'Introduction', 5.
[8] *Authors and Owners*, 1.

Not all names had the resonance of Shakespeare's, and so in certain cases, authorial labelling seemed unimportant or even undesirable. Tiffany Stern has suggested that playbills and title pages worked analogously, and so with both, 'Advertising considerations seem to have determined whether or not to name the playwright.' She quotes Belch in Marston's *Histriomastix* (1610), who says about the playwright Post-hast that 'it is as dangerous to read his name at a playe-dore, as a printed bil on a plague dore', suggesting that authorial naming could be perceived as not only ineffective but even counter-productive.[9] Marcy L. North has pointed out that 'Even as late sixteenth-century book-sellers discovered that popular names could sell books, anonymity remained incredibly common.'[10] The trend towards authorial naming continued in the early seventeenth century, but the omission of the playwrights' names on title pages remained an option for publishers of professional plays.

The context for the occasional authorial misattributions was thus a constellation in which authorship attribution was becoming increasingly common but in which authors had few rights, where 'Attributions of authorship tended to serve business needs' yet where 'There was, usually, no penalty for being wrong.'[11] As James Bednarz has put it, 'If the print market escalated the trend toward literary attribution, the opportunity it afforded stationers to increase profit by fraudulently using a famous author's name also increased the incidence of misattribution.'[12] Insofar as the Stationers' Company normally did not sanction authorial misnaming, the risk a stationer took was slight. And to the extent that a name could help sell books, misattribution was potentially lucrative.

Authorial misattributions of playbooks, 1634–1660: Shakespeare's contemporaries and successors

From 1634 to 1660, plays are misattributed to various contemporaries or successors of Shakespeare. Table 5 provides the list of misattributed professional plays of this period.[13]

---

[9] '"On Each Wall and Corner Poast"', 83.

[10] 'Rehearsing the Absent Name', 20. The fullest study of the functions of early modern anonymity is North's *The Anonymous Renaissance*. See also Starner and Traister, eds., *Anonymity in Early Modern England.*

[11] Peters, *Theatre of the Book*, 38–9.   [12] 'Canonizing Shakespeare', 256.

[13] I consider only those playbooks as misattributions which are assigned to a playwright whom we now believe not to have been involved in the making of that play. When a play is now believed to have been written collaboratively, but the title page does not mention all the collaborators (e.g. *Pericles*, attributed to Shakespeare on the early title pages but not to his likely co-author, George Wilkins),

Table 5 *Authorial misattribution in playbooks, 1634–1660*

Date	Title	Author(s)	Title page attribution
1634	*The Noble Spanish Soldier*	Thomas Dekker, John Ford	S. R.
1635	*The Knight of the Burning Pestle*	Francis Beaumont	Francis Beaumont, and Iohn Fletcher
1638	*Selimus*	Robert Greene (?)	T. G.
1639	*Wit without Money*	John Fletcher	Francis Beamount, and John Flecher
1639	*The Ball*	James Shirley	George Chapman, and James Shirly
1640	*The Coronation*	James Shirley	John Fletcher
1650	*The Elder Brother*	John Fletcher	FRANCIS BEAVMONT, AND JOHN FLETCHER
1652	*The Widow*	Thomas Middleton	BEN: JOHNSON. JOHN FLETCHER. THO: MIDDLETON
1652	*The Wild Goose Chase*	John Fletcher	FRANCIS BEAVMONT, AND JOHN FLETCHER
1654	*Alphonsus, Emperor of Germany*	Anonymous	George Chapman
1654	*Revenge for Honour*	Henry Glapthorne	GEORGE CHAPMAN
1657	*Lust's Dominion*	Anonymous	Christofer Marloe

A closer look at these publications suggests that most misattributions, though probably not all of them, were motivated by the desire to capitalize on the selling power of authors' names. It seems significant, for instance, that two plays were misattributed to George Chapman in 1654: *Revenge for Honour*, published by Richard Marriot, and *Alphonsus, Emperor of Germany*, published by Humphrey Moseley. Modern scholars are

that play is not included on the grounds that the information on the title page is not so much wrong as incomplete. Some cases are borderline: *The Spanish Gypsy*, for instance, ascribed to Middleton and Rowley on the Q1 title page (1653), has sometimes been considered to be by Dekker and Ford (see Harbage, *Annals of English Drama, 975–1700*, 118), but is attributed to all four – Dekker, Ford, Middleton and Rowley – in Taylor and Lavagnino, gen. eds., *Thomas Middleton and Early Modern Textual Culture*, 1105–21. The second quarto of *Thierry and Theodoret* (1648) attributes the play to Fletcher, and the second issue of that edition (1649) to Beaumont and Fletcher, but the first edition of 1621 had appeared anonymously. The play has sometimes been attributed to Fletcher and Massinger, but is attributed to Beaumont, Fletcher and Massinger by Hoy ('The Shares of Fletcher and his Collaborators in the Beaumont and Fletcher Canon (III)' (1958), 97–8). The 1639 first quarto of *The Bloody Brother (Rollo, Duke of Normandy)* attributes the play to 'B. J. F.' (short for Ben Jonson and John Fletcher?). The second quarto of 1640 assigns the play to Fletcher, whereas Hoy attributes it to Fletcher, Massinger, Jonson and Chapman ('The Shares of Fletcher and his Collaborators in the Beaumont and Fletcher Canon (VI)' (1961), 56–63). To the extent that the initials 'B. J. F' point in an authorial direction (Fletcher, Jonson), the direction is not wrong. *The Spanish Gypsy*, *Thierry and Theodoret*, *The Bloody Brother* and other incompletely attributed plays are thus not considered misattributions in this chapter.

unanimous in rejecting these attributions.[14] What may well account for the presence of Chapman's name on the title pages is that he enjoyed considerable prestige following the publication not only of his Folio *Works of Homer* (1616, reissued 1634), but also, more recently, of a collection of six of his plays in 1652: *Comedies, Tragicomedies, and Tragedies*, with *The Blind Beggar of Alexandria*, *An Humorous Day's Mirth*, *All Fools*, *The Gentleman Usher*, *Monsieur d'Olive* and *Bussy d'Ambois*. That this collection led to publications which tried to profit from it is also suggested by the reissues, in 1652 and 1653, of the 1631 edition of Chapman's *Caesar and Pompey*. So it seems likely that the 1654 editions of *Revenge for Honour* and *Alphonsus, Emperor of Germany* constitute deliberate misattributions, by the publishers or those who sold the manuscripts to them, designed to profit from the resonance enjoyed by Chapman's name following the publication of his play collection two years earlier.

The prestige of playwrights whose works had appeared in collections may also have prompted a slightly earlier misattribution in a playbook published by Moseley. The title page of *The Widow*, published in quarto in 1652, ascribes the play to Jonson, Fletcher and Middleton, but Jonson and Fletcher's co-authorship was rejected as early as the seventeenth century, and modern scholars agree that the play is Middleton's unaided work.[15] As Gary Taylor has commented,

Whoever was responsible for the false identification of Jonson and Fletcher as collaborators, its motives are not difficult to discern. No new play attributed to Middleton had been published since 1630; in the intervening 22 years, only a single play quarto – the 1640 reprint of *Mad World* – had carried his name. By contrast, Jonson's works had been published in a prestigious folio as recently as 1640, Fletcher's in 1647. The attributions to Jonson and Fletcher are, in the circumstances, as suspect as the attribution to Middleton is unexpected and therefore credible.[16]

In the case of the 1654 *Alphonsus, Emperor of Germany* and the 1652 *Widow*, both published by Moseley, and the 1654 *Revenge for Honour*, the prestige enjoyed by dramatists who had recently had their plays published in a collection may thus account for the title page misattributions.[17]

[14] For the argument for Henry Glapthorne's authorship of *Revenge for Honour*, see Walter, '*Revenge for Honour*'. For *Alphonsus, Emperor of Germany*, see Chambers, *The Elizabethan Stage*, IV.2–3.
[15] See Taylor, 'Works Included in This Edition', 379–80.
[16] 'Works Included in This Edition', 380.
[17] It is possible that the misattribution of *The Widow* originated not with Moseley but with Alexander Gough, a former actor, who seems to have sold the manuscript to Moseley and written an address 'To the Reader' printed in *The Widow* in which he affirms that the play was written by Fletcher, Jonson and Middleton (see Taylor, 'Works Included in This Edition', 380).

In the light of the two misattributions of plays published by Moseley in 1652 and 1654, it seems relevant to note that Moseley, on 9 September 1653, had entered in the Stationers' Register 'the merry deuil of Edmonton, by W^m: Shakespeare' among a list of plays in which he had obtained the rights. In the case of *The Merry Devil of Edmonton*, something seems to have gone wrong, however, for Moseley did not publish the play and thus had no opportunity to misattribute it to Shakespeare on a title page.[18] When a new edition of the play appeared in 1655, the publisher was William Gilbertson, not Moseley. Rights in the play were transferred on 4 April 1655 to William Gilbertson by the widow of Francis Faulkner, Faulkner having owned those rights since 1624. Conceivably, Moseley had thought that rights in the play had become derelict, but was reminded by Faulkner that this was not so. As it turned out, Gilbertson's edition of 1655 was published anonymously, like the five earlier editions (of 1608, 1612, 1617, 1626 and 1631), though it mentioned performance 'by his Maiesties Seruants, at the Globe', as had its five predecessors. The presence of Shakespeare's name in the Stationers' Register entry of 9 September 1653 does not prove that Moseley deliberately misattributed another play, this time to Shakespeare: after all, there was no point in fooling the wardens of the Stationers' Company if a publisher wanted to sell extra copies through an authorial misattribution. But the entry does suggest that Moseley's interest in publishing prestigiously authored play-books was such that he was quite capable of publishing misattributed playbooks, whether he was aware that the authorship attribution was mistaken or not.

We have seen above that two plays were misattributed to Chapman in the 1650s, but his name had in fact been taken in vain on a title page as early as 1639. James Shirley's *The Ball*, first performed in 1632, was published seven years later by Andrew Crooke and William Cooke and assigned to Shirley and Chapman on the title page, even though the entry in the Stationers' Register of 24 October 1638 correctly attributes the play to Shirley alone. *The Tragedy of Chabot, Admiral of France*, a play originally by Chapman but revised by Shirley, was issued the same year by the same publishers and also attributed, correctly this time, to Chapman and Shirley. It is possible, as Thomas Marc Parrott has argued, that the misattribution happened accidentally during Shirley's residence in Dublin (1636–40),

---

[18] For the authorship of *The Merry Devil of Edmonton* (which has sometimes been attributed to Dekker), see Lancashire and Levenson, 'Anonymous Plays', in *The Popular School*, 208–9. Moseley's list of 9 September 1653 also mentions 'The History of Cardenio, by Mr. Fletcher. & Shakespeare', and, as Stern has pointed out, it is possible that here, too, the attribution to Shakespeare is spurious (see '"The Forgery of Some Modern Author"?', 557–9).

perhaps because Crooke and Cooke found out after entering *The Ball* and *The Tragedy of Chabot*, which are both ascribed to Shirley alone in the Stationers' Register, that the latter play was co-authored by Chapman but mistakenly assumed the co-authorship to apply to both plays.[19] It cannot be ruled out, however, that Crooke and Cooke found *The Ball* and *The Tragedy of Chabot* an attractive pair of plays to promote jointly, and considered identical 'Shirley and Chapman' authorship as part of this promotion. They could be forgiven for believing that Chapman's name would increase the play's marketability.

Another edition which seems to have been misattributed for commercial motives is *The Noble Spanish Soldier* (1634), by Dekker, wrongly ascribed to 'S. R.' on the title page. When the play was entered in the Stationers' Register, Dekker's authorship was correctly stated, so there can be little doubt that the identity of the play's author was known. The initials 'S. R.' have long been assumed to point to Samuel Rowley, and what may have motivated the misattribution is that a popular play of Rowley's about Henry VIII, *When You See Me You Know Me*, had reached its fourth edition in 1632. Similarly, *The Tragedy of Selimus, Emperor of the Turks* was likely assigned to 'T. G.' because the initials suggested Thomas Goffe, author of two plays on Turkish subjects which had appeared earlier in the same decade: *The Raging Turk, or Bajazet the Second* (1631) and *The Courageous Turk, or Amurath the First* (1632). The 1638 title page of *Selimus* is part of a reissue of the original edition of the play which – under the title *The First Part of the Tragical Reign of Selimus* – had appeared in 1594, when Goffe was three years old, so his authorship seems unlikely. The play is now variously considered to be by Greene or treated as anonymous.[20]

An authorial label which had acquired even more cachet by the 1630s than Rowley's or Goffe's is that of 'Beaumont and Fletcher', as is evidenced by playbooks attributed to both, even though the attribution to the one or the other now seems mistaken. For instance, Beaumont's *Knight of the Burning Pestle* was first published in 1613, with no authorship ascription on the title page. In 1616, a first playbook, *The Scornful Lady*, was published in quarto as having been written by Beaumont and Fletcher according to the title page. Many editions followed in the next years: Q1, Q2 and Q3 *A King and No King* (1619, 1625, 1631), Q1, Q2, Q3 and Q4 *Philaster* (1620, 1622, 1628, 1634), Q2, Q3 and Q4 *The Scornful Lady* (1625, 1630, 1635), Q2 and Q3 *Cupid's*

[19] See *The Plays and Poems of George Chapman*, 872. See also Stevenson, 'Shirley's Publishers', 148–9.
[20] Melnikoff and Gieskes list the play among Greene's works, not his 'Apocrypha' (*Writing Robert Greene*, 225, 236), whereas Farmer and Lesser label it anonymous (*DEEP*).

Revenge (1630, 1635; Q1, in 1615, had been published anonymously) and Q3 *The Maid's Tragedy* (1630; Q1 and Q2 (1619, 1622) had been published anonymously). When the second quarto of *The Knight of the Burning Pestle* was attributed to 'Beaumont and Fletcher' in 1635, fourteen playbook editions had appeared in the preceding twenty years with title page ascriptions to 'Beaumont and Fletcher', while not a single playbook had been ascribed on the title page to Beaumont alone. 'Beaumont and Fletcher' authorship was fully established, and the label clearly had considerable cachet. It is not easy to recover whether 'I. S.' (John Spencer?), the publisher of Q2 *Knight of the Burning Pestle*, really believed that the play had been written collaboratively or whether he knew about Beaumont's sole authorship, yet it is easy to understand why he must have considered the 'Beaumont and Fletcher' logo commercially attractive when having the 1635 title page printed.

It comes as no surprise, then, that further playbooks were ascribed to 'Beaumont and Fletcher', despite the fact that modern scholarship disagrees. Modern scholars find Fletcher's but not Beaumont's hand in *Wit without Money*, yet the first quarto of 1639 attributes it to Beaumont and Fletcher.[21] The same applies to *The Wild Goose Chase*: first published in 1652 in folio format, the publication was clearly designed as an addendum to the 1647 'Beaumont and Fletcher' Folio, so the ascription to both playwrights is unsurprising.

The 1650 edition of *The Elder Brother*, attributed to Beaumont and Fletcher on the title page, is likely to be another deliberate misattribution. The play had been correctly assigned to Fletcher alone on the title page when it was first published by John Waterson and John Benson in 1637. Waterson and Benson transferred their rights in the play to Moseley on 31 October 1646, but Moseley did not publish it in the 'Beaumont and Fletcher' Folio the following year, in keeping with his policy of including only plays which had not been printed before. Instead, he issued the play as a separate quarto in 1650, assigning it to Beaumont and Fletcher. Moseley would have had little reason to doubt the accuracy of the 1637 title page attribution to Fletcher alone, all the more so as the entry in the Stationers' Register in October 1646, which records the transfer of rights to Moseley, names 'Mr. Fflesher' (*sic*) as the play's author. Yet having recently published the 'Beaumont and Fletcher' Folio, Moseley had a stake in that label and must have hoped that its appearance on the title page of the 1650 edition of *The Elder Brother* would further its sales.

---

[21] For the authorship of *Wit without Money*, see Smith, 'Francis Beaumont and John Fletcher', 66.

The case of *The Coronation*, attributed to Fletcher in the 1640 quarto but assigned by modern scholars to Shirley on good grounds, is different from those discussed above insofar as the misattribution is most likely to have been accidental.[22] *The Coronation* is one of five plays entered jointly by Andrew Crooke and William Cooke in the Stationers' Register on 25 April 1639, along with Fletcher's *Wit without Money* and *The Night-Walker*, and Shirley's *The Opportunity* and *Love's Cruelty*. Given that the other four plays were attributed correctly, two to Fletcher, two to Shirley, it seems economical to assume that a misunderstanding led the publishers to assign *The Coronation* to the wrong dramatist.[23]

Another play which does not seem to have been misattributed as part of its commercial promotion is *Lust's Dominion*. When the play was first published by Francis Kirkman in 1657, the title page claimed that it was written by 'Christofer Marloe, Gent.', an ascription that modern scholars do not accept. The playbook appeared more than six decades after Marlowe's death, almost a quarter-century after the last edition of a Marlowe play (*The Jew of Malta*, 1633) and exactly two decades after the last edition of his *Hero and Leander* (1637). It is difficult to see, then, how the name of Marlowe on the title page would have been a device to boost sales figures, and it seems more likely that the mistake simply resulted from ignorance. Kirkman or whoever else was responsible for the authorship ascription must have been aware that *Lust's Dominion* was an old play.[24] Its stylistic indebtedness to Marlowe, in particular to *The Jew of Malta*, has been commented upon, which may provide another reason for the misattribution.[25] It has been argued that the quarto 'was brought out for political ends' in 1657, that the play could have been topically construed in that year as 'a critique of Cromwell's regime' and that Marlowe's name on the title page was designed to 'disguis[e] the purpose of the publishing venture': '*This is an old play*, the implication runs, *any connection with current events is wholly unintentional.*'[26] Several explanations for the misattribution to

---

[22] For the authorship of *The Coronation*, see Bentley, *The Jacobean and Caroline Stage*, V.1098–9.

[23] See Stevenson, 'Shirley's Publishers', 149–50. A French play which seems to have been misattributed for similarly accidental reasons is *La Clénide* (1634), by de la Barre, which was reissued in 1635 as *Célidor et Clénide* and ascribed on the title page to de Cormeil (note that the first names of de la Barre and de Cormeil seem to be unknown). See Lancaster, *A History of French Dramatic Literature in the Seventeenth Century*, I.414–15.

[24] The conjectured date of *Lust's Dominion* is *c.* 1600. See Lancashire and Levenson, 'Anonymous Plays', in *The Popular School*, 186.

[25] See, for instance, Cross, 'The Authorship of *Lust's Dominion*', 39.

[26] Cathcart, '"You Will Crown Him King that Slew Your King"', 264, 270.

Marlowe are possible, but the attempt to cash in on his name does not figure prominently among them.[27]

To summarize, from the 1630s to the 1650s, a dozen playbooks appear to have been misattributed, mostly for commercial reasons, usually by stationers, it seems, but conceivably also by those who sold dramatic manuscripts to stationers. There are quite a few dramatists to whom plays were wrongly ascribed: Fletcher, Beaumont, Chapman, Marlowe, Jonson, 'T. G.' (probably for Thomas Goffe) and 'S. R.' (probably for Samuel Rowley). The likely reasons why the misuse of most of these names seems to have been considered a good commercial device are manifold: recent collections and/or folio editions which lent their authors' names prestige (Chapman, Jonson, Fletcher); a well-selling playbook whose success the misattributed play was hoped to replicate (Rowley); plays of a certain genre (Turkish plays) with which a dramatist was then associated (Goffe); an authorial label which had established itself with considerable success on quarto playbook title pages (Beaumont and Fletcher). Clearly, there were many contexts for the creative approach to authorship attribution.

Shakespeare's name is absent from the list of those to whom plays were misattributed in this period. Given that the authoritative canon of his plays appeared in the folios of 1623 and 1632, it may have been perceived to be difficult to pass off other plays as Shakespeare's in the years following their publication. *The Merry Devil of Edmonton*, as suggested above, would likely have been misattributed to Shakespeare in the 1650s if Moseley had obtained the right to publish it. Shortly after the period I have examined here, *The Birth of Merlin* (1662) was published by Francis Kirkman and Henry Marsh and attributed on the title page to 'William Shakespear, and William Rowley'. Scholars agree that while Rowley must have authored or at least contributed to the play, Shakespeare did not.[28] Yet even so, the misattributions of playbooks in the 1630s and the following decades suggest that while the resonance of Shakespeare's name may have been that of one among several with which to sell playbooks, he was no longer in a class of his own.

The preceding examination of misattributed playbooks from the 1630s to the 1650s provides a useful context, I believe, within which to return now to the earlier misattributed playbooks from the 1590s to the 1620s. The multiplicity of motives for misattributions and the number of different authors to

---

[27] Note that reissues of the 1657 edition, with cancel title pages, appeared in 1658 and 1661, also attributing the play to 'Christopher Marloe, Gent.'

[28] For the authorship of *The Birth of Merlin*, see Bawcutt, ed., *The Control and Censorship of Caroline Drama*, 136; and Taylor, 'The Canon and Chronology of Shakespeare's Plays', 135.

whom playbooks were wrongly ascribed between 1634 and 1657, make it all
the more remarkable that all misattributions in the earlier decades, indeed in
the whole fifty-year period between 1584 and 1633, appear to centre on one
playwright, William Shakespeare, also known as 'W. Sh.' or 'W. S.'.

Authorial misattributions of playbooks, 1595–1622: taking Shakespeare's name in vain

A long time ago, E. K. Chambers surveyed the plays mistakenly attributed
to Shakespeare and concluded that 'it looks as if Shakespeare's reputation
had "publicity" value'.[29] Baldwin Maxwell, in 1956, added that misattributions to Shakespeare can be 'interpreted as deliberate designs on the part of
printers to capitalize upon Shakespeare's recognized superiority by misleading hesitant purchasers into thinking they were being offered plays by
William Shakespeare'.[30] I agree with Chambers's and Maxwell's assess-
ments, but a closer examination of the circumstances of these Shakespeare
misattributions is necessary to understand more fully what they tell us about
the place occupied by Shakespeare in the London book trade.

Locrine was entered to Thomas Creede in the Stationers' Register on 20
July 1594 and printed by him the following year. Scholars are agreed that
Shakespeare did not author the play, but whether the initials 'W. S.' on the
title page were intended to mislead potential customers into thinking that
he did is uncertain, as pointed out above.[31] Shakespeare's name is absent
from his previously published playbooks, the 1594 *Titus Andronicus* and
1 Contention as well as the 1595 *Richard Duke of York*, and mentioned only at
the end of the dedications in *Venus and Adonis* (1593, 1594 and ?1595) and
The Rape of Lucrece (1594). The wording on the title page, moreover, is
(perhaps deliberately) ambiguous: the play is said to have been 'Newly set
foorth, ouerseene and corrected, / By W. S.', which leaves open the question
of whether 'W. S.' authored the play or only revised it. It has been argued

[29] *William Shakespeare*, 1.536.   [30] Maxwell, *Studies in the Shakespeare Apocrypha*, 4.
[31] See Proudfoot, 'Is There, and Should There Be, a Shakespeare Apocrypha?', 50. Note that the copy at
the Bodmer Library in Cologny near Geneva contains a manuscript inscription by George Buc
according to which the Babington conspirator Charles Tilney, executed in 1586, a cousin of Edmund
Tilney, Master of the Revels, wrote the play, and Buc wrote dumb shows for it: 'Charles Tilney
wrot[e a] Tragedy of this mattr [which] hee named Estrild [which] I think is this. it was [lost] by his
death. & now s[ome] fellon [or fellou] hath published [it]. I made du[m]be shewes for it. w[hi]ch I yet
haue. G. B.' (Nelson, 'Play Quartos Inscribed by Buc'). Not only Tilney but also several other
dramatists, notably Robert Greene and George Peele, have at various times been proposed as possible
authors of the play, but the evidence remains inconclusive. See Gooch, ed., *The Lamentable Tragedy of
Locrine*, 29–32; and Lancashire and Levenson, 'Anonymous Plays', in *The Predecessors of Shakespeare*,
259–63.

that Shakespeare may indeed have overseen a reworking of the play.[32] Yet the title page of the first extant quarto of *Love's Labour's Lost* (1598) contains a similar formulation, stating that the text has been 'Newly corrected and augmented / By W. Shakespere', and here, at least, Shakespeare is the play's author, not simply its reviser.

What increases the likelihood that the title page insinuates Shakespeare's authorship is that he was establishing himself as an author of 'lamentable' tragedies in the mid-1590s. *Locrine* was advertised as a 'Lamentable Tragedie' in 1595, and the year before, *Titus Andronicus* had been said to be a 'most lamentable Romaine Tragedie' on the title page.[33] The word 'lamentable' had been used before on playbook title pages, but that a Shakespearean resonance seems possible in 1595 is suggested not only by the publication of *Titus* in 1594 but also by *Romeo and Juliet*, which was first performed in 1595 and advertised on the title page of the second, authoritative quarto (1599) as 'The most excellent and *lamentable* Tragedie, of Romeo and Iuliet' (my emphasis), a formulation which may already have been on the playbills four years earlier.[34] *Titus Andronicus* and *Romeo and Juliet* were both published anonymously, and many theatre-goers may have ignored their author's identity, but those with a particular interest in London's theatrical scene probably did not.[35] *Romeo and Juliet*, in particular, soon came to be identified with Shakespeare's name, and John Weever refers to Romeo in a poem, 'Ad Gulielmum Shakespeare', which may have been written as early as 1595.[36] By that time, Shakespeare was the in-house dramatist of one of the two professional companies active in London and a recent author of 'lamentable' tragedies, so it would have been natural for people with an interest in London's theatrical scene to associate 'W. S.' on *Locrine*'s title page with Shakespeare. As Katherine Duncan-Jones has written, persuading book-buyers to identify 'W. S.' with Shakespeare 'would be a good selling point for what is, in truth, a fairly undistinguished "medley" play'.[37]

Thomas Lord Cromwell was entered in the Stationers' Register on 11 August 1602 to William Cotton. Cotton seems to have transferred his rights in the play to William Jones, who had it printed before the end of the year by Richard Read. There can be no reasonable doubt that the attribution to

---

[32] See, for instance, Duncan-Jones, *Ungentle Shakespeare*, 42–3.
[33] See also Robertson, *An Introduction to the Study of the Shakespeare Canon*, 198–216, for possible connections between *Titus* and *Locrine*.
[34] See Stern, '"On Each Wall and Corner Poast"', 83–7. Note that Quince, in *A Midsummer Night's Dream*, calls the Pyramus and Thisbe play the mechanicals are rehearsing a 'lamentable comedy' (Q1, sig. B2r) in what may be a moment of Shakespearean self-parody.
[35] For Peele's likely co-authorship of *Titus Andronicus*, see above, p. 11.
[36] See Ingleby, ed., *Shakspere Allusion-Book*, 1.24.   [37] *Ungentle Shakespeare*, 42.

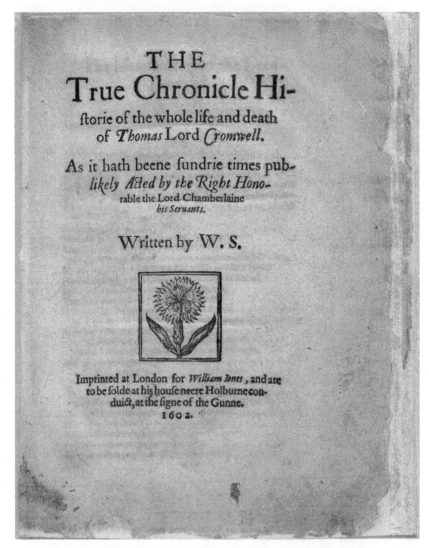

2.1 Title page of *Thomas Lord Cromwell* (Q1, 1602), attributed to 'W. S.'.

'W. S.' was designed to suggest Shakespeare's authorship (Figure 2.1). The title page goes on to affirm that the play 'hath beene sundrie times publikely Acted by the Right Honorable the Lord Chamberlaine his Seruants', and, given the prominence Shakespeare, as the Lord Chamberlain's Men's leading playwright, had reached as a dramatist in print by 1602 the association of

'W. S.' with Shakespeare must have been inevitable. The initials earned the play inclusion in the second issue of the third Folio (1664) and the fourth Folio (1685) of Shakespeare's plays – along with *Pericles*, *The London Prodigal*, *1 Sir John Oldcastle*, *The Puritan*, *A Yorkshire Tragedy* and *Locrine* – but modern scholars agree in regarding the attribution as spurious. No clear candidate, or candidates, for the play's authorship have emerged.[38]

In 1602, Shakespeare's playbooks were enjoying considerable success, in particular his history plays: *Richard II*, *Richard III* and *1 Henry IV*, originally published in 1597 or 1598, had all reached a third edition by 1602. *Henry V* had reached print in 1600, and the *Cromwell* title page may be specifically related to the publication of that play. We now think of the first quarto of *Henry V* as a 'bad quarto', but stationers had every reason to think of it as good since a second edition had become necessary by 1602. That *Thomas Lord Cromwell* may have been trying to emulate *Henry V* is suggested by the similarities of the title page. Q1 *Henry V* is advertised as a 'CRONICLE History', a generic description which came to be used quite frequently on title pages in subsequent years, for instance in Samuel Rowley's *When You See Me You Know Me* (1605), *King Leir* (1605), *Nobody and Somebody* (1606) and Shakespeare's *Lear* (1608), but had in fact not appeared on a title page prior to 1600. *Cromwell* is the second play to use that generic label on the title page, where the play is called a 'True Chronicle Historie'. It did not do as well in print as Shakespeare's bestselling history plays, but there seems to have been enough demand for a second edition, still ascribed to 'W. S.', to become necessary in 1613.[39] It might be argued that the misattribution was not a deliberate marketing ploy but a simple error, based on the publishers' mistaken conviction that the play was indeed by Shakespeare. What argues against this is not only the eminence that Shakespeare had attained by this time but also the use of initials: where the case for Shakespeare's authorship is straightforward, his full name was usually used, but several non-Shakespearean works hinted at his authorship by means of his initials, including *Locrine*, *The Puritan* and the 1612 *Funeral Elegy for Master William Peter*.[40] By contrast, no genuine Shakespeare text was ever ascribed to 'W. S.' or 'W. Sh.' on a printed title page in the late sixteenth or early seventeenth century.[41]

---

[38] See Champion, 'Dramatic Strategy and Political Ideology in *The Life and Death of Thomas, Lord Cromwell*', 219.

[39] Note that by 1613, the rights to the play had been acquired by John Brown.

[40] For the *Funeral Elegy*, see Vickers, *'Counterfeiting' Shakespeare*.

[41] In this respect, too, Shakespeare received unusual treatment in the London book trade: many other dramatists had plays correctly attributed to them through their initials, including Robert Wilson (*The Three Lords and Three Ladies of London*, 1590), Peele (*The Old Wives Tale*, 1595), Greene (*Alphonsus*

The third play to be attributed to 'W. S.' is *The Puritan* which was entered in the Stationers' Register to George Eld on 6 August 1607 and published later the same year. The play is now generally considered to be by Thomas Middleton, in whose Oxford *Collected Works* it has been included.[42] Surprisingly, the 1607 title page states that the play had been 'Acted by the Children of Paules', a company with which Shakespeare seems to have had no association. This led Baldwin Maxwell to believe that 'either [Eld] knew surprisingly little about Shakespeare or he was remarkably careless in his plan of deceit'.[43] Yet, based on a study of Eld's career as a stationer from *c.* 1604 to 1624, David Frost has shown that Eld made his first steps as a publisher (as opposed to printer) in 1607–8 and that 'As a printer attempting to set up on his own as a publisher, Eld needed bestsellers', which may explain his 'sharp practice'.[44] MacDonald Jackson has similarly argued that 'Eld's use of the initials "W.S." on the title page of *The Puritan* was almost certainly intended to mislead.'[45] Brian Vickers has commented on the temptation 'to upgrade the value of some poem or play – whether or not [the stationers] knew its true author – by appending Shakespeare's initials to it',[46] and the publishers of *Thomas Lord Cromwell* and *The Puritan*, William Jones and George Eld, may well have found the temptation too hard to resist.

Given that three professional plays attributed to 'W. S.' were published between 1595 and 1607, it may rightly be asked whether any other playwright could have been referred to. It is true that there were several writers with these initials, but none of them seems a good match for our 'W. S.' William Sampson, playwright and poet, born in 1599 or 1600, first appears in print in 1622 as co-author of the tragedy *Herod and Antipater*, six years after Shakespeare's death. Wentworth Smith wrote plays for Philip Henslowe from 1601, but it is unclear whether any of the plays to which he contributed reached print, and his name figures on no title page.[47] The herald William Smith from Cheshire, born *c.* 1550, wrote about many subjects, including heraldry, the London livery companies and the history and topography of Cheshire. He also composed a historical play – the only one of his texts that appears to have been printed – called *The Hector of Germany, or, The*

King of Aragon, 1599), Chapman (*An Humorous Day's Mirth*, 1599), Jonson (*Every Man Out of His Humour*, 1600) and Marston (*Antonio and Mellida* and *Antonio's Revenge*, both 1602). For the use of initials in early modern paratext, see Williams, 'An Initiation into Initials'.

[42] See Taylor and Lavagnino, gen. eds., *Thomas Middleton: Collected Works*. The edition has been prepared by Donna B. Hamilton.

[43] *Studies in the Shakespeare Apocrypha*, 18.   [44] *The School of Shakespeare*, 261.

[45] *Studies in Attribution*, 171–2.   [46] *'Counterfeiting' Shakespeare*, 73.

[47] It is possible, for instance, that *1 Lady Jane*, on which Smith was working in 1603 with Chettle, Dekker, Heywood and Webster, corresponds to *Sir Thomas Wyatt*, which was published in 1607 and ascribed to Dekker and Webster on the title page. See Kathman, 'Smith, Wentworth (*bap.* 1571)'.

Palsgrave, Prime Elector, written in honour of the marriage of Princess Elizabeth and Friedrich, elector palatine. It was printed in 1615, ascribed to 'W. Smith' on the title page (long misunderstood as referring to Wentworth Smith) and affirmed to have 'beene publickly Acted at the Red-Bull, and at the Curtayne, by a Company of Young-men of this Citie'. As Smith's dedication points out, the play was 'made for Citizens, who acted it well', not for a professional company.[48] Finally, another William Smith authored a sequence of sonnets, *Chloris, or, The Complaint of the Passionate Despised Shepherd* (1596), dedicated to Spenser, and a poem from that volume included in the anthology *England's Helicon* (1600) is indeed ascribed to 'W. S.'[49] Yet nothing indicates that this Smith ever turned his hand to drama. A survey of the available evidence suggests that no other W. S. wrote a professional play between 1590 and 1616 that was deemed worthy of publication in print. As a publisher must therefore have realized, the initials 'W. S.' would probably be construed as a reference to Shakespeare.

Whereas the title pages of *Locrine*, *Thomas Lord Cromwell* and *The Puritan* may have been designed to hint at Shakespeare's name by means of his initials, those of *The London Prodigal*, *A Yorkshire Tragedy*, *The Troublesome Reign of John, King of England* and *1 Sir John Oldcastle* are more straightforward in their misattribution to Shakespeare. *The London Prodigal* and *A Yorkshire Tragedy* were published within three years of each other, in 1605 and 1608, and both not only mention Shakespeare's full name on the title page but also affirm that the play had been performed by his company: 'As it was plaide by the Kings Maiesties seruants' and 'Acted by his Maiesties Players at the Globe'. These company ascriptions are usually considered accurate and may partly explain the misattributions to Shakespeare: a play text from the King's Men which may have been anonymous or composed by a little-known playwright could be rendered more commercially attractive by an ascription to the well-known and well-published in-house dramatist of that company. A misascription to a company would have been easily detected by London's playgoers, but a misattribution of a King's Men's play to that company's leading playwright must have been less likely to be seen through.

No modern scholar of whom I am aware has endorsed the attribution of *The London Prodigal* to Shakespeare (Figure 2.2).[50] The publisher of *The*

---

[48] See Kathman, 'Smith, Wentworth (*bap.* 1571)'.   [49] Rollins, ed., *England's Helicon*, II.31.

[50] The article by Richard Proudfoot, 'Shakespeare's Most Neglected Play', does not argue for Shakespeare's authorship of the play but proposes that the focus on the authorship question has kept scholars from engaging with *The London Prodigal*, which Proudfoot calls 'a play of real interest and modest achievement' (157).

THE
LONDON
Prodigall.

As it was plaide by the Kings Maiesties seruants.

By *VVilliam Shakespeare,*

LONDON.

Printed by T. C. for *Nathaniel Butter*, and
are to be sold neere *S. Austins* gate,
at the signe of the pyde Bull.
1605.

2.2 Title page of *The London Prodigal* (Q, 1605), attributed to 'William Shakespeare'.

London Prodigal, Nathaniel Butter, has been harshly treated by scholars for his obvious misattribution, one of them counting him among 'the most unscrupulous publishers' of his time.[51] It was Butter who published Heywood's *1 If You Know Not Me You Know Nobody* the same year, leading Heywood to protest that the text had been 'copied only by the ear' with 'scarce one word true'. That Butter was convinced of the selling power of Shakespeare's name is also suggested by the first quarto of *King Lear*, which was 'Printed for Nathaniel Butter' in 1608 with a title page on which Shakespeare's name appears first and in by far the largest font: 'M. William Shak-speare: / HIS / True Chronicle Historie of the life and / death of King LEAR and his three / Daughters'. Whereas the non-Shakespearean *King Leir* had appeared anonymously in 1605, Butter's edition, the title page suggests, now provides the real thing, the one by 'M. William Shak-speare'. Butter seems to have considered 'Shakespeare' a name to conjure with, which is ironic given that neither Butter's wrongly attributed *London Prodigal* nor his enthusiastically attributed *King Lear* received a reprint within the next ten years.

A Yorkshire Tragedy may well have been first performed the year *The London Prodigal* appeared in print, although it was not published until three years later, after being entered to Thomas Pavier on 2 May 1608 (Figure 2.3). Like *The Puritan*, it is now generally acknowledged to be by Middleton and is included in Middleton's Oxford *Collected Works* (where the former play receives the title *The Puritan Widow*).[52] The fact that not only the title page but also the entry in the Stationers' Register affirms Shakespeare's authorship of *A Yorkshire Tragedy* may indicate that the manuscript sold to Pavier already contained the false authorship claim. So while Gary Taylor is no doubt correct in arguing that 'The attribution to Shakespeare is probably, in this instance, deliberately dishonest', it is not clear with whom the dishonesty originated.[53] Conceivably, someone associated with the theatre decided to render the playbook more marketable by ascribing it to Shakespeare,

[51] Maxwell, *Studies in the Shakespeare Apocrypha*, 13.

[52] Arguing against the possibility of Shakespeare's authorship, Taylor has written that Shakespeare's 'remarkable late style is nowhere in evidence' ('The Canon and Chronology of Shakespeare's Plays', 140). The chief studies arguing for Middleton's authorship of *A Yorkshire Tragedy* are Lake, *The Canon of Thomas Middleton's Plays*, Jackson, *Studies in Attribution*, and Holdsworth, 'Middleton's Authorship of *A Yorkshire Tragedy*'. A. C. Cawley and Barry Gaines, editors of *A Yorkshire Tragedy* in the Revels Plays series, tentatively support the case for Middleton (4–6). Among the rare dissenters is Duncan-Jones, who has argued for Shakespeare's authorship of *A Yorkshire Tragedy* in *Ungentle Shakespeare*, 209–12.

[53] 'The Canon and Chronology of Shakespeare's Plays', 140. Stanley Wells, editor of *A Yorkshire Tragedy* for the Oxford Middleton, similarly believes that the 'Attribution to Shakespeare both on the title-page and in the Register is probably a deliberate fraud' ('Works Included in This Edition', 356).

A YORKSHIRE

Tragedy.

Not so New as Lamentable and true.

Acted by his Maiesties Players at the *Globe*.

VVritten by VV. Shakspeare.

AT LONDON
Printed by *R. B.* for *Thomas Pauier* and are to bee sold at his
shop on Cornhill, neere to the exchange.
1608,

2.3 Title page of *A Yorkshire Tragedy* (Q1, 1608), attributed to 'W. Shakspeare'.

perhaps thinking that a stationer might be reluctant to invest in a play text which is, after all, extremely short: *A Yorkshire Tragedy* has barely 700 lines, as compared with 2,100 lines for *A Midsummer Night's Dream* (Shakespeare's shortest individually published play) and approximately 3,600 lines for the second quarto of *Hamlet* (Shakespeare's longest play). It is equally possible, however, that Pavier was complicit in the misattribution. *A Yorkshire Tragedy* appeared in the same year that the title page of *King Lear* asserted Shakespearean authorship more emphatically than any previous book had done, and the year before the publication of the *Sonnets*, with their similarly emphatic, large-font title page claim: 'SHAKE-SPEARES / SONNETS'. In 1608, Shakespeare also appeared on the title pages of the fifth quarto of *1 Henry IV* and fourth quarto of *Richard II*, which appeared in two issues, one announcing 'new additions of the Parliament Sceane, and the deposing of King Richard … By William Shake-speare'. Shakespeare's name had publicity value in 1608, as Thomas Pavier or the person who sold him the manuscript of *A Yorkshire Tragedy* or both must have realized.

The 1608 quarto of *A Yorkshire Tragedy* is not Pavier's last involvement in a Shakespeare misattribution. In 1619, he published ten plays by or attributed to Shakespeare – now usually called the 'Pavier Quartos' – which he had printed by William Jaggard. They included not only a reprint of *A Yorkshire Tragedy*, still affirmed to have been 'written by W. Shakespeare', but also the second edition of *1 Sir John Oldcastle*, which was attributed to 'William Shakespeare' on the title page. The venture seems to have originated as a first attempt to publish a collection of Shakespeare's drama, though the fact that the continuous signatures cease after the third play (*The Whole Contention* and *Pericles*) suggests that Pavier changed his mind, leaving him with two possible ways of marketing the playbooks: either as a bound collection or as a series of playbooks to be marketed separately, some with fake imprints and dates, including *1 Sir John Oldcastle* which is misdated 1600 on the title page.[54]

The false date on the title page of the second edition of *1 Sir John Oldcastle* mimics that of the first edition, which Pavier had published in 1600 (after entering the play in the Stationers' Register on 11 August of the same year). Yet, contrary to the second, the first edition contains no

[54] The Pavier Quartos have received sustained attention by scholars. See, for instance, Johnson, 'Thomas Pavier, Publisher'; Jowett, *Shakespeare and Text*, 69–72; Murphy, *Shakespeare in Print*, 36–41; Erne, *Shakespeare as Literary Dramatist*, 255–8 (280–3); and Massai, *Shakespeare and the Rise of the Editor*, 106–35. See also below, pp. 174–9.

authorship ascription. Thanks to Philip Henslowe's *Diary*, we know that the play had been written in 1599 by Anthony Munday, Michael Drayton, Robert Wilson and Richard Hathaway, and that it was written for the Lord Admiral's Men, the main rivals of Shakespeare's company, as is corroborated by the title page of the edition of 1600: 'As it hath been lately acted by the right honorable the Earle of Notingham Lord high Admirall of England his seruants'.[55]

Rather than being by Shakespeare, *1 Sir John Oldcastle* was in fact a response to Shakespeare's disrespectful treatment, in the *Henry IV* plays, of the Protestant martyr Oldcastle (as Falstaff was originally called), the fourth Lord Cobham.[56] This point is made as early as the Prologue to *1 Sir John Oldcastle*: 'It is no pampered glutton we present, / Nor agèd counsellor to youthful sins; / But one whose virtues shone above the rest, / A valiant martyr and a virtuous peer' (ll. 6–9).[57] Shakespeare appears to have been compelled by William Brooke, tenth Lord Cobham, to change Oldcastle's name, yet despite the change to Falstaff, *1 Henry IV*, as John Jowett has pointed out, 'continued to be known as *Oldcastle* as well as *1 Henry IV*', which may partly explain the misattribution in 1619: 'Pavier therefore was able, or had the excuse, to generate a case of mistaken identity.'[58] The excuse may have been all the more welcome as the ten plays included in his collection did not amount to a sizeable portion of Shakespeare's dramatic works. That Pavier could not have ignored the fact that the attribution of *1 Sir John Oldcastle* to Shakespeare was groundless has been argued by Douglas Brooks:

If anyone knew that *Oldcastle* did not flow from Shakespeare's pen, it was precisely Pavier who, nineteen years before he tried to publish a collection of Shakespeare's plays, was as close to the play's point of origin as anyone could be

[55] Foakes, ed., *Henslowe's Diary*, 125. For an unconvincing attempt to credit Shakespeare with part authorship of *1 Sir John Oldcastle*, see Dominik, *A Shakespearean Anomaly*. The flaws in Dominik's methodology are discussed by Jackson in 'Editions and Textual Studies', 224–7. The second part of *Sir John Oldcastle* was never published, but several payments recorded by Henslowe show that it was written in 1599 (see Foakes, ed., *Henslowe's Diary*, 125, 129, 132).

[56] Much ink has been spilled over Shakespeare's use of the name 'Oldcastle', the subsequent change to 'Falstaff' and the controversial decision of the editors of the Oxford *Complete Works* (1986) to revert to 'Oldcastle'. See, for instance, Taylor, 'The Fortunes of Oldcastle' and 'William Shakespeare, Richard James, and the House of Cobham'; Honigmann, 'Sir John Oldcastle'; Goldberg, 'The Commodity of Names'; Kastan, *Shakespeare after Theory*, 93–127; and White, 'Shakespeare, the Cobhams, and the Dynamics of Theatrical Patronage'.

[57] I quote from the edition of *1 Oldcastle* in Corbin and Sedge, eds., *The Oldcastle Controversy*. As Corbin and Sedge point out, 'the dramatists drew heavily on Shakespeare's second tetralogy in the rehabilitation of their hero' (13).

[58] Jowett, 'Shakespeare Supplemented', 45.

└ Shakespeare Yearbook

without having written it or acted in it . . . Knowing full well in 1600 that the play he published in quarto was the collaborative product of four authors as well as the property of Henslowe, how could Pavier republish it nineteen years later as a Shakespeare play?[59]

The answer seems to be that the ascription to Shakespeare suited Pavier's purposes, perhaps even in more than one respect: insofar as he sold the play separately, the misattribution increased the marketability of a text that was already in his possession, and to the extent that the play was included in his Shakespeare collection, it allowed him to swell the size of his meagre corpus.[60]

The last misattribution to Shakespeare ('W. SHAKESPEARE') before the publication of the First Folio was on the title page of the third quarto of the first (sig. A1r) and the second (sig. G4r) parts of *The Troublesome Reign of John, King of England* in 1622, published by Thomas Dewe. The second quarto, published by John Helme, had appeared in 1611 and been ascribed to 'W. Sh.', an abbreviation which leaves little doubt as to whom the initials refer to (Figure 2.4). The first edition of 1591, published by Sampson Clarke, had contained no authorship ascription. The first and second editions mention performance by the 'Queenes Maiesties Players', but when Shakespeare's name was spelled out on the 1622 title pages, the name of that company was omitted and replaced by the simple statement 'As they [the two parts] were (sundry times) lately acted' (sig. A1r).

What complicates the play's pseudo-Shakespearean status is its relationship to the genuinely Shakespearean *King John*. Usually argued to be Shakespeare's main source, though also occasionally believed to have been influenced by it, *Troublesome Reign* entertains a close relationship to *King John*.[61] As L. A. Beaurline has put it, 'the plays match . . . closely in the selection of characters, the sequence of events, and the management of scenes'.[62] Gary Taylor has argued that the attribution of *Troublesome Reign* to Shakespeare 'probably results from or dishonestly exploits confusion with

[59] *From Playhouse to Printing House*, 69–70.
[60] For Pavier as a publisher who was heavily invested in Shakespeare, see below, pp. 174–9. For *1 Oldcastle* and its attribution to Shakespeare, see also Marino, *Owning William Shakespeare*, chapter 4.
[61] For the view that *Troublesome Reign* served Shakespeare as his main source, see Smallwood, ed., *King John*, 365–74; and Taylor, 'The Canon and Chronology of Shakespeare's Plays', 119. For the argument that *King John* preceded *Troublesome Reign*, see Honigmann, ed., *King John*; and Honigmann, *Shakespeare's Impact on his Contemporaries*, chapters 3 and 4. *Troublesome Reign* has usually been considered anonymous but is attributed to George Peele in a recent article by Brian Vickers ('*The Troublesome Raigne*, George Peele, and the Date of *King John*') and in Charles R. Forker's new Revels Plays edition.
[62] *King John*, 195.

THE

Firſt and ſecond Part of

the troubleſome Raigne of
Iohn King of England.

With the diſcouerie of King Richard Cœr-
delions Baſe ſonne (vulgarly named, The Baſtard
Fawconbridge:) Alſo, the death of King *Iohn*
at Swinſtead Abbey.

*As they were (ſundry times) lately acted by
the Queenes Maieſties Players.*

Written by W. Sh.

Imprinted at London by *Valentine Simmes* for *Iohn Helme,*
and are to be ſold at his ſhop in Saint Dunſtons
Churchyard in Fleeteſtreet.
1 6 1 1.

2.4 Title page of *1, 2 The Troublesome Reign of John, King of England* (Q2, 1611),
attributed to 'W. Sh.'.

King John, not published until 1623'.[63] What may support the argument for deliberate misattribution is the use of initials on the title page of the 1611 edition: as pointed out above, none of the playbooks ascribed to 'W. S.' or 'W. Sh.' is now believed to be by Shakespeare. The fact that mention of the 'Queenes Maiesties Players' was omitted on the same title page on which Shakespeare's name was first spelled out may also be significant, perhaps signalling a desire by the publisher not to raise questions about the author-ship attribution to Shakespeare of a play said to have been '(sundry times) lately acted' by a company not associated with him. J. W. Sider, editor of *Troublesome Reign,* seems right in arguing that the 'ascription to "W. Sh." may indicate that the publisher intended to deceive unwary buyers looking for Shakespeare's *King John*'.[64]

I have argued that a good case can be made for each of the seven plays discussed above that it was deliberately misattributed to Shakespeare, obliquely or explicitly, in order to capitalize on the popularity of his name. It is of course possible that in one case, and perhaps even in more than one case, other explanations account for the authorial ascription on the title page, a misunderstanding rather than a fraud, conceivably even another writer with the initials 'W. S.' rather than a hint at Shakespeare. What seems clear, however, is that Shakespeare's name had such publicity value that it was repeatedly used to promote play texts not written by him, and this during a period when, remarkably, no other identifiable playwright had a single playbook misattributed to him. The pattern of misattributed play-books is an eloquent testimony to the remarkable place 'Shakespeare' occupied in the London book trade in the final years of the Elizabethan and in the Jacobean period.

It may well be significant that more than half of the plays misattributed to Shakespeare appeared in the period from 1604 to 1613. This ten-year stretch corresponds to a period during Shakespeare's career as a playwright in which few of his plays reached print: only *King Lear* in 1608 and *Troilus and Cressida* and *Pericles* in 1609. By contrast, no fewer than fifteen of his plays had appeared between 1594 and 1603: *Titus Andronicus, 2* and *3 Henry VI, Edward III, Love's Labour's Lost, Richard III, Richard II, 1 Henry IV, 2 Henry IV, Henry V, The Merchant of Venice, A Midsummer Night's Dream, Much Ado about Nothing, The Merry Wives of Windsor* and *Hamlet.* I have argued in *Shakespeare as Literary Dramatist* that around 1603, Shakespeare and his fellow players appear to have changed their attitude towards the publication

---

[63] 'The Canon and Chronology of Shakespeare's Plays', 140.
[64] *The Troublesome Reign of John, King of England,* xiv–xv.

of his plays. Before then, the plays written for the Lord Chamberlain's Men were usually published unless there was a specific reason to prevent the sale of a manuscript. Yet after 1603, this pattern ceases, and the new supply of Shakespeare playbooks becomes much scarcer. This may partly explain why *The London Prodigal*, *The Puritan*, *A Yorkshire Tragedy* and *Troublesome Reign*, which all first reached print during this period, were attributed to Shakespeare (or 'W. S.' or 'W. Sh.'): as Shakespeare playbooks seemed to be in short supply, misattributions were made to stand in for the real thing.

While various agents in the London book trade thus considered it worthwhile misattributing a play to Shakespeare, it must be pointed out that the strategy had mixed success at best. As shown in Chapter 1, Shakespeare's playbooks had a remarkably high reprint rate, yet the misattributions did not: none of them was reprinted inside ten years; three received an additional edition after eleven years. The idea that the book-buying public was discerning enough to prefer the real Shakespeare to the fake may seem appealing, but the reasons for a playbook's popularity or lack of popularity are often difficult to recover. It is sobering to recall that we still have no real explanation for the astounding popularity of the anonymous comedy *Mucedorus*, first published in 1598, which went through nine editions by 1621, while Shakespeare's *Midsummer Night's Dream* and *Much Ado about Nothing*, which both appeared in 1600, were not reprinted until the First Folio of 1623. Shakespearean authorship, or perceived Shakespearean authorship, was clearly a selling point, but it was not enough to guarantee the success of individual playbooks.

'The author I know much offended': Shakespeare, misattribution and *The Passionate Pilgrim*

What, then, did Shakespeare and his contemporaries make of these misattributions? I pointed out above that stationers had little to fear from them, yet this should not be taken to suggest that the accuracy of title page ascription was considered unimportant. For instance, George Buc went out of his way to identify the playwrights of anonymously published playbooks, successfully identified Greene as the author of *Alphonsus King of Aragon* and Peele as that of *Edward I*, questioned Shakespeare about the authorship of *George a Greene, the Pinner of Wakefield*, found the contents of Q1 *Henry V* (the 'bad' quarto) 'much ye same w[i]th y[a]t in Shakespeare' and tried to correct the misattribution of *Locrine* to 'W. S.' (see below, pp. 199–200). Objections to authorial misattribution are even more explicit in *The Schollers Purgatory* (1625), where George Whither complains about an unnamed stationer who 'makes no scruple to put out the right Authors Name, & insert another in the second edition of a Booke' (sig. H5r).[65] *Brittons Bowre of Delights*, published by Richard Jones in 1591, offers another example which illustrates the irritation an authorial misattribution could provoke. It is assigned to Nicholas Breton, although the volume is a miscellany with poems by various hands, including those of Sir Philip Sidney, the Earl of Surrey and Sir Walter Ralegh. Breton made known his objection in a note which follows a prefatory letter in *The Pilgrimage to Paradise* (1592), protesting that 'it was donne altogether without my consent or knowledge, & many thinges of other mens mingled with few of mine, for except *Amoris Lachrimae*: an epitaphe upon Sir Phillip Sydney, and one or two other toies, which I know not how he vnhappily came by, I haue no part with any of the*m*'.[66] Breton is quite precise in distinguishing between his own poems (the epitaph on Sidney and one or two lesser poems) and those 'many thinges' by others which were misattributed to him. An unidentified 'R. B.' was similarly distraught to find that *Laura* (1597), a poetry collection attributed on the title page to his friend Robert Tofte, contained 'more than thirtie sonnets not his, intermixt with his' and encouraged the 'wel judging Reader' to 'distinguish between them' (sig. KIv) to tell the genuinely attributed from the false.[67] Nicholas Ling must have had such misattributions in mind when, in his address 'To the Reader, if indifferent' prefacing the anthology *England's Helicon* (1600), he proclaimed the care that had been

[65] Complaints about the practice of authorial misattribution persisted well into the eighteenth century, including in the following anonymous essay of 1732 in *Gentleman's Magazine*: 'Of all the Parts of a Book, the Title is the most important; on the *bona fides* of this one Page, half the Commerce of Literature turns; the Title therefore should be most authentick, and composed with the greatest Justness as well as Skill: But so it is, no Part is so subject to Frauds . . . The chief Rule in buying Books is the Author's Name; which is now no Rule at all; since the Booksellers have usurp'd the making Names as well as Titles . . . For the *English* Booksellers, there is no Species of *Legerdemain* which certain among them do not practise daily; especially that of assuming the Name of some celebrated Author . . . either in its proper Form, or with some minute Variation' (*Gentleman's Magazine*, 2 (December 1732), 1099). Among the victims of authorial misattribution was Jonathan Swift, in *A Complete Key to A Tale of a Tub* (1710), 'a flimsy explanation of the prominent points of the allegory' of *A Tale of a Tub*, written by his cousin Thomas Swift, but ascribed on the title page to 'Thomas Swift, grandson to Sir William Davenant, and Jonathan Swift, cousin-german to Thomas Swift, both retainers to Sir William Temple' (Williams, *Jonathan Swift*, 284). In a letter to his bookseller, Benjamin Tooke, Jonathan Swift complained that 'it is strange that there can be no satisfaction against a bookseller for publishing names in so bold a manner, I wish some lawyer could advise you how I must have satisfaction: for at this rate there is no book, however vile, which may not be fastened on me' (Williams, *Jonathan Swift*, 285). Elsewhere, Swift complains about the misattributions by the bookseller-publisher Edmund Curll: 'Curll hath been the most infamous Bookseller of any Age or Country . . . He published three Volumes all charged on the Dean, who never writ three Pages of them: He hath used many of the Dean's Friends in almost as vile a Manner' (Swift's note on line 197 of 'Verses on the Death of Dr Swift', in Swift, *Poems*, II.560).

[66] Breton, *The Pilgrimage to Paradise, Joyned with the Countesse of Pembrookes Love* (1592), sig. ¶3.

[67] See Bennett, *English Books and Readers*, 23–4.

taken to attribute the poems correctly, claiming that the volume could even be used as a check against misattributions elsewhere: 'If any man hath beene defrauded of any thing by him composed, by another mans title put to the same, hee hath this benefit by this collection, freely to challenge his owne in publique, where els he might be robd of his proper due' (sig. A4r).[68] The attributions in *England's Helicon* are genuinely reliable, much more so than those in other anthologies, yet some inaccuracies remained, and when they were discovered, a special effort was undertaken – as is shown by one copy still extant – to amend the misattribution by pasting a cancel slip with the correct name over that of the wrong one.[69] The evidence suggests, as Brian Vickers has pointed out, that 'writers vigorously asserted their moral rights to their own intellectual property' and that readers and stationers were acutely conscious of the possibility of authorial misattribution.[70]

As for Shakespeare, there are few things we know about his views, but we do know, thanks to Heywood's *Apology for Actors* (1612), that he was bothered by the misattribution to him of texts by others. *The Passionate Pilgrim*, originally published in late 1598 or 1599 and reprinted in 1599, received a third edition in 1612, published, like the earlier ones, by William Jaggard, in octavo format.[71] Like the edition of 1599, its title page claims that the collection of poems is by Shakespeare (the only extant copy of the first edition is fragmentary and lacks the title page). Yet fifteen of the twenty poems in the editions of 1598/9 are probably not by Shakespeare, and the third edition added further pieces, extracted from Heywood's *Troia Britannica*, which Jaggard himself had published (and printed) in 1609.[72] Heywood famously objected:

[68] See also Bednarz, 'Canonizing Shakespeare', 261.

[69] For instance, in a copy of the first edition of *England's Helicon*, poem 33 was originally assigned to 'S. Phil. Sidney' but later corrected to 'N. Breton' with a cancel slip. See Rollins, ed., *England's Helicon*, II.110, and Bartlett, *Mr William Shakespeare*, 153.

[70] *Shakespeare, Co-Author*, 51 (See Vickers's 'Appendix II: Abolishing the Author? Theory versus History', 506–41).

[71] For the date of the first edition of *The Passionate Pilgrim*, see Burrow, ed., *Complete Sonnets and Poems*, 74.

[72] There may also be other poems than those in the non-Shakespearean portion of *The Passionate Pilgrim* that were misattributed to Shakespeare in print. A commendatory poem by 'W. S.' appeared in Nicholas Breton's *The Will of Wit* of 1599, but it is unclear whether the initials here signal an oblique suggestion of Shakespearean authorship. A *Funerall Elegy*, 'By W. S.', printed in 1612 by George Eld, was famously attributed to Shakespeare by Donald Foster and Richard Abrams, although they later retracted their argument (see Vickers, *'Counterfeiting' Shakespeare*). It is possible that the initials were meant to hint at Shakespeare. In *Shakespeare, 'A Lover's Complaint', and John Davies of Hereford*, Vickers suggests that 'A Lover's Complaint', ascribed to Shakespeare on a separate title page in the 1609 *Sonnets*, was in fact written by the poet and handwriting master John Davies of Hereford. Vickers's argument has been endorsed in Bate and Rasmussen, eds., *The RSC Shakespeare*, but rejected in Jackson, 'Review'. For ascriptions to Shakespeare in manuscript anthologies and commonplace books, see Chambers, *William Shakespeare*, 1.550–5.

Here, likewise, I must necessarily insert a manifest iniury done me in that worke [*Troia Britannica*], by taking the two Epistles of *Paris* to *Helen* and *Helen* to *Paris*, and printing them in a lesse volume [*The Passionate Pilgrim*, 1612], vnder the name of another [Shakespeare], which may put the world in opinion I might steale them from him [Shakespeare]; and hee to doe himselfe right, hath since published them in his owne name [i.e. in *The Passionate Pilgrim*, 1612]: but as I must acknowledge my lines not worthy his [Shakespeare's] patronage, vnder whom he [Jaggard] hath publisht them, so the Author [Shakespeare] I know much offended with M. Iaggard (that altogether vnknowne to him) presumed to make so bold with his name.[73]

Arthur Marotti has rightly commented on the passage that it 'reveals Shakespeare's sensitivity . . . to the misattribution of the work of others to him'.[74] It is understandable that Shakespeare took offence at Jaggard's action. The textual situation is similar to that in *Brittons Bowre of Delights*: a miscellaneous collection attributed to a single poet who wrote no more than a fraction of the poems it contains. Yet whereas *Brittons Bowre of Delights* was dressed up with additions by poets more reputable than Breton (Sidney, Surrey, Ralegh), *The Passionate Pilgrim* was dressed down with poems by second-rate poets such as Heywood, Richard Barnfield or Bartholomew Griffin. It may be, as James Shapiro has argued, that Shakespeare was also offended because *The Passionate Pilgrim* included inept sonnets from *Love's Labour's Lost* which Shakespeare had not written in his own voice but dramatized as the product of love-sick young men.[75]

While these considerations may have displeased Shakespeare, what he particularly objected to, according to Heywood, is the unwarranted use of his name: that Jaggard 'altogether vnknowne to him) presumed to make so bold with his name'. That Shakespeare made his displeasure known to Jaggard, and that Jaggard seems to have conceded that Shakespeare had a point, are suggested by a cancel title page printed for the 1612 edition of *The Passionate Pilgrim* from which Shakespeare's name has been removed.[76] Nor was Shakespeare alone in taking issue with Jaggard's misattributions in *The Passionate Pilgrim*. Nicholas Ling included four poems from that collection (16, 17, 19 and 20) in *England's Helicon*, yet only the genuinely

---

[73] *An Apology for Actors* (1612), sigs. G4r–v. Note that the words 'hath since published them in his owne name' are governed by the subjunctive mood. It might be thought, Heywood is saying, that Shakespeare is claiming his own in *The Passionate Pilgrim*.

[74] 'Shakespeare's Sonnets as Literary Property', 153.

[75] *A Year in the Life of William Shakespeare*, 194.

[76] Concerning the order in which the two 1612 title pages were printed, see Burrow, ed., *Complete Sonnets and Poems*, 79, note 1. See also Duncan-Jones and Woudhuysen, eds., *Shakespeare's Poems*, 498. For a reproduction of the original and the cancel title page, see Erne, *Shakespeare as Literary Dramatist*, 3–4 (28–9).

Shakespearean poem 16, a version of Dumaine's poem to Katherine in *Love's Labour's Lost*, is assigned to Shakespeare, whereas the others are attributed to 'Ignoto' or their real author (Marlowe). The treatment of poems 16, 17 and 20 is particularly telling: they are printed successively in *England's Helicon*, as poems 34 to 36 of a total of 159. This as well as the poems' close correspondence in *The Passionate Pilgrim* and *England's Helicon* suggests that *The Passionate Pilgrim* is the location from which the poems were taken and inserted into *England's Helicon*. It would have been natural, then, for all three poems to be assigned to Shakespeare, in line with Jaggard's title page attribution. By refusing to follow Jaggard's misattribution, Ling, in other words, was clearly making a statement and signaling his unwillingness to endorse the misattributions to Shakespeare in that volume.[77] When pointing out in his prefatory letter to *England's Helicon* the care he had taken to attribute the poems to their authors, Ling wrote: 'the names of Poets ... haue beene placed with the names of the greatest Princes of the world, by the most autentique and worthiest iudgements' (sig. A4v). His desire to do poets justice clearly exceeded Jaggard's.

When preparing the first edition, Jaggard seems to have been no less shrewd in fabricating a 'Shakespeare' volume. Colin Burrow has pointed out that the original publication of *The Passionate Pilgrim* was 'clearly designed to exploit the excitement which surrounded the name of Shakespeare' at that specific moment in time.[78] The year 1598 had witnessed the massed arrival of Shakespeare's name on playbook title pages and his consecration as an English author of the first order in Meres's *Palladis Tamia*. By late 1598 or early 1599, it must have become clear that Shakespeare's name was a precious commodity with which money could be made, and Jaggard was quick to capitalize upon it (Figure 2.5). Bednarz has convincingly countered the argument that Jaggard's misattribution could have been unintentional, perhaps occasioned by a manuscript which 'may have been written entirely in [Shakespeare's] hand'.[79] Two of the poems, 'If Musique and sweete Poetrie agree' (8) and 'As it fell upon a Day' (20), were in fact faithfully copied from *The Encomion of Lady Pecunia*, which was unambiguously attributed to Richard Barnfield on the title page of a book printed in 1598 by John Jaggard, brother of William Jaggard.[80] As Bednarz puts it, William 'Jaggard knowingly combined

---

[77] See Bednarz, 'Canonizing Shakespeare', 260–2. See also Bednarz, '*The Passionate Pilgrim* and "The Phoenix and Turtle"'.
[78] *Complete Sonnets and Poems*, 74.   [79] 'Canonizing Shakespeare', 258.
[80] See Bednarz, 'Canonizing Shakespeare', 256.

THE
PASSIONATE
PILGRIME.

By W. Shakespeare.

AT LONDON
Printed for W. Iaggard, and are
to be sold by W. Leake, at the Greyhound in Paules Churchyard.

1599.

2.5 Title page of *The Passionate Pilgrim* (O2, 1599), attributed to 'W. Shakespeare'.

whatever manuscript material he had ... with excerpts from at least one printed text by an explicitly identified contemporary poet whose work he fraudulently attributed to Shakespeare.'[81] The motive, Bednarz argues, must have been commercial: 'Jaggard's willful replacement of "Barnfield" with "Shakespeare" was ... part of a shrewd marketing ploy that capitalized on Shakespeare's name to induce readers to buy *The Passionate Pilgrim*, through the sale of which Jaggard alone, as a stationer, benefited financially.'[82]

Part of Jaggard's strategy seems to have been to connect his volume to Shakespeare by means of intertextuality. *The Passionate Pilgrim*'s close relationship to *Venus and Adonis* is established in the subject matter of the so-called 'Venus and Adonis' poems, 4, 6, 9 and 11, and other poems which adopt the sixain stanza form of *Venus and Adonis*, 7, 10, 13, 14 and 18.[83] Other features of the collection clearly establish links with *Romeo and Juliet*: poem 14, it has been suggested, is 'a lyrical spin-off from the ... "balcony" scene',[84] and the title no doubt alludes to the first dialogue between the young lovers in which Romeo is repeatedly figured as a pilgrim. *Romeo and Juliet* was intensely fashionable in 1598, when John Marston's Luscus is said to speak 'Naught but pure *Juliet* and *Romeo*'.[85] Jaggard seems to have drawn on two popular texts which were intimately associated with Shakespeare to construct a collection which is in fact less a Shakespeare misattribution than, as Patrick Cheney has helped us see, a '*fiction* of Shakespearean authorship': 'Fifteen of the twenty poems in Jaggard's octavo proceed in the first-person voice, encouraging Elizabethan readers to identify "The Passionate Pilgrim" with "W. Shakespere".' The suggestion, as Cheney has put it, is that 'W. Shakespeare *is* the passionate pilgrim.'[86] The playbooks which were misattributed to Shakespeare pretend to offer fictional products *by* the author, and, as I have established above, their frequency and the absence of Shakespearean rivals up to the 1630s make them extraordinary enough. Yet *The Passionate Pilgrim*, on top of that, furnishes a fictionalized version *of* Shakespeare, fictionalized by a smart publisher, that is, who rightly anticipated that Shakespeare, the passionate pilgrim, would sell.

---

[81] 'Canonizing Shakespeare', 257.   [82] 'Canonizing Shakespeare', 258.

[83] See, for instance, Burrow, ed., *Complete Sonnets and Poems*, 79. Note that Hobday, in 'Shakespeare's Venus and Adonis Sonnets', argued that the 'Venus and Adonis Sonnets' are in fact by Shakespeare. His argument has not been generally endorsed.

[84] Duncan-Jones and Woudhuysen, eds., *Shakespeare's Poems*, 87.

[85] The passage appears in *The Scourge of Villainy*, quoted by Bednarz, '*The Passionate Pilgrim* and "The Phoenix and Turtle"', 113.

[86] *Shakespeare, National Poet-Playwright*, 163, 159, 155.

Conclusion

Shakespeare's reaction to *The Passionate Pilgrim* suggests that he preferred his own fictions to Jaggard's, and the *Sonnets*, which appeared in 1609 with the title 'SHAKE-SPEARES SONNETS', provide another fictionalization of an authorial persona, a speaker who is an actor called 'Will' (Sonnet 136), clearly pointing to Shakespeare himself. As for the misattributed playbooks, we have no direct evidence which tells us what Shakespeare made of them, but this does not imply that they left him indifferent. As Bednarz has pointed out, it is rare to have evidence of this kind, and it is likely that Shakespeare was offended by any stationer who, like Jaggard, made bold with his name.[87] When John Heminge and Henry Condell, in a prefatory epistle to the First Folio, referred to 'diuerse stolne, and surreptitious copies' with which readers had been 'abused', they were probably alluding to the recent Pavier Quartos, including to those plays among them which had been misattributed to Shakespeare.[88] There is no reason to believe that Heminge and Condell's friend and fellow-actor Shakespeare, when he was still alive, did not share their views of those playbooks. On the other hand, if Shakespeare, in agreement with his fellow players, held back his Jacobean plays in the prospect of a more prestigious (manuscript or print) publication, he may, after 1603, have preferred to see his name on title pages of playbooks he had not authored rather than on those he had but were not yet meant for print.[89] What Shakespeare must have registered and what he cannot have been indifferent to is that the misattributions were a powerful testimony to the influence his name exerted in the London book trade. As Chapter 1 has argued, Shakespeare became a remarkably popular man in print during his own lifetime and the years immediately following it, and, as this chapter has suggested, 'Shakespeare' did so too, so much so that 'Shakespeare' became a coveted book trade construction with which quite a number of stationers tried to make money.

---

[87] 'Canonizing Shakespeare', 264.   [88] See Erne, *Shakespeare as Literary Dramatist*, 255–8 (280–3).
[89] See Erne, *Shakespeare as Literary Dramatist*, 108–14 (132–8).

CHAPTER 3

The bibliographic and paratextual makeup of Shakespeare's quarto playbooks

This chapter examines the bibliographic and paratextual makeup of the Shakespeare playbooks published and disseminated by the London book trade in the late sixteenth and early seventeenth century. My analysis proceeds by comparing and contrasting Shakespeare's playbooks with the makeup of generically related books by his contemporaries. The aim of this examination is to recover as far as possible the meaning Shakespeare's playbooks had in their own time as material and cultural objects, and to contribute to an understanding of the place of the bibliographic author 'Shakespeare' within the early modern book trade.

It is worth reiterating at the outset that my emphasis is on books, not texts. Texts are written before books are produced. Shakespeare wrote his plays and poems in manuscript, many of them alone, some in co-authorship. His manuscripts may have been copied by scribes and annotated by theatre personnel, but there is little doubt that the *texts* now commonly ascribed to Shakespeare are essentially his. Shakespeare's *books*, however, were not made by him. As Roger E. Stoddard famously put it, 'Whatever they may do, authors do not write books. Books are not written at all. They are manufactured by scribes and other artisans, by mechanics and other engineers, and by printing presses and other machines.'[1] The chief responsibility for the material form of Shakespeare's books rested with his publishers, the people who laid out considerable amounts of money in their production in the hope of recouping these costs and making a profit. The makeup of Shakespeare's books – 'what size, what kind and quality of paper, what typeface, what kind of title-page, what paratext' – was shaped by the economic imperatives of publishers who counted on the saleability of such books for their livelihood.[2]

---

[1] 'Morphology and the Book from an American Perspective', 4.
[2] Taylor, 'Making Meaning Marketing Shakespeare 1623', 59–60.

Gérard Genette has defined paratext as a 'zone between text and off-text, a zone not only of transition but also of *transaction*: a privileged place of a pragmatics and a strategy, of an influence on the public'.[3] For publishers, paratext is the locus in which they can intervene between producer and receiver, between author and potential reader, to make of the potential reader a customer. 'Whatever you do, buy,' Heminge and Condell urge in their prefatory address in Shakespeare's First Folio. In one sense, it is the chief role of all paratext to do the same.[4]

Most of us now read Shakespeare in modern editions which precisely conceal the paratextual features and bibliographic makeup of the books in which Shakespeare's plays and poems were first disseminated. The makeup of today's Shakespeare books carries no less cultural meaning than did that of their early modern counterparts, although the meaning has undergone substantial change, in keeping with the change in status of 'Shakespeare' since the early modern period: erudite introductions and annotation reflect classic status; insertion in prestigious series (the Arden Shakespeare; the Oxford Shakespeare in the World's Classics series) indicates canonical prestige; the omnipresence of Shakespeare's name and iconic representations bespeak their saleability. The makeup of Shakespeare's early modern books includes none of these features. Shakespeare books were different cultural objects - in his time from what they are today, reflecting Shakespeare's different status then from what it is now.

Ironically, it is the very rise of Shakespeare's reputation to the top of the literary canon which led to the neglect of the bibliographic and paratextual constitution of the early Shakespeare books. For the attempted recovery of Shakespeare's writings demanded precisely the elimination of accretions by other agents, such as scribes, publishers and compositors. Even textual bibliography, a form of bibliography with which most Shakespeareans are likely to be familiar, focuses on the immaterial linguistic content of books, which we can define most simply as an order of words, rather than the material container in which, and the paratextual apparatus through which, Shakespeare's books first took shape. In fact, the legacy of the New Bibliography, as Sonia Massai has convincingly

---

[3] *Paratexts*, 2. What is now commonly referred to as 'paratext' in English was in fact called 'péritexte' by Genette, which he distinguished from 'épitexte', meaning texts outside the book which relate to it. Genette reserved the word 'paratexte' to the sum of 'péritexte' and 'épitexte'.

[4] This is not to suggest that commercial considerations alone account for the paratext in early modern books. For a recent collection on the topic, see Smith and Wilson, eds., *Renaissance Paratexts*. See also Anderson, 'The Rhetoric of Paratext in Early Printed Books'; and Sherman, 'On the Threshold'.

argued, contributed its share to the neglect of the meaning of the early Shakespeare books:

> One crucial aspect of this legacy is the common tendency to identify the printer's copy rather than the printed text as the ultimate source of textual authority. As a result, all those features that were added to the printer's copy as the dramatic manuscript was transmitted into print and transformed into a reading text tend to be overlooked. The paradox of course is that no dramatic manuscripts used as printer's copy to set up early modern playbooks have survived.[5]

The object of New Bibliographical desire has been a conjectured Shakespearean text which was ideal precisely because it was immaterial. As Massai points out, Shakespeare studies have in fact suffered more from what we might term 'the tyranny of the lost manuscript' than from any alleged 'tyranny of print'.[6]

Until recently, the study of Shakespeare too often neglected his books at the expense of his texts. This chapter takes the opposite approach by surveying precisely those features of the early printed Shakespeare play-books which exceed his dramatic texts. These features are manifold, ranging from prefatory material such as title page, dedication, epistles, commenda-tory poems and dramatis personae, to paratextual notations which are embedded in the text or surround it on the page, such as act or scene divisions and sententiae markers, or bibliographic features such as paper, format, typeface, type size or the arrangement of type on the page. It is true that many of these features have already attracted scholarly scrutiny, some in work devoted to early modern drama as a whole, some in work focusing more specifically on Shakespeare, but I am not aware of a prior attempt at synthesizing these features in order to analyse what they suggest about the meaning of Shakespeare's playbooks as material and cultural objects, and about the status of Shakespeare in the London book trade of his own time.

The cultural status of printed literature, and of printed playbooks more particularly, underwent a significant change in the sixteenth and seven-teenth centuries which provides an important context for my investigation in this chapter. The chief loci in which this change can be observed are the bibliographic and paratextual codes inherent in the playbooks.[7] For part of Elizabeth's reign, most playbooks were little more than 'do-it-yourself'

---

[5] 'Shakespeare, Text, and Paratext', 1.   [6] 'Shakespeare, Text, and Paratext', 1.

[7] The development of the form of printed plays has been ably traced in Voss, 'Printing Conventions and the Early Modern Play', and Howard-Hill, 'The Evolution of the Form of Plays in English during the Renaissance'. See also Massai and Berger, eds., *The Paratext in English Printed Drama to the Restoration*.

staging aids (with doubling charts and the number of actors needed to perform the play indicated on the title page) or records of performance ('As it hath been performed . . .'), yet towards the end of the century, they started being read as literature, and in the course of the seventeenth century, they received the dignity of Folio publication (Jonson in 1616, Shakespeare in 1623 and 'Beaumont and Fletcher' in 1647) as culturally prestigious works.[8] The publication of Jonson's *Works* in 1616, the year of Shakespeare's death, is sometimes considered as having revolutionized the respectability of printed playbooks, but in fact that publication is best understood as one step among many in the process of gentrification that printed drama underwent in the early modern period.[9] Shakespeare's books partly reflect this process and participated in it. How they do so and what that participation suggests about the meaning of 'Shakespeare' and his playbooks in the early modern book trade are the chief questions this chapter tries to address.

Paratext in Shakespeare playbooks and the rise of literary drama

Title pages have attracted more scholarly attention than other paratextual features of early modern playbooks, and with good reason. It is well known that title pages served not only as book covers but also as posters, which were put up on doors, walls and posts in London.[10] No other part of an early modern book gives us more immediate access to what London's publishers and booksellers were counting on to sell their wares. This sheds light on the fact that early modern title pages, including those of playbooks, often praise the book's content ('the most excellent history . . .'; 'the late and much admired play . . .'), a practice which is referred to in *Pericles* when Simonides addresses the Knights in Act 2 Scene 3 by saying that to 'place vpon the volume of your deedes, / As in a Title page, your worth in armes, / Were more then you expect' (Q1, sig. D1r).[11] Despite the adage urging us not to judge a book by its cover, people do, and did so four centuries ago, when Thomas Jackson complained that if a book 'haue a goodly title (be the matter neuer so base and vnprofitable) it is a booke for the nonce'.[12] Book browsing was a common practice, and a glance at a book could decide

---

[8] See Voss, 'Printing Conventions and the Early Modern Play', 98, 102.
[9] See Walker, *The Politics of Performance in Early Renaissance Drama*, 9.
[10] See Stern, *Documents of Performance in Early Modern England*, chapter 2.
[11] The quoted passage appears in the portion of the play which is now commonly ascribed to George Wilkins. See Vickers, *Shakespeare, Co-Author*, 291–332.
[12] See Saenger, *The Commodification of Textual Engagements in the English Renaissance*, 32.

whether it would be bought or not. As Thomas Churchyard regrets, 'on Stationers stall ... in two lines, they giue a pretty gesse, / What doth the booke, contayne'.[13]

What increases the importance of the title page is that other forms of advertising were still largely non-existent. It is true that the first English bookseller's catalogue appeared in 1595, Andrew Maunsell's *The first part of the catalogue of English printed books* (*STC* 17669), but its contents are selective and it contains no playbooks.[14] Catalogues which featured individual stationer's stock (a prominent feature on the Continent from the sixteenth century) did not start appearing until the 1650s.[15] Another reason why title pages were by far the most important locus of the early modern playbooks' promotion is that few professional plays contained any other paratexts. As Paul Voss comments, 'In books without front matter, title pages stand as the only place for the publisher to "sell" the book,' and, as a result, 'the absence of prefatory matter places a greater burden on the title page to advertise and promote the play'.[16] Title pages of playbooks were thus of crucial importance for their promotion.

An ill-judged title page could have serious economic consequences. When Kyd's closet tragedy *Cornelia*, a translation of Robert Garnier's *Cornélie*, was published in 1594, the title page was unusually plain: besides a printer's ornament and the imprint, it contained only a single word, 'CORNELIA', prompting William Covell's bawdy comment in *Polimanteia* (1595) that 'tragicke *Garnier* has his poore *Cornelia* stand naked vpon euery poste' (sig. Q3v). The edition was a commercial failure, despite the promotional efforts suggested by Covell's comment. Before the end of 1595, the play's publishers, Nicholas Ling and John Busby, seem to have identified the book's all-too-plain title page as the reason for its failure to sell. They went through the trouble and expense of reissuing it with a new title page, whose title is more in keeping with contemporary playbooks: 'Pompey the Great, / his faire / *Corneliaes Tragedie*: / Effected by her Father and Hus- / bandes downe-cast, death, / and fortune. / *Written in French, by that excellent / Poet Ro: Garnier, and trans- / slated into English by Thomas / Kid.*' The cancel uses a number of standard rhetorical features of early

---

[13] Churchyard, *The Mirror of Man, and Manners of Men* (*STC* 5242, 1594), quoted in Voss, 'Books for Sale', 754.

[14] See Voss, 'Books for Sale', 736.

[15] See Farmer and Lesser, 'Vile Arts', 78; and McKerrow, 'Booksellers, Printers, and the Stationers' Trade', 61. Note that the 1655 edition of *King Lear* and the 1652 reissue (with a cancel leaf, sig. A1) of the 1637 edition of *The Merchant of Venice* contain advertisements for books 'Sold by Jane Bell' (sig. A1v) and 'Printed and solde by William Leake' (sig. A1v).

[16] Voss, 'Printing Conventions and the Early Modern Play', 101–2.

modern playbook title pages that are conspicuously absent from the title page it replaces: panegyric ('faire . . . *excellent*'), sensationalism ('downe-cast, death'), the appeal of well-known historical figures ('Pompey the Great'), genre ('*Corneliaes Tragedie*') and authorship ('*Ro: Garnier . . . Thomas / Kid*'). Given that Kyd's translation received no further edition before the eighteenth century, we do not know to what extent the editors' strategy was successful, but we can say that the commercial failure of the first issue was such that the publishers considered it worthwhile to try their luck with a completely different, much fuller title page.[17]

One of the changes between original and cancel title page of *Cornelia* is that from anonymous to authored publication. This change mirrors the trend of playbook title pages at the time. The shift from the predominance of anonymous to one of authored publications can be observed on playbook title pages in the late Elizabethan and early Jacobean period. Up to 1593, twenty professional plays had appeared in print, seventeen with no authorial mention on the title page, three with the playwrights' initials and not a single one with the name(s) spelled out.[18] In the next five years (1594–8), eighteen out of forty-three playbook editions feature a title page author ascription, meaning just over 40 per cent, a percentage which remains stable over the next five years (1599–1603), when twenty-five out of sixty editions feature an authorial attribution. As soon as we reach the early Jacobean period, however, a majority of playbooks proclaim their authors on the title page: forty-six out of seventy-seven from 1604 to 1608 (60 per cent), thirty-eight out of fifty-four from 1609 to 1613 (70 per cent), nineteen out of thirty-three from 1614 to 1618 (58 per cent) and thirty-one out of forty-four (71 per cent) from 1619 to 1623. In the late Elizabethan period, the majority of playbooks are still published anonymously, but from the early Jacobean period, the majority are assigned to authors.[19]

A similar shift can be observed in the case of Shakespeare. The earliest Shakespeare playbooks appeared anonymously: *Titus Andronicus* (1594),

---

[17] Ling is the only publisher mentioned on the cancel title page, so it is possible that the initiative was his alone. Clearly, given the radical difference between the two title pages, and the failure of the cancel to acknowledge the earlier issue, part of the strategy was to suggest a new play. An additional incentive for the new title page, and in particular for the foregrounding of Cornelia's father, may have been the popularity of a new play, called 'sesar & pompie' by Henslowe, which received eight performances between 8 November 1594 and 25 June 1595. See Foakes, ed., *Henslowe's Diary*, 25–30.

[18] In three rare instances, the name (or initials) of the author are mentioned in an explicit at the end of the text but not on the title page: *Promos and Cassandra* (1578), by 'G. W.' (i.e. George Whetstone); *Edward I* (1593; 2nd edn, 1599), 'By George Peele Maister of Artes in Oxenforde'; and *Old Fortunatus* (1600), by 'Tho. Dekker'; there are no further examples up to 1660.

[19] See also Leggatt, 'The Presence of the Playwright', 130–2, for the shift from predominantly anonymous to predominantly authored play publications at the turn of the seventeenth century.

1 Contention (1594), *Richard Duke of York* (1595), *Edward III* (1596), *Romeo and Juliet* (1597), *Richard III* (1597) and *Richard II* (1597). *Titus Andronicus* and *Edward III* are likely to have been written collaboratively, and so, perhaps, were *1 Contention* and *Richard Duke of York*, which may partly account for the absence of Shakespeare's name on the title page – collaboratively produced plays were less likely to be assigned to their authors than single-authored ones. This would still leave *Romeo and Juliet*, *Richard III* and *Richard II*, to which can be added *1 Henry IV*, which appeared anonymously in 1598. Yet, in the same year, Shakespeare's name started appearing on playbook title pages, not only of *Love's Labour's Lost* but also of Q2 *Richard III* and Q2 and Q3 *Richard II*, followed by Q2 *1 Henry IV* in 1599.[20] In 1600, four more plays appeared with Shakespeare's name on the title page – *A Midsummer Night's Dream*, *The Merchant of Venice*, *Much Ado about Nothing* and *2 Henry IV* – as compared with one play, *Henry V*, which appeared anonymously. Six more Shakespeare plays appeared in quarto before the First Folio of 1623 – *The Merry Wives of Windsor* (1602), *Hamlet* (1603), *King Lear* (1608), *Pericles* (1609), *Troilus and Cressida* (1609) and *Othello* (1622) – all advertising Shakespeare's name on the title page.

What this means is that, in the case of Shakespeare, the shift from anonymous to authored publication was extraordinarily sudden and its extent striking. After 1598, only one newly published Shakespeare play, *Henry V*, appeared without his name on the title page, as compared with ten with his name on the title page. After the turn of the century, only four of the thirty Shakespeare playbook editions published before the First Folio did not advertise his name on the title page (that is, approximately 13 per cent): Q2 *Henry V* (1602), Q3 *Romeo and Juliet* (1609), Q3 *Titus Andronicus* (1611) and Q3 *Henry V* (1619). Among Shakespeare's contemporaries, the fraction of playbooks without authorial title page ascription remained considerably higher, about 42 per cent (80 editions out of 189) in the twenty-year period from 1601 to 1620.

There is additional evidence to suggest that Shakespeare's name became a crucial feature in the authorization of his drama in print. As a rule, anonymously published playbooks remained anonymous when subsequent editions were published. Exceptions to this rule in late Elizabethan and Jacobean England all seem to have been related to Shakespeare. The first

---

[20] The appearance of Shakespeare's name on the title pages of plays which had previously been published anonymously is all the more remarkable as 'One of the most striking tendencies of title pages is, in fact, their lack of change from one issue or edition to the next' (Farmer and Lesser, 'Vile Arts', 105).

quartos of *Richard II* (1597), *Richard III* (1597) and *1 Henry IV* (1598) were published anonymously, although all subsequent editions of these plays had Shakespeare's name on the title page. *1 Contention* and *Richard Duke of York* were anonymous in their first (1594/5) and second (1600) editions, but when the plays were published jointly as *The Whole Contention* as part of the Pavier Quartos in 1619, the title page attributes them to 'William Shakespeare, Gent.'.[21] The fourth, undated quarto of *Romeo and Juliet* (c. 1623) appeared in two issues, of which one attributes the play to Shakespeare. In addition, two of the spurious Shakespeare plays I dealt with in Chapter 2 started out anonymously before being misascribed to Shakespeare: *1, 2 Troublesome Reign* (1591) is by 'W. Sh.' according to the 1611 edition and by 'W. Shakespeare' according to the 1622 edition (a claim that is repeated on the separate title page for the second part, sig. G4r); and *1 Sir John Oldcastle* (1600) was first attributed to 'William Shakespeare' in the second quarto (a Pavier Quarto) of 1619.

Apart from the frequency of the appearance of Shakespeare's name on playbook title pages, there is the manner of its appearance. In 1598, on the title pages of *Love's Labour's Lost*, *Richard II* and *Richard III*, the name is printed in small type, inconspicuously. Yet by 1600, on the title pages of the first quarto of *The Merchant of Venice* and *A Midsummer Night's Dream*, the type size has increased. On the title page of the first quarto of *Pericles* (1609), Shakespeare's name appears in letters which are larger than the performance information above it ('his Maiesties Seruants at the Globe'), and the third quarto of *Hamlet* (1611) displays Shakespeare's name in nicely spaced out capitals, 'W I L L I A M   S H A K E S P E A R E'. In 1608, on the title page of *King Lear*, finally, Shakespeare's name comes first and largest, like Jonson's in *Volpone* (1607). As has been pointed out, 'given the fact that Q *Lear* is the only quarto to prominently feature Shakespeare's name at the top of the title page . . . Jonson's earlier texts may well have been a model'.[22]

The fact that professional plays were increasingly deemed worthy of authorial ascription contributed to drama's rise in literary status. The presence of an author increases a book's authority; it authorizes the book.

---

[21] The 1619 *Whole Contention* is the first quarto playbook to mention Shakespeare's gentlemanly status, and the only other one before 1660 is the 1634 edition of *The Two Noble Kinsmen*. The social status of dramatists was mentioned far more often on title pages of plays written for elite indoor theatres than on those for outdoor playhouses (see Farmer and Lesser, 'Vile Arts', 92–5).

[22] Brooks, '*King Lear* (1608) and the Typography of Literary Ambition', 149. The only quarto which gives Shakespeare's name even greater prominence is the 1609 *Sonnets*, which not only has Shakespeare's name in large letters on the title page as part of the title – 'SHAKE-SPEARES SONNETS' – but also prints his name in the header on the left-hand page (the verso) of every opening.

Ephemeral publications like ballads or almanacs typically did not have acknowledged authors; books with cultural prestige typically did. The evidence presented above suggests that Shakespeare's playbooks contributed to the process of authorization for printed drama in the sixteenth and seventeenth centuries, and that they did so to an exceptional degree.

Another title page feature which suggests that Shakespeare's playbooks were important for the literary status of playbooks generally is the frequency with which Shakespeare is identified as having 'corrected', 'augmented' or 'enlarged' his dramatic texts. As Alan Farmer has shown, 'no other dramatist . . . was ever identified as a corrector of texts as frequently as Shakespeare was'.[23] In 1598, the title page of *Love's Labour's Lost* announces a 'Newly corrected and augmented' text, 'By W. Shakespeare'. In the following year, *1 Henry IV* is said to have been 'Newly corrected by W. Shakespeare', and so are the following quartos in 1604, 1608, 1613, 1622, 1632 and 1639. Q2 *Romeo and Juliet*, similarly, has been 'Newly corrected, augmented, and amended', as have Q3 in 1609, Q4 in 1622 and Q5 in 1637. Q3 *Richard III*, in 1602, is said to have been 'Newly augmented, / By William Shakespeare', a claim that is repeated in the following editions of 1605, 1612, 1622 and 1629 (though not the one of 1634). Q2 *Hamlet* (1604/5) was 'Newly imprinted and enlarged to almost as much againe as it was, according to the true and perfect Coppie', a claim that is repeated in Q3 (1611) and slightly modified in Q4 (1623?) – 'Newly Imprinted and inlarged, according to the true and perfect Copy lastly Printed. / by / WILLIAM SHAKESPEARE' – and Q5 (1637): 'Newly imprinted and inlarged, according to the true and perfect Copy last Printed. / By WILLIAM SHAKESPEARE'. The second issue of Q4 *Richard II* (1608) announces 'new additions of the Parliament Sceane, and the deposing of King Richard. / . . . / By William Shake-speare', and so do the following editions in 1615 and 1634. The third edition of *The Passionate Pilgrim*, in 1612, announces that the collection has been 'newly corrected and augmented', and the original title page adds: 'By W. Shakespere'. Seven years later, *The Whole Contention* promises a 'newly corrected and enlarged' text, 'Written by William Shakespeare, Gent.' In 1630, finally, *The Merry Wives of Windsor*, 'Written by William Shake-Speare' (*sic*), has been 'Newly corrected'. All in all, I count twenty-seven editions up to 1642 (twenty up to 1623) of Shakespeare playbooks which announce on the title page that the text has been 'revised', 'corrected', 'emended', 'enlarged' or 'augmented', and all but two of them simultaneously feature Shakespeare's name.

---

[23] 'Shakespeare, Revision, and the Ephemerality of Playbooks', 14.

Ironically, even though the modern assumption seems to be that Shakespeare was unconcerned by the quality or completeness of his play texts in print, early modern editions often insisted on the contrary.

Other dramatists, as Farmer has shown, 'were *not* being marketed in this way as often as Shakespeare was. His plays were over three times more likely to carry an advertisement for corrections or additions than other professional plays were.'[24] Particularly typical of Shakespeare's playbooks were 'spurious statements of correction', new editions promising 'Newly corrected' or 'Newly augmented' texts with no or only the most trifling changes. In other words, 'publishers did not gratuitously name authors as revisers of texts, unless that author was Shakespeare'.[25] Not only in the case of authorial attributions (see Chapter 2) but also in that of revision claims did the marketing of Shakespeare thus repeatedly rely on mistaken information. One of the effects of these claims must have been the suggestion that the texts of plays were valuable enough to deserve revision and correction.

Paratext, playbooks and Shakespeare's invisible authorship

The evidence presented so far indicates that Shakespeare's playbooks were crucial agents in the process by which commercial drama was increasingly endowed with literary respectability in the late sixteenth and early seventeenth century. What this needs to be balanced against is the scarcity of other paratextual and bibliographic features in Shakespeare's playbooks by which literary respectability could be suggested: Latin title page mottoes, dedications, prefatory epistles, commendatory poems, dramatis personae, arguments, sententiae markers, continuous printing, and act and scene division. In this section, I will explore the presence or absence of these paratextual and bibliographic features in Shakespeare's playbooks and compare them with the playbooks of his contemporaries. In the following section, I try to account for the tension within the makeup of Shakespeare's playbooks, a makeup which combines conspicuous presence and conspicuous absence of features which endowed playbooks with literary cachet.

---

[24] 'Shakespeare, Revision, and the Ephemerality of Playbooks', 14.

[25] 'Shakespeare, Revision, and the Ephemerality of Playbooks', 15. Massai has analysed the same title page feature from a different angle, insisting on those cases in which title page announcements of textual revision or correction (what she calls 'editorial pledges') genuinely reflect the preparation of dramatic copy. See 'Editorial Pledges in Early Modern Dramatic Paratexts'.

An obvious paratextual feature with which to suggest such literary cachet is Latin title page epigraphs, which, as James G. McManaway has put it, are 'a sign of literary rather than theatrical intention'.[26] Shakespeare's very first publication, *Venus and Adonis*, includes a quotation from Ovid's *Amores* (1.15.35–6) on the title page: 'Vilia miretur vulgus: mihi flavus Apollo / Pocula Castalia plena ministret aqua' ('Let the common herd be amazed by worthless things; but for me let golden Apollo provide cups full of the water of the Muses').[27] The epigraph not only 'invites an elite readership', as Colin Burrow points out, but may also pun on the name of the author, 'Vilia-m', which, although otherwise absent from the title page, reappears at the end of the dedicatory epistle to the Earl of Southampton on the next double page, a suggestive arrival in print in terms of literary ambition.[28] Yet neither *The Rape of Lucrece* nor the *Sonnets* nor any of Shakespeare's playbooks followed up on *Venus and Adonis* with further Latin title page mottoes. The contrast to Jonson could not be starker: with the exception of the 1609 quarto of *The Case is Altered* (a play which, unusually for Jonson, contains no prefatory material and was included in none of the later Folio editions, a 'loose end' in Jonson's canon),[29] all Jonson playbooks published up to 1623 contain Latin title page epigraphs, from the three quarto editions of *Every Man Out of His Humour* in 1600 to the second quarto of *Epicene* in 1620.

Jonson was not alone in having Latin epigraphs on his playbook title pages. Even before 1600, Lodge's *Wounds of Civil War* (1594) and Greene's *The Scottish History of James IV* (1598) featured the same epigraphs which had already appeared on the title pages of a number of non-dramatic publications by Lodge ('O vita! misero longa, foelici brevis') and Greene ('Omne tulit punctum'). Other dramatists whose playbooks appeared with Latin title page epigraphs in the period up to 1623 include Beaumont, Robert Daborne, Dekker, Nathan Field, Heywood, John Mason, William Smith, Webster and George Wilkins. This may convey the mistaken impression that Latin title page epigraphs were a standard feature of professional plays in print. They were not. As Robert Miola has pointed out, Jonson was '[a]lone among contemporary playwrights [in] regularly and consistently us[ing] Latin epigraphs to introduce his publications'.[30] On other dramatists' title pages, the use is often infrequent or does not

[26] 'Latin Title-Page Mottoes as a Clue to Dramatic Authorship', 33.

[27] I quote the translation in Burrow, ed., *Complete Sonnets and Poems*, 173.

[28] Burrow, ed., Complete Sonnets and Poems, 173. For the 'Vilia-m' pun in the *Venus and Adonis* epigraph, see Cheney, *Shakespeare, National Poet-Playwright*, 92–4; and Lecercle, 'Ombres et nombres'.

[29] Loxley, *The Complete Critical Guide to Ben Jonson*, 42.   [30] 'Creating the Author', 36.

occur.[31] Even authors like Marston and Chapman who, in other contexts, did not disguise their literary ambitions, never have a Latin epigraph on a playbook title page. For the period from 1600 to 1623, only 29 of 251, or 11.5 per cent, of all professional plays carried Latin mottoes on the title page.[32] Those that do are typically by Jonson or written for private children's companies or both. The absence of Latin epigraphs on the title pages of Shakespeare's playbooks is thus unsurprising and reflects the situation in the vast majority of comparable contemporary playbooks.

Another paratextual feature which indicates the increasing respectability of printed playbooks is the dedication. Not all forms of Elizabethan literature were deemed equally suitable for dedication to a patron. Satires, pamphlets, ballads and other trivia usually did not include a dedication, whereas works of scholarship, including translations, did.[33] Shakespeare's two narrative poems, *Venus and Adonis* and *The Rape of Lucrece*, included the author's dedications to the Earl of Southampton, and the *Sonnets* contained the mysterious dedication to 'Mr W. H.' by the publisher, Thomas Thorpe. By contrast, not a single Shakespeare playbook published before the First Folio contained a dedication. What, then, is the meaning of this absence? Again, the important point to make is that Shakespeare's playbooks conform to the practice in the vast majority of contemporary playbooks. As a rule, professional plays (contrary to academic plays, translations of ancient or modern drama, or closet drama) contained no dedications at the end of the sixteenth and the beginning of the seventeenth century.[34] As Virgil Heltzel has written, 'during the reign of Elizabeth ... no play prepared for public presentation was deemed worthy of patronage. Toward such plays, however, a change of attitude came about gradually during the first years of the seventeenth century.'[35] The beginning of this change of attitude can be traced in two mock-dedications in the first years of

---

[31] In the case of Heywood, *The Silver Age* of 1612 is exceptional among his early playbooks in having a Latin title page motto, although such an occurrence becomes regular in the 1630s. See also Farmer and Lesser, 'Vile Arts', 99, 101, and Lesser, *Renaissance Drama and the Politics of Publication*, 63–7.

[32] These are Greg, *Bibliography*, 163a, 163b, 163c, 176a, 181a, 186a, 188a, 195a, 216a, 241a, 249a, 249b, 259a, 263a, 286a, 296a, 299a, 300a, 303a, 304c, 305a, 306a, 316a, 317a, 329a, 337a, 388a and 389a. The 1616 Jonson Folio, which has no separate number in Greg, also has a Latin motto on the title page. Note that Latin epigraphs were far more common on title pages of non-professional plays such as closet drama or translations (Farmer and Lesser, 'Vile Arts', 97). See also McManaway, 'Latin Title-Page Mottoes', 33.

[33] For a brief survey of which types of books were dedicated and at what time, see Williams, *Index of Dedications and Commendatory Verses*, x–xi.

[34] See Heltzel, 'The Dedication of Tudor and Stuart Plays', 75–8.

[35] 'The Dedication of Tudor and Stuart Plays', 78. Blayney's statement that 'five of the playbooks first printed in 1583–1602 contained dedications' ('The Publication of Playbooks', 395) is accounted for by the fact that he included in his count plays which were not performed at public playhouses.

the seventeenth century: Dekker's 'To all good Fellowes, Professors of the Gentle Craft, of what degree soeuer' in *The Shoemaker's Holiday* (1600) and Marston's 'To the onely rewarder, and most iust poiser of vertuous merits, the most honorably renowned No-body, bountious Mecaenas of Poetry, and Lord Protector of oppressed innocence' in *Antonio and Mellida* (1602).[36] Two slightly later playbooks contain dedications which, like Dekker's and Marston's, are clearly not pleas for patronage in any traditional sense: Marston's to Jonson in *The Malcontent* (1604) and Jonson's 'To the most noble and most aequall sisters, the two famous universities', in *Volpone* (1607).[37]

As for regular dedications, Voss has singled out Chapman as the 'likely pioneer in this regard', recording the dedications in *The Conspiracy and Tragedy of Charles, Duke of Byron* (1608), *The Widow's Tears* (1612) and *The Revenge of Bussy D'Ambois* (1613).[38] Even slightly before Chapman, Edward Sharpham dedicated *Cupid's Whirligig* (1607) 'To his much honoured, beloued, respected, and iudiciall friend, Maister Robert Hayman', and Barnabe Barnes *The Devil's Charter* (1607) 'To the honorable and his very deare friends Sir William Herbert, and Sir William Pope Knights'.[39] Other playbooks with dedications during Shakespeare's lifetime are Fletcher's *The*

---

[36] Later mock-dedications include John Day's 'To Signior No-body' in *Humour Out of Breath* (1608), Field's 'To any Woman that hath beene to Weathercocke' in *A Woman is a Weathercock* (1612) and Heywood's 'To the honest and hie-spirited Prentises The Readers', in *The Four Prentices of London* (1615).

[37] See also Dekker's slightly later dedication 'To my louing, and loued friends and fellowes, the Queenes Maiesties seruants', in *If It Be Not Good, the Devil Is in It* (1612).

[38] 'Printing Conventions and the Early Modern Play', 108. Contrary to what one might expect, Jonson was not the first one to include a printed dedication in a quarto playbook. For Jonson's earlier practice, going back to at least *Cynthia's Revels* (1601), of including manuscript dedications in printed copies of his playbooks, see Heltzel, 'The Dedication of Tudor and Stuart Plays', 80–1. For dedications added only to select presentation copies of Day, William Rowley and Wilkins's *The Travels of the Three English Brothers* (1607), see Massai, 'Shakespeare, Text, and Paratext', 2. The novelty of Chapman's practice in including a printed dedication is suggested by his prefatory rhetoric: 'if any worke of this nature be worth the presenting to Friends Worthie, and Noble; I presume this, will not want much of that value' ('To the right Vertuous and truly noble Gentleman, Mr Io. Reed of Mitton, in the Countie of Glocester Esquire', *The Widow's Tears*, 1612, sig. A2r); 'Since Workes of this kinds haue beene lately esteemed worthy the Patronage of some of our worthiest Nobles, I haue made no doubt to preferre this of mine to your vndoubted Vertue, and exceeding true Noblesse' ('To the Right Vertuous, and truely Noble Knight, Sr. Thomas Howard', *The Revenge of Bussy D'Ambois*, 1613, sig. A3r). Williams mentions a single leaf with a dedication to Sir Thomas Walsingham inserted into Chapman's otherwise undedicated *All Fools* (1605) in a copy now at the University of Texas, Austin (*Index of Dedications and Commendatory Verses*, 254). Thomas M. Parrott argued that the leaf was a forgery by John Payne Collier (see *The Plays and Poems of George Chapman*, II.726). Parrott's point was endorsed by Chambers (*The Elizabethan Stage*, III.252), but rejected by Freeman and Freeman (*John Payne Collier*, II.1076–8).

[39] For Hayman, see Galloway, 'Robert Hayman (1575–1629)' (concerning Hayman and Sharpham, see p. 83).

Faithful Shepherdess (1609), Jonson's *Catiline* (1611) and *The Alchemist* (1612), Beaumont's *The Knight of the Burning Pestle* (1613) and William Smith's *The Hector of Germany* (1615) – the year in which a publisher commented that 'It is a custome vsed by some writers in this Age to Dedicate their Playes to worthy persons'[40] – with four more following in the years between Shakespeare's death and the publication of the First Folio: Thomas Middleton and William Rowley's *A Fair Quarrel* (1617), Beaumont and Fletcher's *A King and No King* (1619), Jonson's *Epicene* (Q2, 1620, although the first quarto of 1616 had failed to include a dedication) and Gervase Markham and William Sampson's *Herod and Antipater* (1622).

Dedications were thus absent from printed playbooks until most of Shakespeare's plays published in quarto were already in print. No sixteenth-century playbook was dedicated, and only 30 playbook editions appearing between 1600 and 1622 contained dedications, whereas 212 did not.[41] Even including mock-dedications and other unusual dedications, the fraction of playbooks containing dedications (none up to 1599; 12 per cent from 1600 to 1622) was very small. Printed without dedications, the early Shakespeare playbooks thus simply reflect the conventions of the time.[42]

Much the same applies to epistles or addresses to the reader. No Shakespeare playbook contains an authorial address, and the only ones which include an address by a publisher or publishers are *Troilus and Cressida* (1609) and *Othello* (1622). Authorial addresses were largely non-existent in professional plays during the time up to 1603 when most of Shakespeare's separately published plays first appeared. The addresses in Marlowe's *Tamburlaine* (1590) and Lyly's *Endimion* (1591) are by publishers, as is the short note in Jonson's *Every Man Out of His Humour* (1600).[43] Jonson's *Cynthia's Revels* (1601) and *Poetaster* (1602) contain a headline 'Ad lectorem', yet what follow are not epistles but Latin epigraphs from Martial (printed on the play's title page in the 1616 Folio in the case of *Cynthia's Revels*). In fact, the only authorial address up to 1603 is in Thomas Dekker's *Satiromastix* (1602), entitled 'To the World', in which Dekker writes about

---

[40] I quote from 'The Printer to the Reader' prefacing *Cupid's Revenge* (1615), by Fletcher.

[41] The fraction of playbooks including dedications significantly increased after the publication of Shakespeare's First Folio. Blayney writes that 'in 1623–1642, after the Jonson and Shakespeare collections had helped to increase the respectability of printed plays, it [i.e. the number of playbooks containing dedications] soared to seventy-eight (58 percent)' ('The Publication of Playbooks', 395).

[42] Concerning dedications, see also Saenger, *The Commodification of Textual Engagements*, 55–62, and Bergeron, *Textual Patronage in English Drama, 1570–1640*.

[43] The prefatory text in *Troublesome Reign*, although headed 'To the Gentlemen Readers', seems in fact likely to be a prologue conceived for the playhouse ('You that ... Haue ... giuen applause', sig. A2r), written in imitation of the Prologue to *Tamburlaine* (the play to which the prologue refers).

'that terrible Poetomachia ... betweene Horace the second, and a band of leane-witted Poetasters' (sig. A3r) in which he has lately been involved.[44] Only in the early years of James's reign did authorial addresses become more common: by Marston (*The Malcontent* in 1604, *Parasitaster* in 1606 and *Sophonisba*, also in 1606), Jonson (*Sejanus* in 1605 and *Volpone* in 1607), Dekker (*The Whore of Babylon*, 1607), Sharpham (*The Fleir*, 1607), Barry Lording (*The Family of Love*, 1608), John Day (*Law Tricks*, 1608), Heywood (*The Rape of Lucrece*, 1608), Robert Armin (*The History of the Two Maids of More-clacke*, 1609) and Fletcher (*The Faithful Shepherdess*, 1609). Yet even in these years, the number of newly published plays without addresses by far exceeded the number of those with addresses.[45] If Shakespeare and the Lord Chamberlain's Men had a regular policy of publishing Shakespeare's plays up to about 1603 but no longer thereafter, then there is nothing surprising about the absence of authorial addresses to the reader from Shakespeare's early playbooks.[46]

Publishers' addresses to the reader were less frequent than authorial addresses, but they existed in the 1590s (*Tamburlaine* and *Endimion*) and continued to do so in the early seventeenth century, namely in *Every Man Out of His Humour* (1600), Sharpham's *The Fleir* (1607), Fletcher's *Cupid's Revenge* (1615), *The Two Merry Milkmaids* by 'I. C.' (John Cumber?) (1620), Beaumont and Fletcher's *Philaster* (1622) and, most famously, Shakespeare's *Troilus and Cressida* (1609, second issue) and *Othello* (1622).[47] It is instructive to approach the addresses in the two Shakespeare playbooks in the context of the other non-authorial addresses mentioned above. What is striking is that many of the addresses refer to the 'author', although none of them, with the exception of Richard Bonian and Henry Walley's in *Troilus and Cressida* and Thomas Walkley's in *Othello*, praises him in ways which suggest that mention of the author is considered a significant commercial

---

[44] For the 'Poetomachia' or 'war of the theatres', see Bednarz, *Shakespeare and the Poets' War*.

[45] Even in the early 1620s, playbooks with epistles were still less common than those without, even though Thomas Walkley, in 'The Stationers to the Reader' prefacing Q1 *Othello* (1622), suggests the opposite: 'To set forth a booke without an Epistle, were like to the old English prouerbe, A blew coat without a badge' (sig. A2r). Walkley's address is an attempt to make his publication more attractive rather than an accurate description of contemporary publication conventions.

[46] See Erne, *Shakespeare as Literary Dramatist*, 78–114 (102–38). For an analysis of Jonson's prefaces in the context of his contemporary dramatists', see Cannan, 'Ben Jonson, Authorship, and the Rhetoric of English Dramatic Prefatory Criticism'. For a study of authorial prefaces from Luther to Milton and Dryden, see Dunn, *Pretexts of Authority*.

[47] For the epistles in *Troilus and Cressida* and *Othello*, see, for instance, Fiedler, 'Shakespeare's Commodity-Comedy'; Jowett, *Shakespeare and Text*, 61–4; Bevington, ed., *Troilus and Cressida*, 1–3; Voss, 'Printing Conventions and the Early Modern Play', 106–7; and Gregory, 'Shakespeare's "Sugred Sonnets," *Troilus and Cressida*, and the *Odcombian Banquet*'.

advantage. Laurence Chapman, in *Two Merry Milkmaids*, points out that 'the Author was [far] from seeking fame in the publishing' (sig. A2r) of the play. William Holme, in *Every Man Out of His Humour*, expresses his concern not 'to traduce the Authour' (sig. A4v) with his publication. Richard Jones, in *Tamburlaine* (1590), does praise 'the eloquence of the Authour', but since his edition fails to identify the author's name, there is no sense in which the address capitalizes on an identifiable dramatist. Francis Burton informs the reader in *The Fleir* that 'The Author is inuisible to me (viz: ith' Country)' (sig. A3r), and Josias Harrison, in 'The Printer to the Reader' prefacing Fletcher's *Cupid's Revenge*, mentions 'the Authour' only to point out that he is 'not acquainted with him' (sig. A2r). Read in this context, Walkley's assertion that 'the Authors name is sufficient to vent his worke' (sig. A2r) and Bonian and Walley's extravagant praise for 'this authors Commedies' and his 'power of witte' appear in a new light, all the more so as their panegyric follows a title page which has spelled out the author's name, 'William Shakespeare'. Alone among publishers' prefatory epistles to quarto playbooks in the late sixteenth and early seventeenth century, those prefacing *Troilus and Cressida* and *Othello* make of the author a selling point, suggesting, in keeping with the suddenness and frequency with which Shakespeare's name appeared on the title page, as well as in keeping with the commercial success Shakespeare's playbooks had in print, that 'Shakespeare' was an authorial name with which money could be made.

The publishers' addresses in *Troilus and Cressida* and *Othello*, two of the five Shakespeare plays first published separately in the Jacobean period, are the only prefatory material beyond the title page that we have been able to identify in Shakespeare playbooks so far. Yet, as a synthetic view of prefatory material in the late sixteenth and early seventeenth century suggests, Shakespeare's playbooks conform well to the general trend at the time. Paul Voss writes:

Prefaces, epistles, dedications, and other types of front matter . . . became far more common in Jacobean plays. Consider that nearly 50 percent of the ninety-four extant first edition plays printed between 1603 and 1616 contain front matter of some type (the figure for Elizabethan plays, it should be recalled, was less than 10 percent) and one gets the impression that printers, publishers, and authors treated quarto plays differently after, say, 1603.[48]

Up to the end of Elizabeth's reign, when most of Shakespeare's play quartos first appeared, and did so without any prefaces, epistles or dedications, the

---

[48] 'Printing Conventions and the Early Modern Play', 107.

inclusion of front matter was very rare.[49] During the Jacobean period, when the inclusion of front matter became much more common ('nearly 50 percent'), two first-edition Shakespeare plays contain front matter (*Troilus and Cressida* and *Othello*), whereas the other three (*Hamlet*, *King Lear* and *Pericles*) do not. Ironically, it may come as a surprise to us that, considered in the context of contemporary book trade conventions, the scarcity of paratexts in Shakespeare's quarto playbooks is unsurprising.

Like Latin epigraphs, dedications and addresses to the reader, commendatory verses are a paratextual feature which started appearing on title pages of professional plays during Shakespeare's career, with the effect of elevating the status of printed drama. Commendatory verses not only suggested that printed drama *deserved* to be praised and recommended like forms of literature higher up on the scale of generic respectability, but also created 'the sense of a community of authors, presenting themselves to the public *as a community, expecting their names to mean something'.[50] Yet such verses were at first even rarer than the other paratexts previously surveyed, with only seven professional plays published with them prior to 1620, of which four, more than half, are by Jonson: *Sejanus* (1605), *Volpone* (1607), *Catiline* (1611) and *The Alchemist* (1612). The remaining three plays are Fletcher's *The Faithful Shepherdess* (1610?), Field's *A Woman is a Weathercock* (1612) and I. C.'s (Joshua Cooke's?) *Greene's Tu Quoque* (1614). The inclusion of commendatory verses remained highly exceptional up to 1620. Alexander Leggatt has referred to 'the growing custom of affixing commendatory verses to printed plays' in 'the early years of the [seventeenth] century', but it seems clear that the growth was at first very slow.[51] It is thus unremarkable that Shakespeare's playbooks contain no commendatory verses.[52]

---

[49] This point has also been made by Taylor: 'until Ben Jonson's *Sejanus* in 1605 and *Volpone* in 1607, commercial plays had almost always been published without an epistle, or dedication, or front matter of any kind' ('Making Meaning Marketing Shakespeare 1623', 60).

[50] Leggatt, 'The Presence of the Playwright', 137.

[51] 'The Presence of the Playwright', 132. See pp. 132–8 of Leggatt's essay for the rhetoric deployed and the network of writers involved in early seventeenth-century commendatory verses in printed drama. From about 1629, commendatory verses became much more common: no fewer than forty editions of professional plays included them in the next dozen years. See also Saenger, *The Commodification of Textual Engagements*, 72–6, and Williams, 'Commendatory Verses', esp. p. 5, and *Index of Dedications and Commendatory Verses*.

[52] Even rarer was the occurrence of errata sheets in professional plays in print. Only two of these appeared during Shakespeare's lifetime, in Dekker's *Satiromastix* (1602) and Day's *The Isle of Gulls* (1606), with three more following in the 1630s (Ford, *'Tis Pity She's a Whore*, 1633, and Thomas Nabbes, *Hannibal and Scipio* and *Microcosmus*, both 1637).

An additional paratext included in a number of playbooks but in none of Shakespeare's is the 'Argument' (also called 'Fabule argumentum', or simply 'Argumentum', by Marston), a plot summary printed before the dramatic text with the aim of facilitating readerly understanding.[53] In the fifty-year period between 1580 and 1630, only five plays appeared with an 'Argument', three by Jonson (*Sejanus*, 1605, 1616; *Volpone*, 1607, 1616; and *The Alchemist*, 1612, 1616) and two by Marston (*The Dutch Courtesan*, 1605; *Sophonisba*, 1606).[54] In the 1630s and 1640s, seven more plays followed, another three by Jonson (*The New Inn*, 1631; *The Sad Shepherd*, unfinished, 1641; and the equally unfinished *Mortimer His Fall* in the 1640 Folio) and one each by Chapman (*Caesar and Pompey*, 1631), John Mason (*The Turk*, 1632), William Rowley (*All's Lost by Lust*, 1633) and Thomas Nabbes (*Hannibal and Scipio*, 1637). Even though it has recently been argued that in addition to Jonson, 'plenty of other writers published Arguments before theatrical texts – often texts that do not seem to be trying to be "literary"', the non-Jonsonian plays in which 'Arguments' appeared were neither numerous (six in seventy years) nor devoid of other literary pretensions.[55] All six non-Jonsonian plays published with an 'Argument' contain other paratextual features associated with drama's rise to literary respectability: an address to the reader (*Sophonisba*), a dedication (*Caesar and Pompey*), dramatis personae lists (*The Dutch Courtesan*, *Sophonisba*, *The Turk*, *All's Lost by Lust* and *Hannibal and Scipio*), Latin title page mottoes (*The Turk*, *All's Lost by Lust* and *Hannibal and Scipio*) and an errata list (*Hannibal and Scipio*).

Another paratext in which Jonson and Marston took the lead is the character list, variously called 'dramatis personae', 'interlocutores', 'the names of characters', 'the names of the actors', 'the names of the speakers', 'the persons that act', or similar. These lists not only address the specific needs of readers as opposed to spectators but also follow the precedent established in editions of classical drama and its English translations. For instance, the 1581 collection of *Seneca His Tenne Tragedies* prints a character list before each play, and Richard Bernard's *Terence in English* of 1598 similarly includes a list of 'The speakers in this Comedy'. As for English professional plays, after four isolated instances in the 1590s – Robert Wilson's *The Three Lords and Three Ladies of London* (1590), *Dido, Queen of Carthage*, attributed to Marlowe and Nashe on the title page (1594), the anonymous *Mucedorus* (1598) and Henry Porter's *1 The Two Angry Women*

---

[53] Note, however, that Shakespeare's *Rape of Lucrece* does contain an 'Argument'.
[54] Daniel's *Philotas* also appeared with an 'Argument'; concerning *Philotas*, see below, p. 256.
[55] Stern, *Documents of Performance*, 64. Stern devotes chapter 3 of her study to the 'Argument' (63–80).

of Abingdon (Q2, 1599) – Jonson's and Marston's playbooks repeatedly included a list from the turn of the century.[56] With the exception of *The Case is Altered*, a special case as seen above (see p. 100), all of Jonson's single-authored plays included character lists. With Marston, the practice is less regular, but *Jack Drum's Entertainment* (1601), *The Malcontent* (1604), *The Dutch Courtesan* (1605), *Parasitaster* (1606) and *Sophonisba* (1606) all included a list. Playbooks by other dramatists soon conformed to the same practice, three by Chapman (1605–6), two by Dekker (1602, 1607) and one each by Edward Sharpham (1607), John Day (1608) and Heywood (1608), all before the end of the decade. Less than a quarter of all editions of professional plays published in the first decade of the seventeenth century contained lists of characters, a total which went up to more than a third in the next two decades.[57]

As for Shakespeare, according to a statement repeated in standard Shakespeare reference works, none of his quarto editions had a character list.[58] This is not quite true, although the first and only pre-Restoration quarto to contain a list is late, the third quarto of *The Merchant of Venice* (1637) (Figure 3.1). In addition, seven plays in the 1623 First Folio and the 1632 Second Folio print dramatis personae lists at the end of the text: *The Tempest*, *The Two Gentlemen of Verona*, *Measure for Measure*, *The Winter's Tale*, *2 Henry IV*, *Timon of Athens* and *Othello*.[59] Given that the first four of these plays are generally agreed to have been set up from transcripts by Ralph Crane, who was employed as a copyist by the King's Men after Shakespeare's death, it is sometimes believed that the character lists following those four plays originated with Crane. What may argue against this is that the character list following *Measure for Measure* is headed by '*Vincentio: the Duke*', even though the dramatic text never mentions the duke's name. E. A. J. Honigmann has written that 'Shakespeare had a weakness for naming his characters even when names are not strictly necessary: the

[56] Unusually, the 1594 quarto of *Dido, Queen of Carthage* prints the list of characters on the title page.

[57] My figures differ from Taylor's, presumably because he counts plays whereas I count editions: 'For the decade [i.e. the 1600s] as a whole, 39 per cent of texts had tables; in the next decade, the figure rose to 43 per cent' (Taylor, with Daileader and Bennett, 'The Order of Persons', 59–60). See also Beckerman, 'The Persons Personated', which focuses on the names given to character lists, and Howard-Hill, 'The Evolution of the Form of Plays in English during the Renaissance'.

[58] See Dobson and Wells, eds., *The Oxford Companion to Shakespeare*, 115, and Halliday, *A Shakespeare Companion, 1564–1964*, 141.

[59] The second issue of the Third Folio further adds a list to the newly included *Pericles*. It was not until Nicholas Rowe's edition of 1709 that dramatis personae lists preceded all of Shakespeare's plays. For a dramatis personae list in a *c.* 1648–60 manuscript of *The Merry Wives of Windsor*, copied from the Second Folio (Folger MS v.a.73), see Marotti and Estill, 'Manuscript Circulation', 63.

The Actors Names.

The Duke of *Venice,*
Morochus, a Prince, and a Sutor to *Portia.*
The Prince of *Aragon,* Sutor alfo to *Portia.*
Baffanio, an Italian Lord, Sutor likewife to *Portia.*
Anthonio, a Merchant of *Venice.*

Salarino,
Salanio,   } Gentlemen of *Venice,* and Compa-
Gratiano,   }   nions with *Baffanio.*
Lorenfo,

Shylock, the rich Iew, and Father of *Ieffica.*
Tuball, a Iew, *Shilocks* Friend.
Portia, the rich Italian Lady.
Nerriffa, her wayting-Gentlewoman.
Ieffica, Daughter to *Shylock.*
Gobbo, an old man, father to *Lancelot.*
Lancelot Gobbo the Clowne.
Stephano, a Meffenger.
Iaylor, and Attendants.

3.1 'The Actors Names', *The Merchant of Venice* (Q3, 1637), sig. A1v.

M[easure for] M[easure] list could be authorial.'[60] A similar oddity occurs in the character list of *Othello*, in which Montano is referred to as 'Governor of Cyprus', although 'his office cannot easily be deduced from the text itself', which has led Michael Neill to argue for 'an authorial origin for the list'.[61]

Whether or not Shakespeare prepared any of the character lists printed in the First Folio is now impossible to recover. What can be said, however, is that the frequent absence and occasional presence of character lists in Shakespeare's plays is in keeping with what the scarcity of the previously surveyed paratextual features may lead us to expect. When most of his separately published plays first reached print, character lists were still rare. Later, when they had become a relatively common feature, a number of Shakespeare's texts appeared with character lists. Given the prestige of the Folio collection of 1623, we might be surprised that only seven of the thirty-six plays were printed with dramatis personae lists, but even in collections, the feature was not yet standard: Jonson's 1616 and 1640 Folios included character lists, the 'Beaumont and Fletcher' Folio of 1647 did not, while in Marston's quarto collection of 1633, three plays did and the other three did not.

I have so far focused on prefatory material, from title page to dramatis personae list, but the makeup of Shakespeare's playbooks is also shaped by the disposition of the play texts' typographic notation, notably by the typographic layout of dialogue, act and scene division, and *sententiae* markers. Like the more obvious paratexts among the playbooks' prefatory matter, these features are governed by changing book trade conventions and carry socio-cultural meanings to which the early readers and users of Shakespeare's playbooks were exposed.

The form in which the dramatic text appears in playbooks in Shakespeare's time has a history which was principally shaped by the native manuscript tradition and the classical tradition (in particular the Continental method of printing Latin dramatists).[62] While some of the conventions were relatively fixed in Shakespeare's time, others were not. Speech prefixes, for instance, had typically been at the right of the page in native medieval dramatic manuscripts, but started moving leftwards in late medieval manuscripts and were mostly on the left in printed playbooks by the end of the sixteenth century, with every speech starting on a new line, the speech prefix slightly indented. There is a theatrical logic to this typographic arrangement as the new line with the indented speech prefix 'parallels the change in voices, a feature of the auditory experience of the play'.[63] Yet the classical tradition, as mediated by early editions of Seneca, Plautus and Terence, required the text to appear in complete verses, which means that when a line was shared by two or more speakers, the speech prefix(es) appear(s) within the line. As T. H. Howard-Hill has shown, this practice, which is commonly called continuous printing, is not 'congenial to the stage; the early editions of Plautus, Seneca, and Terence were primarily reading texts'.[64] Yet, on the other hand, as Henry Woudhuysen points out, 'it added to the neoclassical dignity of the appearance of the text and contributed a sense of its literary quality'.[65] Zachary Lesser brings together the two aspects by writing that 'Continuous printing values the literary and poetic in the playwright's lines – their meter and form – over the theatrical necessity of clearly identifying the speaker of those lines, helping to turn a stage play into a printed poem.'[66]

Given the literary and cultural associations of continuous printing, it is unsurprising that Jonson became an enthusiastic practitioner, starting with the 1605 quarto of *Sejanus*. Lesser has shown that in the seventy-five years before the publication of Jonson's play, almost all playbooks with continuous printing are academic plays, translations or closet drama, yet in the wake of Jonson, other plays written for the commercial stage appeared with continuous printing, and these plays too were typically fashioned to signal their literary pretensions.[67] Contrary to Jonson's playbooks from 1605, Shakespeare's adhered to the native convention, which remained dominant for professional plays throughout the early modern period. The only exception to this is the first quarto of *King Lear* (1608) in which almost a third of the seventy-nine pages contain continuous printing. Yet the typographic arrangement in this playbook, as Henry Woudhuysen has shown, seems more a matter of saving paper than of claiming literary respectability.[68] As a rule, then, the typographic arrangement of speech prefixes in Shakespeare's playbooks reflects the theatrical imperative of clearly identifying a new speaker on a new line rather than claiming cultural capital by signalling classical descent.

Another feature of the play texts' typographic arrangement is the division, or absence of division, into acts and scenes. Like continuous printing, division of a play into five acts follows classical precedent and conveys

---

[63] McJannet, *The Voice of Elizabethan Stage Directions*, 69.
[64] 'The Evolution of the Form of Plays in English during the Renaissance', 135.
[65] 'Early Play Texts', 56.   [66] *Renaissance Drama and the Politics of Publication*, 67, 70.
[67] See *Renaissance Drama and the Politics of Publication*, 68–9.   [68] See 'Early Play Texts', 57.

literary cachet, whereas its absence conforms to a theatrical logic: the performance of plays by adult companies in public outdoor theatres appears to have been uninterrupted, which made divisions in theatrical manuscripts unnecessary.[69] Performances by boys' companies at the more elite indoor venues, however, were interrupted by act breaks, which is reflected in the printed versions of plays designed for indoor performance.

Shakespeare's playbooks published during his lifetime are undivided, as are almost all contemporary outdoor plays. As Wilfred T. Jewkes shows in *Act Division in Elizabethan and Jacobean Plays, 1583–1616*, the fullest study devoted to the topic to date, there are 'seventy-four plays' written by Shakespeare's contemporaries 'for the adult companies, which survive from the period 1591–1607; not a single one of these is divided, except the five by Jonson'.[70] The first Shakespeare play to contain (imperfect) act and scene division is the 1622 *Othello*, which marks 'Actus 2. Scoena 1.' (sig. D2v) (Figure 3.2), 'Actus. 4.' (sig. I3r) and 'Actus. 5.' (sig. L3r).[71] Even earlier, sheets G–K of the first quarto of *Romeo and Juliet* (1597) contained rows of a printer's ornament inserted between scenes or scenic movements, probably the printer Edward Allde's way of filling the additional space which he had to waste as a result of using unintentionally smaller type than did John Danter, with whom he shared the printing of the playbook.[72] The first three quarto editions of *Pericles* (1609, 1609, 1611) have horizontal strokes before the re-entry of Gower at sigs. C1r and D4v, where modern editions begin acts 2 and 3.[73] In the First Folio, most plays are divided, although the division is sometimes imperfect (e.g. *The Taming of the Shrew, 1 Henry VI* and *Hamlet*) or into acts only (*The Comedy of Errors, Much Ado about Nothing, Love's Labour's Lost, A Midsummer Night's Dream, All's Well That Ends Well, Henry V, Coriolanus, Titus Andronicus* and *Julius Caesar*), and six plays are undivided (*2* and *3 Henry VI, Troilus and Cressida, Romeo and Juliet, Timon of Athens* and *Antony and Cleopatra*). It seems likely, however, that the divisions were added later, either for theatrical reasons or as

---

[69] The absence of division in manuscripts and printed playbooks need not imply that Shakespeare and other playwrights did not at least occasionally organize their material according to a five-act arrangement. See Baldwin, *Shakespeare's Five-Act Structure*, and Jones, *Scenic Form in Shakespeare*, 66–8.

[70] *Act Division in Elizabethan and Jacobean Plays, 1583–1616*, 98. For act and scene division in printed playbooks, see also Howard-Hill, 'The Evolution of the Form of Plays in English during the Renaissance', 134–42.

[71] Q2 *Othello* (1630) similarly marks the beginning of acts 2, 4 and 5, and adds 'Actus 3. Scoena 1.' (sig. F1r). Q1 *Othello* is not only the first Shakespeare playbook to spell out act division, but also the first one with (admittedly erratic) page numbers. The second quarto of 1630 offers little improvement, but the pagination in the 1634 quarto of *The Two Noble Kinsmen* is flawless.

[72] See Erne, ed., *The First Quarto of Romeo and Juliet*, 39–41.

[73] Q2 and Q3 *Pericles* follow the horizontal strokes in Q1, but they are absent from the later quartos.

20　　*The Tragedy of* Othello

And it is thought abroad, that twixt my sheetes
Ha's done my office; I know not, if't be true---
Yet I, for meere suspition in that kind,
Will doe, as if for surety: he holds me well,
The better shall my purpose worke on him.
Cassio's a proper man, let me see now,
To get this place, and to make vp my will,
A double knauery --- how, how, --- let me see,
After some time, to abuse *Othello's* eare,
That he is too familiar with his wife:
He has a person and a smooth dispose,
To be suspected, fram'd to make women false:
The Moore a free and open nature too,
That thinkes men honest, that but seemes to be so:
And will as tenderly be led bit'h nose --- as Asses are:
I ha't, it is ingender'd: Hell and night
Must bring this monstrous birth to the worlds light.

Exit.

Actus 2.

Scœna 1.

Enter Montanio, *Gouernor of* Cypres, *with two other Gentlemen.*

Montanie.

VVHat from the Cape can you discerne at Sea?
　　1 *Gent.* Nothing at all, it is a high wrought flood,
I cannot twixt the hauen and the mayne
Descry a saile.
　　Mon. Me thinkes the wind does speake aloud at land,
A fuller blast ne're shooke our Battlements:
If it ha ruffia'd so vpon the sea,
What ribbes of Oake, when the huge mountaine mes It,

Can

3.2 Act and scene break ('Actus 2. Scoena 1.') in *Othello* (Q1, 1622), sig. D2v.

preparation for publication in the Folio. Contrary to Jonson, Shakespeare habitually seems to have composed his plays without marked act division, nor, it seems, did he impose the neo-classical division on his plays prior to their publication.[74]

Like act divisions, printed sententiae or commonplace markers could increase the literary respectability of playbooks. In an age in which the importance of a piece of writing, including literary writing, was often judged by its perceived usefulness, markers whose purpose was to highlight generally applicable wisdom could lend a text cachet. Commonplacing has received considerable scholarly attention in recent years, and its importance in early modern literary culture has been established.[75] When it comes to professional plays in print, they started to be provided with sententiae markers in 1600, and Jonson again led the way, with *Every Man Out of His Humour*. Just as important for the rise of this practice, however, as Zachary Lesser and Peter Stallybrass have shown, was the commonplacing of plays by non-authorial agents (readers, editors and publishers), most importantly a small circle of people including John Bodenham and the publisher Nicholas Ling (see below, pp. 172–4).[76] Systematic authorial commonplace marking was in fact unusual, and largely confined to Jonson and Marston, whereas other dramatists 'are less likely to have played any significant role in the process'.[77] Shakespeare, then, is not unusual in having little, and probably non-authorial, commonplace marking in his playbooks: fourteen lines in Q1 *Hamlet* (sigs. C2r–v), seven lines in Q2 *Hamlet* (sigs. C3v, K4r) (Figure 3.3), five lines in Q *Troilus and Cressida* (sigs. B3r, B4v, K3v) and a total of fourteen lines in the First Folio, four in *Cymbeline* (sigs. aaa6r, bbb3r), two each in *The Merry Wives of Windsor* (sig. D5v), *1 Henry IV* (sigs. d6v, e5v) and *Measure for Measure* (sigs. F3r, F5v), and one in *2 Henry IV* (sig. g3r), *Henry V* (sig. h2r), *Troilus and Cressida* (sig. ¶1r) and *Two Gentlemen of Verona* (sig. C4r). The only Shakespeare text with more substantial commonplace marking is *The Rape of Lucrece*, which Gabriel Harvey, significantly, singled out with *Hamlet* as being 'for the wiser sort'.[78]

---

[74] See also Greg, 'Act Divisions in Shakespeare', and Taylor, 'The Structure of Performance'.

[75] See, for instance, Sherman, *Used Books* and *John Dee*, and Hackel, *Reading Material in Early Modern England*. Hunter lists twenty books with commonplace markers printed in England before 1600, starting with the 1570 edition of *Gorboduc* ('The Marking of Sententiae in Elizabethan Printed Plays, Poems, and Romances', 172–4).

[76] 'The First Literary *Hamlet*'.   [77] 'The First Literary *Hamlet*', 404.

[78] Harvey's words appear in the margins to his copy of Chaucer's 1598 *Workes*, f. 422v. See also Stern, *Gabriel Harvey*, 126–8, and Lesser and Stallybrass, 'The First Literary *Hamlet*', 393–4. For the 'some twenty-five lines' in *The Rape of Lucrece* highlighted by sententiae markers, see Woudhuysen, 'The Foundations of Shakespeare's Text', 78–9.

Feare it *Ophelia*, feare it my deare sister,
And keepe you in the reare of your affection
Out of the shot and danger of desire,
" The chariest maide is prodigall inough
If she vnmaske her butie to the Moone
" Vertue it selfe scapes not calumnious strokes
" The canker gaules the infants of the spring
Too oft before their buttons be disclos'd,
And in the morne and liquid dewe of youth
Contagious blastments are most iminent,
Be wary then, best safety lies in feare,
Youth to it selfe rebels, though non els neare.

3.3 Q2 *Hamlet* (1604/5), sig. C3v, with commonplace marking.

The bibliographic makeup of Shakespeare's playbooks

Texts cannot mean independently of their materializations. Literature exists, as David Scott Kastan has put it, 'only and always in its materializations', and the materializations are not simple containers within which the texts' meanings are disseminated but the conditions of the meanings they participate in shaping.[79] The work of D. F. McKenzie has been important in teaching us that 'The book itself is an expressive means' and that 'the material forms of books, the non-verbal elements of the typographic notations within them, the very disposition of space itself, have an expressive function in conveying meaning'.[80] Accordingly, an assessment of their meaning is essential 'if we are accurately to reconstruct our literary past'.[81] Jerome McGann has developed McKenzie's idea of the expressiveness of the book form, writing that 'Every literary work that descends to us operates

[79] *Shakespeare and the Book*, 4.
[80] 'Typography and Meaning', 82, and *Bibliography and the Sociology of Texts*, 17.
[81] 'Typography and Meaning', 117.

through the deployment of a double helix of perceptual codes: the linguistic codes, on the one hand, and the bibliographical codes on the other.'[82] Accordingly, McGann urges us to be attentive to 'such matters as ink, typeface, paper, and various other phenomena which are crucial to the understanding of textuality'.[83] Yet despite the well-known scholarship by McKenzie and McGann, Henry Woudhuysen is correct when writing that 'the material forms plays took between, say, 1565 and 1640 or even during the 1590s and 1600s, have attracted surprisingly little attention'.[84]

That it is impossible to dissociate what McGann calls the linguistic and the bibliographic codes must have been implicitly clear not only to stationers but also to readers, such as the Puritan pamphleteer William Prynne who objected in 1633, the year after the publication of Shakespeare's Second Folio, that 'Shackspeers Plaies are printed in the best Crowne paper, far better than most Bibles.'[85] Prynne perceived a shocking inadequacy in the way the materializations of the biblical and Shakespearean texts affected their perceived meaning and importance, whereas the publishers of those books must have found none. On the contrary, the publishers of Shakespeare's Second Folio anticipated that customers would find nothing inappropriate about the rather fine paper on which the plays were printed, and would be willing to pay for it. Here, the quality of paper of the 1632 Folio (a bibliographic code) and Prynne's comment about it (what Genette called an 'épitexte')[86] shed light on the cultural status of 'Shakespeare' by the early 1630s.

The paper used for Shakespeare's quarto playbooks published during and shortly after his lifetime was not of the same quality as that of the Second Folio. The amount of bleed-through in early quarto editions bears witness to the paper's relative thinness, suggesting paper of no more than 'moderately good quality'.[87] The paper size used for playbooks was usually 'the smallest of the common sizes ("pot" paper, named after the watermark most commonly found in sheets of that size), measuring somewhere between fifteen inches by eleven (38 × 28 cm) and sixteen by twelve (41 × 30 cm)'.[88] Paper was an expensive item in the production of printed books (see below, pp. 142–3), and so publishers – whose responsibility it was to provide their printers with paper – would have had every interest in reducing expenses

---

[82] *The Textual Condition*, 77.   [83] *The Textual Condition*, 13.
[84] 'The Foundations of Shakespeare's Text', 82.
[85] *Histriomastix. The Players Scourge, Or, Actors Tragedie*, sig. **6v.   [86] See *Paratexts*, 344–403.
[87] Blayney, *The Texts of King Lear*, 30. Blayney's point about the 1608 quarto of *King Lear* can be applied to Shakespeare's early playbooks more generally.
[88] Blayney, 'The Publication of Playbooks', 405.

related to it as much as possible. Different paper could be used for special presentation copies, and, significantly, several large-paper copies of the 1605 quarto of *Sejanus* are extant, including two which are signed by Jonson.[89] There is an additional reason why the paper used for the 1605 *Sejanus* has attracted scholarly attention, which is that it is the only playbook known to have been printed on English paper, with royal watermarks.[90] The paper was made by John Spilman, 'the only Englishman legally capable at the time of producing white paper'.[91] Paper from Normandy was considerably cheaper than English paper, which means that additional expenses went into the production of Jonson's playbook. It has been argued that 'Jonson arranged to use English paper with royal watermarks in order to give *Sejanus* (1605) the appearance of the king's sanction – which, perhaps, it had.'[92] Independently of whether this is true, the paper used for *Sejanus* is a powerful signifier which goes hand in hand with that playbook's extraordinary paratext to fashion its high-cultural status.[93] None of Shakespeare's early quarto playbooks, by contrast, is made up of paper whose size, quality or provenance would have defied expectations.

It is noteworthy, however, that Shakespeare's earliest playbook, the first quarto of *Titus Andronicus* (1594), is at the same time the first playbook to have been produced with an initial blank leaf. It was followed by a number of playbooks by Shakespeare's contemporaries, with an initial blank leaf, a final blank leaf, or both. Peele's *Old Wives' Tale* (1595), for instance, has a blank leaf at either end, plus a blank title page verso, which means that five of the playbook's forty-eight pages are blank. Blank leaves served as a protection for unbound volumes, but given how expensive paper was, publishers did not want to pay for them if they considered the publication of little value and ephemeral. W. W. Greg pointed out a long time ago that 'In spite of economic reasons to be sparing in the use of paper early printers seem to have rather liked end blanks.'[94] Henry Woudhuysen, who has studied the presence of blank leaves in quarto playbooks, writes that 'The

[89] See Calhoun and Gravell, 'Paper and Printing in Ben Jonson's *Sejanus* (1605)', 19. The *STC* notes that some extant copies of Sir John Harington's translation of Ariosto's *Orlando Furioso* (published by Richard Field in folio in 1591) were printed on 'large or heavy paper, some . . . hand-coloured'. See also Cauchi, 'The "Setting Foorth" of Harington's Ariosto'.

[90] See Calhoun and Gravell, 'Paper and Printing in Ben Jonson's *Sejanus* (1605)'.

[91] Calhoun and Gravell, 'Paper and Printing in Ben Jonson's *Sejanus* (1605)', 18. Mark Bland has written that 'there is no evidence of this paper being employed for other printed books, and its appearance in manuscripts is rare' (*A Guide to Early Printed Books and Manuscripts*, 29).

[92] Calhoun and Gravell, 'Paper and Printing in Ben Jonson's *Sejanus* (1605)', 64.

[93] See Jowett, 'Jonson's Authorization of Type in *Sejanus* and Other Early Quartos'.

[94] Greg, *Bibliography*, IV.cli.

presence of these blanks ... might be taken to challenge received ideas about the relative value placed on printed plays. If they were the unconsidered trifles they are generally taken to have been, it is strange that printers or publishers were so often willing to leave blank paper in them.'[95] Woudhuysen's point corroborates other research which has challenged the once accepted belief that play quartos were ephemera (see also below, Chapter 5), but it seems of significance for the status of professional plays more generally rather than for Shakespeare's in particular.[96]

Most of Shakespeare's plays appeared in quarto, but *Richard Duke of York* was published as an octavo in 1595. As with paper, the format of Shakespeare's early playbooks conforms well to the practice adopted for his contemporaries: plays were usually published in quarto format, although a couple of non-Shakespearean exceptions can be noticed in the 1590s: the two parts of *Tamburlaine* (1590, 1593, 1597) and *The Massacre at Paris* (1594).[97] It has been pointed out that in the case of relatively short books, octavo format had in fact more prestige than quarto: 'A poet like Drayton had his work moved from quarto, to octavo, to folio, that is, from less to more prestigious publication formats.'[98] Perhaps this explains why Shakespeare's narrative poems moved to octavo format after initial publication in quarto. Just as important, however, must have been the force of convention. Once quarto had established itself as the standard format for playbooks, it remained unchanged even when, after the turn of the century, the cultural cachet of playbooks increased and even when single-author playbook collections like Jonson's in 1616 and Shakespeare's in 1623 appeared in folio. Even Jonson's separately published plays, it deserves to be pointed out, all appeared in quarto, not in octavo. A uniform format for playbooks had practical advantages given that they were bound in bulk rather than separately (see below, pp. 219–23). What seems to have happened, then, is that in the first half of the 1590s, when professional plays started being published on an unprecedented scale, there was a period of

---

[95] 'Early Play Texts', 55.

[96] On the subject of paper, see also Heawood, 'Paper Used in England after 1600'; Williams, 'Paper as Evidence'; and Bland, *A Guide to Early Printed Books and Manuscripts*, 22–48.

[97] Woudhuysen notes that Samuel Brandon's closet drama *The Virtuous Octavia* (1598) also appeared in octavo ('The Foundations of Shakespeare's Text', 87).

[98] Marotti, *Manuscript, Print, and the English Renaissance Lyric*, 288 (more generally on format, see 286–90). Note that Joseph A. Dane and Alexandra Gillespie have recently warned us against 'the myth of the cheap quarto', which has contributed to the impression among modern scholars that the quarto format was per se of low prestige. They show that the 'cheap quarto' is 'an often-invoked but imprecise category in discussions of early printing', with 'no firm basis that we can discover in bibliographical fact' ('The Myth of the Cheap Quarto', 40). See also Galbraith, 'English Literary Folios 1593–1623', 63–4.

hesitation about their suitable format, but when octavo playbooks remained a small minority, quarto seems to have imposed itself as the standard format, and remained so even when the cultural prestige of playbooks increased. The format of Shakespeare's playbooks thus conformed to the genre's book trade conventions, or at least it did until 1623 when Shakespeare received the distinction of the first ever folio collection made up entirely of professional plays.[99]

Just as paper and format were bibliographic signifiers, so was typeface.[100] As Henry Woudhuysen has pointed out, 'The forms Shakespeare's printed plays took were not unusual. They were predominantly set in roman type, with italic used for speech prefixes and stage directions, for foreign languages, letters, poems, and … for most proper names.'[101] Roman had become the dominant typeface for playbooks by the time Shakespeare's started appearing in print, but up to 1590, most playbooks had been printed wholly or partly in the more old-fashioned blackletter, the only exceptions being Lyly's *Sappho and Phao* and *Campaspe*, and Peele's *The Arraignment of Paris* (all first published in 1584).[102] Perhaps under the influence of Sidney's *Arcadia* of 1590, roman became the usual typeface for playbooks and other types of imaginative literature.[103] Blackletter did not entirely disappear from playbooks, however. It was used in fourteen new playbooks which appeared between 1591 and 1605. These playbooks include Robert Wilson's *The Three Ladies of London* (1584) and *The Three Lords and Three Ladies of London* (1590), *Arden of Faversham* (1592), Lodge and Greene's *A Looking Glass for London and England* (1594), *A Warning for Fair Women* (1599), Dekker's *The Shoemaker's Holiday* (1600), and Munday's two Robin Hood plays, *The Downfall of Robert, Earl of Huntingdon* and *The Death of Robert, Earl of Huntingdon* (both 1601), all plays of distinctly English character.[104] Other plays in blackletter were starting to grow old when they first reached print, like *Doctor Faustus* (1604) and *The First Part of Hieronimo* (1605) (Figure 3.4), which may illustrate Zachary Lesser's point that 'Black letter

<hr />

[99] For a general examination of format, see Tanselle, 'The Concept of Format'.

[100] See Carter, *A View of Early Typography*, and Isaac, *English Printers' Types of the Sixteenth Century*.

[101] 'The Foundations of Shakespeare's Text', 86–7. Woudhuysen notes the exceptions of Valentine Simmes and, to a lesser degree, Peter Short, who did not consistently italicize proper names as other printers did. For the italic typeface, see also Loewenstein, 'Idem: Italics and the Genetics of Authorship'.

[102] Howard-Hill, 'The Evolution of the Form of Plays in English during the Renaissance', 139–40.

[103] See Bland, 'The Appearance of the Text in Early Modern England', 104, and Voss, 'Printing Conventions and the Early Modern Play', 100.

[104] See Howard-Hill, 'The Evolution of the Form of Plays in English during the Renaissance', 139–40.

# of Ieronimo.

Mary my lēedge miſtake me not I pray,
If friendly phrat'es, honied ſpæch, bewitching accent,
Well timed mellody, and all ſwæt guilts of nature,
Cannot auaile oꝛ win hun to it,
Then let him rai e his gall vp to his tong,
And be as bitter as phyſitions dꝛugs,
Stretch his mouth wider, with big ſwolne phꝛa'es :
Oh hæres a Lad of mettle, ſtout Don Andrea,
Mettle to the crowne
Would ſhake the kings hie court thꝛée handfuls downe.
   Sp i. And well pickt out knight Marſhall,
Spæch well ſtrung,
Ide rather choſe Horatio, were he not ſo young.
   Horꝛ. I humbly thanke your highnes,
In placing me next vnto his royall bo ome.
   Spai Yow ſtand ye Loꝛds to this election.
   Omnes. Right pleaſing our dꝛead Soueraigne,
   Medi. Onely with pardon mighty Soueraigne.
   Caſti. I ſhould haue choſe Don Lorenzo.
I Don Rogero,
   Rog. O no, not me my Loꝛds,
I am wars Champion, and my fées are ſwoꝛds,
Pꝛay king, pꝛay peeres, let it be Don Andrea,
Pées a woꝛthy him,
Loues wars and Souldiers there'oꝛe I loue him.
   Iero. And I loue him, and thee valliant Rogero,
Noble ſpyrits, gallant blouds,
Pour no wi e inſinuating Loꝛds,
You ha no tricks, you ha none o' all their ſlights.
   Lo. So, o, Andrea muſt be ent vnbaſſadoꝛ,
Lorenzo is not thought vpon : good.
Ile wake the Court, oꝛ ſtartle out ſome bloud.
   Spai. Yow ſtand you Loꝛds to this election.
   Omnes. Right pleaſing our dꝛead Soueraigne.
             A iii.   Spaine.

3.4 Page of text in blackletter (with header, speech headings and proper
names in roman), *The First Part of Hieronimo* (Q, 1605), sig. A3r.

is suffused with nostalgia.'[105] Adrian Weiss has called blackletter 'a signifier ... much in the manner of Spenser's archaic diction', creating an atmosphere by means of typography where the author of *The Faerie Queene* uses language.[106]

The dominant typeface for playbooks from the early 1590s, however, was roman. Nonetheless, blackletter remained dominant not only in official documents but also in genres such as ballads, news quartos or horn books, genres, that is, which were aimed at the lower classes. Roman, by contrast, 'became associated, more or less, with middle-class literature'.[107] Significantly, then, most playbooks, and Shakespeare's playbooks among them, were printed with a typeface which the book trade associated 'with a higher level of literacy and education than blackletter', suggesting that readers 'did *not* perceive [playbooks] as belonging to the same market as jestbooks and ballads'.[108]

As for type size, Mark Bland mentions among certain 'generally observed practices' in the book trade that 'plays were set as quartos in pica roman'.[109] The only exception to this among Shakespeare's playbooks of which I am aware are sheets A–D of Q1 *Romeo and Juliet* (1597), which was printed in english roman.[110] A publisher might opt for the slightly larger english type size in the case of exceptionally short plays, but will usually prefer pica in order to save space and thus keep costs down.[111] This seems to have applied equally to Shakespeare's and to his contemporaries' playbooks.

[105] 'Typographic Nostalgia', 99. *1 Hieronimo* is based on the 'doneoracio' (i.e. Don Horatio) mentioned in Henslowe's diary in 1591 (see Erne, *Beyond 'The Spanish Tragedy'*, 14–46).
[106] 'Casting Compositors, Foul Cases, and Skeletons', 205. See also Mish, 'Black Letter as a Social Discriminant in the Seventeenth Century'; the section on 'Black Letter: the Commoner's Typeface?' in Weiss, 'Casting Compositors, Foul Cases, and Skeletons', 202–6; and, for a discussion of 'black letter literacy', Thomas, 'The Meaning of Literacy in Early Modern England'. McJannet has drawn attention to the 'expressive use of different typefaces' in early modern playbooks: 'Italics commonly highlight quotations or dialogue in Latin (such as the conjuring in *Doctor Faustus*). They are also used for dialogue in Romance languages (such as Henry's wooing of Katherine in broken French in *Henry V*). In *Alphonsus, Emperor of Germany* (Q, 1654), in a witty variation, Gothic typeface is used to represent the German spoken by the unfortunate heroine, Hedwick. In the folio edition of *The Alchemist*, Jonson also uses Gothic type for German expressions and names, such as "Ulen Spiegel," one of Face's aliases' (*The Voice of Elizabethan Stage Directions*, 70).
[107] Voss, 'Printing Conventions and the Early Modern Play', 100.
[108] Blayney, 'The Publication of Playbooks', 416–17.
[109] 'The London Book-Trade in 1600', 456. For pica roman, see Ferguson, *Pica Roman Type in Elizabethan England*.
[110] Note that Allen and Muir (*Shakespeare's Plays in Quarto*, 893) mistakenly claim that the first four sheets are printed in pica and the rest in long primer. Pica corresponds to our modern '12 point', english to '13 point'. See Gaskell, *A New Introduction to Bibliography*, 13–15. Weiss has pointed out that Marston's *Antonio's Revenge* (1602) is printed in english roman ('Casting Compositors, Foul Cases, and Skeletons', 207).
[111] Blayney, 'The Publication of Playbooks', 405.

Shakespeare's theatrical playbooks

The evidence so far presented may appear contradictory: the sudden, massed appearance of 'Shakespeare' on title pages, the persistent association of 'Shakespeare' with the revision and expansion of play texts, and the suggestion in the prefatory epistles to *Troilus and Cressida* and *Othello* that Shakespeare is a literary dramatist of unique 'power of witte' whose 'name is sufficient to vent his worke' seem to indicate that Shakespeare's playbooks importantly contributed to the process which increased the literary respectability of printed drama. On the other hand, Shakespeare's playbooks precisely lack many of the paratextual and bibliographic features – Latin epigraphs, dedications, authorial addresses to the reader, arguments, character lists, continuous printing, systematic use of *sententiae* markers, and act and scene division – which played an important part in the rise of respectability of printed drama. In some respects, Shakespeare's playbooks reveal a conspicuous presence of 'Shakespeare', whereas many other paratextual and bibliographic features suggest a conspicuous absence of authorial inscription. Although the evidence seems to suggest that Shakespeare had extraordinary cachet as a dramatic author and, in that capacity, participated in the authorization of printed drama, numerous paratextual and bibliographic features indicate an absence of Shakespearean agency, and this in a double sense: absence of Shakespeare's involvement in the paratextual and bibliographic constitution of his own playbooks as well as absence of Shakespeare's playbooks in the process that turned playbooks into more respectable, more literary publications.

Whereas the preceding parts of this chapter have been chiefly descriptive, the present one is more analytic, trying to come to terms with the tension articulated in the above paragraph and to account for the scarcity of paratext in Shakespeare's early playbooks. This scarcity becomes understandable if we situate Shakespeare's playbooks in the context not just of the most bibliographically visible contemporary playwrights but of professional plays as a whole. I have highlighted Jonson, Marston and Chapman above, for it was these playwrights, and chiefly Jonson, who broke new ground by endowing their playbooks with new paratextual and bibliographic features. An important point follows: at the time when the great majority of Shakespeare's plays published during his lifetime first came into print (1594–1603), the scarcity of paratext conforms to the statistical norm, to standard book trade practices and to what readers of professional plays expected. Up to 1603, few playbooks contained Latin title page mottoes, prefatory matter, character lists, act and scene division, *sententiae* markers or continuous printing, and the majority of those that did are by a small group of playwrights whom we might call Jonson & Sons. More representative than these was Shakespeare or someone like Thomas Middleton, of whom, as Gary Taylor tells us, 'Nine . . . plays were published before 1609', all of them showing a 'consistent poverty of paratext: no dedications, no epistles, no prefatory epigrams'.[112]

Shakespeare thus conforms to the norm when it comes to professional plays in print: title page immediately followed by the beginning of the dramatic text, with an absence of prefatory material in between. What was normal for professional plays was very unusual for books more generally: 'the conspicuous lack of prefatory matter stands as perhaps the most unusual feature of the early modern printed play'.[113] Our scholarship naturally tends to foreground paratextual presence rather than absence, but what must have been striking for book browsers and readers in Shakespeare's time was precisely the absence of prefatory material after turning the title page of most playbooks. One effect is that 'the paucity of conventional mediating factors renders the experience of reading the printed play more immediate and direct – more dramatic – than that of most other printed books'.[114] Prefatory material interposes between title page and dramatic text a series of texts which are extraneous to the theatrical experience, so there is a mimetic relationship between the theatrical experience and the experience of opening a playbook in which no mediatory framework precedes the dramatic text.

What this suggests is not only that Shakespeare did what most playwrights did at the time, but that there is an authorial and bibliographic logic to the absence of paratextual material from his playbooks. Shakespeare found nothing inconsistent about writing texts for performance for which he also anticipated a readership, nor, I believe, did he find anything inappropriate about the appearance of his plays in a form which enacts the immediacy and directness of the theatrical experience. On the contrary, the ideological freedom with which readers could approach a playbook devoid of front matter may well have seemed exactly right to the author of *As You Like It* and *Twelfth Night, or What You Will*, an author who seems to have trusted his spectators and readers as much as Jonson mistrusted his. Given his close involvement with his company, Shakespeare had no reason

---

[112] 'The Order of Persons', 52.
[113] Voss, 'Printing Conventions and the Early Modern Play', 100–1.
[114] Voss, 'Printing Conventions and the Early Modern Play', 101.

to wish his printed plays to appear in a form which would estrange them from the theatre.

In 1594, when the playhouses reopened after a period of closure due to the plague during which Shakespeare had authored his two narrative poems, Shakespeare was faced with the decision between continuing to write poetry and returning to write plays. In a way, he refused to choose by writing plays which were full of poetry, producing the works which an earlier generation of critics used to call the 'lyric phase'.[115] The decision with which Shakespeare was faced was between artistically functioning in solitariness or as part of the community formed by a theatre company. Here, too, he found it most comfortable not to choose: he was a loyal member of the Lord Chamberlain's Men, yet he wrote his plays in sole authorship – contrary to the dominant practice at the time – and saw his plays go into print ascribed to 'William Shakespeare'. Investing his playbooks with the trappings of possessive authorship would have endangered the fine balance with which Shakespeare, member of the Lord Chamberlain's Men and solo-dramatist, must have felt most comfortable, a balance which is also reflected by the makeup of his playbooks.

The difference between texts and books is again important: Shakespeare wrote literary *texts* which he wanted to appear in print and which – as he realized from 1598, still fairly early in his career – did so with greater success than those of any other playwrights. At the same time, he had no desire to see his plays published as '"high" culture' *books*. We can be confident that Shakespeare had his plays published in accord with the Lord Chamberlain's Men, and it seems likely that the published playbooks served the purpose of recommending the play in the theatre.[116] The Lord Chamberlain's Men were not '"high" culture' and elite (like the children's indoor playhouses) but popular, and this is reflected by Shakespeare's playbooks (of which many mention the play's performance by the company on the title page).

The difference between Shakespeare, on the one hand, and Jonson and his followers, on the other, is not, as we were too long led to believe, that the latter cared about the publication of their plays, whereas the former did not. Rather, what distinguishes them is that the latter were the first to promote what Zachary Lesser has called 'a "high" culture of drama written in English', something Shakespeare never did.[117] For Shakespeare, the two media of stage and page were complementary; for Jonson they were

---

[115] See Erne, 'Print and Manuscript', 64–8.
[116] See Erne, *Shakespeare as Literary Dramatist*, 84–91 (108–15).
[117] *Renaissance Drama and the Politics of Publication*, 71.

antithetical. The '"high" culture of drama' did not simply mean transposing the theatrical experience into a different medium but turning away from it. Jonson's anti-theatricality is well established, and the paratextual and biblio-graphic form his playbooks took was important in displaying it.[118] Several of Jonson's Latin epigraphs, for instance, are explicitly anti-theatrical.[119] The practice of continuous printing favoured by writers like Jonson and Chapman from early on is precisely not 'congenial to the stage' but mimics the convention in 'the early editions of Plautus, Seneca, and Terence', which 'were primarily reading texts', serving to 'distance the play from its theatrical origins and from the "vulgar" spectacles that win the favor of audiences in the commercial theatre'.[120] To borrow the words of Stephen Orgel, the aim of the paratextual and bibliographic presentation of '"high" culture drama' is that it 'no longer requires the mediation of an acting company for its realization. The play is now a transaction between the author and the individual reader, and the only performance takes place in the reader's imagination.'[121]

During Shakespeare's lifetime, only one of his playbooks was fashioned so as to reach the elite readership to which Jonson and his followers catered, and that is the 1609 edition of *Troilus and Cressida* or, to be more precise, the second issue of that edition, with the new title page which omits mention of performance 'by the Kings Maiesties / seruants at the Globe' and inserts the famous address 'A neuer writer, to an euer reader. Newes' (Figure 3.5 and 3.6) Independently of whether or not it is true that the play was 'neuer stal'd with the Stage, neuer clapper-clawd with the palmes of the vulger' (sig. ¶2r), what is significant is that the address presents us with the kind of anti-theatrical rhetoric characteristic of the '"high" culture of drama' *à la* Jonson *et al*. Spectators at public playhouses are 'dull and heauy-witted worldlings' (not unlike Jonson's 'understanding gentlemen o' the ground here' whose only redeeming feature is that they leave the playhouse 'better wittied than they came').[122] What counts as praise here is that 'the most displeased with Playes, are pleasd with his Commedies' (sig. ¶2r). Dislike of publicly performed, vulgarly clapper-clawed 'Playes' and appreciation of Shakespeare's 'Commedies' allegedly go hand in hand. The sales pitch is

---

[118] A good starting point for Jonson's anti-theatricality is still Barish, 'Jonson and the Loathèd Stage' in *The Anti-Theatrical Prejudice*, 132–54.

[119] See Lesser, *Renaissance Drama and the Politics of Publication*, 63–5.

[120] Howard-Hill, 'The Evolution of the Form of Plays in English during the Renaissance', 135, and Lesser, *Renaissance Drama and the Politics of Publication*, 67.

[121] *Imagining Shakespeare*, 2. Orgel makes this point specifically about the 1605 quarto of *Sejanus*, but it applies more generally to the '"high" culture drama' Jonson and others promoted.

[122] Horsman, ed., *Bartholomew Fair*, Induction, lines 49–50.

A neuer writer, to an euer reader. Newes.

Ternall reader, you haue heere a new play , neuer ſtal'd with the Stage, neuer clapper-clawd with the palmes of the vulger, and yet paſſing full of the palme comicall; for it is a birth of your braine, that neuer vnder-tooke any thing commicall, vainely : And were but the vaine names of commedies changde for the titles of Commodities, or of Playes for Pleas ; you ſhould ſee all thoſe grand cenſors , that now ſtile them ſuch vanities , flock to them for the maine grace of their grauities : eſpecially this authors Commedies , that are ſo fram'd to the life , that they ſerue for the moſt common Commentaries, of all the actions of our liues. ſhewing ſuch a dexteritie, and power of witte, that the moſt diſpleaſed with Playes, are pleaſd with his Commedies. And all ſuch dull and heauy-witted worldlings, as were neuer capable of the witte of a Commedie , comming by report of them to his repreſentations , haue found that witte there , that they neuer found in them ſelues, and haue parted better wittied then they came : feeling an edge of witte ſet vpon them , more then euer they dreamd they had braine to grinde it on. So much and ſuch ſauored ſalt of witte is in his Commedies, that they ſeeme (for their height of pleaſure) to be borne in that ſea that brought forth Venus. Amongſt all there is none more witty then this: And had I time I would comment vpon it , though I know it needs not, (for ſo

¶ 2   much

3.5 Address from 'A neuer writer, to an euer reader. Newes.', *Troilus and Cressida* (Q, second issue, 1609), sig. ¶2r.

THE EPISTLE.

much as will make you thinke your testerne well be-
stowd) but for so much worth, as euen poore I know to be
stuft in it. It deserues such a labour, as well as the best
Commedy in Terence *or* Plautus. *And beleeue this,*
that when hee is gone, and his Commedies out of sale,
you will scramble for them, and set vp a new English
Inquisition. Take this for a warning, and at the perrill
of your pleasures losse, and Iudgements, refuse not, nor
like this the lesse, for not being sullied, with the smoaky
breath of the multitude; but thinke fortune for the
scape it hath made amongst you. Since by the grand
possessors wills I beleeue you should haue prayd for them
rather then beene prayd. And so I leaue all such to bee
prayd for (for the states of their wits healths)
that will not praise it.
Vale.

3.6 Address from 'A neuer writer, to an euer reader. Newes.', *Troilus and Cressida*
(Q, second issue, 1609), sig. ¶2v.

awkward insofar as many of Shakespeare's comedies had been and continued to be performed and applauded by audiences at public playhouses like
the Globe. The address's strategy seems potentially counter-productive
insofar as it cries down public playhouse theatre ('sullied, with the smoaky
breath of the multitude', sig. ¶2v) while trying to advertise a play by a public
playhouse playwright. It may be significant that the address appears not in a
whole edition but only in one of its two issues. We do not know whether
and, if so, when the issue sold out, but the fact that *Troilus and Cressida*
received no single-play reprint in the rest of the century does not suggest
that Bonian and Walley's strategy was a spectacular success.

Conclusion

Shakespeare's paratextual absence from his quarto playbooks long contributed to the flawed belief in his indifference to the afterlife of his plays in
print. Bentley, for instance, wrote that Shakespeare 'did not himself take to
the printers any of the plays he wrote for the Lord Chamberlain-King's
company. When his plays were published they appeared without any
indication of the author's sponsorship – no dedications, no epistles, no
addresses to the readers, no commendatory verses from friends, not even a
list of characters.'[123] For Bentley, Shakespeare's indifference to the publication of his plays could be inferred from the absence of authorial paratext in
his playbooks, as if the wish to have one's plays published in itself required
the production of prefatory material, independently of the paratextual
conventions of the time. Even a recent scholar has called 'the lack of any
signed or unsigned dedication, address or postscript in the early editions of
plays published during Shakespeare's lifetime' a 'glaring anomaly for a
playwright supposedly committed to dramatic publication'.[124] A close
look at the evidence shows that it is not.

   This does not mean that Shakespeare was as visibly and aggressively
protective of his published writings and authorial persona as Ben
Jonson.[125] The real opposition between Shakespeare and Jonson was not
between an author invested in the publication of his plays and a playwright
indifferent to it. Rather, the contrast seems to have resided in their different
degrees of possessiveness. In contrast to Jonson, Shakespeare, in keeping
with most other playwrights of the time, did not oversee the printing of any

---

[123] *The Profession of Dramatist in Shakespeare's Time, 1590–1642*, 280.
[124] Massai, 'Shakespeare, Text, and Paratext', 4.
[125] This paragraph is indebted to my 'Afterword' in *Shakespeare's Book*, 258–9.

of his play texts, nor did he provide them with an epistle or dedication. Jonson did what he could to inscribe his keenly possessive authorship into his publications; Shakespeare did not, but entrusted them to the care of his publishers and readers. Whereas Jonson mistrusted his readers and tried to shape the reception of his texts as best he could, Shakespeare did not. Rather, as Jane Rickard has put it, for Shakespeare 'the relationship between texts and their readers was a source not of anxiety but of creative potential', a relationship in which 'myriad-minded Shakspear', who 'never promulgates any party-tenets', instead allows his spectators and readers to define their own position.[126]

Patrick Cheney has identified in Shakespeare a self-effacing authorship which he terms 'counter-laureate', in contrast to the self-advertising laureate authorship of a number of his contemporaries: 'Shakespeare forges theatrical self-concealment in response to the laureate self-presentation of Spenser and indeed most authors of the 1590s, from Marlowe to Jonson.'[127] Spenser's and later Jonson's laureate authorship proceeds through authorial self-presentation by means of characters like Colin Clout or Horace (in *Poetaster*); Shakespeare's authorial self-presentation precisely does not but is oblique and refracted.[128] The form of authorship which Cheney finds in the fiction of Shakespeare's writings in fact applies remarkably well to what we can gather about Shakespeare's bibliographic authorship. Shakespeare's paratextual silence in all his dramatic publications becomes understandable if we read it in the context of Cheney's argument in *Shakespeare's Literary Authorship*: Shakespeare's counter-laureate authorship, which precisely avoids authorial self-presentation, is in keeping with his absence from the bibliographic locus which foregrounds the authorial self.

---

[126] 'The "First" Folio in Context', 222. The two other passages are quoted from Coleridge, *Biographia Literaria*, 19, and *Lectures 1808–1819*, 272.
[127] *Shakespeare's Literary Authorship*, 63.
[128] See Cheney, *Shakespeare's Literary Authorship*, chapters 1 and 2.

CHAPTER 4

Shakespeare's publishers

Prologue: William Leake's reissue of Q3
The Merchant of Venice in 1652

In 1652 appeared what is perhaps the least known of all Shakespeare publications up to the Restoration, a reissue, by William Leake, of the third
quarto of *The Merchant of Venice*. It had originally been published by
Lawrence Hayes in 1637, but the rights in the play passed to Leake after
Hayes's death.[1] When reissuing the play, Leake updated the edition by
providing the remaining copies with a cancel title page according to which
the books had been 'Printed for William Leake' and were being 'solde at his
shop at the signe of the Crown in Fleetstreet, between the two Temple Gates.
1652' (Figure 4.1).[2] The title remained the same as in 1637, announcing the
'most excellent Historie of the Merchant of Venice', with the lengthy subtitle
still singling out 'the extreame cruelty of Shylocke the Jew', though the
spelling of the last word was updated from 'Iewe' to 'Jew'.

Leake's objective was to pass off the remnants of an old edition as a new
one. His customers may well have been taken in, and so were some modern
scholars, who claimed that Leake published a new edition.[3] But why did
Leake reissue the third quarto edition fifteen years after the text was printed?
Multiple issues of Shakespeare editions were not particularly rare: the 1600 *2
Henry IV*, the 1604/5 *Hamlet*, the 1608 *Richard II*, the 1609 *Troilus and*

---

[1] Hayes died shortly after publishing the third quarto of *The Merchant of Venice*, before the end of 1637.
When exactly Leake acquired the rights in the play is not clear: the assignment to him is not recorded
in the Stationers' Register until 17 October 1657, although the cancel title page of *The Merchant of
Venice* suggests that the remaining stock of the third edition must have been in his possession by 1652
(see Greg, *Bibliography*, 1.281).

[2] In addition to printing a cancel title page, Leake added to the 1652 reissue a list of books he had recently
published. Such publishers' booklists, of which Leake made several, started appearing in the mid-
seventeenth century. For a 'systematic examination of the catalogues of . . . William Leake', see Hooks,
'Booksellers' Catalogues and the Classification of Printed Drama in Seventeenth-Century England'
(I quote from p. 446). See also Lindenbaum, 'Publishers' Booklists in Late Seventeenth-Century London'.

[3] See, for instance, Wright, 'The Reading of Plays during the Puritan Revolution', 79.

The moſt excellent

HISTORIE

OF THE

Merchant of Venice:

With the extreame cruelty of *Sbylocke*
the *Jew* towards the ſaid Merchant, in cutting a
juſt pound of his fleſh: and the obtaining
of *Portia* by the choyce of three Cheſts.

As it hath been diverſe times acted by the
Lord Chamberlaine his Servants.

Written by WILLIAM SHAKESPEARE.

LONDON:
Printed for *William Leake,* and are to be folde at his ſhop at the
ſigne of the Crown in *Fleetſtreet,* between the two
Temple Gates. 1652.

4.1 Title page of the 1652 reissue of Q3 *The Merchant of Venice.*

Cressida, the undated *c.* 1623 *Romeo and Juliet* and the 1630 *Pericles* all exist in two issues, but in these cases, the second issue appeared soon after, or was even published at the same time as, the first. Leake is in fact the first publisher of a Shakespeare playbook who issued the remainder of an edition many years after its original appearance. It is true that there are other instances of a publisher quietly updating an edition by providing the unsold stock with a new title page. In 1610, for instance, the 1589 edition of Thomas Lodge's *Scillaes Metamorphosis* was reissued with a new title as *A moste pleasant Historie of Glaucus and Scilla*.[4] And in 1611, Robert Chester's *Love's Martyr* of 1601 (with various appended poems, including Shakespeare's 'The Phoenix and the Turtle') was reissued as *The Anuals* [*sic*] *of Great Brittaine*. Nonetheless, Leake's decision may require an explanation.

In search for it, we may rephrase my earlier question as follows: was there a particular reason why, in 1652, Leake wanted his customers to think *The Merchant of Venice* was a new publication rather than an old one? The Stationers' Register contains a piece of information which seems suggestive: on 9 September 1653, Leake's fellow stationer Humphrey Moseley entered a lost play by Dekker called *The Jew of Venice*.[5] It is unclear whether Moseley went on to publish the play; if he did, no copy is extant. Yet its mention in 1653 is intriguing. Dekker had died in 1632; most of his extant plays were published during his lifetime, and no single-authored play assigned to Dekker was published after the 1630s. Moseley's entrance in the Stationers' Register of Dekker's *Jew of Venice* in 1653 thus seems in some ways as surprising as Leake's reissue of the third quarto of *The Merchant of Venice* in 1652.

What may explain why Leake and Moseley were both contemplating or faking the publication of a play about a Jew in the early 1650s is that the question of the readmission of the Jews – officially expelled since 1290 – was being vigorously debated in London at the time.[6] The Commonwealth led

---

[4] See McKerrow, *An Introduction to Bibliography*, 177.

[5] See Chambers, *William Shakespeare*, 1.375.

[6] Investigating the publication of another 'Jew' play, Zachary Lesser has argued that Marlowe's *Jew of Malta* was published in 1633 – more than forty years after its original composition – because Nicholas Vavasour, the publisher, 'apparently believed that *The Jew* had gained new relevance in the religious climate of the 1630s and felt the play could be made to participate in the debates over the ecclesiastical program of Archbishop Laud' (*Renaissance Drama and the Politics of Publication*, 24). Lesser argues that 'If the publisher considered Marlowe's play in the Laudian context, *The Jew* must have seemed to him to be as much about puritans as about Jews. Malta provided a discouraging image of what England might become if it continued to countenance disunity in the Church' (101–2). Lesser's argument is sophisticated and less straighforward than my present one about the reissue of *The Merchant of Venice* in 1653: Leake, I believe, reissued a play which dramatizes a Jew's fraught position in society because he was counting on his customers' interest in the question of the Jews' position in society.

to hopes of religious toleration, and as early as 1649, *The Petition of the Jewes for the Repealing of the Act of Parliament for their banishment out of England* (Wing C695) as 'Presented to his Excellency and Generall Councill of Officers' (title page) was published in London.[7] In 1650, *The Hope of Israel* (Wing M375) by the famous Amsterdam rabbi Menasseh ben Israel, dedicated to Parliament, led to further 'discussion of whether or not to permit Jews to enter the country'.[8] Owing to the Anglo-Dutch war (1652–4), ben Israel's planned visit to London was delayed until 1655, when Cromwell received him and, in December, went on to preside over a national conference at Whitehall devoted to the question of readmission.[9] Although Cromwell stopped the discussion in order to prevent an adverse decision, he seems to have informally granted Jews conditional permission to reside in England the following year.[10]

During the years in which the readmission was being debated, numerous publications testify to the intensity of public interest in Jewish questions in England. For instance, in 1652, Eleazar Bargishai ('a born Jew', according to the title page) published *A Brief Compendium of the vain Hopes of the Jews Messias. The Ignorant Fables of their Rabbies, and the Confuting of the Jewish Religion* (Wing E332A), a 'small and short Book, expressing and revealing the wickedness of the Jews' (sig. B1r). In the same year, John Bellamie published a treatise about Jewish forms of worship by William Pinchion, called *The Jewes synagogue* (Wing P4309). Still in 1652, Livewell Chapman published a second edition of *The Hope of Israel*, and an anonymous publisher, 'M. S.', issued *The Great Deliverance of the Whole House of Israel*, by 'J. E.', written, as stated on the title page, 'in Answer to a Book called The Hope of Israel'. In it, Menasseh ben Israel is urged to repentance – 'you must with sorrowfull heart . . . confesse your sin unto God' (sig. E1v) – and conversion to Christianity: 'that you might know and understand the greater misteries which are contained in the Gospel of Jesus Christ' (sig. E1v). The following year, 1653, saw the publication of a sarcastic pamphlet, called *Two Centuries of Pauls Church-yard* (Wing B2973), which lists among a series of supposed 'new Acts of Parliament': 'An Act for admitting Jews into England, with a short proviso for banishing the Cavaliers' (26–7). In the same year, several

---

[7] For a slightly earlier publication which advocated Jewish resettlement in England, see Edward Nicholas, *An Apology for the Honorable Nation of the Jews, and All the Sons of Israel* (1648, Wing N1081).

[8] Osterman, 'The Controversy over the Proposed Readmission of the Jews to England (1655)', 301.

[9] See Osterman, 'Controversy', 301–2.

[10] See Osterman, 'Controversy'; Jordan, *The Development of Religious Toleration in England, 1640–1660*; Patinkin, 'Mercantilism and the Readmission of the Jews to England'; and Katz, *The Jews in the History of England 1485–1850*, 107–44.

pamphlets circulated that activated fears about Jews and Catholics alike by telling the story of Thomas Ramsey, a Scottish Catholic, who had claimed to be a Jew converting to Protestantism, including *The Counterfeit Jew* (Wing C6520A) and *A False Jew* (Wing W1266), which was reprinted in 1654 (Wing W1267). In 1656, the Puritan polemicist William Prynne weighed in on the question with *A Short Demurrer to the Jewes Long Discontinued Barred Remitter into England* (Wing P4078 and P4079), to which a second part was added later in the same year (Wing P4073), passionately advancing political, economic and theological reasons against the Jews' readmission.[11] From the late 1640s to at least the mid-1650s, a spate of pro- and anti-Jewish publications testified to the intensity of the debate about the readmission of the Jews.

In this climate, Leake's *Merchant of Venice* reissue of 1652 with a title page announcing the 'extreame cruelty of Shylocke the Jew', appearing in the same year in which Bargishai had published his treatise 'revealing the wickedness of the Jews', would not have lacked topicality.[12] That Venice – with its reputation for intense trade, cosmopolitanism and licentiousness – was understood as an indirect way of representing London is a critical commonplace.[13] Leake may have counted on the updated title page to convey the impression that his book – even though containing an old play text by a dead dramatist – constituted a relevant intervention into a lively debate of the moment, and Moseley, when envisaging the publication of Dekker's *Jew of Venice*, may well have hoped to do the same.

Shakespeare's publishers and the early modern book trade

The brief opening section about William Leake has exemplified this chapter's focus on Shakespeare's publishers, although the rest of the chapter is devoted to an earlier period, namely the first thirty years of Shakespeare publishing, from the first quarto of *Venus and Adonis* in 1593 to the first quarto of *Othello* in 1622. After an introduction to the economic and institutional contexts in

---

[11] For further evidence of interest in the question of the Jews' readmission, see *Anglo-Judaeus, or The History of the Jews, whilst here in England* (1656, Wing H3321); D. L., *Israels Condition and Cause Pleaded; or Some Arguments for the Jews Admission into England* (1656, Wing L9); John Dury, *A Case of Conscience, whether it be lawful to admit Jews into a Christian common-wealth* (1656, Wing D2838); and Alexander Ross, *A View of the Jewish Religion* (1656, Wing R1983A).

[12] See Hales, '*The Merchant of Venice* in 1652'. Hales is quoted in Furness's Variorum edition of *The Merchant of Venice*, 273–4.

[13] See, for instance, Gillies, *Shakespeare and the Geography of Difference*, 122–40, and Levith, *Shakespeare's Italian Settings and Plays*, 12–39.

which Shakespeare's early publishers functioned, I demonstrate that more than a dozen of them had a significant investment – economically and culturally – in Shakespeare, the author. Their engagement with Shakespeare took different forms and was often commercially thoughtful and at other times daring. It is still routinely asserted that 'a published play text [was] a cheap pamphlet', and we have been told that publishing plays was precisely not 'a shortcut to wealth' and that, in any case, 'plays never accounted for a very significant fraction of the trade in English books'.[14] As I will show more fully in Chapter 5, the view modern critics tend to remember about early modern playbooks is Thomas Bodley's, who called them 'baggage bookes' and considered that 'Hardly one in fortie' was 'worthy the keeping'.[15] As a result, it is easily assumed that publishers did not much value them either. According to a recent Shakespeare biographer, 'the publishing trade, [Shakespeare's] conduit to posterity, served him ill ... His texts, cheaply bound, held together until the day of sale. They weren't ... much honored on Stationers' Row.'[16] I argue instead that a considerable number of publishers took his plays and poems very seriously and repeatedly invested in them. In a very real sense, these publishers *made* Shakespeare, and they did so in the course of his lifetime and the years immediately following it. Another important conclusion at which this chapter arrives concerns genre: although Shakespeare was a poet-playwright whose poems and plays were both successful in print, all his early publishers issued either his poems or his plays, but not both. The segregation of poems and plays in the history of Shakespeare publishing, which is usually considered to have started with the First Folio in 1623, in fact began considerably earlier.

It is important to clarify early on what this chapter is *not* devoted to: Shakespeare's printers. Publishers engaged in economic ventures by acquiring texts and speculating on their popularity, and they hired printers to have those texts set in type and mechanically reproduced. Shakespeare's printers have received a great deal of scholarly attention, far more than his publishers.[17]

---

[14] Kastan, 'Plays into Print', 29; Blayney, 'The Publication of Playbooks', 389, 385.

[15] Wheeler, ed., *Letters of Sir Thomas Bodley to Thomas James, First Keeper of the Bodleian Library*, 221–2.

[16] Fraser, *Shakespeare*, 170.

[17] For comprehensive studies devoted to individual Shakespeare printers, see Ferguson, *Valentine Simmes*, and Yamada, *Thomas Creede*. See also Blayney, *The Texts of King Lear*. No such comprehensive studies have been undertaken about individual Shakespeare publishers. For shorter treatments, see, for instance, Johnson, 'John Busby and the Stationers' Trade', 'Nicholas Ling, Publisher 1580–1607', 'John Trundle and the Book Trade, 1603–1626', 'Succeeding As an Elizabethan Publisher', and 'Thomas Pavier, Publisher'; Lesser, *Renaissance Drama and the Politics of Publication*, 157–225; Massai, *Shakespeare and the Rise of the Editor*, 91–105; and Straznicky, ed., *Shakespeare's Stationers*. For Thomas Thorpe and Nathaniel Butter, see Rostenberg, *Publishing, Printing and Bookselling*, 1.49–73, 1.75–96.

Given the scholarly interest in Shakespearean texts, this is easily understand-able: 'If we want to investigate the text of a play – the relationship between what the typesetter saw in the manuscript and what appears on the printed page – we need to study the printer.' But, as Peter Blayney adds, if we are interested in 'the reasons why *that* play was published *then*, . . . we must focus not on the printer but on the publisher'.[18] Interest in publishers and printers leads to important questions about Shakespeare's plays and poems, but the functions fulfilled by the two groups of people were very different, and it is important to clarify this difference at the outset. This seems all the more necessary as the word 'publisher' was not in use in the early modern book trade, and as, confusingly for us, the word 'printer' was often used instead: 'when publishers discussed their activities in prefaces, they generally used the word *print* in the sense "cause to be printed." The formulaic heading, "The Printer to the Reader," was therefore commonly used by publishers who were not strictly speaking printers at all.'[19] Early modern books thus easily lead us to confuse printer and publisher, but the distinction is of crucial importance.

I have been keeping the functions of publisher and printer distinct in order to stress differences which early modern terminology at times collap-ses. Yet few stationers were active in the book trade exclusively as publishers. With the sole exception of Thomas Thorpe, all of Shakespeare's early publishers seem to have acted simultaneously as printers or booksellers: 'Most books were published by stationers whose daily trade was book-selling; a few were published by stationers who were also printers.'[20] The same applies to Shakespeare's publishers.

The two chief sources of information about early modern publishers are imprints (usually at the bottom of the title page) and the records of the Stationers' Company (most importantly the Stationers' Register).[21] Unfortunately, neither source provides a full guide to publishing arrange-ments. When a publisher had secured a manuscript he wanted to publish, he was officially obliged to have it first allowed by a church or state authority and licensed by officers of the Stationers' Company, the allow-ance and the licence both being marked on the actual manuscript. There

[18] 'The Publication of Playbooks', 391.   [19] 'The Publication of Playbooks', 391.

[20] Blayney, 'The Publication of Playbooks', 391. Blayney adds in a footnote that the fraction of books published by booksellers was about '74 percent in 1583–1602' and '88 percent in 1603–1622' (417). Note that Kathman believes that Thorpe may have worked in William Aspley's bookshop ('Thorpe, Thomas (1571/2–1625?)').

[21] The colophon, which became less common in the course of the sixteenth century, provides similar information to the imprint but is placed at the end of the book. For the records of the Stationers' Company, see Arber, *Transcript*; Greg and Boswell, eds., *Records of the Court of the Stationers' Company 1576 to 1602*; and Jackson, ed., *Records of the Court of the Stationers' Company 1602 to 1640*.

was no obligation, however, to have the text entered in the Stationers' Register, and about one-third of the books published in the period were not.[22] Entrance was 'voluntary', 'an insurance policy' providing 'the best possible protection' but whose 'price had to be weighted against the risk'.[23] As a result, the record provided by the Register is far from complete: before their texts first reached print, Richard Field entered *Venus and Adonis* (18 April 1593), Thomas Millington *1 Contention* (12 March 1594), John Harrison *The Rape of Lucrece* (9 May 1594), Cuthbert Burby *Edward III* (1 December 1595), Andrew Wise *Richard II* (29 August 1597), *Richard III* (20 October 1597), *1 Henry IV* (25 February 1598) and, with William Aspley, *2 Henry IV* and *Much Ado about Nothing* (23 August 1600), Thomas Fisher *A Midsummer Night's Dream* (8 October 1600), Thomas Thorpe the *Sonnets* (20 May 1609) and Thomas Walkley *Othello* (6 October 1621).[24] On the other hand, *Richard Duke of York*, *Romeo and Juliet*, *Love's Labour's Lost* and *Henry V* were not entered before reaching print.

Even when a text was entered, the record in the Stationers' Register does not necessarily reflect its ownership. *Pericles*, for instance, was entered to Edward Blount on 20 May 1608, but when the play appeared in print the following year, the publisher acknowledged on the title page was Henry Gosson. The rights in a text could be transferred from one stationer to another, and such reassignment could be recorded in the Stationers' Register, or not. The ownership of texts, as M. A. Shaaber pointed out, was 'subject to modification by private contracts among the stationers', and, as a rule, such contracts do not survive.[25] They could be concluded by means of the kind of 'bill of sale' repeatedly mentioned in the Stationers' Register.[26] Two plays whose transfers are recorded are *The Merchant of Venice* and *The Merry Wives of Windsor*: *Merchant* was entered to James Roberts on 22 July 1598, transferred from Roberts to Thomas Hayes on 28 October 1600 and published by Hayes the same year. *Merry Wives* was entered to John Busby on 18 January 1602 but transferred the same day to Arthur Johnson, who published it that year. For *Pericles*, however, the Stationers' Register records no transfer from Blount to Gosson.

[22] See Blayney, 'The Publication of Playbooks', 396–405.

[23] Blayney, 'The Publication of Playbooks', 404.

[24] All early Shakespeare-related entries in the Stationers' Register are reproduced in Schoenbaum, *William Shakespeare: Records and Images*, 208–35.

[25] 'The Meaning of the Imprint in Early Printed Books', 124.

[26] See, for instance, Arber, *Transcript*, III.564. See also Kirschbaum, *Shakespeare and the Stationers*, 75.

As for the imprints in early modern printed books, their meaning is sometimes less transparent than the modern book historian desires.[27] In the most transparent case, the functions of printer, publisher and bookseller are held by three stationers who are all mentioned in the imprint: 'By G. Eld for T. T. and are to be solde by William Aspley' (Q *Sonnets*, 1609). 'T. T.' was the publisher, George Eld the printer and William Aspley the bookseller, and since Thomas Thorpe had Shakespeare's *Sonnets* entered in the Stationers' Register on 20 May 1609, it is clear that he was the publisher.[28] More commonly, the imprint mentions only one or two stationers, the one the book was printed 'for' (i.e. the publisher, who often also functioned as retail bookseller) and, on many occasions, the one whom it was printed 'by' (i.e. the printer): 'Printed by Valentine Simmes, for Mathew Law, and are to be solde at his shop in Paules Churchyard, at the signe of the Fox' (Q4 *1 Henry IV*, 1604). Simmes acted as printer and Law as both publisher and bookseller. This imprint or a version thereof is the most common formulation in early Shakespeare books.[29]

Some imprints name the printer and the bookseller but fail to mention for whom the book was printed: Printed by A, and are to be sold by B. Shaaber has shown that this imprint usually means that A functioned as printer-publisher, who had B act as bookseller, although he also notes that in a large group of exceptions it means the opposite, namely that B was a publisher-bookseller who hired A for the printing.[30] To this group of exceptions belong Q4 (1605), Q5 (1612) and Q6 (1622) *Richard III* and Q6 *1 Henry IV* (1622), whose imprints read: 'Printed by Thomas Creede [or 'Thomas Purfoot', or 'T. P.'], and are to be solde by Mathew Law'. We know thanks to the Stationers' Register that Andrew Wise transferred *1 Henry IV*, *Richard II* and *Richard III* to Law on 25 June 1603, and Law kept publishing the three plays until 1622.[31]

---

[27] The best guide to an understanding of the various formulations in early modern imprints is Shaaber, 'The Meaning of the Imprint in Early Printed Books'. Greg, in *Some Aspects and Problems of London Publishing between 1550 and 1650*, has a section devoted to 'The Interpretation of Imprints' (82–9) that shows no awareness of, and is less full and less reliable than, Shaaber. For a more recent article about early modern imprints, see Smith, '"Imprinted by Simeon Such a Signe"'.

[28] Some extant copies mention a different bookseller: John Wright.

[29] See Q1–5 *1 Henry IV*, Q1 *The Merchant of Venice*, Q2 *The Passionate Pilgrim*, Q1–2 *Pericles*, Q1–3 *Richard III*, Q2–4 *Romeo and Juliet*, Q1 *Thomas Lord Cromwell*, Q2–3 *Titus Andronicus* and all pre-1623 editions of *1 Contention*, *Richard Duke of York*, *Edward III*, *Hamlet*, *2 Henry IV*, *Henry V*, *King Lear*, *The London Prodigal*, *Love's Labour's Lost*, *The Merry Wives of Windsor*, *Much Ado about Nothing*, *Othello*, *1 Sir John Oldcastle*, *The Rape of Lucrece*, *Troilus and Cressida*, *The Troublesome Reign of King John*, *Venus and Adonis* and *A Yorkshire Tragedy*.

[30] Shaaber, 'The Meaning of the Imprint in Early Printed Books', 132–4.

[31] Greg believed that 'The form "Printed by A to be sold by B" indicates that the printer-publisher has entrusted the distribution to a bookseller' (*Some Aspects and Problems of London Publishing between*

The only other instance of this type of imprint in a Shakespeare book is the first quarto of *Titus Andronicus*, which constitutes a particularly thorny case. The imprint reads: 'Printed by Iohn Danter, and are to be sold by Edward White & Thomas Millington, at the little North doore of Paules at the signe of the Gunne. 1594.' John Danter was a printer-publisher, and so it is usually assumed that he published *Titus*, all the more so as he had entered it in the Stationers' Register on 6 February 1594.[32] Yet several things are unusual about the imprint. None of the books Danter printed were sold by Edward White or Millington. The shop 'at the little North doore of Paules at the signe of the Gunne' was White's, but Millington was not associated with it. So why does the imprint mention two booksellers and the shop of one of them but not the other? Danter got into trouble with the Company's authorities in 1597 and died in 1599, following which his widow assigned rights in some of his copies, though not, perhaps significantly, in *Titus*.[33] The second edition of *Titus* was published by Edward White in 1600, and when the play was next mentioned in the Stationers' Register on 19 April 1602, the rights were being transferred from Millington to Thomas Pavier. What this suggests is that both White and Millington believed they had a claim to the play. Greg wrote that 'After Danter's death in 1599 both White and Millington seem to have based a claim to the copy on the fact that they had acted jointly as booksellers for the original edition.'[34] Yet this is surely wrong: if Danter owned the rights in *Titus Andronicus* up to 1599, and White and Millington only acted as wholesale booksellers of the 1594 edition, then the only person who inherited the copyright of *Titus* on Danter's death was his widow.[35] The explanation which best accounts for the evidence is that Danter transferred the rights in *Titus* to White and

1550 and 1650, 85) and seems to have been unaware of the many exceptions to this rule mentioned by Shaaber. This led Greg to misinterpret the imprints of Q4, Q5 and Q6 *Richard III* and Q6 *1 Henry IV* (*Some Aspects and Problems of London Publishing between 1550 and 1650*, 88–9).

32 See, for instance, Chambers, *William Shakespeare*, 1.130; Halliday, *A Shakespeare Companion 1564–1964*, 385; Maguire, 'The Craft of Printing (1600)', 434; and Kastan, *Shakespeare and the Book*, 44. Chambers pointed out that the ornament above the head-title incorporates Danter's initials: 'I. D.' (sig. A3r). Yet Danter used the same ornament in Wilson's *The Cobler's Prophecy* and in Greene's *Orlando Furioso* (where it also appears on the title page), both of which he printed 'for Cuthbert Burbie' the same year. The ornament thus provides no evidence that Danter considered Q1 *Titus Andronicus his* publication.

33 See Arber, *Transcript*, III.173.

34 Greg, *Bibliography*, 1.197. Jonathan Bate has similarly written that 'Q1 was "to be sold by Edward White & Thomas Millington", so it seems reasonable to suppose that this gave White the authority to have the editions of 1600 and 1611 printed for him, while Millington assigned his share to Pavier' (*Titus Andronicus*, 113n).

35 I am grateful to Peter Blayney for a conversation about this matter.

Millington after entering it but before the play was published, an explanation which is strengthened by the fact that Danter did just that with
Greene's *Orlando Furioso*. The play was entered to Danter on 7 December
1593 (two months before *Titus*), transferred from Danter to Cuthbert
Burby on 28 May 1594 and 'Printed by Iohn Danter for Cuthbert
Burbie', as spelled out in the imprint, in the same year. Whereas Burby
chose to have the transfer entered, White and Millington seem to have felt
no need to do so. They functioned as booksellers of *Titus* in 1594, and the
cumulative evidence suggests that they may well have functioned as
publishers, too.[36]

Another imprint formulation which is potentially confusing only
states by whom the book was 'Printed' or 'Imprinted'. In the majority
of such cases, the stationer mentioned both printed and published the
book. For instance, we know that the 1612 edition of *The Passionate
Pilgrim*, 'Printed by W. Iaggard', was also published by Jaggard (see
below, pp. 154–5). Similarly, *Locrine* was registered by Thomas Creede
on 20 July 1594 and 'Printed by' (i.e. published by) him the year after;
and *The Puritan* was entered by George Eld on 6 August 1607 and
published by him the same year with an imprint reading 'Imprinted at
London: By G. Eld'.

A more complex case is the second quarto of *Thomas Lord Cromwell* of
1613 – by 'W. S.' according to the title page – whose imprint reads 'Printed
by Thomas Snodham'. With only the imprint to go by, we would conclude
that Snodham printed and published the play. Yet the Stationers' Register
records that the rights in the play had been transferred from William Jones
to John Browne in 1611. Snodham was Browne's favourite printer: in the
period from 1609 to 1615, Browne published thirty books of which eighteen,
more than half, were printed by Snodham.[37] It seems likely, therefore, that
Q2 *Thomas Lord Cromwell* was published by Browne, although the imprint
fails to mention this fact.

[36] As Shaaber wrote, it 'appears from the registers that a stationer would sometimes enter a copy for the
purpose of selling it to a publisher rather than publishing it himself' ('The Meaning of the Imprint in
Early Printed Books', 125), which may well apply to Danter's entrance of *Titus* in 1594. A few years
later, James Roberts did the same, having plays entered in the Stationers' Register before selling the
rights to fellow stationers who hired him to print the plays when they published them (see below,
pp. 159–61). It is worth noting that Danter entered several other titles which were published by fellow
stationers when they first reached print (see *STC* 21082, entered by Danter in 1593, 'Printed by
Thomas Creede' in 1598; *STC* 3696, entered by Danter in 1595, published by William Barley in 1598;
STC 14032, entered by Danter in 1595, published by Millington in 1598).

[37] See *STC* 3691.7, 4542, 4546, 4546.5, 5769, 7098, 10827, 10828, 15588, 17355, 17356, 17356a, 17749, 18132,
18299, 19923, 21333 and 25619a.

Even less transparent is the third quarto of *Pericles* (1611), which was 'Printed at London by S. S.' according to the imprint. The initials refer to Simon Stafford, a printer who seems to have published or co-published a few books (though no playbooks), including in 1611 (*STC* 1729.5) and 1612 (*STC* 18014a). On 20 May 1609, Edward Blount had entered *Pericles* in the Stationers' Register, although the two quarto editions of that year were published by Henry Gosson according to the imprint. The *STC* does not know of any books which Stafford printed for Gosson. The fourth quarto of *Pericles* of 1619 was published by Thomas Pavier (one of the Pavier Quartos), and *Pericles* is among the plays which Pavier's widow transferred to Edward Brewster and Robert Bird on 4 August 1626. No entry in the Stationers' Register records any reassignment of *Pericles* between 1609 and 1626. We can only speculate, therefore, as to whether the imprint of q3 *Pericles* means that Stafford published the play or printed it for Gosson, Pavier or another publisher. Similarly unclear is the case of *A Funeral Elegy in Memory of the Late Virtuous Master William Peter* (1612): it was 'Imprinted at London: By G. Eld', but the poem had been entered to Thomas Thorpe on 13 February 1612. It is therefore impossible to know with certainty who published the poem.[38]

Imprints and the Stationers' Register thus provide occasionally unclear but nonetheless the best information about who published an early modern book. They provide little help, though, in understanding exactly what the publisher's role in the book trade was. The publisher has been described as 'the person who acquired the text' and who 'paid for several hundred copies of it to be manufactured'.[39] As part of this process, he hired a printer, to whom he lent the copy text (in manuscript for a first edition, usually in print for a subsequent edition) and whom he furnished with the appropriate amount of paper. The printer's job was to produce the agreed number of copies of as good a text as possible in the format, type font and type size requested by the publisher. For these services, the publisher paid the printer a previously agreed sum. In other words, the amount of money a printer earned was entirely independent of the success the edition had when it was made available by the bookseller.[40]

---

[38] The only other Shakespearean instances of the 'Printed by' imprint are the second quartos of *The Merchant of Venice* and *A Midsummer Night's Dream*, both of 1619, two so-called 'Pavier Quartos' with fake imprints: 'Printed by J. Roberts, 1600'; 'Printed by Iames Roberts, 1600'.

[39] Blayney, 'The Publication of Playbooks', 391. See also Shaaber's account of the publisher's role: 'It is the publisher who decides that a piece of copy is worth publishing, who treats with the author for the right to publish it . . . , who risks his money in the venture, and who therefore may exercise some editorial supervision of the copy' ('The Meaning of the Imprint in Early Printed Books', 121).

[40] This and the following paragraphs are indebted to Blayney's incisive introduction to early modern playbook publishing ('The Publication of Playbooks', 394–415).

The publisher, by contrast, depended on the book's success to make money.[41] Independently of whether he sold the book himself or had booksellers do so for him, the money he earned was proportional to the book's popularity as a saleable commodity. Whereas a printer could agree to print any text as long as he was able to fit it into his schedule (and had the necessary equipment and skills), a publisher had to choose his texts with care and discrimination. If he correctly anticipated consumer demand for a certain book at a certain time, he could make considerable money; if he wrongly anticipated it, he lost money. While the printer's task was thus one of manufacture and mechanical reproduction, the publisher – trying to anticipate and create future consumer demand – engaged in a form of speculation. He was, as Lesser has nicely put it, 'the capitalist of the book trade'.[42]

The publisher's speculation involved a considerable amount of money even in the case of a single quarto playbook.[43] According to the best-informed estimate we have, a publisher would have had expenses of approximately £9 for an edition of 800 copies, which he had to pay before he could start selling the edition.[44] This sum includes about £2 for the acquisition of the manuscript, allowance by church or state authorities, and the Stationers' Company's licence and registration; a little under £3 for paper; and a little over £4 for the printing (wages for compositors and pressmen, and the printer's overheads). In a very real sense, an edition of a text was first and foremost the publisher's, chosen and paid for by him, produced according to his orders, all its copies owned by him before they went up for sale. This was signalled not only in the imprint but also, on some occasions, by means of the device. On the title page of Q1 and Q2 *Hamlet*, the device includes a fish, specifically a ling, as well as Nicholas Ling's initials.[45] In other puns on

---

[41] My chapter deals exclusively with speculative publications. For non-speculative publications (such as proclamations), see Farmer and Lesser, 'The Popularity of Playbooks Revisited', 13–14.

[42] *Renaissance Drama and the Politics of Publication*, 28.

[43] For a useful online calculator with which to convert early modern pounds, see 'How Much is That?'.

[44] As Lesser has pointed out, 'In most industries, the amount of capital necessary to start production is far less than the overall amount that will be invested in a given project – the initial capital, in other words, can be augmented by money from the sale of goods produced early in the process, which is then rolled back into further production, thereby diminishing risk. In the book trade, however, virtually all of the capital necessary to produce an edition must be laid out before the investment can begin to be recouped' (*Renaissance Drama and the Politics of Publication*, 27).

[45] The ling is entwined in honeysuckle, which may have been intended as an anagram of Ling's first name: Honisocal – Nicholas (see Carroll, ed., *Skialetheia or A Shadowe of Truth, in Certaine Epigrams and Satyres*, 100). See also Marino, *Owning William Shakespeare*, 83. For Richard Jones's initials in one of his devices, see Melnikoff, 'Jones, Richard (*fl.* 1564–1613)'. For other punning devices, including a graft and a tun in a device of Richard Grafton, see Raven, *The Business of Books*, 55–7. The Ling/ling is device 301 in McKerrow, *Printers' and Publishers' Devices*.

the publisher's name, Thomas Fisher used a device with a kingfisher, Nicholas Okes one with an oak tree and John Smethwick one with a bird, 'presumably a smee or smew ... bearing the word "wick" in its bill'.[46] The publishers' sense of ownership of the books in which they had invested their money was clearly visible on many title pages.

At the typical wholesale price of 4d. and retail price of 6d., a publisher – having spent approximately £9 on a first edition – had to sell hundreds of copies before breaking even. The more copies the publisher had printed, the higher the loss if the edition failed to sell, or the higher the profit if it sold out. If an edition sold out, the publisher could have a reprint made at considerably lower costs since copy, allowance, licence and registration had already been paid for. A first edition of 800 copies cost about £9, but the expenses for a second (or any subsequent) edition were lower, approximately £7. Whereas the total profit for a sell-out first edition would have been about £6 (or closer to £6 10s. if the edition sold out fast), the profit would have been around £8 (or *c.* £8 10s.) for a subsequent edition.[47] The risk a publisher was taking was thus considerably higher for a first than for a subsequent edition: to break even, he had to sell about 480 of his 800 copies (almost 60 per cent) of a first edition, but only about 350 copies (about 45 per cent) of any subsequent edition.

These figures are based on an edition of 800 copies, but publishers could take greater risks by opting for a higher press-run. The only playbook edition for which we have a precise figure is the second quarto of *Philaster*, published by Thomas Walkley in 1622: it consisted of 1,500 copies.[48] Walkley's venture paid, for the edition sold out in a few years, and a third quarto appeared in 1628. If we extrapolate from the above figures, Walkley would have paid about £5 3s. for paper and £5 11s. for the printing (the wages for the compositors being the same but those for the pressmen almost double those for the 800-copy edition), total costs thus amounting to approximately

---

[46] McKerrow, *Dictionary*, 105, 206, 248.

[47] Blayney imagines that a stationer may have sold about 40 per cent of the copies to fellow stationers at the wholesale price of 4d., about 50 per cent to non-stationers in London and elsewhere at the retail price (6d.) 'discounted by 3s. in the pound', and most of the remaining 10 per cent (a few copies would have been given away for free) in his own bookshop for 6d. ('The Publication of Playbooks', 412). On average a copy would thus have returned just over 4.7d.

[48] See Blayney, 'The Publication of Playbooks', 422. Note that in 1639, John Benson asked the court of the Stationers' Company for permission 'to print an Imp[r]ssion of the play called The Tragedy of Albouine made by M[r] Davenant w[ch] was printed in 1629'. The play had not been entered and was therefore considered 'in the disposall of this Co[m]' which decided 'that the said mr Benson should haue leaue to print an Imp[r]ssion of 1500. paying to the Poore of this Company xl[s]' (Jackson, ed., *Records of the Court of the Stationers' Company 1602 to 1640*, 325). Despite this decision, the planned edition does not seem to have been published.

£10 14s. Whereas an 800-copy edition, if selling out, would have returned about £15 14s., 1,500 copies (minus a few copies that were given away) sold for a total of approximately £29 9s. On a small to average-size edition of 800 copies, a publisher could thus gain or lose as much as £8 or £9. With a large 1,500-copy edition, a publisher took an even greater risk, but, if as lucky as Walkley was with *Philaster*, he could gain as much as £18, and this at a time when the average yearly wage of a London labourer was £12.[49] Farmer and Lesser have argued that the profit publishers could hope to derive from playbooks 'would not have been paltry, as many have claimed', a judgment which these figures support.[50]

Publishing the kind of book in which Shakespeare's plays and poems first appeared thus involved risk-taking, which could result in the loss or gain of considerable sums of money. In order to maximize profit and minimize risks, publishers needed a thorough understanding of the book trade and sound analytical skills. In *The schollers purgatory* (1625), George Wither complained about a generic publisher that 'If he gett any written Coppy into his powre, likely to be vendible, ... he will publish it.'[51] For the publisher, however, the question was precisely what texts would be vendible. Wither may be taken to imply that low-brow fare would sell particularly well, but, as Tessa Watt has argued, 'there is no straight equation between "popularity" in numerical terms and print for the "popular" classes' since 'literacy was weighted at the top of the social scale'.[52] In a very real sense, publishers, in order to anticipate consumer behaviour, had to be good readers.[53] What literary and cultural meanings a book would have when its purchase was being considered by book-buyers ultimately decided whether it would be a commercial success or not. The decision to publish thus had to be preceded by a reading of the text in which its meanings were analysed.

The considerations which led to the decision to publish a certain text could be manifold. A publisher might decide to issue a text – as I have argued William Leake did with *The Merchant of Venice* in 1652 – because

---

[49] Boulton, 'Wage Labour in Seventeenth-Century London', 288.

[50] 'The Popularity of Playbooks Revisited', 6. Compare Blayney: 'on a reprint of 1,500 copies at the same rates, the total profit would be a little under £19 less overhead', which he estimates would have amounted to about 18d. a year ('The Publication of Playbooks', 412–13). Blayney's accountancy for a slow-selling low-press-run first edition led him to the point that not much money was to be made from playbooks ('a profit of £1 10s. a year'; 'The Publication of Playbooks', 412), yet his own figures show that a high-press-run reprint could result in an appreciable profit.

[51] Wither, *The schollers purgatory* (1624), 121.   [52] *Cheap Print and Popular Piety*, 259.

[53] As Lesser has put it, 'publishers ... are themselves actual readers (among the first and most critical), although the material evidence for and traces of their readings lie not in marginalia but in the specialized corpus of books that they produced' (*Renaissance Drama and the Politics of Publication*, 18). On early modern literature and consumer behaviour, see Baker, *On Demand*.

he anticipated that recent history or current affairs would lend it topical appeal. If a publication was particularly successful, a text on a related subject could be published in the hope of capitalizing on its success. Another important consideration could be a publisher's profile: publishers specialized and might be inclined to publish a text because it fitted their list.[54] Some, like Richard Field, never published a playbook, whereas others, like Thomas Millington, specialized in playbooks or, like Humphrey Moseley, in what we now call 'literature'.[55] Henry Gosson chiefly published news pamphlets and ballads, John Wright specialized in 'tried and true' fare, whereas William Ponsonby was an elite publisher who issued texts which reflected 'the political and religious views of the Leicester faction and . . . his business contact with [Philip] Sidney's relations and friends'.[56] Many publishers had an output which was predominantly religious, although this did not prevent some of them – like Thomas Pavier – from also publishing more secular texts, including plays.

Success in the publishing trade also required awareness of genre: if the demand for a certain kind of text was in excess of its supply, publishers had every interest to increase the supply. But if the supply exceeded the demand, their publications lost them money. This mechanism may be observed in the playbook market around the turn of the seventeenth century. In 1598 and 1599, a remarkable number of plays (seventeen) reached a (commercially highly desirable) second or third edition, the number of new playbooks being inferior to that of the reprints. Clearly, there was considerable demand for playbooks, and those available on the market were doing remarkably well. Several publishers (including John Busby) therefore decided to join the playbook publishing business in 1600. The number of newly published plays consequently soared, going up to fourteen (as opposed to five in 1598 and eight in 1599). The majority of these plays (eleven of fourteen) were not reprinted in the next fifteen years, and the average number of reprint editions of plays during the next ten years was no more than four, significantly fewer, that is, than in the closing years of the previous century.

This does not mean that playbooks generally constituted a bad investment. We saw in Chapter 1 that about half of the playbooks published

---

[54] See Lesser, *Renaissance Drama and the Politics of Publication*, 43–51 (for early modern publishers – like John Trundle and Nathaniel Butter – whose specialization seems to have been familiar enough to be the object of casual puns and allusions, see p. 42).

[55] See Kastan, 'Humphrey Moseley and the Invention of English Literature'.

[56] Brennan, 'William Ponsonby', 103. For Wright, see Lesser, 'Typographic Nostalgia', 108.

between 1583 and 1622 received at least a second edition within twenty-five years. Farmer and Lesser have compared the reprint rates of 'professional plays' with those of sermons and speculative books in general and concluded that playbooks 'turned a profit more reliably than most other types of books'.[57] Whereas 39.9 per cent of the plays that first appeared in 1576–1625 were reprinted at least once inside twenty years, the reprint rate for sermons in the same period was only 19.3 per cent and that for speculative books more generally even lower, at 18.1 per cent. Lesser succinctly sums up the evidence: 'playbooks were in fact more popular than many other kinds of books, judging by the rates at which they were reprinted. Nonetheless, plays were far from a guaranteed success, as more than half of all first editions of plays from the professional theatres were not reprinted before 1660. In other words, like most kinds of books, playbooks were *speculative*.'[58] It is thus easy to understand why a publisher might have considered putting money in a playbook, although the fact that more than half the plays were not reprinted means he would have wanted to seize not just any opportunity but the right one.

As for Shakespeare's playbooks, in Chapter 1 we saw that their reprint rate was significantly higher still than that of professional plays in general: 85 per cent of the plays first published up to 1622 were reprinted at least once inside twenty-five years. Some of them, like *Romeo and Juliet* and *Henry V*, did not acknowledge Shakespeare's authorship on any title pages. Clearly, for a publisher, a Shakespeare publication could have an appeal which had little or nothing to do with Shakespeare. Yet, as we will see below, quite a number of stationers repeatedly published texts which made Shakespeare's authorship clearly visible. Appendix C provides a concise summary of the evidence with an alphabetic list of all the stationers who published Shakespeare in the period up to 1622.

The chief publishers of Shakespeare's poems

Several publishers showed considerable interest in Shakespeare's narrative poems, yet the publisher we most readily remember – Richard Field – showed in fact little commitment to them. One of the leading London printers, Field had grown up in Stratford, like Shakespeare, and published *Venus and Adonis* in 1593, the first Shakespeare text to appear in print. He is also the only stationer to whom Shakespeare alludes in one of his works:

---

[57] 'The Popularity of Playbooks Revisited', 6.
[58] *Renaissance Drama and the Politics of Publication*, 36.

'Richard du Champ' (*Cymbeline*, 4.2.377).[59] Field printed several of Shakespeare's most important sources, including the 1587 edition of Holinshed's *Chronicles* (in the last year of his apprenticeship) and North's translation of Plutarch's *Lives of Noble Grecians and Romans* (1595 and 1603), which has prompted the theory that Shakespeare may have used Field's printing house 'as a kind of library'.[60] Yet even though Field helped his fellow countryman to get into print, he cannot be said to have had more than a passing interest in publishing Shakespeare. He sold the rights in *Venus and Adonis* little more than a year after acquiring them, on 25 June 1594. Perhaps because Field *printed* the first edition of *The Rape of Lucrece* in 1594, it is sometimes wrongly assumed that he also *published* that poem, but it is significant that he did not.[61] Shakespeare may well have asked Field to publish *The Rape of Lucrece* in 1594, but if he did, Field declined, as we shall see.

Venus and Adonis was an atypical text for Field to publish. The only other poetry he seems to have published before the turn of the century is Sir John Harington's translation of Ariosto's epic romance *Orlando Furioso* (1591, *STC* 746), a volume of Thomas Campion's Latin poetry (1595, *STC* 4544) and an Italian book of poetry by Petruccio Ubaldini (1596, *STC* 24483), a scholar, illuminator and poet who was in London as a Protestant. Thus, *Venus and Adonis* was Field's only original vernacular poetry.[62] Field may have felt that *Venus and Adonis* did not really fit his list and therefore sold the rights in the poem in 1594, a decision he might not have taken if he had anticipated its commercial success: the poem went through at least ten more editions in Field's lifetime.[63]

Having functioned as wholesale bookseller of *Venus and Adonis* from 1593, John Harrison acquired the rights in the poem by transfer from Field on 25 June 1594. The previous month, he had entered 'a booke intituled the Ravyshement of Lucrece', and the first edition of Shakespeare's second narrative poem appeared later that year. Harrison's customers 'at the signe

---

[59] The fullest article about Field is Kirwood, 'Richard Field, Printer, 1589–1624' (for Field as publisher as opposed to printer, see 16–19). See also Kathman, 'Field, Richard (*bap.* 1561, *d.* 1624)'. For the *Cymbeline* allusion to Field, see Wilson, Rickard and Meek, 'Introduction', 1–2; and Kane, '"Richard du Champ" in Cymbeline'.

[60] Duncan-Jones, *Ungentle Shakespeare*, 5.

[61] See, for instance, Bevington, *Shakespeare*, 12, and Kastan, 'Plays into Print', 23.

[62] Note, however, that Field also published George Puttenham's *The Arte of English Poesie* (1589, *STC* 20519).

[63] I am in agreement with Hooks who writes that 'Field's presumed biographical link with Shakespeare has granted Field ... an exaggerated prominence in the creation of the poet's authorial persona, eclipsing the contributions of others by privileging a single moment in Shakespeare's textual life' ('Shakespeare at the White Greyhound', 262).

of the white Grey-hound in Paules Church-yard' could thus purchase Shakespeare's narrative poems from the same shop as companion volumes. That joint purchase was encouraged by Harrison is suggested by the change in format: Field had published *Venus and Adonis* in quarto in 1593 and 1594, which explains why Harrison chose the same format for the first edition of *The Rape of Lucrece*. But when Harrison published *Venus and Adonis* in 1595 and 1596, he decided on the more prestigious octavo format, which he also adopted for the second edition (and all following editions) of *The Rape of Lucrece*.[64]

An additional reason why Harrison may have chosen to issue Shakespeare's narrative poems in octavo is that he had another handsome pair of octavos on his shelves: Ovid's *Metamorphoses* (*STC* 18952) and a volume with the *Heroides* and parts of the *Amores*, the *Ars Amatoria* and the *Remedia Amoris* (*STC* 18929).[65] Both books were printed by Field for Harrison, in the original Latin, in 1589 and 1594 respectively. As any reader of *Venus and Adonis* and *The Rape of Lucrece* would have known, Shakespeare took the stories of his narrative poems from Ovid. Shakespeare's Ovidianism was clear to his early readers: 'the sweete wittie soule of *Ovid* lives in mellifluous & hony-tongued *Shakespeare*', wrote Francis Meres in 1598.[66] The title page of the early editions of *Venus and Adonis* proclaims its Ovidian indebtedness with an epigraph from the *Amores* (see above, p. 100). Ovid, the epigraph implies, is Shakespeare's 'source of inspiration and his guarantor of high cultural status', as Jonathan Bate puts it.[67] The epigraph affirms what the book simultaneously performs, its cultural status made visible in the bookstall by occupying a space shared with Ovid. The constellation in Harrison's bookshop was thus intertextually compelling and commercially shrewd: in the mid-1590s, as Shakespeare's reputation as the English Ovid was establishing itself, Harrison had published and was selling in his bookshop the chief poems of Ovid and the English Ovid, two pairs of octavos.[68]

All in all, Harrison published seven editions of Shakespeare's narrative poems, more than any other early modern publisher. He kept the rights in *The Rape of Lucrece* until 1614, but he sold those in *Venus and Adonis*

---

[64] The date of the third edition of *Venus and Adonis* is conjectural as the only extant copy lacks the first gathering (see Duncan-Jones and Woudhuysen, eds., *Shakespeare's Poems*, 514). Concerning the relation between bibliographic format and prestige, see above, p. 118.

[65] The format of the 1589 *Metamorphosis* is technically a 16° in 8s, meaning an octavo in size, printed on extra-large paper torn in half.

[66] I quote from Ingleby, ed., *A Shakespere Allusion-Book*, 1.46.   [67] *Shakespere and Ovid*, 2.

[68] See also Hooks, 'Shakespeare at the White Greyhound', 267–72, and Hooks, 'Book Trade', 132.

considerably earlier: for reasons which are unknown, Harrison, sometime in 1596, ceded his shop at the White Greyhound in St Paul's Churchyard to William Leake and transferred the rights in the poem to Leake around the same time, on 25 June 1596.[69] I started this chapter with William Leake, junior, who reissued *The Merchant of Venice* in 1652 (and, incidentally, published the third quarto of *Othello* in 1655). His father, William Leake, senior, had already published Shakespeare more than half a century earlier.[70] Having acquired the rights to *Venus and Adonis*, he published two octavo editions before the turn of the century, both dated 1599.

Leake did not specialize in poetry or even literature: by far the greatest part of his output was religious. Yet once he had secured the rights to Shakespeare's exceptionally popular poem, he may have thought of ways of maximizing sales. The year after acquiring the rights to *Venus and Adonis*, he entered *Hecatonphila: The Art of Love*, an anonymously published translation, by Anthony Munday, of the fifteenth-century Italian Leone Battista Alberti, which Leake went on to publish in octavo, with a commendatory poem by Francis Meres (*STC* 257). Described by a modern critic as a conversation on 'how to choose and enjoy lovers from the female point of view',[71] the topic seems suggestive in the context of *Venus and Adonis*. Both books were available from Leake's bookshop, and he may well have felt that customers interested in the one might decide to purchase also the other.

Whether Leake published Munday's translation because he was hoping the simultaneous presence of Shakespeare's narrative poem in his bookshop would help sales is not clear. There is another volume, however, whose sale Leake certainly hoped would be boosted by *Venus and Adonis*. This was *The Passionate Pilgrim*, 'By William Shakespeare', according to the title page, and, as the imprint points out, 'Printed for W. Iaggard' and 'sold by W. Leake, at the Greyhound in Paules Churchyard'. Jaggard barely disguised that his miscellany was designed to cash in on the success of *Venus and Adonis*. For instance, the fourth poem, a sonnet, begins: 'Sweet Cytherea, sitting by a Brooke, / With young Adonis'. Three more 'Venus and Adonis Sonnets' follow slightly later in the volume, and another five non-Shakespearean poems formally conform to *Venus and Adonis* by adopting its sixain stanza form (see above, p. 88). Jaggard published more than a hundred books in the thirty-year period from 1594 to 1624 and functioned as the printer of many

---

[69] See McKerrow, *Dictionary*, 171. From 1596, Harrison dwelt in Paternoster Row at the Greyhound (first mentioned in the imprint of *STC* 20804).

[70] For the three generations of Leake publishers, see Phelps, 'The Leakes of St Dunstan's in the West'.

[71] Hull, *Chaste, Silent* and *Obedient*, 86.

more, his name appearing in the imprints of almost 250 titles. Yet only a single one of these imprints points to a connection between Jaggard and Leake, that of *The Passionate Pilgrim*, published by Jaggard and sold by Leake. Jaggard and Leake's scheme of selling the two books as companion volumes seems to have worked: not only did *Venus and Adonis* go through two octavo editions in 1599, but so did *The Passionate Pilgrim*.[72] That *The Passionate Pilgrim* must have served as an appealing companion volume to Shakespeare's narrative poem is also suggested by the fact that two volumes have survived to this day which bind 1599 copies of *Venus and Adonis* and *The Passionate Pilgrim* between the same covers (see below, p. 222).[73]

Venus and Adonis was not Leake's only literary bestseller: George Cawood had owned the rights in Lyly's *Euphues, the Anatomy of Wit* and *Euphues and His England* since they first reached print in 1578/80 and had published eleven and ten editions respectively by the time he died, following which Leake acquired the rights in them on 2 July 1602. He went on to publish three editions of either text, all in quarto, from 1605 to 1613. Following his experience with Shakespeare, Leake may have been confident that a popular literary seller which had been going through quite a number of editions would be worth the initial expenses and would keep selling. Experience proved him right. The success of *Venus and Adonis* and its companion volume, *The Passionate Pilgrim*, may have encouraged Leake to acquire other paired titles, designed to be sold, and perhaps bound, jointly, in the hope of increasing his profit. *Euphues, the Anatomy of Wit* and *Euphues and His England* kept appearing and selling in parallel. Slightly earlier, on 1 December 1600, Leake decided to enter two closely related plays, Munday's *The Downfall of Robert, Earl of Huntingdon* and *The Death of Robert, Earl of Huntingdon*. Both were printed in 1601 'for William Leake'. Contrary to the Shakespeare and Lyly diptychs, the plays did not sell well and failed to reach a second edition.

I have mentioned Leake's two *Venus and Adonis* editions of 1599 (*STC* 22358 and 22358a), but he published three more after the turn of the century. Of one (*STC* 22359), printed by Richard Bradock, the only extant copy lacks the title page, but there is strong evidence to suggest that it was published in 1602.[74] The other two editions (*STC* 22360a and 22360b), of one of which (*STC* 22360b) no more than a title page survives, are dated '1602', yet it has been shown that the dates are wrong.[75] The reason for the misdating is

[72] See also Duncan-Jones and Woudhuysen, eds., *Shakespeare's Poems*, 515.
[73] See also Burrow, ed., *Complete Sonnets and Poems*, 75.
[74] Farr, 'Notes on Shakespeare's Printers and Publishers', 244.   [75] See Rollins, ed., *The Poems*, 376–7.

unclear. Harry Farr attributed it to 'the more rigid supervision of the printing-press under the primacy of Richard Bancroft (1604–10)', Archbishop of Canterbury, adding that 'Leake must have been well aware of the views of the ecclesiastical authorities, for he acted as Warden of the Stationers' Company in 1604–5, 1606–7, 1610–11, and 1614–15, and was Master in 1618–19.' Farr considered it therefore 'a reasonable assumption that occupying the position he did [Leake] would neither publish nor reprint openly anything likely to give offence to the authorities'.[76] Whatever the precise motives are that led Leake to the misdatings, he published five editions of a Shakespeare text within about a decade. No other publisher produced as many editions of a Shakespeare poem or play in such a short period.[77]

There is a third edition of *Venus and Adonis* misdated '1602' (*STC* 22360). Like the other two, it claims on the title page that it was 'Imprinted at London for William Leake', but contrary to the other two, it was not. Instead, the edition is a piracy published by Robert Raworth. Raworth took up his freedom as a stationer on 31 March 1606 and is known to have printed fourteen books from 1606 to 1608.[78] In 1608, he printed for Leake two sermons by Henry Smith (*STC* 22767).[79] The title page (Figure 4.2) displays Leake's winged-skull device (McKerrow, device 341), which was also used for several other books, including the two *Venus and Adonis* editions of '1602'.[80] What happened is that Raworth seized the opportunity when Leake had lent him his device for the printing of the Smith sermons, forging an edition which looked like Leake's of 1602 and surreptitiously using the winged-skull device for the title page.[81] Having Leake's device conveniently to hand provided a starting point for Raworth's pirated edition, but if he

---

[76] Farr, 'Notes on Shakespeare's Printers and Publishers', 238–40. Farr's argumentation has been called 'faultless in every detail' by John Roe (*The Poems*, 288), while Duncan-Jones and Woudhuysen have considered it 'unlikely' (*Shakespeare's Poems*, 515). Chambers was also sceptical, writing that he did not 'see any very clear evidence here of a belated treatment of *Venus and Adonis* as licentious' (*William Shakespeare*, 1.545).

[77] For a good description of the early editions of *Venus and Adonis*, see Rollins, ed., *The Poems*, 369–80.

[78] The *STC* titles Raworth printed (or printed in part) are: in 1606: 11215; in 1607: 1692, 3471, 3671, 5491, 5492, 14526.5, 14696 and 22360; and in 1608: 1968.7, 11403, 12494, 22767 and 24414.

[79] See Arber, *Transcript*, III.683 and IV.31.

[80] The device was used in the following books (I provide the *STC* numbers and indicate the printer's name parenthetically): in 1602: 18163 and 19165 (both James Roberts); in 1603: 12311 and 14599 (both Richard Bradock); in 1605: 190, 17077 (both Bradock) and 22766 (Valentine Simmes); in 1606: 17061 (Humphrey Lownes); in 1607?: 22360 (Raworth); in 1608: 22767 (Raworth); in 1608/9 (?): 22360a (Lownes); in 1609: 17079 (William Hall), 22953 (Thomas East) and 22961 (Lownes); in 1609/10 (?): 22360b (?); and in 1610: 22768 (William Hall).

[81] See Farr, 'Notes on Shakespeare's Printers and Publishers', 244.

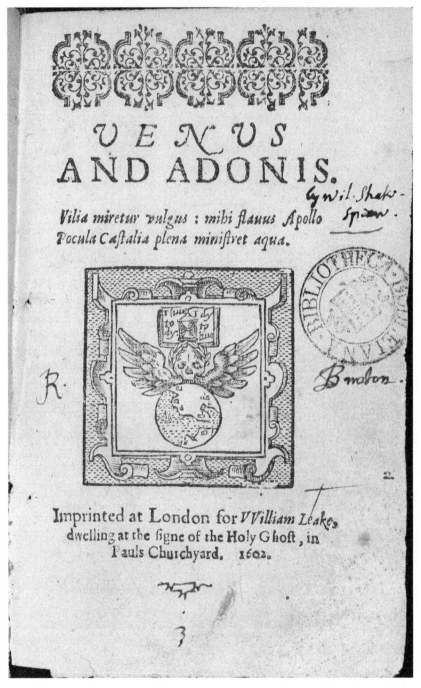

V E N V S
AND ADONIS.

Vilia miretur vulgus : mihi flauus Apollo
Pocula Castalia plena ministret aqua.

Imprinted at London for VVilliam Leake,
dwelling at the signe of the Holy Ghost, in
Pauls Churchyard. 1602.

4.2 Title page of Robert Raworth's 1607/8 forgery, misdated '1602', of *Venus and Adonis*
(*STC* 22360), with William Leake's winged-skull device.

4.3 Printer's ornament on sig. A2v of Leake's 1602 edition of *Venus and Adonis* (STC 22359), printed by Richard Bradock.

wanted his edition to look much like Leake's, Raworth needed to overcome the problem posed by the printer's ornaments used by Bradock. The ornament at the end of the dedicatory epistle (sig. A2v) and the initial 'R' at the beginning of the dedication (sig. A2r) of Raworth's edition are almost but not quite identical with the ornaments in Leake's edition of 1602 (STC 22359), a 'close imitation', according to Farr, a 'forgery' according to Peter Blayney (Figures 4.3 and 4.4).[82] Raworth must also have purchased or borrowed the designs of 'printer's flowers' on sig. A3r to imitate those used by Bradock.[83] Raworth thus went out of his way to fabricate copies of *Venus and Adonis* which looked almost exactly like those Bradock had printed for Leake in 1602.

Publishing a text without the permission or knowledge of its author was not unusual in the early modern period and was something to which the

[82] Farr, 'Notes on Shakespeare's Printers and Publishers', 233–4. Blayney (private communication, 30 October 2011) points out that Bradock's 'R' on sig. A2r of *STC* 22359 had been previously used by him in 1601 (*STC* 3648 and 3700.5) and 1607 (*STC* 5300.7, of which Bradock printed sheets A–O), following which it passed to Hall (20629 in 1609). Raworth's 'R' on sig. A2r of *STC* 22360 had not been used before and was next employed by Felix Kingston in 1609 (19677.3) and 1610 (20096). Bradock's ornament on sig. A2v of *STC* 22360 was used again in 1608 (*STC* 5334), after which it passed to William Hall, Bradock's successor, who used it in 1610 (*STC* 25795) and 1611 (*STC* 7182 and 13424.2). Raworth's ornament on sig. A2v of *Venus and Adonis* (*STC* 22360) also appears on sig. A5r in his share of *STC* 24414, of which Nicholas Okes printed sheets D–E (see Blayney, *The Texts of King Lear*, 397–9). *STC* 24414 was entered in the Stationers' Register on 1 February 1608 and seems to have been printed very soon thereafter (see Blayney, *The Texts of King Lear*, 78–9). This means that Raworth's pirated edition of *Venus and Adonis* can be dated with unusual precision: 'if Leake's device was lent to him for use on [*STC* 22767, the two Smith sermons,] it is unlikely to have arrived much before the end of 1607. And if we assume that *Venus and Adonis* saw the first appearance of ornament 7543 [i.e. the ornament on sig. A2v of *Venus and Adonis*], then it can't have been printed any later than February 1608' (Blayney, private communication, 31 October 2011). I am greatly indebted to Peter Blayney for sharing with me his insights into the Raworth forgery.

[83] Blayney, private communication, 30 October 2011. Blayney adds that the 'printer's flowers' 'used on A1r and A2r ... were extremely common, and also used by Raworth in 1607 ([*STC*] 14526.5) and 1608 ([*STC*] 1968.7, 18258), so those he probably owned already'.

4.4 Printer's ornament on sig. A2v of Raworth's 1607/8 edition, misdated '1602', of *Venus and Adonis* (STC 22360).

authorities of the Stationers' Company usually did not object. But surreptitiously publishing a text which had been purchased by a fellow stationer and to which one had no claim was a very different matter. Many stationers took a risk by publishing Shakespeare, but no stationer risked as much as Raworth. That he took the risk tells us something about the perceived attractiveness of Shakespeare's narrative poem: first published fifteen years earlier, *Venus and Adonis* was considered by Raworth commercially attractive enough in 1608 for him to risk his livelihood for it. The risk did not pay. When Raworth's action came to light, he was 'supprest' by the Stationers' Company 'for printing anothers Copy'.[84] A document produced in the 1630s reports more specifically that Raworth 'about 26 yeeres since [was] supprest (for printing Venus and Adonis)'.[85] Raworth's press was seized, and he stopped all activity as a printer for twenty-five years; from 1633 to 1636, he printed some twenty more books.

Four years after Raworth's piracy of *Venus and Adonis*, another Shakespeare publisher incurred displeasure, although with less drastic consequences. In 1612, Jaggard published 'THE PASSIONATE PILGRIME. OR Certaine Amorous Sonnets, betweene Venus and Adonis, newly corrected and augmented. By W. Shakespere. The Third Edition. Where-unto is newly added two Loue-Epistles, the first from Paris to Hellen, and Hellens answere backe againe to Paris. Printed by W. Iaggard. 1612.' Jaggard owes to this edition the distinction of being the only publisher at whom Shakespeare is known to have

---

[84] Arber, *Transcript*, III.703.
[85] Arber, *Transcript*, III.701. Peter Blayney has argued that the Court of Assistants disapproved of Adam Islip's sale of 'part of his equipment to Robert Raworth and John Monger in 1606, despite the fact that neither had been officially admitted as a master printer', and that in this situation, 'Raworth's piracy of *Venus and Adonis* forced the issue' (*The Texts of King Lear*, 24–5).

taken offence, as reported by Thomas Heywood's *Apology for Actors* in 1612 (see above, pp. 84–6). What seems particularly interesting in the context of the present chapter is the commercial rationale which informed Jaggard's publication. The added material mentioned on the title page – 'two Loue-Epistles . . . from Paris to Hellen, and Hellens answere backe againe to Paris' – were translated from Ovid, as anyone familiar with the *Heroides* would have realized. What the volume does, therefore, is bring together two kinds of Ovidian material: the Venus and Adonis material, going back to the *Metamorphoses*, and the Paris and Helen epistles, translated from the *Heroides*. Like Harrison, Jaggard thus tried to capitalize not just on Shakespeare's name but more specifically on his reputation as the English Ovid, the contemporary poet in whom 'the sweete wittie soule of Ovid lives'. Since no suitable material by Shakespeare himself was available, he turned to Heywood's *Troia Britannica*, which he had published in 1609. Jaggard's original 1612 title page did not go as far as asserting that the added material is by Shakespeare, but since Shakespeare is the only author mentioned on the title page, Jaggard may well have counted on his customers' inference that it is.

Jaggard thus went to considerable lengths to publish a 'Shakespeare' collection, although the only Shakespearean material he actually managed to get his hands on was versions of Sonnets 138 and 144 and of three poems previously published in *Love's Labour's Lost*: in 1599, Jaggard built a collection by means of fifteen other poems by various hands; in 1612, he added the two love epistles and seven other poems (translated) by Heywood. Eventually, Jaggard marketed as a Shakespearean poetry collection a volume of sixty-four leaves of which no more than five short poems are actually by Shakespeare. Jaggard's 'Shakespeare' construction paid: with three editions in fourteen years, *The Passionate Pilgrim* was far more successful than the average poetry collection of the same period.[86]

Jaggard's 1612 edition of *The Passionate Pilgrim* asserted Shakespeare's authorship before a cancel title page retracted it; another volume published the same year insinuated Shakespeare's authorship without spelling it out: 'A FVNERALL Elegye In memory of the late Vertuous Maister William Peter of Whipton neere Excester. By W. S.' The poem attracted considerable attention when Donald Foster attributed it to Shakespeare in 1995, although scholars now seem to agree that it is in fact by John Ford.[87] It was

---

[86] See Badcoe and Erne, 'The Popularity of Poetry Books in Print, 1583–1622'. For Jaggard, see Willoughby, *A Printer of Shakespeare*. For the 1612 edition of *The Passionate Pilgrim*, see also Reid, '"Certaine Amorous Sonnets, Betweene Venus and Adonis"'.

[87] See Vickers, *'Counterfeiting' Shakespeare*.

entered to Thomas Thorpe on 13 February 1612 and 'Imprinted at London by G. Eld.' This leaves unclear whether Thorpe acted as publisher, having the volume printed by George Eld without being mentioned in the imprint, or whether he sold the rights in the poem to Eld before it was published.[88] In either case, the initials must have made the poem commercially more attractive and may well have increased Thorpe's interest in it. Three years earlier, Thorpe had published a book, entered by him on 20 May 1609, to which Shakespeare's name was of crucial importance, as suggested by the large capitals on the title page: 'SHAKE-SPEARES SONNETS'.[89] The combination of the misleading initials on the title page of *The Funeral Elegy* and the prominence of Shakespeare's name on that of the *Sonnets* suggests that Thorpe, like Jaggard, may have invested in Shakespeare because he believed in the drawing power of his name.

Uniquely among Shakespeare's publishers, Thorpe appears to have been neither a printer nor a bookseller. Admitted as a freeman of the Stationers' Company on 4 February 1594, nothing is known about his activities before the turn of the century, following which he is involved in some forty publications until 1625. His career as a publisher falls into three parts: in the third (1616–25), he published relatively little, less than one book a year. In the second, 1611–15, he published more than a dozen books 'of varied interest', with no discernible specialization.[90] In the first part, Thorpe was not only more active as a publisher than ever after, but also more focused: from 1604 to 1610, Thorpe entered or published eighteen titles, of which eleven were plays or masques by Jonson, Marston and Chapman.[91] He published Jonson's *Sejanus His Fall* (1605), *Hymenaei* (1606), *Volpone* (1607) and *The Character of Two Royal Masques* (1608); Chapman's *All Fools* (1605), *The Gentleman Usher* (1606) and *Charles, Duke of Byron* (1608);

---

[88] See Shaaber, 'The Meaning of the Imprint in Early Printed Books', 124. Note that if Eld published the elegy, it may be significant that he also entered and published *The Puritan* in 1607 which was attributed to 'W. S.' on the title page.

[89] For a convenient short-cut through the endless debate triggered by the dedication in the 1609 *Sonnets*, see Burrow, ed., *Complete Sonnets and Poems*, 98–103.

[90] Rostenberg, *Publishing, Printing and Bookselling*, 1.70. My account of Thorpe's publishing career is indebted to Rostenberg's chapter on Thorpe (1.49–73), which is a revised version of her article, 'Thomas Thorpe, Publisher of "Shake-speares Sonnets"'. For Thorpe, see also Kathman, 'Thorpe, Thomas (1571/2–1625?)'.

[91] The other titles were Thomas Wright's *Passions of the Mind* (1604, *STC* 26040) and the same author's *A succinct philosophicall declaration of the nature of clymactericall yeeres, occasioned by the death of Queene Elizabeth* (1604, *STC* 26043.3), a sermon by Samuel Walsall (1607, *STC* 24996), Joseph Hall's *The discovery of a new world, or, A description of the South Indies* (1609, *STC* 12686), John Healey's translation, from the Greek, of *Epictetus his Manuall* (1610, *STC* 10424; with a dedication by Thorpe to John Florio) and two books of poetry: Richard West's *Wits A. B. C. Or A Century of Epigrams* (1608, *STC* 25262), a collection of epigrams, and Shakespeare's *Sonnets*.

Marston's *What You Will* (1607) and *Histriomastix* (1610); and, with William Aspley, Marston's *The Malcontent* (1604), and *Eastward Ho* (1605), by Marston, Jonson and Chapman.[92] Thorpe thus appears to have been well acquainted with several of Shakespeare's fellow dramatists.

It has not been conclusively established whether Shakespeare authorized Thorpe's publication of the *Sonnets* or whether they appeared despite Shakespeare's intentions to keep them out of print.[93] What seems clear, however, is that Thorpe 'was a publisher of some deserved status and prestige, handling works by close associates of Shakespeare, and producing, in many cases, highly authoritative texts'.[94] As the preceding chapter documents, in the years in which Thorpe published their plays, Jonson, Marston and Chapman formed a trio of dramatists engaged in raising the respectability of printed drama. In other words, Thorpe published plays of the dramatic avant-garde, 'the most intellectual of the leading dramatists', whose playbooks made a claim to literary respectability.[95] Thorpe's recurrent dealings with the same dramatists suggests the identity of the author was an important selection criterion for Thorpe. This may be corroborated by the insistence with which several of Thorpe's title pages are headed by the name of the author in capital letters: 'LUCANS FIRST BOOKE' (1600), 'BEN: JONSON his VOLPONE' (1607), 'SHAKE-SPEARES SONNETS' (1609), 'EPICTETVS his Manuall' (1610). Shakespeare's *Sonnets* must have fitted Thorpe's desire to publish high-profile literary titles by prominent contemporary authors and may well have been published because of Thorpe's association with the circle of dramatists he had previously brought into print.

Thorpe was not the first to publish Shakespeare alongside Jonson, Marston and Chapman: in 1601, Edward Blount had done the same. Appended to Robert Chester's long and tedious poem, *Love's Martyr*, appeared a short twenty-page collection of poems, called 'Diuerse Poeticall Essaies on the former Subiect; viz: the Turtle and Phoenix',

---

[92] These plays were entered by Thorpe, but Aspley, with whom Thorpe repeatedly collaborated, is the only name mentioned in the imprint. For Thorpe's Catholic connections and the light they may throw on some of his publications, see Martin and Finnis, 'Thomas Thorpe, "W. S.", and the Catholic Intelligencers'.

[93] For the argument that the 1609 publication was authorized, see Duncan-Jones, 'Was the 1609 Shake-Speares Sonnets Really Unauthorized?' For a skeptical response to Duncan-Jones's argument, see Burrow, 'Life and Work in Shakespeare's Poems', 48–50.

[94] Duncan-Jones, 'Was the 1609 Shake-Speares Sonnets Really Unauthorized?', 154–5. Rostenberg writes even more emphatically: 'During the period of his greatest fecundity Thorpe demonstrated an almost unerring judgment in the choice of manuscripts for publication' (*Publishing, Printing and Bookselling*, 53).

[95] Duncan-Jones, 'Was the 1609 Shake-Speares Sonnets Really Unauthorized?', 161.

'Done' as the inserted title page continues, 'by the best and chiefest of our moderne writers' (sig. z1r).[96] The four writers to whom the poems are attributed are, in order, Shakespeare (the poem often referred to as 'The Phoenix and the Turtle'), Marston, Chapman and Jonson. Thorpe and Blount were close associates. In 1600, *Lucan's First Book* included a dedication by Thorpe addressed 'To His Kind and Trve Friend: Edward Blvnt', and the dedication suggests that Thorpe had received the manuscript of Marlowe's translation from Blount.[97] Blount, as has been pointed out, was 'no mere trade publisher' but 'a man of literary instinct and appreciation'.[98] He had, in Gary Taylor's words, 'an unparalleled gift for recognizing new works that would eventually become classics'.[99] He published not only Shakespeare's First Folio but also the earliest English translations of Miguel de Cervantes's *Don Quixote* and Michel de Montaigne's *Essays*, dramatic collections like William Alexander's *The Monarchick Tragedies* and Lyly's *Six Court Comedies*, and other significant texts by, among others, Jonson, Samuel Daniel and Chapman. It has been surmised that 'Blount's literary associations and perception could well have exercised a beneficent influence upon [Thorpe,] his younger colleague.'[100] Given that the volume Blount published in 1601 referred to Shakespeare, Jonson, Marston and Chapman as 'the best and chiefest of our moderne writers' (sig. z1r), Thorpe may have felt that he could do worse than publish books by the same four authors.

Blount eventually became 'the person who most heavily invested in William Shakespeare's name ... the dominant figure in the syndicate that published the famous first folio edition of Shakespeare's *Comedies, Histories, and Tragedies*'.[101] Yet the only Shakespeare text he published prior to 1623 was 'The Phoenix and the Turtle'. Blount entered *Antony and Cleopatra* and *Pericles* on 20 May 1608, but *Antony and Cleopatra* was not published until 1623, and when *Pericles* appeared in 1609, it was published by Henry Gosson.[102] Even though Blount owned the rights in 'The Phoenix and

[96] For 'The Phoenix and the Turtle' and the publication of *Love's Martyr*, see Bednarz, *Shakespeare and the Truth of Love*.

[97] 'This spirit was sometime a familiar of your own, *Lucans first booke translated*; which (in regard of your old right in it) I haue rais'd in the circle of your Patronage' (sig. A2r).

[98] Rostenberg, *Publishing, Printing and Bookselling*, 50–1.

[99] 'Blount, Edward (*bap.* 1562, *d.* in or before 1632)'.

[100] Rostenberg, *Publishing, Printing and Bookselling*, 51.

[101] Taylor, 'Making Meaning Marketing Shakespeare 1623', 61. For Blount and the First Folio, see also Massai, 'Edward Blount, the Herberts, and the First Folio'.

[102] Blayney has argued that 'one possible reason why Edward Blount left *Pericles* unpublished after registering it in 1608 may be that he failed to reach an agreement with the publisher of George Wilkins's novel, *The Painful Adventures of Pericles* (1608), which explicitly describes itself as "The true History of the Play of *Pericles*"' ('The Publication of Playbooks', 399).

the Turtle', *Pericles* and *Antony and Cleopatra*, he thus cannot be said to have been either among the significant publishers of Shakespeare's poems, or, prior to 1623, among those of his plays. The publishers with the most significant interest in Shakespeare's poetry were, I have argued, John Harrison, William Leake, Robert Raworth, William Jaggard and Thomas Thorpe. The publishers with significant investments in Shakespeare's plays were even more numerous.

The chief publishers of Shakespeare's plays

James Roberts, like Richard Field, could have published several of Shakespeare's works but chose not to do so. He was the playbill printer from 1594 to 1615, which must have brought him into regular contact with the theatre companies in London.[103] His dealings with Shakespeare or his company are confirmed by the fact that he entered three Shakespeare plays in the Stationers' Register: *The Merchant of Venice* on 22 July 1598, *Hamlet* on 26 July 1602 and *Troilus and Cressida* on 7 February 1603. Yet he published none of them. He transferred *The Merchant of Venice* on 28 October 1600 to Thomas Hayes, who had it printed by Roberts before the end of the year. Q1 *Hamlet* was published by Nicholas Ling and John Trundle in 1603 and Q2 *Hamlet* (1604/5) by Ling alone, who had it printed by Roberts.[104] *Troilus and Cressida* was entered on 28 January 1609 to Richard Bonian and Henry Walley who had the play printed by George Eld the same year.

A recent scholar has tried to account for Roberts's unwillingness to publish these plays by arguing that he was 'a printer rather than a publisher', but for an accurate assessment of Roberts's attitude towards playbooks, it is important to know that he was both.[105] As early as 1594, Roberts published *Fiue godly and learned sermons* (*STC* 19858), by George Phillips, which Roberts had entered on 13 December 1593. As late as 1606, he published an edition (following his earlier one of 1600) of *Spiritus est vicarius Christi in terra. The poore mans garden* (*STC* 18669). In between, he published several works by Edward Dering, the evangelical preacher and Puritan spokesman

---

[103] The only exception to Roberts's exclusive right to print playbills for London's theatre companies was Worcester's Men: in 1602, Roberts transferred the right to print their bills to William Jaggard in return for a regular fee of 4s. per month. Roberts further shared with Richard Watkins a lucrative monopoly on the printing of almanacs.

[104] For an account of what seems to have led to this succession of events, see Erne, *Shakespeare as Literary Dramatist*, 81 (105).

[105] Kastan, *Shakespeare and the Book*, 29.

(not to be confused with the slightly later antiquary and religious controversialist, Sir Edward Dering), whose early death in 1576 at the age of thirty-six made him a 'living legend':[106] three editions (1596–1603) of *A sermon preached before the Queenes Maiestie* (*STC* 6708–10), four editions (1595–1603) of *A short catechisme for housholders* (*STC* 6715.7–17) and four editions (1597–1605) of *A briefe and necessarie catechisme or instruction, very needfull to be known of all housholders* (*STC* 6681–3). Roberts also published works of satire, including Marston's *The scourge of villanie* (1598, *STC* 17485) and, in the last years of his career, several anti-Catholic tracts, among them Samuel Harsnett's *A declaration of egregious popish impostures* (1603, *STC* 12880) and Jean Chassanion's *The merchandises of Popish priests* (1604, *STC* 5062).[107] All in all, Roberts was the publisher of almost forty books, of which by far the greatest share was religious.

Given that Roberts printed two of the three Shakespeare plays he had entered, it has been argued that Roberts pursued the strategy of selling copyrights so as to secure the printing rights in the process: 'The entries seem to be for him usually a way of reserving work for himself without risking the capital that publication would involve.' What is adduced as evidence is that 'Roberts ... had on numerous occasions entered material that was eventually published by another stationer but that Roberts himself printed.'[108] Yet an examination of Roberts's output as printer suggests that apart from the Shakespeare plays, only two titles were entered to him before being printed by him for another stationer: *The most honorable tragedie of Sir Richard Grinuile, Knight* (1595, *STC* 17385), entered to Roberts on 20 September 1595 and printed by him for Richard Smith the same year, and *Fitzharberts booke of husbandrie* (*STC* 11004), entered to Roberts on 31 May 1594 and printed by him for Edward White in 1598.[109] Most of the books Roberts entered he in fact published himself.[110]

As playbill printer, Roberts was in an ideal situation to publish Shakespeare's and others' playbooks, but he chose not to do so. The reason for this is clearly not that Roberts was generally averse to taking the commercial risks that come with publishing in the book trade. Nor, I

---

[106] Collinson, 'Dering, Edward (*c*. 1540–1576)'.
[107] Kathman includes Everard Guilpin's *Skialetheia* (1598) among the books of satire Roberts published (see 'Roberts, James (*b*. in or before 1540, *d*. 1618?)'), but this book seems to have been *printed* by Roberts and published by Nicholas Ling.
[108] Kastan, *Shakespeare and the Book*, 29.   [109] Arber, *Transcript*, II.651, III.48.
[110] Note, moreover, that when another Lord Chamberlain's Men's play (*Alarum for London*), which Roberts had previously entered (on 29 May 1600), was published by William Ferbrand in 1602, it was printed not by Roberts but by Edward Allde (*STC* 16754); and *Troilus and Cressida*, originally entered by Roberts, ended up being printed by George Eld.

believe, did he refrain from publishing the plays he had entered solely because he wanted to secure a well-remunerated printing job from the publisher to whom he sold the copyright. Instead, the evidence suggests that Roberts simply did not want to publish plays. Strikingly, he printed eleven playbooks between 1594 and 1606 – including the first quarto of *The Merchant of Venice* (1600) and the second quartos of *Titus Andronicus* (1600) and *Hamlet* (1604/5) – but he never published a single one. As playbill printer, Roberts may have been close enough to Shakespeare and his fellow actors to agree to buy and enter the plays when asked, but as a publisher who specialized in religious fare, he may have been disinclined to add them to his list.[III]

The beginning of Roberts's publishing career overlaps with that of another publisher who is likely to have had a direct connection to Shakespeare: Andrew Wise, active from 1593 to 1602, with a bookshop in St Paul's Churchyard ('at the Angel'). Wise and Roberts were both involved in the publication of Nashe's *Christs teares ouer Ierusalem* (*STC* 18366) in 1593 (of which more below). Both entered several Shakespeare plays during the same period, yet their attitude towards publishing them could not have been more different: whereas Roberts did not publish a single one, Wise published all of them and did so with considerable commercial success.

Wise published the first edition of five different Shakespeare plays, more than any other publisher before 1623: *Richard III* (1597), *Richard II* (1597), *1 Henry IV* (1598) and, with William Aspley, *2 Henry IV* and *Much Ado about Nothing* (both 1600). The last two plays were not reprinted before the First Folio, but the first three were bestsellers, with three editions each by 1603, when Wise sold the rights to Matthew Law. With a profit of about £6 10s. for each of the five first editions (of which two were shared with Law) and about £8 10s. for each of the six subsequent editions (see above, p. 143), Wise would have made a total profit of more than £75, or more than £10 per year, from publishing Shakespeare from 1597 to 1603. If Wise opted for large-print-run reprints, as Walkley did in 1622, the total must have been close to £18 per subsequent edition, or approximately £140 overall, meaning £20 per year. By comparison, as pointed out above, the average labourer's yearly wage in London at the time

---

[III] Roberts has been unconvincingly linked to the famous entry in the Stationers' Register of 4 August 1600 of Lord Chamberlain's Men's plays which were 'to be staied': *As You Like It, Henry V, Every Man in his Humour* and *Much Ado about Nothing* (see Hirrell, 'The Roberts Memoranda'). Hirrell's belief that 'Roberts regularly acquired and sought to publish the [Lord Chamberlain's Men's] play manuscripts without the company's own permission' (728) is contradicted by the fact that Roberts never published a single play. Nor is there any evidence which relates the entry of 4 August 1600 to Roberts.

was £12. The statement that 'a published play text [was] a cheap pamphlet' easily disguises how much money could be made from playbooks.[112]

It has been argued that 'Wise's output is largely made up of works by three authors, namely Thomas Nashe, Thomas Playfere and Shakespeare ... who were all under the direct patronage of Sir George Carey', that Wise had 'a long-standing working relation' with them and that he is 'likely to have had a personal connection with at least one of the three authors whose works he published, and to have met the other two as a result of such a connection'.[113] Yet the only Nashe book Wise took a share in publishing is *Christs teares ouer Ierusalem*, of which the copy demonstrably did not pass directly from Nashe to Wise. It was entered on 8 September 1593 to Alice Charlewood, whose husband, John, had died earlier in the year.[114] Before the end of September 1593, Alice had married James Roberts, who thus owned the rights in *Christs teares* through marriage. *Christs teares* is dated 1593, 'Printed by Iames Roberts' and 'to be solde by Andrewe Wise'. It was reissued in 1594, with the imprint now reading 'Printed for Andrew Wise'. What the publishing arrangement between Wise and Roberts exactly was is beyond recovery (was the edition published jointly, or did Roberts function as publisher in 1593 but sell the remainder of the edition to Wise in 1594?), but it is clear that Wise's original connection to the text was through Roberts, not Nashe.

As for Playfere, in 1596, Wise published two of his sermons which had both been entered on 30 April of that year and, as the *STC* notes, were issued jointly: *The meane in mourninge* (*STC* 20015) and *The pathway to perfection* (*STC* 20020).[115] They reached a second edition the following year. Wise had in fact published three editions of one of these sermons in 1595 under a different title (*A most excellent and heavenly sermon*) and without attribution to Playfere (*STC* 20014–4.5). In the 'Epistle Dedicatory' prefacing the 1596 edition, Playfere complains about the earlier editions, in which his sermon was 'mangled' and published unbeknownst to him (sig. A2r). Wise's publication not only distressed its author but also got him into trouble with the court of the Stationers' Company. On 28 June 1595, he was fined 40s. for 'pritinge [*sic*] m^r Playforde sermon twyce without aucthoritie', which, according to an entry of 18 April 1597, was reduced to 'onlye v^s wch hee [i.e. Wise] hath paide'.[116] What seems to have happened is that Wise and Playfere came to an arrangement between the publication of the unauthorized editions in 1595 and the

[112] Kastan, 'Plays into Print', 29.   [113] Massai, *Shakespeare and the Rise of the Editor*, 100, 221n23.
[114] Arber, *Transcript*, II.635.   [115] Arber, *Transcript*, III.64.
[116] Greg and Boswell, eds., *Records of the Court of the Stationers' Company*, 51. See also Arber, *Transcript*, II.823, 827.

authorized one in 1596, which may well be the reason why the fine was reduced.[117] Playfere's words in the 'Epistle Dedicatory' – 'in whom the fault resteth I cannot learn certainly' (sig. A2v) – imply that Wise pleaded that he was not to blame for the mishap, and Playfere may well have believed him.

Nothing thus suggests that Wise had 'a long-standing working relation' with Nashe or Playfere, or – with the exception of Shakespeare – with any other author. Wise published only five other books: John Racster's *A booke of the seuen planets* (1598, *STC* 20601), a response to a pamphlet in which William Alabaster justifies his conversion to Catholicism; a report (no more than seven quarto pages long) of 'The BATTAILE FOVGHT BET-VVEENE Count Maurice of Nassaw, and Albertus Arch-duke of Austria, nere Newport in Flaunders ... Written by a Gentleman imploied in the said seruice' (1600, *STC* 17671a); two short books of elegies on the death of Sir Horatio Palavicino, in Latin and English respectively (1600, *STC* 19154–4.3), collected and partly authored by Theophilus Field, later Bishop of Hereford, who received his MA from Cambridge in 1599 and 'was incorporated at Oxford on 16 July 1600';[118] and Thomas Campion's *Obseruations in the art of English poesie* (1602, *STC* 4543). Apart from Wise's publication of five Shakespeare plays in eleven editions, his small output is thus a medley ranging from religion to ephemera.

In fact, Wise had only one publishing speciality: the plays of Shakespeare. This raises the question of why a relatively minor stationer came to be such a major publisher of Shakespeare. A plausible connection between Wise and Shakespeare, as I have argued elsewhere, is James Roberts: as playbill printer, he had regular dealings with Shakespeare's company, yet, as we have seen above, he did not want to publish his plays.[119] Roberts collaborated with Wise in 1593/4 over *Christs teares* and again in 1597, when he printed the two Playfere sermons for Wise. In the very same year, Wise started publishing Shakespeare's plays. Both the texts Roberts entered and went on to print and those Wise published are generally believed to have been set up from an authoritative manuscript. The conclusion that Wise and Roberts repeatedly did business with Shakespeare or his company is hard to resist.

---

[117] Massai, who does not refer to Wise's fine by the Court of the Stationers' Company, argues that 'Playfere's claim ... that he never authorized the earlier editions ... seems disingenuous' (*Shakespeare and the Rise of the Editor*, 221n23), an opinion I am unable to share.

[118] Atherton, 'Field, Theophilus (*bap.* 1575, *d.* 1636)'. Atherton explains that Field, by means of the two books of elegies, 'thanked Palavicino for being his patron for six years'. Note that Racster's pamphlet was reissued in 1598 with a cancel title page (*STC* 20601.5).

[119] See *Shakespeare as Literary Dramatist*, 87–8 (111–12). For Massai's different explanation, see *Shakespeare and the Rise of the Editor*, 95–102.

4.5 Entrance in the Stationers' Register, dated 23 August 1600, of *2 Henry IV* and *Much Ado about Nothing*, 'Wrytten by master SHAKESPERE'.

Wise's special interest in Shakespeare may also be inferred from two unusual measures he took. As Sonia Massai has convincingly argued, Wise invested not only in the publication of Shakespeare's plays but also 'in the perfection of his dramatic copies for the press': 'substantive variants in speech prefixes, stage directions and dialogue in the second and third quartos of *Richard II*, *Richard III* and *1 Henry IV* suggest that they were corrected as they were repeatedly reprinted between 1598 and 1602'.[120] Moreover, although the first quartos of *Richard II* (1597), *Richard III* (1597) and *1 Henry IV* (1598) were published anonymously, in conformity with the majority of professional playbooks up to that period, they were reprinted, each in the year following the first edition, with authorship attributions to Shakespeare on the title page, the earliest title page appearances of his name besides that of the 1598 quarto of *Love's Labour's Lost*.[121] Given how important Shakespeare and his name were to Wise, it also seems significant that Shakespeare's name appears for the first time in the Stationers' Register when Wise, with Aspley, entered *2 Henry IV* and *Much Ado about Nothing* on 23 August 1600: 'Wrytten by master SHAKESPERE' (Figure 4.5).[122]

Another minor publisher had an output which was strongly focused on the plays of Shakespeare: Thomas Millington. He published, or co-published, no more than seventeen titles from 1594 to 1603. The dates of

[120] *Shakespeare and the Rise of the Editor*, 95, 102.
[121] For the role Francis Meres's *Palladis Tamia* may have played in increasing the book trade value of 'Shakespeare' as reflected in Wise's decision to add the name to the playbook title pages, see *Shakespeare as Literary Dramatist*, 58–69 (82–93).
[122] Arber, *Transcript*, III.170. For Wise, see also Hooks, 'Wise Ventures'.

his books suggest that he stopped publishing in 1600, but that he seized the opportunity of Queen Elizabeth's death and King James's ascension to resume his activities for two editions of Henry Chettle's *England's Mourning Garment* and an account of James's progress from Edinburgh to London (*The true narration of the entertainment of his Royall Maiestie*), all published in 1603.[123] Among Millington's fourteen titles dated 1594 to 1600, there are five short news pamphlets, two single-sheet ballads and a translation by Gervase Markham of a French elegy on the death of the Earl of Essex's brother.[124] The six remaining books are: *Titus Andronicus* (1594), of which I have argued above that Millington is likely to be the co-publisher (see pp. 139–40); *1 Contention* (*2 Henry VI*) in 1594; *Richard Duke of York* (*3 Henry VI*) in 1595; reprints of *1 Contention* and *Richard Duke of York* in 1600; and, with John Busby, *Henry V*, also in 1600. In other words, the core of Millington's publishing output consists of six editions of plays written – alone or in co-authorship – by Shakespeare.

Before we jump to the conclusion that Millington must have known Shakespeare and made a conscious decision to specialize in him, we need to remind ourselves that none of these playbooks bears Shakespeare's name on the title page. *Titus, 1 Contention* and *Richard Duke of York* reached print well before the first play was attributed to Shakespeare, and, contrary to Wise, Millington did nothing to lift their anonymity when he had them reprinted. Nor does anything suggest that Millington tried to market the three history plays he published in 1600 as a trilogy: *1 Contention* and *Richard Duke of York* were for sale at 'his shoppe vnder Saint Peters Church in Cornewall', whereas *Henry V* was available at Busby's 'house in Carter Lane'. Massai has plausibly suggested that Millington's 'decision to invest in dramatic publication seems linked to [his] coming into contact with a specific company, or with an agent acting on the company's behalf'.[125] Indeed, the reason why Millington published three Shakespeare plays in 1594/5 has probably less to do with Shakespeare than with the Earl of Pembroke's Men, in whose repertory they had all been.[126] Millington thus presents us with the paradox of a publishing profile centred on one author who, however, is never acknowledged in any of the books and whom the publisher may not have known or cared about. Millington published several plays by Shakespeare, but he did nothing to market them as Shakespeare's.

Yet there is a third publisher besides Roberts and Wise who may have had a direct connection to Shakespeare or the Lord Chamberlain's Men,

[123] See *STC* 5121–2 and 17153.
[124] See *STC* 5066, 5631.3, 13119, 14032, 18654, 18895.5, 19793 and 24093.
[125] *Shakespeare and the Rise of the Editor*, 98.   [126] Chambers, *The Elizabethan Stage*, 11.128–9.

although, as we will see, his interest in Shakespeare was short-lived: Cuthbert Burby. He published the 1598 quarto of *Love's Labour's Lost*, the 1599 quarto of *Romeo and Juliet* and two editions of the probably collaborative *Edward III* in 1596 and 1599.[127] The 1599 edition of *Romeo and Juliet* supersedes and the 1598 edition of *Love's Labour's Lost* claims to supersede an inferior edition.[128] The plays Burby published seem to be have been set up from authorial manuscripts, and the moment when the plays reached print conforms to the publication pattern of the plays Shakespeare wrote for the Lord Chamberlain's Men, which increases the likelihood that Burby had direct dealings with Shakespeare or his company.[129]

Burby was a prolific stationer, publishing close to 120 books from 1592 to 1607. In the 1590s, almost two-thirds of his titles were literature, mostly prose fiction (Greene, Munday, Nashe, Lodge and others) and plays (including by Jonson, Lyly, Greene and Nashe) but hardly any poetry.[130] After 1601, however, Burby's publishing profile underwent a sudden and astonishing conversion: he ceased to publish any literary titles (first editions or reprints), and about four-fifths of the approximately fifty titles he issued from 1602 to 1607 deal with religious matters.[131] The reasons for this change are hard to assess. It has been pointed out that Burby became an unusually wealthy stationer, and it is possible that he decided to put his money only where his heart lay.[132] Judging by contemporary allusions, *Romeo and Juliet* was an exceptionally popular play at the time, yet after the second quarto of 1599, no new edition of it appeared for ten years (by which time it had been assigned to John Smethwick), while several other plays, *Richard II*, *Richard III*, *1 Henry IV*, *Henry V* and *Hamlet*, received reprints during the same period. It is not impossible that *Romeo and Juliet* failed to do so because Burby, after what looks like a short period of intense interest in Shakespeare, ceased to publish not only any Shakespeare but also any other literature.

---

[127] See Melchiori, ed., *King Edward III*, 3–17. Burby also published the probably non-Shakespearean *Taming of a Shrew* and Francis Meres's *Palladis Tamia* (1598) with its famous references to Shakespeare.

[128] For the lost edition of *Love's Labour's Lost* to which the title page of the 1598 edition alludes, see above, p. 13.

[129] See Erne, *Shakespeare as Literary Dramatist*, 88–9 (112–13).

[130] The only poetry book in Burby's large output is *England's Parnassus* (1600), the anthology of verse extracts, which he published with Nicholas Ling and Thomas Hayes.

[131] The only scholarly article devoted to Burby of which I am aware is Johnson, 'Succeeding as an Elizabethan Publisher'. Johnson does not comment on the sudden generic change in Burby's publications, nor does McKerrow (*Dictionary*, 55) or Kirschbaum (*Shakespeare and the Stationers*, 285–9). The *ODNB* has no entry for Burby.

[132] See Johnson, 'Succeeding as an Elizabethan Publisher', 71–2.

Roberts, Wise and Burby all entered or published Shakespeare's plays in the last years of Queen Elizabeth's reign but not beyond. Wise did not publish after 1602 and transferred the rights in *Richard II*, *Richard III* and *1 Henry IV* to Matthew Law on 25 June 1603.[133] We do not know how much the three copyrights were worth, but we may assume that Law paid a handsome sum for them. By 1603, *Richard II*, *Richard III* and *1 Henry IV* were Shakespeare's bestselling plays. And they kept selling. Law published two editions of *Richard II* (Q4–5; 1608, 1615) and four editions each of *Richard III* (Q4–7; 1605, 1612, 1622, 1629) and *1 Henry IV* (Q3–6; 1604, 1608, 1613, 1622). With a total of ten editions, Law published even more Shakespeare books than did Wise – indeed, more Shakespeare books than any other publisher in early modern England.

Law was active as publisher and bookseller from 1595 to 1629, although he published only two books before 1601 and eleven after 1617, as opposed to more than sixty from 1601 to 1617.[134] He specialized in two areas, drama and, chiefly, religion. Thirteen of his books were sermons and other writings by William Barlow, Bishop of Rochester and Lincoln (whose chosen publisher he appears to have been). He published some forty additional books devoted to religion, chiefly sermons (almost thirty) by various divines, including, on six occasions, by Thomas Playfere, whose copyrights he had also purchased from Wise. As for drama, Law published sixteen playbook editions, including the ten of Shakespeare's three history plays, making Shakespeare the second most significant author in Law's output after Barlow. Shortly after the turn of the century, when the market in playbooks had just peaked, Law acquired the copy of five different plays in the space of approximately two years: Robert Yarington's *Two Lamentable Tragedies* (published in 1601), *How a Man May Choose a Good Wife from a Bad* (published in 1602) and the three Shakespeare plays (transferred from Wise in June 1603).[135] Perhaps Law realized that the market in playbooks was on the wane, for he acquired no other playbooks, but four of those he owned kept selling, not only the three by Shakespeare but also *How a Man May Choose a Good Wife from a Bad*, which went through five editions between 1602 and 1621.

The early popularity of this anonymously published, now little-known comedy may seem surprising. It is possible that it profited from the

---

[133] Arber, *Transcript*, III.239.

[134] As Kirschbaum mentions, 'Along with thirteen others Law was transferred to the Stationers' Company from the Drapers' in June, 1600' (*Shakespeare and the Stationers*, 304).

[135] For Thomas Heywood's likely authorship of *How a Man May Choose a Good Wife from a Bad*, see below, p. 245.

simultaneous sale of Shakespeare's history plays at 'his shop in Paules Church-yard, neere vnto S. *Augustines* gate, at the signe of the Foxe'.[136] That the plays sold at an approximately parallel rhythm can be inferred from the dates of the reprints: *1 Henry IV*, *Richard III* and *How a Man* in 1604–5, *Richard II*, *1 Henry IV* and *How a Man* in 1608, all four plays in 1612–15 and *Richard III*, *1 Henry IV* and *How a Man* in 1621–2.[137]

Nothing indicates that Law, like Wise, had a direct connection to Shakespeare and his company. The texts of Law's editions were simple reprints, except for the deposition episode in *Richard II*, first included in 1608, which appears to have been 'printed from a source inferior to the Folio text and of doubtful origin'.[138] That Law was nonetheless conscious of the value of his Shakespeare plays is suggested not only by the number of editions he published but also by an incident in the preparation of the First Folio. In the printing of the histories, quires a–c, ending with the first half of *Richard II*, were followed not by quire d (with the rest of *Richard II* and the beginning of *1 Henry IV*), but with quires h–o, containing *Henry V* and *1, 2 Henry VI*. Only then followed the printing of quires d–g.[139] 'These irregularities, otherwise inexplicable, are', as Charlton Hinmann wrote, 'almost certainly the results of difficulties raised by Law . . . over the use of [his] plays in the Folio.'[140] Whether Law was 'angered by the printing syndicate', as one critic put it, is not known, but he was clearly aware that he owned three valuable copyrights and, since he was not a member of the group of First Folio publishers, it was in his interest to drive up their price.[141] In addition, he tried to capitalize on the increased interest in Shakespeare occasioned by the First Folio by having *Richard III* and *1 Henry IV* republished in 1622.

In the First Folio of 1623, the 'Histories' section contains ten plays, yet their publication record (or lack thereof) prior to that date suggests that *Richard III*, *Richard II* and *1 Henry IV* formed the heart of the canon of his playbooks about English history while Shakespeare was still alive. Their popularity made them an enviable book trade commodity, and publishers such as John Busby seem to have tried to capitalize on their popularity by means of plays closely related to them. Busby published Q1 *Henry V* in 1600

---

[136] I quote from the title page of the 1608 edition of *1 Henry IV*. The bookshop is mentioned in the imprints of all the playbooks Law published.

[137] I am here building on John Jowett, who has commented on the grouped reprinting of Law's three Shakespeare plays (see *Richard III*, 117).

[138] Forker, ed., *King Richard II*, 532.

[139] See Hinmann, *The Printing and Proof-Reading of the First Folio of Shakespeare*, II.523.

[140] *The Printing and Proof-Reading of the First Folio of Shakespeare*, I.27–8.

[141] Marder, *His Exits and his Entrances*, 91.

(with Thomas Millington) and entered *The Merry Wives of Windsor* on 18 January 1602, although he transferred the rights to the play to Arthur Johnson on the same day.[142] The Stationers' Register entry of *Merry Wives* stresses the connection to *1 Henry IV*: 'An excellent and pleasant conceited commedie of Sir JOHN FFAULSTOF and the merry wyves of Windesor.'[143] So does the title page of Q1 *Henry V*, which evokes another popular character from *1 Henry IV*: 'Togither with Auntient Pistoll'. That these two characters from *1 Henry IV* were used as promotion is also suggested by the title page of *2 Henry IV*, which mentions both: 'With the humours of sir Iohn Falstaffe, and swaggering Pistoll'.

Whereas Wise had access to authorial manuscripts and, quite possibly, Shakespeare himself, Busby seems to have had access to neither. Q1 *Henry V* and Q1 *Merry Wives*, traditionally labelled as 'bad quartos', offer texts vastly different from, and much shorter than, those printed in the Folio. In several respects, then, Wise had the real thing, whereas Busby did not: authorial vs. non-authorial texts, bestseller vs. occasional seller, original vs. commercial spin-off.

Given scholarly interest in the provenance of the 'bad quartos', it may be significant that Busby has been called 'primarily a procurer of manuscripts who depended upon other publishers for help in financing and selling the editions at their shops'.[144] Busby published many books with someone else, and he entered quite a few more which he may have sold before publication. Imprints point out that Busby published with George Loftus, Thomas Gubbin, Thomas Millington and, on no fewer than ten occasions, Nicholas Ling.[145] In a number of other cases, the imprint acknowledges only one publisher, although Busby entered the title with another stationer, suggesting joint publication arrangements of some kind, with John Trundle, Arthur Johnson, Ling, Nathaniel Butter, Gubbin and John Oxenbridge.[146] As Gerald D. Johnson has commented, Busby collaborated

---

[142] Significantly, Q1 *Henry V* was printed by Thomas Creede. As Blayney explains, 'When Millington and Busby tried to license Shakespeare's *Henry V* in 1600 ... the wardens ... would have required the consent of Thomas Creede, who had published (and printed) *The Famous Victories of Henry the Fifth* in 1598. Creede presumably did consent, on condition that he be hired (and therefore paid) to print the rival play' ('The Publication of Playbooks', 399).

[143] Arber, *Transcript*, III.78.

[144] Johnson, 'John Busby and the Stationers' Trade, 1590–1612', 14. Johnson's is the fullest assessment of Busby's career as publisher to date. See also Massai, *Shakespeare and the Rise of the Editor*, 98–9.

[145] See *STC* 19936 (Loftus), 16664 and 16665 (Gubbin), 22289 (Millington) and 7205, 7206, 7214, 11622, 12253, 16657, 22656, 22657, 23633a and 26124 (Ling).

[146] See *STC* 22384 (Trundle), 22380 (Johnson), 7214.5 and 16656 (Ling), 13360–1 and 22292 (Butter), 5654.5–6 (Gubbin) and 13341 (Oxenbridge).

with a series of other publishers . . . Since these men were all publishing independently of these joint ventures, the inference may be drawn that Busby, after finding a
marketable manuscript, brought it to them for help in financing its publication.
This inference gains support from the fact that in most cases, as evidenced by
reprints and assignments, the collaborator retained or gained control of the
copyright.[147]

Busby's Shakespeare publications are cases in point: he published *Henry V*
not alone but with Millington, and, before the end of 1600, the rights to the
play had passed to Thomas Pavier.[148] He entered *The Merry Wives of
Windsor* on 18 January 1602, but, curiously, transferred the rights in the
play to Johnson on the same day, perhaps, as has been suggested, because
Busby 'entered the copy with the intent to speculate [and] may have found a
customer on the same day'.[149] As for *King Lear*, Busby entered the play with
Nathaniel Butter, on 26 November 1607, although Butter is the only
publisher mentioned in the imprint when the play was published the year
after. Whereas, as we have seen above, William Leake, senior, liked to pay
for copyrights of proven sellers, Busby seems to have preferred the opposite:
purchasing copyrights but then sharing the costs (and risks) of publication,
or selling the copyrights for a profit.

   Busby specialized in what we now call literature.[150] He published and/or
entered just over fifty titles between 1590 and 1610, of which thirty-six are by
well-known authors: Thomas Lodge, Robert Greene, Thomas Nashe and
George Peele (all 'University Wits'), Michael Drayton, Thomas Kyd,
Robert Southwell, John Marston, Thomas Heywood, Edward Sharpham
and Shakespeare. Busby's literary output falls into two distinct groups:
poetry and prose in the 1590s and playbooks in the 1600s. The first group
includes prose works such as Greene's *The defence of conny-catching* (1592)
and *Ciceronis amor* (1597), Nashe's *Pierce Penilesse* (1592) and Lodge's
A margarite of America (1596), books of verse like Lodge's *Phillis* (1593),
Peele's *The honour of the garter* (1593), Drayton's *Matilda* (1594), *Peirs
Gaueston* (1594) and *Endimion and Phoebe* (1595), Southwell's *Moeoniê*
(1595) and Marston's *The scourge of villanie* (1598), or books of prose and
verse, including Lodge's *Rosalynde: Euphues golden legacie* (1590) and
Euphues shadow (1592), and Greene's *Greenes neuer too late* (1590). The
only dramatic work Busby published in this period is Kyd's closet tragedy
Cornelia, translated from Robert Garnier (1594). Yet after 1598, Busby's

---

[147] Johnson, 'John Busby and the Stationers' Trade', 2.   [148] Arber, *Transcript*, III.169.
[149] Johnson, 'John Busby and the Stationers' Trade', 10.
[150] Note that a second John Busby was active as stationer in London 1607–31 (as opposed to 1590–1619
   for the one in whom I am here interested).

publications of verse and prose fiction ceased almost completely.[151] Instead he turned to professional plays. He entered Heywood's two parts of *Edward IV* on 28 August 1599, Shakespeare's *Merry Wives* on 18 January 1602, Sharpham's *The Fleir* on 13 May 1606 and *Cupid's Whirligig* on 29 June 1607, and Shakespeare's *King Lear* on 26 November 1607, and he published *Henry V* in 1600 and Heywood's *The Rape of Lucrece* in 1608, issuing a second edition in 1609.

This sharp generic and chronological division in Busby's activities suggests that he took a conscious decision in or around 1599 to change his publishing profile, and he probably did so in the wake of the increasing popularity of playbooks. The most immediate motivation may well have been provided by the unusual interest in *Richard III*, *Richard II* and *1 Henry IV*, which together went through the stunning total of eight editions from 1597 to 1599. This would explain his interest not only in *Henry V* and *The Merry Wives of Windsor* but also in Thomas Heywood's two-part history play *Edward IV*. The playbooks in whose publication Busby was involved from 1599 to 1602 can all be read, in other words, as commercial spin-offs of the Shakespeare history plays owned by Wise. Busby's publication of Heywood's *The Rape of Lucrece* in 1608 is also suggestive in this context: Shakespeare's *Rape of Lucrece* remained popular, reaching its fifth edition in 1607. Not only did Busby repeatedly invest in Shakespeare; it looks like he also allowed several successful Shakespeare texts which he did not own to have an impact on his commercial decisions.

Two publishers with whom Busby collaborated also showed conspicuous interest in Shakespeare: Nathaniel Butter and Nicholas Ling. Busby and Butter entered *King Lear* on 26 November 1607, although Busby fails to appear in the imprint of Q1 in 1608, and Butter seems to have published the play alone. *King Lear* stands out from among Shakespeare's quarto playbooks in that it is the only one that highlights his name on the title page to the point of putting it first, at the top of the page, and in largest letters. The 1608 *King Lear* has been called the 'one important exception in the prefolio printing history of Shakespeare's plays which . . . places him for a moment in the self-consciously literary company of Webster and Jonson'.[152] The foregrounding of Shakespeare's name in the playbook published by Butter is interesting insofar as Butter also published *The London Prodigal* in 1605, whose title page claims it is 'By William Shakespeare'. Jointly, the two

---

[151] The only book of poetry Busby published after 1598, with George Loftus, is *Pimlyco. Or, Runne Red-cap* (1609, *STC* 19936). He published no prose fiction in this period.

[152] Brooks, '*King Lear* (1608) and the Typography of Literary Ambition', 148.

publications suggest that Butter, although he was not among Shakespeare's most successful publishers, may have been sensitive to the potential value of Shakespeare's *name*.[153]

As for Nicholas Ling, his track record may not suggest that he was an important publisher of Shakespeare: he published Q1 *Hamlet*, with John Trundle, in 1603, and Q2, alone, in 1604/5. On 22 January 1607, the rights in *Romeo and Juliet* and *Love's Labour's Lost* were transferred to him by Cuthbert Burby, but on 19 November of that year, these plays and *Hamlet* were assigned to John Smethwick. Ling specialized in literary titles, which account for the greatest part of the approximately sixty books he published between 1590 and 1607, publishing books of verse (most notably seventeen by Drayton, whose chosen publisher he clearly was), prose (by Greene, Nashe and Lodge, among others) and a few playbooks, including the third quarto of Jonson's *Every Man Out of His Humour* (1600). Ling had been made free of the company as early as 1579 and published a few books in 1584 and 1585, after which he returned to his native Norwich and only reappears in the London book trade in 1590, at which point he resumed activities as a bookseller with a shop in St Paul's Churchyard.[154]

What accounts for Ling's significance is his contribution to the commonplacing of professional plays, which was helping to elevate their cultural status and turn Shakespeare into a literary dramatist in print. In the final years of the sixteenth century, a small group of people comprising John Bodenham, Robert Allot and Nicholas Ling started compiling and publishing commonplace books. *Politeuphuia wits common wealth* (*STC* 15685), published by Ling in 1597, organizes, as he explains in the dedication, excerpts from classical and Christian authorities compiled by Bodenham into a 'methodicall collection of the most choice and select admonitions and sentences' (sig. A2r). In 1600, *Bel-vedére or The Garden of the Muses* (*STC* 3189) contained excerpts of 'Moderne and extant Poets' (sig. A5v), collected and edited by Bodenham, with the help of Anthony Munday, and in the same year, Robert Allot's *England's Parnassus* (*STC* 378), co-published by

[153] For *The London Prodigal*, see also above, pp. 73–5. Apart from *King Lear*, the publications for which Butter is now best remembered are those of Chapman's Homer, *The Iliad* in 1611, twelve books of the *Odyssey* in 1614, the complete *Odyssey* in 1615 and *The whole works of Homer* in 1616. He published a few professional plays, by Heywood, Dekker, Samuel Rowley and Edward Sharpham, but his publishing speciality, particularly in the second half of his long career (1604–41), was news tracts, making of him, in Shaaber's words, the 'premier news-publisher of the first half of the seventeenth century' (quoted in Kirschbaum, *Shakespeare and the Stationers*, 293). For Butter, see also Baron, 'Butter, Nathaniel (*bap.* 1583, *d.* 1664)', and Rostenberg, *Publishing, Printing and Bookselling*, 1.75–96.

[154] See Johnson, 'Nicholas Ling, Publisher, 1580–1607'. For Ling, see also Kirschbaum, *Shakespeare and the Stationers*, 305–7, and Bourus, 'Shakespeare and the London Publishing Environment'.

Ling, did the same. These books drew extensively on professional plays, including, as we will see, those by Shakespeare. At the same time that Ling was contributing to the dissemination of commonplace books, he was publishing or co-publishing some of the earliest English literary texts printed with commonplace markers: Kyd's *Cornelia* (1594, *STC* 11622), Michael Drayton's *Matilda* (1594, *STC* 7205) and Edward Guilpin's *Skialetheia* (1598, *STC* 12504), which, significantly, are all repeatedly quoted in *England's Parnassus*.

From 1600, playbooks also received the distinction of being printed with commonplace markers. At a time when the cultural value of playbooks still needed to be fully established, these markers, as Lesser and Stallybrass have shown, served 'as a way to elevate ... playbooks and to indicate their suitability as serious reading matter'.[155] Significantly, two early instances of playbooks with commonplace markers are Ling's Q1 and Q2 *Hamlet*. With the exception of the 1609 *Troilus and Cressida*, they are the only pre-Folio Shakespeare playbooks to have them. Given its commonplace markers, Lesser and Stallybrass have called Q1 *Hamlet* 'a literary publication' and added that it was 'offered to readers at the moment of its production as an early example of the professional theater's capacity to produce literature and as the first play of Shakespeare's to assert such a literary claim'.[156] In other words, Ling made his Shakespeare publications participate in the rise of literary drama.[157]

In this context, Ling's acquisition of the rights to *Romeo and Juliet* and *Love's Labour's Lost* in 1607 seems significant. *England's Parnassus*, the commonplace book Ling co-published, contains passages from five Shakespeare plays: *Love's Labour's Lost*, *Romeo and Juliet* and the three bestsellers owned by Wise, *1 Henry IV*, *Richard III* and *Richard II*. *Belvedére* similarly includes quotations from *Love's Labour's Lost* and *Romeo and Juliet* as well as five other Shakespeare plays. In addition to his involvement in commonplacing, Ling has been identified as the editor of the literary miscellany *England's Helicon* (*STC* 3191), also published in 1600 and dedicated to Bodenham, which contains a poem excerpted from *Love's Labour's Lost*.[158] As early as 1600, in other words, several books appeared with

---

[155] 'The First Literary *Hamlet*', 410. This and the following paragraph are indebted to Lesser and Stallybrass's incisive article.

[156] 'The First Literary *Hamlet*', 410–11.

[157] For Ling and Q1 *Hamlet*, see also Melnikoff, 'Nicholas Ling's Republican *Hamlet* (1603)'.

[158] For Ling's editorship of *Englands Helicon*, see Hebel, 'Nicholas Ling and *Englands Helicon*'; Rollins, ed., *England's Helicon 1600, 1614*, I.1–6; and Bednarz, 'Canonizing Shakespeare', 260–1. See also Honigmann, *John Weever*, 23.

passages from *Love's Labour's Lost* and *Romeo and Juliet*, by means of which Ling and his colleagues suggested that playbooks were 'serious reading matter'.[159]

Ling thus used *Hamlet, Romeo and Juliet* and *Love's Labour's Lost* for the commonplacing and anthologizing of literary drama years before he came to own the rights to them. He died in 1607, and while the exact date of his death is not known, we may assume that it was before the copyrights in his Shakespeare plays passed to Smethwick. In all likelihood, the assignment of the copyrights to Smethwick does not suggest Ling's lack of interest in them; instead, his growing interest in owning and publishing Shakespeare's plays may well have been cut short by his death. Perhaps without knowing each other, Ling and Shakespeare collaborated on the construction of the latter's literary drama.

Another stationer made a significant contribution to Shakespeare's standing as dramatist in print before the First Folio: Thomas Pavier. He did so by being the first publisher to envisage and at least partly realize a collection of Shakespeare plays, now called the 'Pavier Quartos', in 1619. Pavier's engagement with Shakespeare started well before that date. Having entered the rights to *Henry V* on 14 August 1600, he published its second quarto in 1602. This was followed six years later by the first quarto of *A Yorkshire Tragedy*, ascribed to Shakespeare on the title page.[160] As early as 1600, he had published *1 Sir John Oldcastle*. Although it appeared without authorship attribution in that year, it was included – like *A Yorkshire Tragedy* – in the Shakespeare collection of 1619, where it was assigned to 'William Shakespeare'.[161]

The separate playbooks of the 1600s and the collection of 1619 belong to two different phases of Pavier's career. Publishing close to two hundred titles from 1600 to 1625, he focused on news pamphlets, ballads and plays in the first decade of the seventeenth century, after which his emphasis shifted to sermons and other religious titles.[162] Between 1600 and 1610, he published thirteen editions of playbooks: Lodge and Greene's *A Looking Glass for London and England* (1602), Kyd's *Spanish Tragedy* (1602, 1603 and 1610/

---

[159] Lesser and Stallybrass, 'The First Literary *Hamlet*', 410. See also below, pp. 228–9.

[160] I also address Pavier's publication of plays which were misattributed to Shakespeare in Chapter 2 (see pp. 75–9).

[161] It should be added here that Pavier first published *The Spanish Tragedy* in 1602, with additions which have recently been attributed to Shakespeare (see Craig, 'The 1602 Additions to *The Spanish Tragedy*').

[162] Johnson, 'Thomas Pavier, Publisher, 1600–25', 12, 25, 31. Pavier is one of twelve bookselling drapers to have been admitted to the Stationers' Company in June 1600. See Arber, *Transcript*, 11.725, and Johnson, 'The Stationers versus the Drapers'.

11), *Jack Straw* (1604), *The Fair Maid of Bristow* (1605), *Captain Thomas Stukeley* (1605), *The First Part of Hieronimo* (1605) and Heywood's *1 If You Know Not Me, You Know Nobody* (1608 and 1610), in addition to the three editions mentioned above. Yet after these, he published no other plays for the rest of his career, with the exception of the Shakespeare collection in 1619.

Given that the majority of playbooks published after the turn of the century appeared with an authorship attribution on the title page, it is remarkable how many of Pavier's plays did not. *A Looking Glass for London and England* had originally appeared in 1594 with Lodge and Greene's names on the title page, and this attribution was repeated in Pavier's edition of 1602. Of the twelve other Pavier playbooks published 1600–10, eleven appeared anonymously, and only one did not: *A Yorkshire Tragedy*, 'Written by W. Shakspeare'. *A Yorkshire Tragedy* is also unusual among Pavier's plays in that it is one of only two which he originally entered in the Stationers' Register instead of acquiring it from a fellow stationer (the other exception being *The Fair Maid of Bristow*). When Pavier entered *A Yorkshire Tragedy* on 2 May 1608, Shakespeare's name, unusually, is mentioned: 'A booke Called *A Yorkshire Tragedy* written by WYLLIAM SHAKESPERE.'[163] The evidence may suggest that Pavier had initially little investment in dramatic authorship, but that by 1608, he had started to become interested in Shakespeare's.

This interest is again in evidence in the Pavier Quartos in 1619. From our modern point of view, the collection consists of an unlikely gathering of plays: *The Whole Contention* (meaning *1 Contention* and *Richard Duke of York*), *Pericles*, *A Yorkshire Tragedy*, *The Merry Wives of Windsor*, *King Lear* (misdated 1608), *Henry V* (misdated 1608), *The Merchant of Venice* (misdated 1600), *A Midsummer Night's Dream* (misdated 1600) and *1 Sir John Oldcastle* (misdated 1600). Not until the early twentieth century did scholars realize that these ten plays were produced as a group, under the initiative of Pavier and printed by William Jaggard.[164] That the plays were originally intended as a collection is clear: the first three plays, *The Whole Contention* and *Pericles*, were printed with continuous signatures. That the original plan was abandoned is equally clear: after the third play,

---

[163] Arber, *Transcript*, III.377. This is the third of four mentions in the Register during Shakespeare's lifetime, the others being Wise and Aspley's entrance of *2 Henry IV* and *Much Ado about Nothing* on 23 August 1600, Butter and Busby's of *King Lear* on 26 November 1607 and Thorpe's of the *Sonnets* on 20 May 1609.

[164] See Greg, 'On Certain False Dates in Shakespearian Quartos', and Neidig, 'The Shakespeare Quartos of 1619'.

the continuous signatures cease, and of the seven remaining plays, five are misdated. The playbooks appear to have been issued both separately and jointly: several copies of the collection are known to have survived, although the order in which the ten plays were bound differed.[165]

Why did Pavier change his plan and publish several plays with fake imprints? It is possible that the King's Men got wind of the undertaking, perhaps through Jaggard, who had taken over from Roberts as playbill printer, and, since they had started planning their own Shakespeare collection, secured the help of William Herbert, the third Earl of Pembroke and Lord Chamberlain, future dedicatee of the First Folio, to prevent Pavier's.[166] The records of the court of the Stationers' Company contain an entry, dated 3 May 1619, which notes that 'vppon a lér [i.e. letter] from the right ho[ble] the Lo. Chamberleyne It is thought fitt & so ordered That no playes that his Ma[tyes] players do play shalbe printed w[th]out consent of some of them'.[167] Whether this order applied – and whether the King's Men wanted the order to apply – only to previously unpublished plays or to all of their plays is now difficult to ascertain. As a rule, the Stationers' Company would no doubt have considered it their members' right to republish previously printed plays. This may explain why 'the faked imprints were not intended to deceive the copyright-holders' but may have been considered a smart move to placate the King's Men and their powerful patron.[168] A different explanation has been advanced by Massai, who believes that the initial publication plan was not abandoned in response to the Lord Chamberlain's letter. Instead, she argues, William Jaggard's son, Isaac, 'rather than the actors, was first inspired by Pavier's projected collection and persuaded the King's Men to invoke the Lord Chamberlain's support to prevent other stationers – and *not* Pavier – from securing previously unpublished plays from their repertory'.[169] Isaac, Massai claims, 'also persuaded Pavier to issue his ten Quartos either individually or as a nonce

[165] For bound volumes with the Pavier Quartos, see below, pp. 222–3.

[166] For the standard account of the genesis of the Pavier Quartos, see Pollard, *Shakespeare Folios and Quartos*, 81–107; Chambers, *William Shakespeare*, 1.133–7; Greg, *The Shakespeare First Folio*, 9–17; Kirschbaum, *Shakespeare and the Stationers*, 227–42; Kastan, *Shakespeare and the Book*, 57; and Murphy, *Shakespeare in Print*, 36–41.

[167] Jackson, ed., *Records of the Court of the Stationers' Company 1602–1640*, 110.

[168] Johnson, 'Thomas Pavier', 40. As Johnson has noted, 'at the time these quartos [i.e. the Pavier Quartos] appeared [Pavier] was enjoying his promotion into the governing councils of the Stationers' Company, having been elected to the Court of Assistants on 14 June 1619. It seems unlikely that Pavier, at this stage in his career, would have perpetrated a fraud that put his reputation at risk' ('Thomas Pavier', 35). Indeed, Pavier's new position within the company may have made him eager to avoid causing trouble.

[169] *Shakespeare and the Rise of the Editor*, 107.

collection ... in order to whet, rather than satisfy, readers' demand for a new collection of Shakespeare's dramatic works', allowing Pavier to minimize the risks of his undertaking and secure 'further revenue from lending his rights to Isaac and to the other members of the Folio syndicate'.[170]

Pavier and William Jaggard had started collaborating well before 1619: *A View of all the Right Honourable the Lord Mayors of this Honorable Citty of London* (*STC* 14343), authored by Jaggard, was jointly published by him and Pavier in 1601. From 1603 to 1610, Jaggard printed several prose texts published by Pavier: *Present remedies against the plague* (*STC* 5871.7) in 1603; *The Case is Altered* (*STC* 23615), by 'F. T.', in 1605; Henry Arthington's *Principall points of holy profession* (*STC* 797) in 1607; and *The way to true happines* (*STC* 25132) in 1610. In 1604/5, Jaggard also printed three plays for Pavier: *The Fair Maid of Bristow, 1 Hieronimo* and *Captain Thomas Stukeley*. Perhaps surprisingly, Pavier did not hire Jaggard to print any of the almost fifty titles he published from 1610 to 1618. Yet the Pavier Quartos show that they continued to do business together, and Jaggard's will – which names Pavier as overseer – suggests they remained lifelong friends.[171]

What is at the origin of Pavier's intention to publish a collection of plays by Shakespeare? Andrew Murphy has plausibly argued that 'Pavier may have been motivated to embark on his collection ... because he had spotted a potential gap in the publishing market. Shakespeare had died in 1616 and none of his plays had appeared in print since 1615.'[172] In 1619, the most recently published Shakespeare plays were *Richard II* (Q5, 1615), *1 Henry IV* (Q6, 1613) and *Richard III* (Q5, 1612), the three plays then owned by Law. Clearly, Shakespeare's English history plays kept selling. Pavier, a shrewd businessman, therefore intended to open the collection with two of *his* history plays, *1 Contention* and *Richard Duke of York*, and included one of which he may have known that the attribution to Shakespeare was a bit of a stretch: *1 Sir John Oldcastle*.

---

[170] *Shakespeare and the Rise of the Editor*, 107–8. Massai's revisionary account grants Isaac Jaggard considerable agency at an early stage of his career, asking us to believe that young Isaac persuaded old Thomas Pavier to reduce the risks of his publishing venture, and this at a time when Pavier did not shy away from commercial risks, as suggested by the slightly later Folio *Works of Joseph Hall* (1625). What seems particularly unclear is why Pavier would have felt the need to reduce the publishing risks of his Shakespeare collection if Isaac had persuaded him that a larger and more ambitious collection was viable (see *Shakespeare and the Rise of the Editor*, 106–21). Nor am I sure that the help of the Earl of Pembroke would have been enlisted to prevent the publication of previously unpublished Shakespeare plays given that not a single new Shakespeare play had appeared in ten years. Nonetheless, Massai rightly reminds us that the exact genesis of the Pavier Quartos may still elude us.

[171] See Murphy, *Shakespeare in Print*, 38.

[172] *Shakespeare in Print*, 41. See also Johnson, 'Thomas Pavier', 36–7.

Another reason why a Shakespeare collection may have recommended itself as a gap in the market is the Jonson Folio of 1616: William Stansby was creating a market for single-authored collections containing professional plays, and Pavier may well have hoped to capitalize on it. Pavier's earlier interest in Shakespearean authorship has been documented, and the plays whose copyright he owned or secured in 1619 gave him enough material for a collection. Pavier had ceased to publish single playbooks in 1610, but a collection was clearly a different matter. In 1625, he published another, even more ambitious single-authored collection, *The Works of Joseph Hall*, in Folio.[173] The Shakespeare collection thus marks a distinct stage in Pavier's evolution as an increasingly ambitious publisher who started with ephemera in 1600 and ended with Folio *Works* a quarter-century later.[174]

Whereas we may safely assume that Pavier initiated the collection, it is less clear whether he bore its commercial risks alone or in partnership. The imprints of *The Whole Contention, Pericles, A Yorkshire Tragedy, Henry V* and *Sir John Oldcastle* all state that the plays were 'printed for T. P.', suggesting that Pavier functioned as their publisher.[175] *Merry Wives* was 'Printed for Arthur Johnson' and *King Lear* 'for Nathaniel Butter', and since Johnson and Butter were still active in 1619, they must have agreed to their plays' inclusion in the collection, either financing the printing of their play or granting Pavier permission to reissue it for 'a share of the copies of the new edition'.[176] As for *A Midsummer Night's Dream* and *The Merchant of Venice*, the original publishers, Thomas Fisher and Thomas Hayes, were dead by 1619, so that Pavier may have considered the rights derelict, meaning the copyright officially became 'the property of the Stationers' Company, though in practice it might be appropriated by any enterprising stationer'.[177] The imprints claim the editions were 'Printed by Iames [or 'J.'] Roberts' and misdate them '1600'.

---

[173] See Johnson, 'Thomas Pavier', 40–2.

[174] The evolution of Pavier's publishing career is also indicative of his success. As Johnson has commented, 'Pavier's career may be seen as a "success story" in the book-trade of the time' ('Thomas Pavier', 45). The earlier view of Pavier as a rogue publisher is now discredited (see Johnson, 'Thomas Pavier'; Massai, *Shakespeare and the Rise of the Editor*, chapter 4; and Murphy, *Shakespeare in Print*, 36–41).

[175] There is no record of how the rights in *Pericles* passed to Pavier, but its 1619 imprint and the publication of the following edition, in 1630, by Robert Bird, to whom Pavier's widow had transferred 'Master Paviers right in SHAKESPERES plaies or any of them' on 4 August 1626, indicates that they did. See Arber, *Transcript*, IV.165.

[176] For the two possibilities, see, respectively, Halliday, *A Shakespeare Companion 1564–1964*, 384–6, and Massai, *Shakespeare and the Rise of the Editor*, 225n29.

[177] Halliday, *A Shakespeare Companion 1564–1964*, 135. See also Johnson, 'Thomas Pavier', 38–9; and Murphy, *Shakespeare in Print*, 39. Thomas Hayes's son, Lawrence, may well have been prompted by the reprint of *The Merchant of Venice* to enter the play along with another title, which 'were the Copies of Thomas Haies his fathers' (Arber, *Transcript*, III.651).

At least one scholar speculates that William Jaggard functioned as publisher of these two plays, although there is no evidence that he did, and the collection as a whole is now rightly considered Pavier's.[178]

The contents of Pavier's collection may seem to us surprising, but what is in some ways even more surprising is what it does not contain: in 1602, Pavier had acquired Millington's share in the rights to *Titus Andronicus*, and although Pavier's name does not appear in the 1611 edition of that play (which was published by Edward White), Pavier clearly held on to these rights, as evidenced by the presence of *Titus* in a list of assignments of his copyrights in 1626.[179] *Titus* is an early and collaborative play and remained anonymous until 1623, so did Pavier not know that he could have included it in his Shakespeare collection? No less puzzling is the omission of *The London Prodigal*, which had been published in 1605 by Butter and attributed to 'William Shakespeare'. *King Lear*, owned by Butter, was included in the collection, so why is it that *The London Prodigal* was not? Since Pavier included in his Shakespeare collection two plays whose copyrights were owned by active fellow stationers (*Merry Wives* by Johnson and *King Lear* by Butter), it is quite possible that he also tried but failed to persuade other publishers to collaborate, notably Matthew Law (*Richard III, Richard II, 1 Henry IV*), William Aspley (*2 Henry IV, Much Ado*), John Smethwick (*Romeo and Juliet, Love's Labour's Lost, Hamlet*) and Richard Bonian and Henry Walley (*Troilus and Cressida*).

Given the uncertainties of its genesis and the oddity of its makeup, what we mostly remember today about the Pavier Quartos is their mixed credentials. Yet they should not blind us to the fact that Pavier was a pioneer. No one before him had published a collection consisting entirely of plays written for the commercial stage; no one before him had published a collection of plays by Shakespeare. He has rightly been called 'the main investor in Shakespeare the dramatist among London stationers in the 1610s'.[180]

Incidental Shakespeare publishers

An objective of the preceding pages has been to demonstrate that publishers did not wait until 1623 to show significant interest in Shakespeare's plays and poems. It is true that there is a publisher whose engagement with

---

[178] Halliday, *A Shakespeare Companion 1564–1964*, 385.   [179] See Arber, *Transcript*, IV.165.

[180] Massai, *Shakespeare and the Rise of the Editor*, 106. For corrections to dialogue and stage directions in several of the Pavier Quartos, which may reflect the care with which the texts were prepared for the press, see Massai, *Shakespeare and the Rise of the Editor*, pp. 128–30.

Shakespeare strikingly intensified with the publication of the First Folio, but he is an exception rather than the rule: John Smethwick. On 19 November 1607, he had registered sixteen titles, which, the entry specified, previously 'dyd belonge to Nicholas Lynge', including four plays: *Hamlet, Romeo and Juliet, Love's Labour's Lost* and *The Taming of a Shrew*.[181] In the next fifteen years, he published only two of these, *Romeo and Juliet* in 1609 (Q3) – still not assigned to Shakespeare on the title page – and *Hamlet* in 1611 (also Q3). It was only when he became a junior member of the syndicate publishing the First Folio that Smethwick started investing more heavily in Shakespeare. Probably in the expectation that the First Folio would lend Shakespeare considerable cachet, he published quarto editions of *Romeo and Juliet* (probably in 1623) and *Hamlet* (probably in 1625).[182] The title page of *Romeo and Juliet* appeared in two states, of which one assigns the play to Shakespeare, in contrast to all the earlier editions. In the 1630s, Smethwick not only contributed to the Second Folio but published separate editions of all the Shakespeare plays to which he owned the rights – *The Taming of the Shrew* and *Love's Labour's Lost* in 1631 and *Romeo and Juliet* and *Hamlet* in 1637 – all four plays being assigned to Shakespeare on the title page. No one else published as many Shakespeare playbooks in the 1630s. From 1623 to 1637, Smethwick thus repeatedly invested in Shakespeare, without, incidentally, publishing any playbooks by any other dramatist in the 1620s or the 1630s. Yet this must not blind us to the fact that prior to 1623, Smethwick's interest in Shakespeare had been no more than incidental.

Other publishers' involvement with Shakespeare, it seems important to add, was incidental. Although most publishers had a clearly discernible profile and focused on certain types of books more than on others, few never published outside their generic field of specialization. Henry Gosson, for instance, specialized in popular literature – 'ballads, broadsides, newsbooks, romances and jest books' – and published only one professional play in his entire career (1601–40), namely *Pericles* (Q1 and Q2, 1609).[183] Arthur Johnson, 'an extensive publisher and dealer in all kinds of literature', published only five plays in twenty years (1602–21): *The Merry Wives of Windsor* in 1602 and four more in 1607/8 (Middleton's *Phoenix* and *Michaelmas Term*, Edward Sharpham's *Cupid's Whirligig* and the anonymous *Merry Devil of Edmonton*), with four reprints appearing 1611–17.[184] Similarly, John Trundle published few plays

[181] The last play refers to the probably non-Shakespearean *The Taming of a Shrew* (first published in 1594), not Shakespeare's *The Taming of the Shrew*, which first reached print in 1623.
[182] For the dates of these editions, see Hailey, 'The Dating Game'.   [183] McKerrow, *Dictionary*, 115.
[184] McKerrow, *Dictionary*, 157.

beside Q1 *Hamlet* (five in twenty-three years) and specialized instead in sensational news and other ephemeral pamphlet literature.[185]

Even William Aspley, a junior partner in the syndicate that financed the first two Folio editions of Shakespeare's plays in 1623 and 1632, seems to have had no more than an intermittent interest in drama. He published books over more than forty years (1599–1640), but – apart from the Shakespeare Folio – there were only two brief periods during which he tried his luck on playbooks, with bad and good results respectively. None of the four plays he published in 1599–1600 (the anonymous *A Warning for Fair Women*, Dekker's *Old Fortunatus* and Shakespeare's *2 Henry IV* and *Much Ado about Nothing*) was reprinted in the next twenty years. Yet in the middle of the following decade, he struck gold twice by publishing Marston's *The Malcontent* (1604) and Chapman, Jonson and Marston's *Eastward Ho* (1605), which both went through three editions in the first year. Chapman's *Bussy D'Ambois* (1608) met with less success and remained without reprint during Aspley's lifetime, however, and Aspley seems to have soon lost interest in playbook publication and focused his output on religious texts.[186]

Other publishers repeatedly published playbooks, but the identity of the playwright probably mattered little to them. Besides specializing in ballads, Edward White came out with several early stage hits, including *The Spanish Tragedy* (1592), *Arden of Faversham* (1592 and 1599), *1* and *2 Tamburlaine* (1605/6) and *Titus Andronicus* (1594 (see above, pp. 139–40), 1600 and 1611), but published no Shakespeare other than that play. Thomas Walkley, to give another example, published *Othello* in 1622, but he may have done so more because he had a working relationship with the King's Men from 1619 to 1630 – during which period he published several of their plays, including ones by Beaumont, Fletcher and Massinger (*A King and No King*, *Philaster*, *Thierry and Theodoret* and *The Picture*) – than because of a specific interest in Shakespeare.[187] In other words, Shakespeare was by no means always the main reason why a publisher issued a play by Shakespeare.

Some stationers published so few titles that little can be said about the place of Shakespeare within their output. Thomas Hayes published only

---

[185] According to Johnson, Trundle 'devoted most of his twenty-three years in the trade to the publication of pamphlet literature meant to catch the eye of the lower-class reading public' ('John Trundle', 177). He has been described as 'enterprising and versatile in his pursuit of copy', which seems suggestive given the unknown provenance of the copy behind the 'bad' quarto of *Hamlet* (Johnson, 'John Trundle', 198).

[186] For Aspley, see Travers, 'Aspley, William (*b*. in or before 1573, *d*. 1640)'.

[187] For the argument that Walkley had a strategy of selling books on matters of state to Members of Parliament and followers of the court, see chapter 5 of Lesser's *Renaissance Drama and the Politics of Publication*.

two books besides *A Midsummer Night's Dream* (1600) – *Englands hope, against Irish hate* (1600, *STC* 7434.7), a poem about the Irish wars, and *The flowers of Lodowicke of Granado* (1601, *STC* 16901), a translation from the Latin by Thomas Lodge – plus he co-published *England's Parnassus* (1600, *STC* 378), a miscellany with extracts from contemporary poets, with Nicholas Ling and Cuthbert Burby. Richard Bonian and Henry Walley had short careers as publishers, 1607–12 and 1609–10 respectively, and Walley published exclusively in partnership with Bonian, mostly rather exclusive literary fare: Chapman's *Euthymiae raptus; or The teares of peace,* Jonson's *The Case Is Altered* and *The Masque of Queens,* Fletcher's *The Faithful Shepherdess* and Shakespeare's *Troilus and Cressida.*[188]

A little more can be gathered about Thomas Fisher, a draper who transferred from the Drapers' to the Stationers' Company in January 1600.[189] He published *A Midsummer Night's Dream* the same year and is responsible for three more books – Nicholas Breton's *Pasquils mistresse* (1600, *STC* 3678) and Marston's *Antonio and Mellida* and *Antonio's Revenge* (*STC* 17473/4), both published in 1602 – following which nothing more is heard of Fisher. Breton, like Shakespeare, was an author for whom there was vivid demand in 1600, with particularly intense interest in his Pasquil satires: besides *Pasquils mistresse, Melancholike Humours* (*STC* 3666), *Pasquils Mad-cap* (*STC* 3675), *Pasquils Fooles-cap* (*STC* 3677) and *Pasquils Passe, and Passeth Not* (*STC* 3679) all appeared in 1600, *Pasquils Mad-cap* and *Pasquils Fooles-cap* even going through two editions that year. With seven editions in 1600 alone, Breton was 'perhaps the most popular contemporary poet', and Shakespeare, with eight playbook editions that same year, was clearly the most popular dramatist.[190] Although he had no prior experience in the publishing business, Fisher must have assumed that with authors as popular, he could not go wrong.[191]

Conclusion

I have offered in this chapter the first examination of Shakespeare's early publishers as a group. Related to this chapter, Appendix C lists the forty-one stationers who published and/or owned rights in plays and poems by or

---

[188] See also Lesser, *Renaissance Drama and the Politics of Publication*, 1–4.

[189] For the fraught relationship between the drapers and the stationers in the late sixteenth and early seventeenth century, see Johnson, 'The Stationers versus the Drapers'.

[190] Bland, 'The London Book-Trade in 1600', 461.

[191] Whether Fisher's assumption was correct is another matter: *Pasquils mistresse* was not reprinted, and *A Midsummer Night's Dream* did not receive a second edition until 1619, when Fisher's copyright seems to have been considered derelict.

assigned to Shakespeare up to 1622. For at least two publishers, Thomas Millington and Andrew Wise, Shakespeare books constituted a large part of their output. Publishers like Nicholas Ling and Thomas Pavier made significant contributions to configuring Shakespeare as a literary dramatist, and John Harrison, William Leake, William Jaggard, John Busby and Nathaniel Butter considered and implemented commercial strategies to increase the saleability of their Shakespeare books. Several publishers (notably Wise and Matthew Law) earned considerable money by publishing Shakespeare. One publisher, Robert Raworth, risked his livelihood for a Shakespeare publication – and lost it, having his press seized and his publishing activity interrupted for the next thirty years. Several publishers considered Shakespeare's name an asset that justified extraordinary measures, such as issuing a nonce collection of playbooks (Pavier), or a 'Shakespeare' miscellany of which no more than the smallest fraction was by Shakespeare (Jaggard). They illustrate Adam Hooks's point that 'Shakespeare was a distinctly vendible commodity, and his value – the authorial status and artistic merit ascribed to him – was inextricably tied to his commercial viability'.[192] The view that, prior to 1623, Shakespeare was a *quantité négligeable* for publishers, issued in cheap, commercially insignificant pamphlets, and that it was not until the First Folio that his name acquired what publishers considered marketable prestige, is a myth.

This chapter has suggested that a sizeable group of publishers had significant investments in Shakespeare's poems and plays. The overall effect of these publishers' interest in Shakespeare was that he must have been perceived by anyone familiar with the English literature produced by the book trade as not solely a poet or solely a dramatist but both. Nonetheless, separate sections on the publishers of the poetry and the publishers of the plays have seemed appropriate: none of the notable publishers of Shakespeare's poetry, Harrison, Leake, Raworth, Jaggard and Thorpe, published a Shakespeare play before 1623, nor did any publisher of Shakespeare's plays publish any of his poems.[193] Blount may have come closest to publishing both: he included 'The Phoenix and the Turtle' in the 'Diuerse Poeticall Essaies' appended to Robert Chester's *Love's Martyr*, and he entered *Pericles* and *Antony and Cleopatra* in 1608. Yet Shakespeare's presence in *Love's Martyr* – in terms of both the texts it contains and the way it was advertised – is at best marginal; *Pericles* was published by Henry

---

[192] 'Book Trade', 127.
[193] By being among the publishers of the First Folio, Jaggard and Blount thus became the first to have published poems and plays by Shakespeare. See also de Grazia, *Shakespeare Verbatim*, 167.

Gosson in 1609; and *Antony and Cleopatra* was not published at all prior to the First Folio. The argument has been made that the reason why we have lost from sight Shakespeare's authorial profile as a 'poet-playwright' is the First Folio of 1623 which, unlike the Jonson Folio of 1616, excludes the poetry.[194] The evidence for this is compelling, but we may want to add that even prior to 1623, individual publishers invested in Shakespeare's drama or Shakespeare's poetry, but not in both.

If the publishers' interest in Shakespeare – in particular Shakespeare's plays – seems to us surprising, then this has much to do with scholarly views which became so entrenched in the twentieth century that we may now find it difficult to free ourselves from them. One is that which reduces Shakespeare to a 'man of the theatre',[195] whose early modern existence is firmly located at the playhouse, not at the printing house, only in Southwark, not in St Paul's Churchyard. Another is that which reduces early modern playbooks, including Shakespeare's playbooks, to cheap ephemeral pamphlets not worth keeping, allegedly marginal presences in the book trade (see pp. 186–93). A third fallacy is that which we encountered in Chapter 1, namely the view that Shakespeare simply was not very popular, that 'Jonson, and not Shakespeare, was the dramatist of the seventeenth century' and that 'Jonson's general popularity was greater than Shakespeare's from the beginning of the century to 1690.'[196] Jointly, these views not only suggested that publishers, before 1623, had little to gain from Shakespeare but also discouraged a close look at the evidence by keeping the scholarly focus elsewhere.

Given more recent scholarly insights, however, there is really nothing surprising about the interest of Shakespeare's early publishers in his books. Farmer and Lesser have presented a full case for the importance of printed playbooks in the book trade, arguing that they 'turned a profit more reliably than most other types of books, and this profit would not have been paltry, as many have claimed, but rather would have been fairly typical for an edition of books'.[197] Not only did playbooks thus sell rather well, but Shakespeare's playbooks, as I have shown in Chapter 1, sold particularly well, with considerably higher reprint rates than those of his fellow

[194] See Cheney, *Shakespeare, National Poet-Playwright*, 1–12. For the possible reasons why the poems were excluded from the Folio – the theatrical origins of those who initiated the publishing project, the difficulty in securing what might have been expensive copyrights or the textual quality of the available editions – see Burrow, ed., *Complete Songs and Sonnets*, 2; Cheney, *Shakespeare, National Poet-Playwright*, 67–9; and Duncan-Jones and Woudhuysen, eds., *Shakespeare's Poems*, 9.

[195] Wells, 'General Introduction', xxxix.　　[196] Bentley, *Shakespeare and Jonson*, 1.133, 139, 138.

[197] 'The Popularity of Playbooks Revisited', 6.

dramatists. Given that Shakespeare's plays clearly led a double life, success-ful in performance and in print, publishers had good reasons to expect to make a profit from them.

The number of publishers with a significant interest in Shakespeare before 1623 suggests that the success of Shakespeare in the book trade was a process in which many participated. In 2006, Gary Taylor delivered the McKenzie Lectures at the University of Oxford, entitled 'The Man Who Made Shakespeare: Edward Blount and the Shakespeare First Folio' (not yet pub-lished).[198] I disagree in two ways with the implications of this title: firstly, to the extent that the book trade 'made' Shakespeare, the making was the result of many publishers, not a single one; secondly, although Blount clearly made a significant investment in Shakespeare, it was not the First Folio but the earlier quarto (and, more rarely, octavo) editions which created Shakespeare's value in and for the book trade. I here concur with Farmer and Lesser: 'However much the Jonson and Shakespeare folios may have elevated the cultural value of drama, they seem to have had little or no effect on its economic value. Instead, what created value and finally established the market for printed drama was not these imposing folios but rather the more humble quarto reprints from the end of the 1590s.'[199] At least as far as the book trade is concerned, not Blount and the First Folio but the publishers studied in this chapter and their pre-1623 quartos and octavos 'made' Shakespeare.

Shakespeare himself did not live far from his publishers. From his lodgings in Bishopsgate in the second half of the 1590s, it may have taken him no more than fifteen minutes to walk to St Paul's Churchyard, where he surely browsed in the bookshops and perhaps met some of his publishers.[200] How many of them he personally knew we do not know, but we can safely assume that he was neither oblivious nor indifferent to the books they published.[201]

---

[198] For the argument that Isaac Jaggard and not Blount initiated the First Folio, see Massai, *Shakespeare and the Rise of the Editor*, 118–21.

[199] 'The Popularity of Playbooks Revisited', 13.

[200] Shakespeare 'was living in St Helen's parish, Bishopsgate, at some date before October 1596', and he stayed there until no later than 1599, when he had moved to Southwark, so 'Shakespeare crossed the river around the time that his company did' (Schoenbaum, *Compact Documentary Life*, 223). In Schoenbaum, *Documentary Life*, the corresponding passage reads: 'Shakespeare crossed the river when his company did' (164). Given the limitations of our knowledge, the vaguer formulation in the revised *Compact Documentary Life* seems preferrable.

[201] Disappointingly, we know nothing about the books Shakespeare bought and owned, although it has been speculated that a copy of Henry Estienne's *A mervaylous discourse vpon the lyfe … of Katherine de Medicis* (1575, STC 10550), which a seventeenth-century title page inscription shows to have been the gift of a 'Susanne Hall', had originally been Shakespeare's and was inherited by his daughter (Schoenbaum, *Documentary Life*, 249).

CHAPTER 5

The reception of printed Shakespeare

The early status of playbooks and survival rates

The last two chapters have focused on the bibliographic and paratextual constitution of Shakespeare's playbooks and on his publishers. This chapter is devoted to what happened to Shakespeare's books once they had been sold. Shakespeare's books were popular, but what impact did this popularity have on their early bibliographic reception? Were the quartos read to pieces, out of existence, the early modern equivalents of our modern comics? Was a Shakespeare quarto 'a self-destructing artefact', an object whose physical vulnerability and lack of social status meant that its popularity inevitably led to its disappearance?[1] For books, popularity can be a double-edged sword: repeated consumption of a fragile bibliographic object can lead to its disintegration, but interest in it might also engender a desire to preserve and to continue to engage with it.

The long dominant opinion, summed up by Fredson Bowers, is that there was little such desire. Playbooks, Bowers and others believed, were considered in Shakespeare's time 'ephemeral entertainment reading', to be consumed and discarded.[2] This opinion lives on among important scholars today: 'Shakespeare wrote in an environment in which plays, at least English plays, had not yet emerged as a literary genre; they were much like film scripts in the movie industry today.'[3] Yet dissenting voices have been trying to make themselves heard. One scholar, after examining early libraries with books by Shakespeare, has even come to the conclusion, 'against the grain of much modern criticism, that Shakespeare's poems and plays ought to be approached, if we are to respect history . . . as verbal and dramatic art, as – dare I think it? – English Literature'.[4] The chief aim of this chapter is to add

---

[1] Birrell, 'The Influence of Seventeenth-Century Publishers on the Presentation of English Literature', 166.
[2] 'The Publication of English Renaissance Plays', 414.   [3] Kastan, *Shakespeare and the Book*, 21.
[4] Nelson, 'Shakespeare and the Bibliophiles', 70.

to the evidence which suggests that from early on, many considered Shakespeare's books worth preserving and engaging with.

One reason why the enduring interest of early modern readers and collectors in Shakespeare's books was often belittled by scholars is that, for a long time, surprisingly little research was devoted to the subject. As John Jowett has recently pointed out, it is 'striking that, although Andrew Gurr ... has studied the social composition and attitudes of theatre audiences and assembled a list of all known London playgoers, there are no comparable accounts of the readers of early modern English writers'.[5] There is clearly a paradox here: the investment of the scholarly community in Shakespeare is huge, and our own engagement with Shakespeare – no matter how often we see his plays on stage or on screen – is always also, and for many predominantly, a readerly engagement. We have long left behind the heydays of the New Criticism, and historicism, in various guises, has been of central importance to Shakespeare scholarship. Yet despite our investment in historicism and in reading Shakespeare, 'little attention has been paid to how his works were *read* in early modern England'.[6]

Another reason why scholars long held that Shakespeare's playbooks were considered ephemeral publications in their own day is that most of the copies that were printed in the sixteenth and seventeenth centuries have not come down to us. Of at least one edition, the earliest edition of *Love's Labour's Lost*, not a single copy is extant. Of the earliest edition of *1 Henry IV* (1598) all we still have is a fragment of one copy, and two more editions, Q1 *Titus* (1594) and O1 *Richard Duke of York* (1595), survive in a single copy. Yet these editions are not representative. Table 6 lists the number of extant copies of Shakespeare playbooks from 1594 to 1660. It shows that a considerable number of copies of several editions dating from as early as the turn of the century are extant: twenty-two copies of Q1 *2 Henry IV* (1600), eighteen of Q1 *The Merchant of Venice* (1600), seventeen of Q1 *Much Ado about Nothing* (1600), and somewhere between ten and thirteen of Q2 *Love's Labour's Lost* (1598), Q3 *1 Henry IV* (1599), Q2 *Edward III* (1599) and Q2 *Romeo and Juliet* (1599). With editions dating from the second decade of the seventeenth century or later, it becomes the norm for a two-digit number of copies to have survived, and some editions – chiefly but not only the Pavier Quartos of 1619 – are extant in more than thirty copies. The average number of extant copies of playbooks published during Shakespeare's lifetime is 8.2, and if we extend the terminus ad quem to 1623, the year of the publication of the First Folio, the average even goes up to 11.9.

---

[5] 'Middleton's Early Readers', 286.
[6] Roberts, *Reading Shakespeare's Poems in Early Modern England*, 3.

Table 6 *Number of extant copies of Shakespeare playbooks, 1594–1660*

Title	Edition	Date	Number of copies
Titus Andronicus	QI	1594	I
1 Contention	QI	1594	3[a]
Richard Duke of York	QI	1595	I[b]
Edward III	QI	1596	7[c]
Love's Labour's Lost	QI	1597	0
Richard II	QI	1597	4
Richard III	QI	1597	5
Romeo and Juliet	QI	1597	5
1 Henry IV	QI	1598	I
1 Henry IV	Q2	1598	3
Love's Labour's Lost	Q2	1598	14[d]
Richard II	Q2	1598	8
Richard II	Q3	1598	3[e]
Richard III	Q2	1598	8
Edward III	Q2	1599	12[f]
1 Henry IV	Q3	1599	10
Romeo and Juliet	Q2	1599	13
1 Contention	Q2	1600	5[g]
2 Henry IV	QI [issue 1]	1600	II
	[issue 2]		10
	[issue 1 or 2]		I
	Total		22[h]
Henry V	QI	1600	6
The Merchant of Venice	QI	1600	18
A Midsummer Night's Dream	QI	1600	8
Much Ado about Nothing	QI	1600	17
Titus Andronicus	Q2	1600	2
Richard Duke of York	Q2	1600	9[i]
Henry V	Q2	1602	3
The Merry Wives of Windsor	QI	1602	6
Richard III	Q3	1602	4
Hamlet	QI	1603	2
1 Henry IV	Q4	1604	5[j]
Hamlet	Q2 [issue 1]	1604	3
	[issue 2]	1605	4[k]
	Total		7
Richard III	Q4	1605	7
1 Henry IV	Q5	1608	8
King Lear	QI	1608	12
Richard II	Q4 [issue 1]	1608	6
	[issue 2]		I
	[issue 1 or 2]		3
	Total		10

Table 6 (*cont.*)

Title	Edition	Date	Number of copies
Pericles	Q1	1609	11[l]
Pericles	Q2	1609	6[m]
Romeo and Juliet	Q3	1609	7
Troilus and Cressida	Q1 [issue 1]	1609	4
	[issue 2]		12
	Total		16
Hamlet	Q3	1611	19
Pericles	Q3	1611	4[n]
Titus Andronicus	Q3	1611	17[o]
Richard III	Q5	1612	12
1 Henry IV	Q6	1613	13
Richard II	Q5	1615	14
Henry V	Q3	1619	39
King Lear	Q2	1619	32
The Merchant of Venice	Q2	1619	31
The Merry Wives of Windsor	Q2	1619	35
A Midsummer Night's Dream	Q2	1619	30
Pericles	Q4	1619	39[p]
The Whole Contention	Q3	1619	39[q]
Othello	Q1	1622	19
1 Henry IV	Q7	1622	13
Richard III	Q6	1622	7
Romeo and Juliet	Q4 [issue 1]	n.d.	3
	[issue 2]	(1623?)	9[r]
	Total		12
Hamlet	Q4	n.d. (1625?)	20
Richard III	Q7	1629	17
The Merry Wives of Windsor	Q3	1630	11
Othello	Q2	1630	34
Pericles	Q5 [issue 1]	1630	7
	[issue 2]		11
	Total		18[s]
Love's Labour's Lost	Q3	1631	27
The Taming of the Shrew	Q1	1631	24
1 Henry IV	Q8	1632	13[t]
Richard II	Q6	1634	22
Richard III	Q8	1634	19
The Two Noble Kinsmen	Q1	1634	62[u]
Pericles	Q6	1635	19[v]
Hamlet	Q5	1637	31
The Merchant of Venice	Q3 [issue 1]	1637	20
	[issue 2]	1652	14
	[issue 1 or 2]	1637/52	2
	Total		36

Table 6 (*cont.*)

Title	Edition	Date	Number of copies
Romeo and Juliet	Q5	1637	28
1 Henry IV	Q9	1639	27
King Lear	Q3	1655	17[w]
Othello	Q3	1655	25

Notes:

Unless otherwise noted, the figures in this table correspond to those in Bartlett and Pollard, *A Census of Shakespeare's Plays in Quarto*. They have been checked against the *ESTC* and other sources such as scholarly articles or textual introductions of recent scholarly editions (which, however, do not systematically mention the number of extant copies of the first edition and even less that of subsequent editions). The list of copies in Greg, *Bibliography*, is not complete and, as Greg pointed out, was 'not intended to be complete' (1.xviii). If the *ESTC* records copies not mentioned in Bartlett and Pollard's *Census*, I add them to the total and note this fact in a footnote. Bartlett and Pollard did not include *1 Contention, Richard Duke of York, Pericles, Edward III* and *The Two Noble Kinsmen* in their *Census*, so the figures for these plays have been obtained from other sources, as indicated in footnotes. The figures in the table, especially for the later editions, are unlikely to be wholly accurate: Bartlett and Pollard's *Census* is more than seventy years old, and the *ESTC* does not systematically record all copies, not even of early Shakespeare quartos. Nor should we underestimate the number of unrecorded copies that may still be hidden away in country houses or elsewhere, unknown to the Shakespearean community – and perhaps to the owners, too. A new census of early Shakespeare quartos is a scholarly desideratum, made more evident by the publication of Rasmussen and West's excellent descriptive catalogue of all extant First Folio copies (*The Shakespeare First Folios*). That, however, would be a separate project, and not one which I undertake as part of this chapter.

[a] Q1 *1 Contention* is extant in 'two complete copies: one in the Bodleian Library, Oxford; the other at the Folger. A fragment of a third copy, A–C4, is in the Elham Church Deposit at Canterbury Cathedral' (Montgomery, ed., *The First Part of the Contention 1594*, v).
[b] See *ESTC*.
[c] See Lapides, ed., *The Raigne of King Edward the Third*, 66. The *ESTC* also lists seven copies.
[d] See Werstine, 'The Hickmott–Dartmouth Copy of *Love's Labour's Lost* Q1 (1598)'. Bartlett and Pollard, *Census*, mention twelve copies, as does the *ESTC*.
[e] See *ESTC*. Bartlett and Pollard, *Census*, are aware of two copies.
[f] The *ESTC* lists twelve copies, whereas Fred Lapides mentions ten (*The Raigne of King Edward the Third*, 72–3).
[g] 'Five copies of Q2 have been traced ... Location of copies of Q2 ... are listed in William Montgomery, *The Contention of York and Lancaster: A Critical Edition*, 2 vols., unpublished D. Phil. thesis, Oxford, 1985, vol. 2, pp. xxxii, xxxiii' (Montgomery, ed., *The First Part of the Contention 1594*, v, note 2). The *ESTC* lists the same five copies.
[h] See Berger and Williams, 'Variants in the Quarto of Shakespeare's *2 Henry IV*'. Note that the Bodmer copy (which I count among the first issue) inserts sheet E of the second issue into a copy that is otherwise of the first issue. Berger and Williams mention the Lambeth Palace Library copy, which is not listed in Bartlett and Pollard. This copy had long been reported as lost (see Jowett and Taylor, 'The Three Texts of *2 Henry IV*', 33) but was finally recovered in 2011.
[i] See *ESTC*.

Notes for table 6 (cont.)

[j] See *ESTC*. Bartlett and Pollard, *Census*, mention four copies.

[k] See *ESTC*. Bartlett and Pollard, *Census*, are aware of only three copies of the second issue.

[l] See *ESTC*. Hoeniger, ed., *Pericles*, was aware of nine copies (xxxvii).

[m] See *ESTC*.

[n] See *ESTC*.

[o] See Metz, 'How Many Copies of *Titus Andronicus* Q3 are Extant?'. Bartlett and Pollard, *Census*, list sixteen copies.

[p] See *ESTC*.

[q] The *ESTC* lists thirty-nine copies, whereas Montgomery mentions thirty-five. 'Location of copies of . . . Q3 are listed in William Montgomery, *The Contention of York and Lancaster: A Critical Edition*, 2 vols., unpublished D. Phil. thesis, Oxford, 1985, 2: xxxii, xxxiii' (Montgomery, ed., *The First Part of the Contention 1594*, v, note 2).

[r] See *ESTC*. Bartlett and Pollard, *Census*, list eight copies of the second issue.

[s] See *ESTC*.

[t] See *ESTC*. Bartlett and Pollard, *Census*, list twelve copies.

[u] See Proudfoot and Rasmussen, eds., *The Two Noble Kinsmen*, v–vii.

[v] See Lee, ed., '*Pericles*', 35. The *ESTC* mentions sixteen copies. For all other early editions of *Pericles*, Lee mentions fewer copies than are recorded in the *ESTC*.

[w] See *ESTC*. Bartlett and Pollard, *Census*, mention sixteen copies.

Editions of which very few copies have survived were typically published early in Shakespeare's career or received a subsequent edition shortly after. In the 1590s and the 1600s, eight playbooks were followed by subsequent editions of the same play in the same year or the year after: Q1 and Q2 *Richard II*, Q1 *Richard III*, Q1 *Love's Labour's Lost*, Q1 and Q2 *1 Henry IV*, Q1 *Hamlet* and Q1 *Pericles*. Of these, only Q1 *Pericles* survives in more than eight copies, and the average number of extant copies is 4.25. In the same two decades, eleven editions appeared which did not receive a quarto reprint in the next fifteen years: Q2 *Love's Labour's Lost*, Q2 *Edward III*, Q2 *1 Contention*, Q2 *Richard Duke of York*, Q1 *2 Henry IV*, Q2 *Henry V*, Q1 *Merchant*, Q1 *Dream*, Q1 *Much Ado*, Q1 *Merry Wives* and Q1 *Troilus*. Of these, the average number of extant copies is 11.6, or almost three times as many. The exact reason for this difference is not clear. Editions which sold out quickly suggest the play was popular so that many copies may have been read to pieces. Alternatively, some editions may have taken long to sell out because a great number of copies had been printed, and so the large number of extant copies may at least partly reflect the large number of originally produced copies. Having seen *Richard II*, *Richard III* and *1 Henry IV* go through two or three editions each in 1597–9, Andrew Wise, when publishing *2 Henry IV* and *Much Ado about Nothing* with William Aspley in 1600, had good reasons to believe that his two most recent plays would sell well too, and so may have ordered a large edition. Significantly, more copies are extant of *2 Henry IV* and *Much Ado* than of any of the seventeen Shakespeare playbook editions published from 1594 to 1599.

Table 6 suggests that Shakespeare's early playbooks are now rare but that by no means all editions are very rare. Of those published during his lifetime, some 370 copies are still known to exist today. Much time went by until Shakespeare's books became genuine collector's items in the eighteenth and then even more so in the nineteenth century, securing their subsequent preservation. The many copies from Shakespeare's lifetime have survived despite the fact that early editions were often discarded when later ones became available, as famously happened to the First Folio at the Bodleian after the Third Folio had been acquired.[7] The significant number of surviving copies does not suggest that Shakespeare's playbooks were considered discardable ephemera in his own time.[8]

The survival rate of genuinely ephemeral print material, which included ballads, chapbooks, primers, almanacs, ABCs and books of popular piety, is considerably lower. In the period from 1660 to 1700, approximately 14,000 psalters were printed annually, so hundreds of thousands over the forty-year period, yet only four copies are known to have survived. As for primers, 'in 1676/7, 84,000 passed through the Treasurer's hands' of which only 'a single 16mo black-letter copy in the British Library, dated *c.* 1670' is known to exist today.[9] Thomas Deloney's prose narrative *Jack of Newbery* was entered in the Stationers' Register on 7 March 1597, and the earliest extant edition, of 1619, claims to be the eighth on the title page. John Pennyman compiled a list of sixty-seven titles he published from 1670 to 1680, yet of only twenty-eight of these is at least one copy still extant.[10] Of Thomas Dyche's *Guide to the English Tongue*, thirty-three editions appeared

---

[7] The story of the loss and recovery of the Bodleian First Folio copy is told in Smith, 'Why a First Folio Shakespeare Remained in England'.

[8] There are a number of databases which make digitally available early Shakespeare quarto playbooks. For instance, the British Library's 'Shakespeare in Quarto' website provides access to '107 copies of the 21 plays by Shakespeare printed in quarto before the 1642 theatre closures' ('Shakespeare in Quarto'); 'The Shakespeare Quartos Archive' puts online 'cover-to-cover digital reproductions and transcriptions of thirty-two copies of the five earliest editions of the play *Hamlet*' ('The Shakespeare Quartos Archive'); and 'The Folger Digital Image Collection' contains 'digitized copies of 218 of the Folger Shakespeare Library's pre-1640 Shakespeare texts, including poems, plays, and "apocryphal" editions now known to have been written by someone else' ('Folger Digital Image Collection').

[9] Barnard, 'The Survival and Loss Rates of Psalms, ABCs, Psalters, and Primers from the Stationers' Stock, 1660–1700', 149.

[10] See McKenzie, 'Printing and Publishing 1557–1700', 558.

between 1733 and 1749, a total of some 275,000 copies, of which only five are known to be extant.[11]

Nor does the number of surviving copies of other, roughly contemporary publications suggest that Shakespeare's playbooks were considered particularly discardable. *The Faerie Queene* (1590, 1596) established Edmund Spenser as England's national poet, yet of his *Amoretti and Epithalamion* (1595), only eleven copies have survived.[12] Sir Philip Sidney was considered the paragon of his age, and his *Astrophel and Stella* paved the way for the contemporary sonnet craze, yet of the first edition (1591) of his sonnet sequence, only three copies are now known to be extant.[13] Of Emilia Lanyer's volume of poems, *Salve Deus Rex Judaeorum*, published in 1611, nine copies are now known to exist.[14] A great number of copies of Milton's *Paradise Lost* and his shorter epics have survived, yet of his *Poems*, the third edition (1695), for instance, survives in no more than sixteen copies.[15] Of the first two editions, both of 1597, of Francis Bacon's *Essays*, which hardly qualify as ephemera, only nine and three copies respectively have been preserved.[16] In fact, many books which no one would accuse of having constituted 'ephemeral entertainment reading' survive in about the same number of copies as Shakespeare's playbooks.

A full investigation of early owners and readers of Shakespeare would fill far more than a chapter, so my aim here is more modest, namely to survey the evidence in response to the following questions: What do we know about early owners and collectors of Shakespeare's playbooks? What kind of evidence do we have in Shakespeare's early playbooks of readerly engagement with them? How were Shakespeare's playbooks processed, bibliographically and textually, to turn them into something new: bibliographically new by binding them along with other books; textually new by excerpting passages for the purpose of commonplacing? What do the answers to these questions tell us about the status of Shakespeare's books in the early modern period? My focus remains on the quartos. The reception history of the First Folio has been recently told in exhaustive detail elsewhere, and there is no need to return to it here.[17]

---

[11] See McKenzie, 'Printing and Publishing 1557–1700', 560 (for more about the enormous loss rates of certain publications, see 557–60). See also Blayney, *The Texts of King Lear and their Origins*, 38–9; Bland, 'The London Book-Trade in 1600', 458; and Bennett, *English Books and Readers, 1558–1603*, 300.

[12] See Larsen, ed., *Edmund Spenser's Amoretti and Epithalamion*, 255.

[13] Ringler was aware of only two copies (*The Poems of Sir Philip Sidney*, 542); the *ESTC* now adds a third. It is unknown how many copies of this edition had already been sold when it was suppressed in September 1591.

[14] See Woods, *Lanyer*, viii.   [15] See Parker, *Milton*, 1208.

[16] See Kiernan, ed., *The Essayes or Counsels, Civill and Morall*, lxv, lxviii–lxix.

[17] See West, *The Shakespeare First Folio: Volume I*, and *Volume II*; and Rasmussen and West, *The Shakespeare First Folios*.

Early owners and collectors of Shakespeare's quarto playbooks

If one person is chiefly responsible for the modern belief that Shakespeare's playbooks were considered disreputable ephemera, it is Sir Thomas Bodley, founder of the Bodleian Library in Oxford. In a letter of 15 January 1612 addressed to Thomas James, First Keeper of the Library, Bodley explains his decision to exclude certain types of books, including playbooks:

> I can see no good reason to alter my opinion, for excluding suche bookes, as almanackes, plaies, & an infinit number, that are daily printed, of very unworthy maters & handling . . . Happely some plaies may be worthy the keeping: but hardly one in fortie . . . Were it so againe, that some litle profit might be reaped (which God knows is very litle) out of some of our playbookes, the benefit therof will nothing neere conteruaile, the harme that the scandal will bring vnto the Librarie, when it shalbe giuen out, that we stuffe it full of baggage bookes.[18]

Bodley's restrictive admissions policy did not prevail for long. Within a few years of his death in 1613, the Bodleian Library had added the first playbooks to its collection.[19] And when a large number of playbooks were bequeathed to John Rous, who had become Bodley's Librarian in 1620, he gladly accepted them (see below, p. 210). Nonetheless, Bodley's exclusion of playbooks from his library is still read as representative of the low status they allegedly enjoyed. 'Plays were not "works",' Marjorie Garber writes: 'Plays were more like potboilers or comics. Thomas Bodley . . . called them "riff-raff" and "baggage books," and ordained that no plays be shelved in his grand new space.'[20] 'Printed plays were generally considered ephemera' – David Scott Kastan writes – 'among the "riffe-raffes" and "baggage books" that Thomas Bodley . . . would not allow in his library lest some "scandal" attach to it by their presence.'[21] The introduction to the Arden Shakespeare *Complete Works* informs us that 'plays remained sub-literary, the piece-work of an emerging entertainment industry. "Riff-raffe", Thomas Bodley called them in 1612, and ordered his librarian not to collect such "idle books".'[22] Having referred to Pierre Bourdieu's concept of

---

[18] Wheeler, ed., *Letters of Sir Thomas Bodley to Thomas James, First Keeper of the Bodleian Library*, 221–2. Note that Bodley's scepticism about the suitability of certain books also manifested itself elsewhere: he was 'at first inclined to regard books of octavo size as generally unsuitable . . . for the shelves of a library'; at another point, he showed himself unsure about the fitness of some 'lesser bookes' on religious topics, which ended up being rejected by the library (Wheeler, ed., *Letters of Sir Thomas Bodley to Thomas James*, xvi, 3).

[19] See Hackel, '"Rowme" of its Own', 119–20.   [20] *Shakespeare after All*, 12.

[21] *Shakespeare and the Book*, 22.

[22] Proudfoot, Thompson and Kastan, eds., *The Arden Shakespeare*, 7.

'cultural capital', Stephen Greenblatt writes that 'Early seventeenth-century plays in the vernacular by modern playwrights had no such capital. In 1612 Thomas Bodley instructed the first keeper of his library in Oxford to exclude from the shelves "such books as almanacs, plays, and an infinite number, that are daily printed, of very unworthy matters." "Baggage books," he called them.'[23] Bodley's exclusion of the kind of books librarians and collectors came to value most in later centuries, and the alliterative expressions he used to qualify playbooks – 'riffe-raffe', 'baggage books' – are so memorable that they prove irresistible for modern scholars, who make them central to their account of the early status of playbooks.[24]

Research on the early status of the First Folio reinforces this scholarly tendency. Anthony James West quotes the famous passage from Bodley and goes on to write: 'I have found only one early reference to the First Folio in library catalogues or donors' books or inventories.'[25] West's research provides further ammunition to those who believe that Bodley's attitude reflects that of his contemporaries: Greenblatt continues: 'Bodley was evidently not alone: though an estimated 750 copies were printed and the edition sold out in less than a decade, an exhaustive census has turned up only a single early reference to the First Folio in any library catalogue or donors' inventory.'[26]

If Bodley is considered representative, and if even the grand First Folio is almost entirely absent from early catalogues and inventories, then we are certainly tempted to infer that the prospect for Shakespeare's slighter quartos to have entered libraries and their catalogues, or to have left other traces of early interest in their preservation, is bleak. Yet the documentary record of early ownership and collecting of Shakespeare's quarto playbooks is less blank than we might assume.

For instance, the books owned by the poet and pamphleteer Sir William Drummond of Hawthornden (1585–1649) tell a very different story from Bodley's. Drummond is known to have assembled a sizeable library of about 1,300 books. From 1606 to 1614, he composed lists of 'Bookes red be me' which show that he was not only a diligent collector but also an avid reader.

---

[23] *Shakespeare's Freedom*, 98.

[24] Note that in the sixteenth and seventeenth centuries, 'baggage' could have the meaning of 'rubbish' (see *OED*, 'baggage', n.4). It is possible that Bodley's 'baggage books' was also prompted by the Italian 'libri da bisaccia' (see Petrucci, 'Alle origini del libro moderno'). Given that Bodley may well have been considering the primary needs of university readers, whose academic curriculum included no vernacular literature, there is of course no reason to expect his opinion to be normative for his time. For thoughtful responses to the famous Bodley quotation, see Murphy, *Shakespeare in Print*, 31; and Lesser, 'Playbooks', 529.

[25] *The Shakespeare First Folio: Volume 1*, 3.   [26] *Shakespeare's Freedom*, 98–9.

Among the forty-two titles on the 1606 list, Drummond mentions eight plays, including 'Romeo and Iulieta Tragedie', 'loues labors lost comedie', 'A midsommers nights Dreame comedie' and 'The Tragedie of Locrine'. In the same year, he also read 'The rape of lucrece' (which must be Shakespeare's poem, given that Heywood's play of the same title was not published until 1608), 'The passionat pilgrime' and 'loues martir' (with Shakespeare's 'The Phoenix and the Turtle').[27] Drummond repeatedly focused on one writer in a specific year. In 1609, he read a lot of Ronsard, and in 1611 a lot of Tasso.[28] Clearly 1606 was his Shakespeare year. In 1611 Drummond drew up a catalogue of the books he owned by language, a 'Table of my Italian bookes' (61 titles), a 'Table of my Spanish bookes' (8 titles) and the same for French (120), English (50), Greek (35), Hebrew (11) and Latin (109). The list of his English books includes 'Venus and Adon. by Schaksp.', on the next line 'The Rape of Lucrece, idem.' and, further down, 'The Tragedie of Romeo and Julieta' and 'A Midsumers Night Dreame'.[29]

In 1626/7, Drummond donated more than 360 books and manuscripts to the University of Edinburgh, of which a catalogue was printed in 1627: *Auctarium bibliothecae Edinburgenae, sive Catalogus librorum quos Guilielmus Drummondus ab Hawthornden bibliothecae* (*STC* 7246).[30] The books are listed alphabetically, by author, including 'William Shakespeare / Loues Labours lost, Comedie, Lond. 1598.' (sig. F1v) (Figure 5.1). The other Shakespeare book Drummond donated, 'Romeo / And Iuliete Tragedie, Lond. 1599.' (sig. E4v), appears under 'R', no doubt because the second quarto of *Romeo and Juliet* had been published anonymously.[31] Whereas Bodley refused to include quarto playbooks in his library, Edinburgh University Library gladly accepted them and even mentioned Shakespeare and his playbooks in a printed catalogue, probably Shakespeare's earliest appearance in a printed catalogue published in Britain.[32] Yet while Shakespeare scholars regularly repeat Bodley's exclusion of plays from his library, they seem entirely unaware of the Edinburgh catalogue testifying to the presence of Shakespeare's quarto playbooks in another university library.

---

[27] MacDonald, *The Library of Drummond of Hawthornden*, 228–9.
[28] See MacDonald, *The Library of Drummond of Hawthornden*, 229–30.
[29] Laing, ed., *Extracts from the Hawthornden Manuscripts*, 21.
[30] See Spiller, 'Drummond, William, of Hawthornden (1585–1649)'. Note that the 1627 catalogue was reprinted in the early nineteenth century (Laing, ed., *Auctarium*).
[31] Another Shakespeare playbook Drummond seems to have donated to the University of Edinburgh Library – although it does not appear in the 1627 catalogue – is the second quarto of *Titus Andronicus* (1600). See Bartlett and Pollard, *Census*, §1189.
[32] In Oxford, the First Folio was 'entered in the 1635 printed appendix to the library catalogue' (Smith, 'Why a First Folio Shakespeare Remained in England', 257).

34   Avctarivm Biblioth.

Ioannes Secundus

Opera. Trajecti *Batavorum*, 1541.

Ioannes Selden

Analecton Anglo-Britannicon libri duo, *Francofurti*, 1614.

Sendebar Indiano Philofopho.

Trattati diverfi, in *Vinegia*, 1552.

William Shakefpeare

Loues Labours loft , Comedie, *Lond.* 1598.

Theod. Shervelius

Alexicacon, five de Patientia libri, *Lugd. Bat.* 1623.

Alexander Siluayn

The Orator : *London* 1596.

Marcus Simon Hatherflebienfis

Parentalia Fraederici Secundi *Daniæ* Regis, 1589.   *Captaine Ihon Smith*

A Map of *Virginia*, *Oxford*, 1612.

A Defcription of New-*England*, *Lond.* 1616.

Somnium.

Scipionis Chriftiani.

Ioannes Spangerburgus.

Pfalterium Univerfum Elegiaco Carmine explicatum.

Sr. *Henrye Spelman Knight,*

De non temerandis Ecclefiis, *Edinb.* 1616.

Edmund Spenfer

Amoretti and Epithalamion, *Lond.* 1595.

Achilles Statius Alexandrinus

De Clitophontis & Leucippes amoribus libri 8. *Cantabrigiæ.*

Henricus Stephanus

Epiftola, quâ ad multas amicorum refpondet, Index librorum qui ex officina ejus prodierunt, 1569.

Ro-

5.1 Catalogue of books donated by Sir William Drummond of Hawthornden to the University of Edinburgh: *Auctarium bibliothecae Edinburgenae, sive Catalogus librorum quos Guilielmus Drummondus ab Hawthornden bibliothecae* (Edinburgh, 1627, *STC* 7246), sig. F1V, mentioning '*William Shakespeare* / Loues Labours lost, Comedie, *Lond.* 1598.'

Like Drummond, Sir John Harington (*bap.* 1560–1612) not only read but also collected and recorded Shakespeare playbooks as early as the dramatist's lifetime. Towards the end of his life, probably in 1610, he drew up two lists, now in the British Library, of playbooks in his possession, which seems to have 'formed part of a more extensive catalogue of his library'.[33] The first list consists of forty plays, arranged in no discernible order, whereas the second incorporates 130 plays (including two duplicates, so 128 different plays), divided into eleven volumes of nine to thirteen plays each. Of the forty plays in the first list, thirty-three reappear in the second list, meaning Harington owned at least 135 different plays. Among these are, in volume I, 'The Marchant of Venice', 'The London prodigall', 'Henry the fourth. I', 'Henry the fourth : 2', 'Richard ye 3d:. tragedie', 'Locryne' and 'Hamlet'; in volume II, 'Lord Cromwell'; in volume III, 'Romeo and Iulyet'; in volume IV, 'Moch adoe about nothing', 'Loves labor lost', 'Midsomer night dream' and 'Richard the 2'; in volume VII, 'Henry the fift. Pistol' and 'York and Lanc. j. part'; in volume VIII, 'Merry wyves winsor. w.s.', 'King Leyr. W. Sh.', 'Ed the third' and 'Yorksh. Traged. w.s.'; in volume IX, 'Pericles'; and in volume XII, 'Puritan wyddow. w.S.'. Harington thus owned twenty-one of the twenty-four playbooks by or attributed to Shakespeare (or to 'W. S.' or 'W. Sh.') which had been published before 1610 – the three exceptions being *Titus Andronicus*, *Richard Duke of York* and *Troilus and Cressida* – making Shakespeare by far the best represented playwright in the collection. The second list contains seventeen notes of authorship (often no more than initials), including one to each of Jonson, Fletcher and Heywood, two to Marston, three to Dekker and four to Shakespeare. Interestingly, *Merry Wives* and *A Yorkshire Tragedy*, which had been published with Shakespeare's full name on the title page, have Shakespeare's initials as their authorship note; *The Puritan*, which had been assigned to 'W. S.', did too. As far as we can tell, Harington had no reason to doubt *A Yorkshire Tragedy*'s title page attribution to Shakespeare and believed that 'W. S.' on the title page of *The Puritan* referred to Shakespeare.

Even earlier than Drummond and Harington, in fact as early as 14 February '1595' (which may be 1595 or 1596 depending on whether Old Style or New Style dating was used), a Cambridge physician, whose name has not come down to us, recorded in his library catalogue the acquisition of several new titles, including two playbooks, Shakespeare's *Richard Duke of*

---

[33] Greg, *Bibliography*, III.1306–13 (I quote from page 1306); BL Add. MS 27632, fol. 43. See also Furnivall, 'Sir John Harington's Shakespeare Quartos'; and Scott-Warren, 'Harington, Sir John (*bap.* 1560, *d.* 1612)', and *Sir John Harington and the Book as Gift*.

York and Marlowe's *Edward II*.[34] And some years after Drummond and Harington, in 1632, Scipio Le Squyer (1579–1659), Deputy Chamberlain of the Exchequer, drew up a catalogue of his 487 printed books and 296 manuscripts, sorting them according to subject headings like 'Divinity', 'History' and 'Law'. Among the eighty titles listed under 'Poesy' are *Venus and Adonis* and *Romeo and Juliet*.[35]

Henry Oxinden (1609–70), a Kentish country squire, compiled a catalogue with 122 playbooks in his library, of which 91 are mentioned with publication date.[36] The list includes 'Titus & Andronicus', 'Hamlet Prince of Denmark 1603', 'Yorkshire Tragedy 1608', 'Richard the second by Shakespeare 1615', '2d part of Heny [*sic*] the 4th 1600', 'Chronicle history of Hen. 5. 1600', 'Troylus & Cresseid. 1609', 'Romeo & Iuliet' and 'Reign of K Ed. 3'.[37] Oxinden was born in 1609, and the catalogue he compiled dates from 1647, yet three-quarters of the dated playbooks are from between 1591 and 1615, so 'clearly', as Greg pointed out, 'the main collector was not Henry Oxinden himself, who must have inherited or otherwise acquired the collection', although the name of the original owner is now unknown.[38]

Other early collectors of playbooks, including of Shakespeare's, are Humphrey Dyson (*c.* 1582–1633) and George Buc (1560–1622). Dyson, who 'started his library well before 1610', owned several hundred books, including at least sixteen plays, whose publication dates range from 1533 (John Heywood's *Pardoner and the Friar*) to 1613 (Beaumont's *Knight of the Burning Pestle*) and which include Chapman's *Gentleman Usher* (1606), Lyly's *Endymion* (1591) and Shakespeare's *Troilus and Cressida* (1609, first issue).[39]

As for Buc, he served as Master of the Revels from 1610 to 1622, although the reversion of the mastership had been granted to him as early as 1603 by

---

[34] The physician paid 8d. for *Richard Duke of York* and 6d. for *Edward II*. See Bodleian Library MS Rawlinson D 213, cited in Johnson, 'Notes on English Retail Book-Prices, 1550–1640', 91. Concerning extant records of early modern book prices, see Johnson, 'Notes on English Retail Book-Prices, 1550–1640', and McKitterick, '"Ovid with a Littleton"'.

[35] See Birrell, 'Reading as Pastime', 119–20; Nelson, 'Shakespeare and the Bibliophiles', 62–4; and Taylor, 'The Books and Manuscripts of Scipio le Squyer, Deputy Chamberlain of the Exchequer, 1620–1659', 157–8.

[36] Greg, *Bibliography*, III.1313. Oxinden's playlist is now at the Folger. For a short biography of Oxinden, see Hingley, 'Oxinden, Henry (1609–1670)'.

[37] Greg, *Bibliography*, III.1315–16.

[38] Greg, *Bibliography*, III.1314. See also Hingley, 'Elham Parish Library'; and Dawson, 'An Early List of Elizabethan Plays'.

[39] Nelson, 'Shakespeare and the Bibliophiles', 64–9. No full catalogue of Dyson's library is known, but his notebooks (now at All Souls College, Oxford, MS 117) from about 1630 contain a 'Catalogue of all such Bookes touching aswell the State Ecclesiasticall as Temporall of the Realme of England which were published vpon seuerall occasions'. This catalogue does not list playbooks. See also Steele, 'Humphrey Dyson'; and Jackson, *Records of a Bibliographer*, 135–41.

King James and perhaps even earlier by Queen Elizabeth.[40] Nelson has identified no fewer than twenty playbooks which are certain or likely to have belonged to Buc's collection. None of them dates from later than 1605, which 'may suggest that Buc had formed his collection prior to his tenure as Master of the Revels'.[41] Buc marked many of his playbooks with an 'E' on the title page, including a copy, now at the British Library, of Q1 *2 Henry IV* (1600), on which the inscription is now barely visible.[42] A copy of Q1 *Henry V* (1600), now at the Huntington Library, may also have belonged to the collection.[43] Buc's manuscript notations on the title pages repeatedly show an interest in the authorship of anonymously published plays. *Edward I*, for example, is 'By George Peele', and *Alphonsus, King of Aragon* was 'Made by R. Green'. Most interestingly, on the title page of the 1599 quarto of *George a Greene, the Pinner of Wakefield*, Buc noted: 'Written by . . . . a minister, who ac[ted] the pin[n]ers part in it himself. Teste W. Shakespea[re]' (Figure 5.2).[44] Buc, in other words, knew Shakespeare personally and consulted him on the question of the authorship of *George a Greene* (which had been performed in 1593 and 1594). As Nelson has written, 'Although Shakespeare recalled important details concerning the playwright, either he (during the presumed interview) or Buc (subsequently) failed to recall his name.'[45] What Buc thus offers is a collection of playbooks – undertaken as early as the turn of the century and probably completed by 1605 – which not only appears to have included playbooks by Shakespeare but to which Shakespeare himself contributed by providing 'a detailed response to a bibliographic query', leaving a trace on the title page of one of the playbooks in the collection.[46]

Sir Edward Dering (1598–1644), a courtier and antiquary, acquired a great number of playbooks – at least 221 of them and possibly as many as 240 – in the period from 1619 to 1624. During the same years, he recorded twenty-eight payments to see plays (mostly in London), which means his taste for plays demonstrably straddled the stage and the page.[47] Dering acquired playbooks in bulk, usually between twenty and thirty at a time,

---

40 For Buc, see Kincaid, 'Buck, Sir George (*bap.* 1560, *d.* 1622)', and Dutton, *Mastering the Revels*, 194–217.
41 'George Buc', 80.   42 See Nelson, 'Play Quartos Inscribed by Buc'.
43 See Bartlett and Pollard, *Census*, §349.
44 For the question of the authenticity of the *George a Greene* title page inscription, see Nelson, 'George Buc'.
45 'George Buc', 80. Note that Buc also tried to correct the misattribution of *Locrine* to 'W. S.' by writing on the title page that 'Charles Tilney wrot[e a] Tragedy of this mattr [which] hee named Estrild [which] I think is this' (Nelson, 'Play Quartos Inscribed by Buc').
46 Nelson, 'George Buc', 83.
47 Lennam, 'Sir Edward Dering's Collection of Playbooks, 1619–1624', 147. See also Krivatsy and Yeandle, 'Sir Edward Dering', 141; and Salt, 'Dering, Sir Edward, first baronet (1598–1644)'.

5.2 Title page of the Folger copy (STC 12212) of *George a Greene, the Pinner of Wakefield* (Q, 1599), with George Buc's manuscript notation: 'Written by . . . . a minister, who ac[ted] the pin[n]ers part in it himself. Teste W. Shakespea[re]'.

and had them bound into volumes, of which he had fourteen by spring
1624.[48] How many Shakespeare playbooks he acquired is unclear, but we
know that among them were the two parts of *Henry IV*, of which he produced
a shorter version for private performance. On 27 February 1622/3, he records
a payment of 4s. for the copying of *Henry IV*, probably the manuscript
which is now at the Folger Shakespeare Library (v.b.34).[49] In an entry of 5
December 1623, Dering's 'Booke of expences' also records the purchase of '2
volumes of J Shakespear's playes - - 02 00 00', followed on the next line by
'Jhonson's playes - - - - 00 09 00'. 'J Shakespear's' suggests Dering started
writing Jonson's name but changed his mind and first completed
Shakespeare's. In all likelihood the entry refers to Dering's acquisition of
two copies of the First Folio.[50]

Frances Egerton (née Stanley), Countess of Bridgewater (1583–1636), is
another early collector who owned printed plays by Shakespeare, as we
know thanks to the 'Catalogue of my Ladies Bookes at London; Taken
October. 27th. 1627'.[51] The main inventory (two updates followed on 26
April 1631 and 17 April 1632) is divided into 'Bookes in Folio' (thirty-one),
'Bookes in Quarto' (fifty-nine), 'Bookes in Octavo and Lesse' (ninety-four)
and 'French Bookes' (seventeen), a total of more than two hundred titles.[52]
Among the 'Bookes in Quarto', title 44 reads:

Diuers Playes by Shakespeare _____ 1602.

(see Figure 5.3.) The inventory goes on to list other bound volumes of plays,
which, however, are not associated with a particular dramatist: 'Diuerse
Playes in 5 thicke Volumes in velum', 'A Booke of Diuerse Playes in Leather'
and 'A Booke of Diuerse Playes in Velum'.[53] Egerton's collection thus
featured seven volumes of 'Diuers Playes' (including five 'thicke' ones),
plus one volume attributed to and with plays by Shakespeare.

---

[48] For Dering's purchase of multiple copies of the same playbooks, probably for domestic performances
at Surrenden, see Lennam, 'Sir Edward Dering's Collection of Playbooks, 1619–1624', 148.

[49] See Krivatsy and Yeandle, 'Sir Edward Dering', 141; and Yeandle, 'The Dating of Sir Edward Dering's
Copy of "The History of King Henry the Fourth"'. Yeandle 'confidently' dates Dering's manuscript of
Henry IV to 'no later than February 1623' (226), thus almost a year before the publication of the First
Folio. For a modern edition of the manuscript, see Williams and Evans, eds., *The Dering Manuscript*.

[50] Lennam, 'Sir Edward Dering's Collection of Playbooks, 1619–1624', 148. Dering's 'A Booke of
expences from ye yeare 1619' is now in the Kent Archives Office, Cat. No. U350/E4.

[51] The manuscript (EL 6495) is now part of the Ellesmere manuscript collection at the Huntington
Library.

[52] For a full transcription of the 1627 inventory and of two later updates of 26 April 1631 and 17 April 1632
(which raise the total number of titles to 241), see Hackel, *Reading Material in Early Modern England*,
258–81.

[53] Hackel, *Reading Material in Early Modern England*, 266–7. 'The Tragaedy of Mustapha', Fulke
Greville's closet drama, is the only separately listed playbook in the 1627 catalogue.

5.3 'Catalogue of my Ladies [Frances Egerton (née Stanley), Countess of Bridgewater's] Bookes at London; Taken October. 27th. 1627', Ellesmere manuscript collection (EL 6495). The excerpt mentions 'Diuers Playes by Shakespeare _____ 1602' (see item 44)

Egerton's books became part of the Bridgewater House Library, which was sold to the Huntington Library in 1917. Heidi Brayman Hackel has identified fifty-nine books with Bridgewater House provenance that are mentioned in the countess's inventory.[54] Yet none of the playbook volumes survive. They were disbound and rebound separately. To make things worse, in the years after the acquisition of the Bridgewater House Library, the Huntington sold many pre-1627 playbooks that may have been in the countess's collection. Lawrence Manley has argued that it may nonetheless be possible to reconstruct the lost volumes in part, thanks to a 'ubiquitous feature of playbooks from the Bridgewater collection: the presence of a handwritten numeral inside a square bracket in upper right hand corner of the title page of most plays'.[55] Manley believes that the numbers were 'keyed to a manuscript table of contents written in the opening flyleaf of each bound pamphlet volume'.[56] He has identified copies of the following editions of Bridgewater House provenance, with successive square-bracketed numerals on the title page, suggesting they may have belonged to the 1602 volume of 'Diuers Playes by Shakespeare': Q2 *Titus Andronicus* (1600), Q1 *Much Ado about Nothing* (1600), Q2 *Romeo and Juliet* (1599), Q2 *Richard II* (1598), Q3 *1 Henry IV* (1599), Q1 *2 Henry IV* (1600), Q2 *Love's Labour's Lost* (1598), Q1 *The Merchant of Venice* (1600), Q2 *Richard III* (1598), Q1 *A Midsummer Night's Dream* (1600), Q1 *1 Contention* (1600) and Q2 *Richard Duke of York* (1600).[57] That makes no fewer than twelve plays, in fact almost all of Shakespeare's plays available at the time. As Manley states, 'here, more than twenty years in advance of the First Folio, is a "complete" volume containing every one of Shakespeare's plays that were in print by 1602, with the exception of the bad quarto of *Henry V* . . . and the bad quarto of *The Merry Wives of Windsor*'.[58]

---

[54] 'The Countess of Bridgewater's London Library', 158.

[55] 'Shakespeare and the Countess of Bridgewater', 2.

[56] 'Shakespeare and the Countess of Bridgewater', 3. He shows that a volume of fourteen pamphlets, still in its original binding, survives at the Huntington with such a manuscript table of contents (Huntington E-PV 12314–28).

[57] Strictly speaking, the 1600 edition of *Richard Duke of York* is the first quarto; the 1595 edition was published in octavo format.

[58] 'Shakespeare and the Countess of Bridgewater', 6–7. Hackel thought that the date '1602' in the inventory for the volume of 'Diuers Playes by Shakespeare' might suggest that the volume contained playbooks 'the first of which was printed in 1602' (*Reading Material in Early Modern England*, 266). Even if we understand 'first' spatially (i.e. the first within the bound volume) – as I think we are supposed to – rather than temporally, Manley's research suggests that her hunch is wrong: the Shakespeare editions which made up the volume date from 1598 and 1600. '1602', as Manley points out, probably refers to 'the date of the binding of the volume' ('Shakespeare and the Countess of Bridgewater', 6).

5.4 Frances Egerton, Countess of Bridgewater, by Paul van Somer, 1619.

In 1602, Frances was nineteen years old and newly married – or, less likely, on the point of being married – to John Egerton.[59] Her father was Ferdinando Stanley, Lord Strange, later fifth Earl of Derby (1559?–1594), who had patronized a company of players, Lord Strange's Men, some of whom later joined the Lord Chamberlain's Men and whose repertory may have included plays by Shakespeare.[60] She had good reason, in other words, to be interested in plays, and especially in Shakespeare's plays, from an early age. Thomas Pavier has been singled out as the man whose 1619 nonce collection (the 'Pavier Quartos') constituted 'the first serious attempt to materialize Shakespeare as a dramatic author in the form of a bound book'.[61] That distinction should instead go to Frances Egerton (Figure 5.4):

---

[59] See O'Donnell, 'Egerton, Frances, Countess of Bridgewater (1583–1636)'; and Knafla, 'Egerton, John, First Earl of Bridgewater (1579–1649)'.
[60] See Gurr, *The Shakespearian Playing Companies*, 258–77.
[61] Stallybrass and Chartier, 'Reading and Authorship', 42.

the 1602 volume makes of the countess an extraordinary figure in the early bibliographic history of Shakespeare, a collector of almost his complete dramatic works then available before the end of the reign of Queen Elizabeth.

The 1602 volume, in the context just provided, may invite us to reconsider some of our prejudices about the cultural status of dramatic authorship among readers and collectors in Shakespeare's own time. It has been argued that 'when play-pamphlets from the Renaissance have survived, it is usually because collectors treated them *as plays* rather than as authored texts and bound them together as miscellanies'.[62] While the countess's collection, with its five non-authorial volumes of 'Diuerse Playes', confirms that this could be the case, the Shakespeare volume shows that it need not. Clearly, the countess was not deterred by the allegedly low cultural status of quarto playbooks or dramatic authorship from forming a bound collection of Shakespearean drama in 1602.

Further evidence of the value Shakespeare's quarto playbooks were accorded is provided by a volume which was once in the Royal Library. It has long been known that King Charles I owned a copy of the Second Folio (1632), but we have only recently discovered that his Royal Library also housed a remarkable volume of 'Shakespeare apocrypha' which appears to have come into existence in the early 1630s, perhaps in the year of publication of the Second Folio.[63] Called 'Shakespeare. Vol. 1' on the back cover, it was made up of eight playbooks, bound in the following order: *The Puritan* (Q, 1607), *Thomas Lord Cromwell* (Q2, 1613), *The Merry Devil of Edmonton* (Q5, 1631), *The London Prodigal* (Q, 1605), *Mucedorus* (Q1, 1598), *Fair Em* (Q2, 1631) and *Love's Labour's Lost* (Q3, 1631).[64] *The Puritan* and *Thomas Lord Cromwell* were attributed to 'W. S.' on their title page, and *The London Prodigal* ascribed to 'William Shakespeare', which explains their inclusion in the volume. Neither *The Merry Devil of Edmonton* nor *Mucedorus* was, as far as we know, associated with Shakespeare before the 1630s, though they were performed by his company, as various title pages pointed out, and they were assigned to him in the booksellers' catalogues of Edward Archer and Francis Kirkman in 1656 and 1661. *Fair Em*, by contrast,

[62] Stallybrass and Chartier, 'Reading and Authorship', 42.

[63] See Kirwan, 'The First Collected "Shakespeare Apocrypha"'. As Kirwan points out, Shakespeare scholars long believed that the volume goes back to the library of Charles II, not Charles I, and that it contained only three plays, *The Merry Devil of Edmonton*, *Mucedorus* and *Fair Em*. For King Charles I and the Second Folio, see Rasmussen, *The Shakespeare Thefts*, 113–21. For a 1642 volume of nine 'Beaumont and Fletcher' quarto playbooks which belonged to King Charles I, see Simpson, 'King Charles the First as Dramatic Critic'.

[64] See Kirwan, 'The First Collected "Shakespeare Apocrypha"', 598.

was never ascribed to Shakespeare in the seventeenth century except in the volume of the Royal Library, so it may have served to pad out the volume – like *Love's Labour's Lost*, whose canonical status was undisputed – simply because it had recently been printed in 1631.[65]

Perhaps the most voracious seventeenth-century book collector with an interest in Shakespeare was Edward Conway, second Viscount Conway (1594–1665). Conway maintained two libraries of considerable size, one at his Irish seat of Brookhill, Lisnagarvey (now Lisburn), Co. Antrim, the other one in London. Conway had a catalogue drawn up for his Brookhill library from 1636 to 1640, which survives in Armagh Public Library. It lists approximately 8,000 volumes, under more than eighty classifications, including 'English Playes', of which he had no fewer than 349, published between 1560 and 1640.[66] With twenty quartos by or attributed to him, Shakespeare is 'the best-held playwright in the Conway library', as Arthur Freeman and Paul Grinke put it, 'a reminder that his popularity with readers as well as theatre-goers in his own era was never in question'.[67] The holdings included first quartos of *Love's Labour's Lost* (1597, the only record of a dated copy of the lost edition; Figure 5.5), *Much Ado about Nothing* (1600), *Troilus and Cressida* (1609), *Othello* (1622) and *The Two Noble Kinsmen* (1634, with Fletcher), *Locrine* (1595, by 'W. S.'), *The Puritan* (1607, also by 'W. S.') and 'The London Prodigal by William Shakes: 1605'; second editions of *Edward III* (1599), *1 Contention* (1600), 'A Yorkshire Tragedy by W: Sh: 1619' and 'The first parte of Sr John Oldcastle, by W. Shak. 1600' (the Pavier Quarto of 1619); the third edition of *Pericles* (1611); the sixth edition of *Richard II* (1634); the eighth edition of *Richard III* (1629); undated editions of *Romeo and Juliet* and 'The history of Henry the 4 by William Shakespeare'; an edition of 'The Taminge of the Shrew by W. Sh:' dated '1621' (probably a slip of the pen for 1631 when Shakespeare's *Taming of the Shrew* – as opposed to the anonymous *The Taming of a Shrew* – was first published in quarto); and 'Henry 4 the first and second parte(s), 1619' (where '4' – IV in roman numbers – may well be a mistake for

---

[65] It is surprising that *Pericles* was not included in the volume given that a new edition, the fifth quarto, had appeared in 1630, that all five early quartos of *Pericles* had assigned the play to Shakespeare, and that the play had not been included in the First and Second Folios.

[66] See Birrell, 'Reading as Pastime'; and Starza-Smith, '"La conquest du sang real"'.

[67] 'Four New Shakespeare Quartos?', 17. Freeman and Grinke's total of Shakespeare quartos in the Conway library was initially twenty-one, but, as they pointed out in a subsequent letter to the *TLS*, the 1617 edition of a Henry V play is in fact 'The victoryes of Henry 5, 1617', in other words the 'second quarto of [the] source or analogue of Shakespeare's play, *The Famous Victories of Henry the Fifth*' (Freeman and Grinke, 'Four New Shakespeare Quartos?').

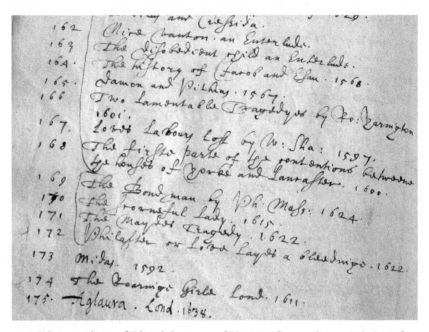

5.5 Library catalogue of Edward Conway, 2nd Viscount Conway (1594–1665), Armagh
Public Library. The excerpt records, among other plays, a copy of the now lost 1597 edition
of *Love's Labour's Lost* (see item 167)

'6' – VI in roman numbers – meaning *The Whole Contention*, published by
Pavier in 1619).[68]

The dates of some of these editions suggest that Conway started collecting his Shakespeare playbooks before the 1630s and probably before 1623.
For instance, of *Pericles*, he owned the third quarto (1611), not the fourth
(1619), fifth (1630) or sixth (1635); of *Othello*, the quarto in his library was the
first (1622), not the second (1630); and of *Love's Labour's Lost*, he had a copy
of the first quarto (1597), not the third (1631). Conway's book-buyers may
well have purchased certain copies second hand, but even if they did, they
must have found it easier to obtain copies of recent editions rather than old
ones. Conway was an avid reader and, according to Edward Hyde, first Earl
of Clarendon, reserved 'so much time for his books and study that he was

---

[68] Two minor slips in Freeman and Grinke's *TLS* article should be noted: for *Edward III*, the date they
indicate is '1595' (when no edition was published) instead of '1599' (the publication date of Q2); and
for *Richard III*, 'eighth edition' should be 'sixth edition' and '1614' should be '1634' (see 'Four New
Shakespeare Quartos?'). I am grateful to Thirza Mulder of Armagh Public Library for making
available to me a print-off of the digitized catalogue.

well versed in all parts of learning'.[69] His extant correspondence shows him to be a perceptive reader, who, in a letter written to his daughter-in-law, Lady Anne Conway, makes a prescient comment about the quality of early modern English drama: 'Our English Playes are not written according to the rules of Antient Comoedies or Tragedies, but if the English language were understood by other nations, they would certainly imitate them.'[70] Conway's more detailed response to the plays he read would be well worth having, but if he provided the playbooks with marginal comments, they seem to have been lost. None of the Shakespeare playbooks once in his possession is now known to be extant, perhaps because his library was severely damaged by fire on 27 November 1641, during the Irish Rebellion, in an attack by the rebel forces under Sir Phelim O'Neill.[71] Four years earlier, in November 1637, a list, now among the Conway papers, had been drawn up of 488 titles of 'double and imperfect bookes' to be sent from his Irish to his London library, which includes 'Shakespeare's Works' (no doubt one of the two Folios then in print), *Othello* and *Henry IV*, providing further evidence of the place of Shakespeare books in Conway's collections.[72] Conway's London library, housing some 3,000 books, was inventoried in 1643, when it was seized by the Committee for Sequestration. The catalogue occupies pages 141 to 229 of a volume, now in the Public Record Office (SP 20/7), containing a 'valuation of the libraries of London Royalists and Catholics, which were seized by the Committee in 1643'; it is 'an almost complete record of the activities of the Committee in this field'.[73] No record of any Shakespeare books seems to have been traced in the 1643 inventory, and Roy wrote that 'The presence of the collected edition of Jonson's plays is as noticeable as the apparent absence of the Shakespeare folios.'[74] Yet, given the evidence of the 1637 list of books to be transferred from Ireland, it seems likely that Conway's London library at one point also housed some Shakespeare.

---

[69] Roy, 'The Libraries of Edward, 2nd Viscount Conway, and Others', 44, quoting from Cokayne, *The Complete Peerage*, II.§83.

[70] Nicolson, ed., *The Conway Letters*, 31.

[71] See Freeman and Grinke, 'Four New Shakespeare Quartos?', 17. Note, however, that some of his books – though none by Shakespeare – are now in Armagh Public Library, recognizable by their armorial bindings (see Knowles, 'Conway, Edward, Second Viscount Conway and Second Viscount Killultagh (*bap.* 1594, *d.* 1655)'). The *ESTC* knows of 265 books in Armagh Public Library which were published between 1475 and 1641.

[72] See Freeman and Grinke, 'Four New Shakespeare Quartos?', 17. For the 1637 book list, see PRO, SP 16/372/III.

[73] Roy, 'The Libraries of Edward, 2nd Viscount Conway, and Others', 35.

[74] Roy, 'The Libraries of Edward, 2nd Viscount Conway, and Others', 43.

Another early collector of playbooks is Robert Burton (1577–1640), who bequeathed his collection of books to the Bodleian Library and to Christ Church, Oxford. After surveying Burton's more than 1,700 books, John Rous, the Bodleian's second head librarian, took 872 volumes, including 417 books which he described as 'English books' in quarto and octavo, of which sixty-six were labelled 'Maskes, Comedies, & Tragedies'.[75] Among the books of poetry were Shakespeare's narrative poems, which Rous recorded as 'Venus and Adonis by Wm Shakespear Lond.' and 'The rape of Lucrece by Wm Shakespear Imperfet.'[76] Rous's attitude towards playbooks was very different from Bodley's: he retained 'ten plays and entertainments by Heywood, nine by Beaumont and Fletcher, eight by Shirley, six by Chapman, six by Middleton, four by Jonson and three by Webster', but, as far as we know, no Shakespeare.[77] Nicholas K. Kiessling, in *The Library of Robert Burton*, has written that 'Burton must have owned at least one copy of a play by Shakespeare,' but he provides no evidence to suggest that this is more than a hunch.[78] The hunch is not implausible, though. Burton, in the second edition of *The Anatomy of Melancholy* (1624), quotes the final couplet of *Romeo and Juliet*: 'Who ever heard a story of more woe, / Then that of Juliet and her Romeo.' He also refers to *Much Ado about Nothing* and *Hamlet*.[79] A possible explanation is that Rous did not retain the Shakespeare quarto playbooks because he remembered that the Bodleian had already acquired the Shakespeare Folio in 1624.[80]

It is possible that Sir Thomas Mostyn (*c.* 1542–1618) and his son Sir Roger Mostyn (1567/8–1642) should also be counted among the early collectors of Shakespeare playbooks. As A. D. Carr informs us in the *Oxford Dictionary of National Biography*, 'According to the family history, it was Sir Thomas Mostyn who began to assemble the famous Mostyn library.'[81] Little is known about the exact composition of the early library, but when parts of the Mostyn library were sold by Sotheby's on 31 May 1907, three books which changed hands may have been acquired by Sir Thomas: copies of Q1 *1 Contention* (1594), *The Merchant of Venice* (1600) and *King Lear* (1608).[82] If Sir Roger continued the collection, he may have acquired the other copies of Shakespeare playbooks sold at the 1907 and at a later, 1919, sale: Q4 *Hamlet* (*c.* 1625), Q2 *The Merry Wives of Windsor* (1619), Q2 *Othello* (1630) and Q7

---

[75] Kiessling, *The Library of Robert Burton*, viii.

[76] See Bodleian. Arch. G. F. 31 and Bodleian 8° L 2(2) Art. BS.

[77] Hackel, '"Rowme" of its Own', 120. See also Nelson, 'Shakespeare and the Bibliophiles', 56–8.

[78] *The Library of Robert Burton*, 335.   [79] Burton, *The Anatomy of Melancholy*, III.107, 199, 227.

[80] For Rous's disposal of duplicates, see Kiessling, *The Library of Robert Burton*, xiv–xv.

[81] 'Mostyn Family (*per.* 1540–1642)'.

[82] For *The Merchant of Venice* and *King Lear*, see Bartlett and Pollard, *Census*, §502, §616. For *1 Contention*, see 'Notes on Sales: the Mostyn Plays'.

Richard III (1629), Q2 *A Yorkshire Tragedy* (1619), Q2 *Sir John Oldcastle* (1619) and Q6 *Pericles* (1635).[83]

The library of the ninth and tenth Earls of Northumberland, Henry Percy (1564–1632) and Algernon Percy (1602–68), at Petworth House (West Sussex), contained 149 early modern English playbooks (including eight duplicates), with publication dates ranging from 1585 to 1638.[84] They were bound together in seemingly random order in sixteen volumes in seventeenth-century calf binding, with six to eleven plays per gathering.[85] They survive in this form at Petworth House to this day. The collection includes many plays by Shakespeare: Q1 *Richard II* (1597), Q5 *Richard III* (1612), Q3 *Henry V* (1619), Q3 *King Lear* (1655), Q2 *Merry Wives* (1619), Q1 *Othello* (1622), Q4 *Hamlet* (n.d., 1625?), Q3 *Love's Labour's Lost* (1631), Q8 *1 Henry IV* (1632) and Q5 *Romeo and Juliet* (1637). In addition, the collection included the collaborative *Two Noble Kinsmen* (Q1, 1634, with Fletcher) and the spurious *Thomas Lord Cromwell* (Q2, 1613, by 'W. S.') and *Troublesome Reign* (Q3, 1622, by 'W. Shakespeare').[86]

In an article published in 1975, Edward Miller argued that the collection was initiated not by Henry Percy, the ninth Earl (who 'does not appear to have been interested in contemporary drama or literature'), nor by Algernon Percy, the tenth Earl (an 'austere and upright supporter of the Parliamentary cause'), but by William Percy (1575–1648), a younger brother of Henry and uncle to Algernon.[87] William Percy is the dedicatee of Barnabe Barnes's

---

[83] See Bartlett and Pollard, *Census*, §40, §728, §841 and §1077; 'Notes on Sales: the Mostyn Plays'; de Ricci, *English Collectors of Books and Manuscripts (1530–1930) and their Marks of Ownership*, 180–1; and de Ricci, ed., *Fulgens and Lucres*, 7–11.

[84] All in all, the library contained 2,873 volumes by 1690, of which 2,339 had been published in 1632 or earlier. See Batho, 'The Library of the "Wizard" Earl Henry Percy, Ninth Earl of Northumberland (1564–1632)'.

[85] See Miller, 'A Collection of Elizabethan and Jacobean Plays at Petworth', 63. According to Matthew Dimmock and Andrew Loukes, 'the quartos seem to have been bound together some time subsequent to the 1690 catalogue of the library (the "Catalogus Librorum Bibliothecae Petworthianae"), in which these plays are catalogued individually and in a different order' ('Plays and Playing at Petworth House (1590–1640)'). The *Catalogus Librorum Bibliothecae Petworthianae* (occasionally referred to as the Leconfield MS) is now in the West Sussex Record Office, Chichester (PHA/5377). Thanks to an AHRC Collaborative Doctoral Award between the School of English at the University of Sussex and The National Trust at Petworth House, a project devoted to 'Plays and Playing at Petworth House (1590–1640)', supervised by Dimmock and Loukes, is currently investigating the origin and composition of the Petworth collection.

[86] Bartlett and Pollard record nine of the ten Shakespeare copies in the second edition of their *Census* (the copy of *Merry Wives* is unaccountably absent). Note that Miller ('A Collection of Elizabethan and Jacobean Plays at Petworth', 63) erroneously states that the *King Lear* copy in the collection is a second quarto (1619); it is in fact a third (1655).

[87] 'A Collection of Elizabethan and Jacobean Plays at Petworth', 62. Writing fifteen years earlier, Batho had assumed that the playbook collector was Algernon Percy, the tenth Earl (see 'The Library of the "Wizard" Earl Henry Percy, Ninth Earl of Northumberland (1564–1632)').

sonnet collection, *Parthenophil and Parthenophe* (1593) and the author of *Sonnets to the fairest Coelia* (1594) and several manuscript plays, which seem to have been written for performance by the Children of Paul's.[88]

With the exception of Frances Egerton, the collectors I have mentioned so far are all men, but at least one other seventeenth-century woman is known to have had a collection which included books by Shakespeare. Frances Wolfreston (1607–1676/7) spent her married life in Statfold, near Tamworth, and gave birth to ten or eleven children.[89] In her will, she bequeathed her books to one of her sons, Standford, and most of them remained at Statfold Hall, unbound and uncut, stitched as originally issued, until they were sold at an auction by Sotheby and Wilkinson on 24 May 1856.[90] The auction catalogue, *The Remains of a Library Partly Collected During the Reign of King James the First*, contains more than 400 titles published before Wolfreston's death, of which 240 date from earlier than 1641. They 'represent the leisure reading of a literate lady in her country house', with some history and theology, and a considerable number of titles (about half the total) in what we now call English literature.[91] We do not know when she started her collection, but she clearly continued adding to it until relatively late in her life, the latest book inscribed by her having been published in 1670.[92]

Wolfreston inscribed her books 'frances wolfreston hor [or her] bouk'; almost one hundred of them have been identified in modern libraries, some with annotations in her hand.[93] They include copies of the first edition of *Venus and Adonis* (1593), the sixth edition of *The Rape of Lucrece* (1616), Q4 *Hamlet* (undated, 1625?), Q6 *Richard II* (1634), the sixteenth edition of *Venus and Adonis* (1636), Q3 *King Lear* (1655) and Q3 *Othello* (1655).[94] The 1856 auction catalogue mentions a few more Shakespeare quartos which, however, have not been identified in modern libraries: Q1 *The Taming of the Shrew* (1631), Q3 *The Merchant of Venice* (1637), Q5 *Romeo and Juliet* (1637)

---

[88] See Miller, 'A Collection of Elizabethan and Jacobean Plays at Petworth', 62; and Hillebrand, 'William Percy'.

[89] See McElligott, 'Wolfreston, Frances (*bap.* 1607, *d.* 1677)'.

[90] Morgan, 'Frances Wolfreston and "Hor Bouks"', 199–202. Some books left the collection earlier though, including the only surviving copy of the first edition of *Venus and Adonis* (1593), now in the Bodleian Library, which Edmond Malone acquired from a Manchester bookseller, William Ford, in 1805 (see Morgan, 'Frances Wolfreston and "Hor Bouks"', 202). See also Gerritsen, '*Venus* Preserved'.

[91] Morgan, 'Frances Wolfreston and "Hor Bouks"', 200, 203–4. On Wolfreston's reading, see also Roberts, 'Reading the Shakespearean Text in Early Modern England'; and Watt, *Cheap Print and Popular Piety, 1550–1640*, 315–17.

[92] Morgan, 'Frances Wolfreston and "Hor Bouks"', 211–19.

[93] Morgan, 'Frances Wolfreston and "Hor Bouks"', 200.

[94] See Morgan, 'Frances Wolfreston and "Hor Bouks"', 217–18; and Bartlett and Pollard, *Census*, §543, §870 and §1017.

and unidentified quartos of *Richard II* and *Richard III*, with missing title pages.[95]

After this survey of early collectors with an interest in Shakespeare, it must be added that there were of course plenty of libraries and library catalogues without plays. For instance, the library of Griffin Higgs (1589–1659), Dean of Lichfield, contained no playbooks but instead a copy of John Rainolds's anti-theatrical tract, *Th'overthrow of stage-playes* (Middleburgh, 1600, *STC* 20617).[96] Other collections clearly marginalized quarto playbooks. The massive catalogue, made between 1653 and 1655, of the Penshurst library of Robert Sidney, second Earl of Leicester (1595–1677), contained a copy of Shakespeare's Second Folio but no Shakespeare quarto playbook, nor, indeed, any pre-1630 playbook other than the 1605 quarto of *Sejanus*, which is notable for its elaborate, neo-classical, anti-theatrical apparatus.[97] It is further noticeable that several slightly later collections, from the second half of the seventeenth century, tend to marginalize Shakespeare, even though a fair number of other playbooks are listed – evidence that not only among publishers but also among collectors, Shakespeare's reputation was waning.[98] For instance, the library of Sir Joseph Williamson (1633–1702), with some 6,000 volumes, was formed 'towards the end of the 17th century'.[99] The only Shakespeare it is known to contain is a Restoration edition of *The Tempest*, included in a volume called 'Collection of Plays'.[100] Anthony Wood's library, which was constituted in the second half of the seventeenth century, did not contain much Shakespeare either: *Venus and Adonis* (1630), *Othello* (1655) and the 1640 *Poems*.[101] The library of Sir Edward Bysshe (1610–79), consisting of roughly 2,500 books, was sold at an auction in 1680. It contained a substantial

[95] *Catalogue of the Remains of a Library Partly Collected during the Reign of King James the First* (London, 1856), 34. The catalogue also mentions *1 Sir John Oldcastle*, of '1600' (34), assigned to Shakespeare, no doubt a copy of the 1619 Pavier Quarto.

[96] Morrish, *Bibliotheca Higgsiana*, 52.

[97] See Warkentin, 'The World and the Book at Penshurst'. Joseph L. Black, William R. Bowen and Warkentin's critical edition of the manuscript catalogue of the seventeenth-century library of the Sidney family is forthcoming from the University of Toronto Press (*The Library of the Sidneys of Penshurst Place, ca. 1665*). I wish to thank the editors for their answer to my query about the holdings of the Penshurst library.

[98] For Shakespeare's reputation in the second half of the seventeenth century, see Dobson, *The Making of the National Poet*, chapter 1; and Taylor, *Reinventing Shakespeare*, chapter 1.

[99] Birrell, 'Reading as Pastime', 127.

[100] Williamson's library catalogues (an alphabetical catalogue and two subject catalogues) are now in Queen's College Library, Oxford, MS 42, 'A Catalogue of Sir Joseph Williamson's Library'. For the 'Collection of Plays' with *The Tempest*, see Queen's College Library MS 44, f. 115. I am grateful to Helen Powell and Amanda Saville for their help with the Williamson catalogues.

[101] Kiessling, *The Library of Anthony Wood*, 544.

collection of erotica, a good share of English poetry and eight volumes of plays, including one of '16 Old Plays, by Beaumont and Fletcher', but no Shakespeare other than the collaborative *Two Noble Kinsmen*, which was part of the 'Beaumont and Fletcher' volume.[102]

Nonetheless, the amount of evidence of ownership and collecting of Shakespeare playbooks, particularly in Shakespeare's own lifetime and the period shortly after it, is remarkable and difficult to reconcile with the belief that Shakespeare's contemporaries considered his playbooks discardable ephemera or 'riffe-raffe' unfit for inclusion in libraries. As we have seen, quite a number of individuals made Shakespeare playbooks part of their personal library before 1623, including Sir William Drummond of Hawthornden, Sir John Harington, an anonymous Cambridge physician, the original owner of the Oxinden collection, Humphrey Dyson, George Buc, Sir Edward Dering, Frances Egerton, Countess of Bridgewater, and possibly also Edward Conway, second Viscount Conway, Sir Thomas Mostyn and William Percy. Of these, Drummond, Harington, Egerton and Conway produced library catalogues in which Shakespeare playbooks are mentioned. Several collections seem to have made a point of highlighting their Shakespearean presence. Egerton had a book in her collection which had bound into one volume almost all Shakespeare playbooks published by 1602. Harington owned more than twenty playbooks by or attributed to Shakespeare, virtually the complete dramatic works of Shakespeare available in print by 1612, the year of his death. Others are known to have collected and catalogued Shakespeare playbooks slightly later, notably Henry Oxinden and Scipio Le Squyer. In the early 1630s, a volume of Shakespeare apocrypha, ascribed to Shakespeare on the binding, was made part of the Royal Library. As early as 1627, a printed catalogue of the Drummond collection bequeathed to the University of Edinburgh records the presence of Shakespeare quarto playbooks among its holdings. We may be tempted to think that whereas the First Folio had prestige, the quartos were 'riffe-raffe', but if a leading expert of the 1623 edition has 'found only one early reference to the First Folio in library catalogues or donors' books or inventories', then the number of early traces of the quartos is surely remarkable.[103] If we remember that a large part of the once existing evidence of the early collecting and cataloguing must have perished, we may recognize that many took Shakespeare's quarto playbooks more seriously than Bowers and others made us believe.

---

[102] *Bibliotheca Bissaeana, sive, Catalogus librorum in omni arte & linguâ praestantissimorum* (1680, Wing 1351), 66. See also Birrell, 'Reading as Pastime', 125–6. The manuscript catalogue of Bysshe's library is now in the British Library (MS Harl. 813 ff. 174–99). For Bysshe, see Sherlock, 'Bysshe, Sir Edward (*c.* 1610–1679)'.

[103] West, *The Shakespeare First Folio: Volume 1*, 3.

Shakespeare owned and bound

Other evidence of early ownership likewise suggests that Shakespeare's quarto playbooks were considered more than ephemera. The inscription of the owner's name (and, more rarely, date of purchase) into a copy indicates that that book had been bought to be preserved, not to be read and discarded, so it is significant that a number of extant early Shakespeare playbooks feature the owner's name, like 'An Bosvil', in a seventeenth-century hand, in the 'G. Wells' copy, now in the Huntington, of Q5 *Richard II* (1615).[104] The title page of the Huntington copy of Shakespeare's *Sonnets* (1609) shows the initials of an early owner, 'N: L: S:' (which, as Katherine Duncan-Jones has speculated, might refer to 'Nicholas Ling, Stationer').[105] The title page verso of a copy, now at the Folger, of Q1 *Edward III* (1596, STC 7501) bears the initials of one 'G:. K:.', dates the inscription to 'festo diui Jacobi. [i.e. St. James's day, 25 July] 1610' and adds that the copy was purchased at least twelve years earlier (meaning before 25 July 1598).[106] Humphrey Dyson (*c*. 1582–1633) signed his copy of *Troilus and Cressida* (1609): 'Hum: Dyson'.[107] Scipio Le Squyer (1579–1659) inscribed his copy of the first quarto of *Pericles* (1609): 'Scipio Squyer 5. Maij 160[9]'.[108] He also left his name on a copy of the second edition (1600) of *Richard Duke of York*.[109] The owner of a now lost copy of *2 Henry IV* (1600) also noted the exact date of purchase and added the price: '11 December 1610. price vd.'[110] The case of Frances Wolfreston, who inscribed several Shakespeare play-books and *Venus and Adonis* with her name, has been touched upon above.[111] Thomas Skynner, buying a copy of the 1619 *Merry Wives of Windsor* two years after its publication, wrote on it: 'Thomas Skynner 1621'.[112] And Edward Gwynn (*d. c.* 1645), who entered the Middle Temple in 1610, collected books on which he stamped his name 'in gold on their upper covers and the initials, E G, on their lower' (Figure 5.6).[113]

[104] See Bartlett and Pollard, *Census*, §999.

[105] *Shakespeare's Sonnets*, 6. It is difficult to date the inscription with precision.

[106] The full inscription reads: 'G:. K:. festo diui Jacobi. 1610: cum duodecim ad minimum annos librum hunc ante possederat:. Mihi solatium Jesus.' I am grateful to Richard Proudfoot for drawing my attention to this inscription and providing me with an offprint of the relevant page.

[107] Nelson, 'Shakespeare and the Bibliophiles', 67. Dyson's copy of *Troilus and Cressida* is now in the Huntington Library (RB 59072).

[108] Nelson, 'Shakespeare and the Bibliophiles', 63. The copy is now in the Elizabethan Club, Yale.

[109] The copy is now in the Bodleian Library, Arch. G d.43(5). See Birrell, 'Reading as Pastime', 119–20; Nelson, 'Shakespeare and the Bibliophiles', 62–4; and Taylor, 'The Books and Manuscripts of Scipio le Squyer, Deputy Chamberlain of the Exchequer, 1620–1659', 157–8.

[110] Bartlett and Pollard, *Census*, 127.   [111] Morgan, 'Frances Wolfreston and "Hor Bouks"', 217–18.

[112] Bartlett and Pollard, *Census*, §695. The copy is now in Balliol College Library, Oxford.

[113] Jackson, 'Edward Gwynn', 90, 94.

5.6 Calf binding of Edward Gwynn's copy of the Pavier Quartos (1619), with his name and
initials stamped in gold on the covers. Folger Shakespeare Library (STC 26101, copy 3).

William A. Jackson identified 'seventy odd examples' of books with Gwynn's name, including a full set of the 1619 Pavier Quartos, in original binding, now housed at the Folger.[114]

As Blayney has pointed out, 'Relatively few seventeenth-century owners inscribed their books, and fewer still used bookplates or personal binding stamps. Those who did so . . . usually recorded their ownership on the most vulnerable parts of the book, which in most cases have now disappeared.'[115] Writing about the Shakespeare First Folio, Blayney added that 'When its unique importance began to be more widely recognized, collectors who obtained copies usually had them cleaned, rebound and (if necessary) perfected with leaves from copies in worse condition. That process often destroyed all evidence of earlier ownership.'[116] What is true for the First Folio also applies to the quartos. For every surviving owner's inscription in a Shakespeare playbook, we can be confident that many others existed.

Other surviving traces of acquisition or ownership of early Shakespeare books add to the evidence that some people considered them worth recording and preserving. For instance, William Freke, born in 1605, who went to Oxford in 1619 and was at the Middle Temple from 1622 to 1639, kept an account book in which he listed receipts and expenses during his years in Oxford and London. It survives in its original vellum binding, now at the Bodleian Library.[117] Freke purchased a fair number of books, including playbooks. Under February 1627, he lists 'a booke of Playes', without further specification, which cost him 3s., but the other plays he acquired are mentioned by title: 'Lingua and Othello', purchased jointly in June 1624 for 8d., and 'The Game at Chess', which he bought in April 1625 for 6d.[118] Freke also recorded the acquisition of several books of poetry, among them

---

[114] 'Edward Gwynn', 93. See also Nelson, 'Shakespeare and the Bibliophiles', 55, and Greg, *Bibliography*, III.1108. The British Library copy of *2 Henry IV*, shelfmark C.34.k.13, contains an unusual ownership inscription, not on the title page but in the margin of sig. D4r: 'Edward Sulyard his Book 1613'. I have found no reference to this person in modern scholarship, and it may now be impossible to identify him, although it is tempting to speculate that he was the son of the Edward Sulyard of Flemyngs in the parish of Runwell, Essex, to whom William Webbe dedicated his *Discourse of English Poetrie* in 1586 (*STC* 25172). Edward Sr was knighted in 1603 and died in 1610. Webbe seems to have been private tutor to his two sons, Thomas and Edward, in *c*. 1583–4 (see Heale, 'Webbe, William (*fl.* 1566?–1591)'). Edward Jr is repeatedly mentioned in Edward Sr's will of 1 June 1610, now at the National Archives (PROB 11/116), which makes it likely that Edward Jr was still alive in 1613. For additional ownership inscriptions in early Shakespeare quarto playbooks, see Massai, 'Shakespeare's Early Readers', 153–4.

[115] *The First Folio of Shakespeare*, 32.   [116] *The First Folio of Shakespeare*, 32.

[117] See MSS Eng. misc. c. 338.

[118] *Lingua, or the Combat of the Tongue and the Five Senses for Superiority*, probably by Thomas Tomkis, is a university play, in English, which first appeared in 1607 (*STC* 24104) and went through further editions in 1610, 1617, 1622, 1632 and 1657.

'Venus and Adonis' in February 1630, for 8d.[119] A few years later, the London bookseller Richard Whitaker compiled a bill with the books purchased by a country client of his, Sir Thomas Barrington of Hatfield Broad Oak, Essex, from 1635 to 1639. Under 20 December 1637, he lists 'Shakespeares Works' for '00–18–[0]6' and '2 Playes of Henry 4th' for '[00–0]1–[00]', no doubt one of the two Folios then in existence and probably two copies of *1 Henry IV*, which had been reprinted most recently in 1632.[120]

The earliest known owner of a Shakespeare book, Richard Stonley (*c.* 1520–99), recorded his acquisition of a copy of the first edition of *Venus and Adonis* almost immediately after its publication, noting in his diary on 12 June 1593: 'For the Survay of Fraunce, with the Venus and Athonay p[r] Shakspere, xii.d.'[121] Shakespeare's poem had been entered in the Stationers' Register by Richard Field on 18 April of the same year. The other book purchased by Stonley on 12 June is John Eliot's *Survey, or topographical description of France*, which was first published in 1592 and reached a second edition in the following year (*STC* 7575). Interestingly, Stonley mentions Shakespeare's name. Even in the earliest extant record of ownership, Shakespeare's authorship seems to matter. When Edward Alleyn, the famous actor and theatre businessman, recorded the purchase of Shakespeare's *Sonnets* on the back of a letter, he similarly mentioned the author's name, 'a book. Shakesper sonetts 5d', though given the fact that Shakespeare's name is on the title page and that Alleyn knew him, this seems less remarkable.[122]

Playbooks are rarely mentioned by title in wills or probate inventories, but there are exceptions, such as the inventory compiled in 1613 on the death of Walter Brown, cleric and scholar from Oxfordshire, which includes 'The

[119] See Prothero, 'A Seventeenth-Century Account Book', 97.
[120] McKerrow suggested that '2 Playes of Henry 4th' refers to the two parts of *Henry IV* (see Bohannon, 'A London Bookseller's Bill', 441). Yet given that the second part had not been printed in quarto since 1600, it seems more likely that Barrington was buying two copies of the first. He also purchased two copies of other books, for instance William Bradshaw's *A Preparation to the Receiuing of Christs Body and Blood* (1634, *STC* 3515) and Charles Aleyn's *Historie of that Wise and Fortunate Prince, Henrie the Seventh* (1638, *STC* 353) (see Bohannon, 'A London Bookseller's Bill', 441, 445).
[121] Three of Stonley's diaries survive for 1581, 1593 and 1597. They are now at the Folger, MSS v. a. 459–461. Stonley and the books he purchased have attracted considerable attention: see Scott-Warren, 'Books in the Bedchamber'; Nelson, 'Shakespeare and the Bibliophiles', 59–62; Schoenbaum, *Documentary Life*, 130–1; and Hotson, 'The Library of Elizabeth's Embezzling Teller'. For a photographic facsimile of the relevant page of Stonley's diary, see Scott-Warren, 'Books in the Bedchamber', 248.
[122] Dulwich College MS 11 f.44v, reproduced in Greg, ed., *The Henslowe Papers*, vol. 11, item 12. See also Piggott, 'Edward Alleyn's Books', 64, Duncan-Jones, ed., *Shakespeare's Sonnets*, 6; and Nelson, 'Shakespeare and the Bibliophiles', 56.

History of Henr. 4'.[123] Nor, usually, do we keep a record of playbook gift giving, but we know that Thomas Twysden (1602–83) – a Member of Parliament who was knighted in 1660 and became a baronet in 1666 – made a gift of his jointly bound copies (now at the Folger) of the fourth quarto of *1 Henry IV* (1604) and the first quarto of *2 Henry IV* (1600) because the verso of the title page tells us so: 'These two plays are particularly esteemed by me because they were giv'n me by my Dear Friend ye late Sr Thomas Twysden of Peckam in Kent.'[124] More typically, however, what records of ownership once existed have no doubt long perished. In the case of Charles Blount, Baron Mountjoy (1563–1606), for instance, we know that he 'enjoyed reading playbooks for recreation' and 'owned a number of printed quartos of the drama', but no trace of actual ownership is now extant.[125]

Other evidence that some of Shakespeare's books were bought to be preserved comes in the form of book-binding. In the early modern period, thin quartos or octavos were usually sold unbound, no more than stitched together, with nothing firm around them to protect against wear and tear.[126] Left unbound, a book's survival prospects were not good. Shakespeare's Lady Capulet, hoping that Count Paris will marry Juliet, says of Paris that 'This precious book of love, this unbound lover, / To beautify him only lacks a cover' (1.3.89–90). When they were first sold, Shakespeare's quarto and octavo books, too, lacked a cover, which, when added, not only made the book aesthetically more appealing but also reduced the chances that they would perish. Yet book-bindings were expensive. In a broadsheet book-binders' price list of 1619, entitled 'A generall note of the prises for binding of all sorts of bookes' (*STC* 16768.6), the prices mentioned for quartos range from 10d. to 5s. 6d. By comparison, a usual price for a single quarto

---

[123] See Fehrenbach, Poston and Wolfe, 'PLRE.Folger', the online database devoted to private libraries in Renaissance England. As the entry in the database points out, 'The History of Henr. 4' is likely to refer to Shakespeare's play, although it cannot be ruled out that it designates Sir John Hayward's *The first part of the life and raigne of king Henrie the IIII* (1599; *STC* 12995) or Edmond Skory's *An extract out of the historie of the last French king Henry the fourth* (1610, *STC* 22629).

[124] I quote from the quarto's holdings notes in the 'Folger Digital Image Collection'. See also Bartlett and Pollard, *Census*, §222.

[125] Pitcher, 'Literature', 357. See also Falls, *Mountjoy*.

[126] For an unbound volume, with the 1609 quarto of *Pericles* and Samuel Daniel's 1606 quarto of *The Queen's Arcadia*, stitched together, see Knight, 'Making Shakespeare's Books', 330–2. For stitched books, see Pickwoad, 'Onward and Downward', 89–91; Woudhuysen, 'The Foundations of Shakespeare's Text', 76; and Clegg, '"Twill Much Enrich the Company of Stationers"', 251. See also Blayney, 'The Publication of Playbooks': 'Until copies of the play reached the bookshops they would remain in quires. Most booksellers who bought a batch would have at least some of them turned into something more closely resembling books, although few copies (if any) would be actually bound. The basic minimum would be to fold each sheet in four and to stack them in order as if for binding, to take a bodkin and stab three or four holes through the whole stack about a quarter-inch from the spine fold, and to stitch through the holes with packthread – essentially the equivalent of side stapling' (413).

playbook was 6d. Having a single quarto playbook bound would have been uneconomic since its price would have at least doubled or tripled.[127]

We have come across several bound volumes above: John Harington, in 1610, lists 130 plays bound in eleven volumes of nine to thirteen playbooks each. Edward Dering assembled fourteen volumes made up of playbooks by 1624. Frances Egerton's 1627 catalogue lists a volume of 'Diuers Playes by Shakespeare ... 1602', 'Diuerse Playes in 5 thicke Volumes in velum', 'A Booke of Diuerse Playes in Leather' and 'A Booke of Diuerse Playes in Velum'. The Royal Library, under Charles I, housed a bound volume made up of Shakespeare apocrypha. Petworth House Library holds sixteen volumes with a total of 149 early modern English playbooks, bound in seventeenth-century calf binding. And Thomas Twysden made a gift of his jointly bound copies of *1 Henry IV* (1604) and *2 Henry IV* (1600). Another composite volume, whose original ownership we know nothing about, contains a masque (Thomas Carew's *Coelum Britanicum*, 1634) and fourteen plays by various playwrights, dated between 1615 and 1635, including *Richard III* (1629), *1 Henry IV* (1632) and the 1622 *Troublesome Reign of John, King of England*, by 'W. Shakespeare'.[128] The volume, still in its original binding, is now at the Folger.[129] A copy of Q5 *Hamlet* (1637) in the Cambridge University Library has a dramatis personae list for *1 Henry IV*, in a seventeenth-century hand, on the last page, suggesting that it was once bound up with that play, and perhaps others. The verso of the title page of a British Library copy of Q1 *The Merchant of Venice* (1600) contains a list of plays 'in early hand, which appears to be the contents list for a bound volume of fifteen plays, in which this play was the first item' (Figure 5.7).[130] The list begins with 'The merchant of venice', 'A mid-somernights dreame' and 'Much adoe about nothinge', and is followed by twelve plays (all first published between 1601 and 1608) by other playwrights.[131]

---

[127] See Foot, *Studies in the History of Bookbinding*, 15–67.

[128] The non-Shakespearean playbooks are Jonson's *Catiline*, Chapman's *Caesar and Pompey*, Shirley's *Triumph of Peace*, Massinger's *The Roman Actor*, Heywood's *1, 2 Edward IV*, *The Troubles of Queen Elizabeth* and *The Four Prentices of London*, Davenant's *The Just Italian*, Dekker's *The Noble Spanish Soldier*, Thomas Randolph's *Aristippus* and the anonymous *Tragedy of Nero*.

[129] See Knight, 'Making Shakespeare's Books', 318. Note that the formerly composite volumes of plays in the Hunter Collection of Glasgow University Library were bound in the eighteenth century, not in the seventeenth (see Knight, 'Making Shakespeare's Books', 314–17).

[130] Kahrl and Anderson, *The Garrick Collection of Old English Plays*, 232.

[131] The other plays listed are, in order (I indicate parenthetically the name of the author(s) and the date of first publication): *Law Tricks* (Day, 1608), *Sir Giles Goosecap* (Chapman, 1606), *The Woman Hater* (Beaumont and Fletcher, 1607), *The Puritan* (Middleton, though ascribed to 'W. S.', 1607), *Lingua* (Tomkis?, 1607), *Michaelmas Term* (Middleton, 1607), *A Trick to Catch the Old One* (Middleton, 1608), *Your Five Gallants* (Middleton, 1608), *Cynthia's Revels* (Jonson, 1601), *Cupid's Whirligig* (Edward Sharpham, 1607), *The Fleir* (Sharpham, 1607) and *The Phoenix* (Middleton, 1607). The list 'cannot be identified with any existing bound volume', nor do we have any knowledge of its history (Kahrl and Anderson, *The Garrick Collection of Old English Plays*, 232).

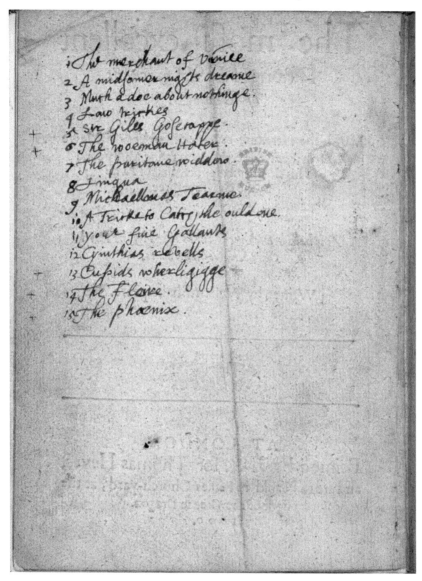

5.7 Title page verso (sig. A1v) of a British Library copy (C.34.k.22) of *The Merchant of Venice* (Q1, 1600) with a list of plays, in manuscript, probably the contents list of a previously bound volume of plays, beginning with 'The merchant of venice', 'A midsomernights dreame' and 'Much adoe about nothinge'.

Other composite volumes contain poems by Shakespeare. Thomas Isham (*d.* 1605), founder of the Lamport Hall Library, owned a volume, now at the Huntington Library, with copies of *Venus and Adonis* (1599) and *The Passionate Pilgrim* (1599), jointly bound with a copy of Sir John Davies's *Epigrammes* (1599).[132] Another volume of around 1600, now at the Folger, includes *The Passionate Pilgrim* (1599), *Venus and Adonis* (1599) and *The Rape of Lucrece* (1600), along with Thomas Middleton's *The Ghost of Lucrece* (1600) and the sonnet sequence *Emaricdulfe* (1595), by 'E. C. Esquier', according to the title page.[133]

A special case of bound Shakespeare playbooks is the 1619 Pavier Quartos (see above, pp. 175–9). Although only *The Whole Contention* and *Pericles* were printed with continuous signatures and the eight playbooks seem to have been issued separately, they were nonetheless part of a single commercial undertaking, and, given their generic and authorial coherence, lent themselves to joint binding. The fact that a considerable number of copies of the Pavier Quartos have survived (see above, p. 189) suggests that many sets were bound, even though most of them, in keeping with later practice, have since been disbound and rebound separately. However, not all of them have. I have previously mentioned Edward Gwynn's calf-bound volume, with his name stamped on the cover, now at the Folger. Another copy, with a rebacked spine but original front and back covers, is now at the Mary Couts Burnett Library, Texas Christian University.[134] A few other copies are known to have existed but no longer do. One was 'given early in the nineteenth century by T. M. Randolph to the University of Virginia and burned in 1895'.[135] Another one was disbound when it was – or before it became – part of the Garrick collection. The separately bound volumes were bequeathed to the British Museum in 1779, where they survive today as

[132] See Gordon, 'The Book-Collecting Ishams of Northamptonshire and their Bookish Virginia Cousins', 175. The volume was rediscovered among a 'group of Elizabethan books … in a garret at Lamport Hall in 1867'. It was 'sold in 1893 to the Britwell library' and became the possession of Henry E. Huntington at the Britwell sale in 1919, where it fetched the record-breaking price of £15,100 (de Ricci, *English Collectors of Books and Manuscripts (1530–1930) and their Marks of Ownership*, 27). See also Knight, 'Making Shakespeare's Books', 327–30; Adams, ed., *The Passionate Pilgrim*, xi–lxiii; and Jackson, 'The Lamport Hall–Britwell Court Books', 587–99.

[133] The volume was rediscovered in 1920 in Longner Hall, an English country house near Shrewsbury, and believed to have been there since the early seventeenth century (see 'Notes on Sales' (26 February 1920)). If so, the first owner may have been Thomas Burton, esq., of Longner (1542–1619), ancestor of Richard Francis Burton, the owner of Longner Hall in 1920. For Thomas Burton, see Burke, *A Genealogical and Heraldic History of the Commoners of Great Britain and Ireland*, IV.263. A somewhat later volume, now also at the Folger, binds *The Rape of Lucrece* (1632) together with Charles Fitz-Geffry's *The Blessed Birth-Day* (Oxford, 1636, STC 10936). See Knight, 'Making Shakespeare's Books', 333–5.

[134] Knight, 'Making Shakespeare's Books', 323–7. 　　[135] Greg, *Bibliography*, III.1108.

quartos of 'uniform and unusually large size'.[136] Similarly, a copy once in the Capell collection, presented to Trinity College Library, Cambridge, survives today bound in two volumes, one with histories (*1 Oldcastle*, *Henry V*, *The Whole Contention*) and one with comedies and tragedies (*A Yorkshire Tragedy*, *Merry Wives*, *Dream*, *Lear*, *Merchant*).[137] Another volume whose copies are now bound separately, at the Folger, contained Heywood's *A Woman Killed with Kindness* in addition to the nine Pavier Quartos, an eloquent reminder that the composition of such bound volumes was typically determined not by the playbooks' publishers or booksellers but by their owners, who could choose to constitute their bound volumes as they pleased.[138]

The extant evidence of early modern composite volumes with Shakespeare in them is no more than the tip of the iceberg that once existed. Many such volumes have inevitably perished, and many others were disbound in centuries past. As Jeffrey Todd Knight has pointed out, 'Particularly in the eighteenth and nineteenth centuries, texts of exceptional value were "cut out of old covers and put into new ones," erasing evidence of earlier reading practices.'[139] In fact, the more important a quarto or octavo book is now considered to be, the less likely it is to have remained in the composite volume to which it once belonged. We can be confident that many of the extant Shakespeare quartos and octavos survive because their early owners chose to have them bound in composite volumes. As T. A. Birrell has put it, 'Shakespeare quartos that have survived were mostly bound up in the seventeenth century as part of tract-volumes, and were disbound and rebound as individual items in the eighteenth, nineteenth, or twentieth century.'[140] The bindings for these volumes were expensive and indicate that their owners did not consider their Shakespeare books discardable 'riffe-raffe' but thought that their preservation was worth paying for.

---

[136] Greg, *Bibliography*, III.1108. See also Bartlett and Pollard, *Census*, §358, §512, §627, §701 and §752; and Kahrl and Anderson, *The Garrick Collection of Old English Plays*, 237.

[137] Greg, *Bibliography*, III.1108, and see Bartlett and Pollard, *Census*, §391, §538, §649, §726 and §778.

[138] Knight, 'Making Shakespeare's Books', 326. Note that the Bibliothèque Nationale in Paris today houses copies of all Pavier Quartos except *A Yorkshire Tragedy* and *1 Oldcastle*, and the copies recorded in Bartlett and Pollard's *Census* (§354, §508, §623, §696 and §749) are of uniform size, which may suggest that they too once belonged to a bound set. Greg also knew of a once-bound volume of Pavier Quartos 'from the library of Edward Hussey of Scotney Castle, Kent' which had been 'broken up and sold at Sotheby's in 1906' (*Bibliography*, III.1108). I have been unable to locate the individual copies of this set. For the discovery of the 'Pavier Quartos' on the basis of various sets of (formerly) bound copies of the ten plays, see Pollard, *Shakespeare Folios and Quartos*, 81–104.

[139] 'Making Shakespeare's Books', 309.

[140] 'The Influence of Seventeenth-Century Publishers on the Presentation of English Literature', 166.

Early readers and commonplacers of Shakespeare in print

Readers of Shakespeare's early quartos and octavos provide corresponding evidence of *textual* engagement. From 1593, when *Venus and Adonis* first appeared, readers left traces which suggest that Shakespeare's poems and plays were taken more seriously than the word 'ephemera' suggests. In a letter of 21 September 1593, William Reynolds, a Londoner who had served in the West Indies, the Netherlands and elsewhere, wrote that 'within thees few dayes ther is another boke made of Venus and Adonis wherin the queene represents the person of Venus', thereby anticipating those modern critics who have read the poem allegorically.[141] Reynolds adds that the poem has 'much ado with redde & whyte' which, as has been pointed out, betrays 'a definite literary perception' given that these colours 'do indeed pervade the whole poem'.[142] Given their frequent reprints, it is perhaps unsurprising that *Venus and Adonis* and *The Rape of Lucrece* stimulated much interest among early readers, as has been fully documented by Sasha Roberts.[143] Yet Shakespeare's quarto playbooks received similarly thoughtful engagement. The scholar Gabriel Harvey, in a marginal note to his copy of Thomas Speght's edition of Chaucer, wrote that 'the younger sort takes much delight in Shakespeares Venus, & Adonis: but Lucrece, & his tragedy of Hamlet, Prince of Denmarke, have it in them, to please the wiser sort'.[144] Harvey was clearly not alone in thinking that a Shakespeare play no less than a Shakespeare poem repaid close attention.

William Scott is a case in point. Born in or around 1579 and having entered the Inner Temple in 1595, he wrote a scholarly treatise of almost a hundred pages, called *The Model of Poesy*, which can be dated to no later than 1601.[145] In it, he repeatedly turns to Shakespeare and provides 'precise close criticism of [his] style', as Stanley Wells has shown.[146] For instance, at one point, Scott probes Shakespeare's versification by drawing on a passage from *The Rape of Lucrece*; at another point, he praises 'the very well-penned Tragedy of Rich. the 2d' and quotes a substantial passage from it when discussing amplification. For Sir Philip Sidney, in his *Defence of Poesy*

---

[141] See, for instance, Erickson, *Rewriting Shakespeare, Rewriting Ourselves*, 41. For Reynolds's letters, see BL MS Lansdowne 99, ff. 81r–87v.

[142] Duncan-Jones, 'Much Ado with Red and White', 489–90.

[143] See *Reading Shakespeare's Poems in Early Modern England*.

[144] Moore Smith, ed., *Gabriel Harvey's Marginalia*, 232. For other, probably later, Harvey marginalia in a copy of Lodovico Guicciardini's *Detti et fatti piacevoli et gravi* (Venice, 1571), with mention of 'the Tragedie of Hamlet: Richard 3', see Hoeniger, 'New Harvey Marginalia on *Hamlet* and *Richard III*'.

[145] See Wells, 'A New Early Reader of Shakespeare', 235.

[146] 'A New Early Reader of Shakespeare', 238. See also Crummé, 'William Scott's Copy of Sidney'.

(*c.* 1579), English drama was basically live theatre, and what the stage produced was 'gross absurdities', 'with neither decency nor discretion', resulting in 'nothing but scurrility, unworthy of any chaste ears'.[147] Some twenty years later, Scott's *Model of Poesy* treats Shakespearean drama as poetry, dramatic poetry, which Scott draws on to illustrate his analysis. The place Scott's poetics grants to Shakespeare makes it seem less surprising than it might otherwise be that – as has recently been discovered – 'from as early as 1628 some schoolboys and university students encountered Shakespeare as an important and authoritative writer in the vernacular in a formal educational setting'.[148]

Scipio Le Squyer and William Drummond of Hawthornden, both of whom we met above as collectors of Shakespeare, also left evidence of their close reading of Shakespearean drama. Le Squyer's copy of Q1 *Pericles* contains emendations in his own hand which are worthy of (and repeatedly anticipate) modern editors, changing 'warmth' to 'warm' (sig. E4r), 'vnsisterd' to 'vnsisserd' (sig. E4v), 'will' to 'wild' (sig. E4v), 'peasure' to 'pleasure' (sig. F4v) and 'mum' to 'Nunn' (sig. I2v).[149] Drummond overlined passages in his copies of the 1599 quarto of *Romeo and Juliet* and the 1598 quarto of *Love's Labour's Lost* which he thought were particularly noteworthy.[150] He seems to have been partial to Shakespeare's personifications, highlighting in *Romeo and Juliet* the 'alcheering Sunne' (sig. B1r), the 'well appareld Aprill' (sig. B2v) and the 'frozen bosome of the North' (sig. C2v), among other passages.[151]

Most manuscript traces in Shakespeare's quarto playbooks were left by anonymous readers. Many books had their margins so mercilessly cropped or white-washed in the nineteenth century that their readers' notes do not survive or are now scarcely legible,[152] but enough evidence survives to show that it was not uncommon for readers to respond to the text in the margins. Some readers added stage directions: a reader of Q1 *Lear* (BL, C.34.k.17) clarified the addressee of certain speeches in Latin: 'ad Regē Gal.' (to the French King) and 'loq. ad Emundū' (spoken to Edmund) (sigs. B3v, H1r) (Figure 5.8);[153] and the annotating reader of Q1 *Othello* (Huntington Library 69337) repeatedly spelled out the implied stage action: 'Lets fall the napkine'

[147] Sidney, *Miscellaneous Prose*, 114–15.
[148] Shakespeare is referred to in the third edition of Thomas Vicars's manual of rhetoric, Χειραγωγία, *Manuductio ad artem rhetoricam* (1628), sig. D11v. See Schurink, 'An Unnoticed Early Reference to Shakespeare'.
[149] See Nelson, 'Shakespeare and the Bibliophiles', 64.
[150] See MacDonald, *The Library of Drummond of Hawthornden*, 140.
[151] See Greg, ed., *Romeo and Juliet*.
[152] See, for example, the Bodleian copy of Q4 *1 Henry IV* (1604, Arch. G d.43.2), sig. D1r.
[153] Massai, 'Shakespeare's Early Readers', 154. This paragraph draws on Massai's important work on playbook annotations by early readers. See, in particular, 'Shakespeare's Early Readers', 149–56, and *Shakespeare and the Rise of the Editor*, 24, 93.

The Historie of King Lear.

Corn. Leaue him to my difpleafure, *Edmūd* keep you our fifter
- (company.
The reuenge we are bound to take vpon your trayterous father,
Are not fit for your beholding, aduife the Duke where you are
To a moft feftuant preparatiō, we are bound to the like, (going
Our poft fhall be fwift and intelligence betwixt vs,
Farewell deere fifter, farewell my Lord of *Glofter,* *loq. ad Edmundū*
How now whers the King ?   *Enter Steward.*

5.8 Manuscript stage direction added to British Library copy (C.34.k.17) of *King Lear* (Q1, 1608), sig. H1r: 'loq. ad Emundū' ('spoken to Edmund').

(sig. H1v), 'othello kneeles' (sig. H3v) and 'he strikes her' (sig. K2v).[154] Even more readers provided alternative readings or corrections, which suggests that textual accuracy was of importance to them. Some manuscript variants betray considerable learning. For instance, in the Folger copy of Q1 *Titus Andronicus* (STC 22328), 'obsequies' (derived from classical Latin) was substituted for 'exequies' (derived from a 'corrupt' medieval form), and 'bereaud in blood' (which most modern editors change to 'berayed [i.e. defiled] in blood') was imaginatively changed to 'heere reau'd of lyfe'. A reader of Q1 *Richard II* (Huntington Library 69343) noticed that a speech heading on sig. I3r was wrong and modified it from 'yorke' to 'King'. Another reader changed 'pangs of office' in Q4 *Hamlet* (1625?, BL C.34. k.3) – an eye-skip error induced by the word 'office' in the line below – to 'pangs of dispis's loue', the reading in Q2 and Q3. And a third reader noted a series of problems in Q1 *Othello* (Huntington Library 69337), changing, for instance, 'Not hot and moist' (emended to 'Hot, hot and moist' in modern editions) to 'both hot and moist'. The above-mentioned reader of Q1 *King Lear* made dozens of local changes to the text, correcting errors or substituting words or phrases he preferred, for instance 'halfe persuaded' for 'false perswaded' (sig. D1v).[155]

Some early readers produced dramatis personae lists, a paratextual feature characteristic of classical drama that was increasingly in evidence in English playbooks (see above, pp. 107–10), including in copies of Q1 *Much Ado*

---

[154] For other stage directions added by an early reader, see the copy of Q3 *Titus Andronicus* (1611), sig. K2v, in the Library of Trinity College, Cambridge.

[155] For other early copies with manuscript notes, see Bartlett and Pollard, *Census*, §1, §284, §519, §1082, §1084 and §1109; and Massai, 'Shakespeare's Early Readers', 149–56.

(1600), Q4 *1 Henry IV* (1604), Q1 *Othello* (1622), Q4 *Hamlet* (1625?), Q7
Richard III (1629) and Q7 *1 Henry IV* (1632).[156] Other playbooks show act or
scene divisions in early hands, for instance a British Library copy of Q6 *1
Henry IV* (1613), which adds scene divisions, and a Bodleian copy of Q3
Love's Labour's Lost (1631), which corrects 'Actus Quartus' to 'Actus
Quintus' on sig. F3v.[157] Other manuscript comments exhibit an interest
in questions of authorship. George Buc wrote on his copy of Q1 *Henry V* (a
'bad quarto'): 'much ye same w[i]th y[a]t in Shakespeare'.[158] Drummond's
copy of Q2 *Romeo and Juliet* has 'Wil. Sha.' on the title page, 'probably in
Drummond's hand'.[159] Anthony Wood added to his copy of *Venus and
Adonis* (1630): 'Written by Will. Shakspeare'.[160] Humphrey Dyson provides
on the title page of his copy of the 1609 quarto of *Troilus and Cressida* what
has been called 'the earliest known bibliographical note on Shakespeare'. To
the printed authorship inscription, 'Written by William Shakespeare', he
added: '& printed amongest his workes'.[161]

Numerous quarto playbooks have traces of readers pointing to specific
passages by means of underlining or marginal signs such as manicules or
vertical strokes.[162] For instance, in a British Library copy of the 1599 edition
of *1 Henry IV* (c.34.k.6), a reader (perhaps a female reader?) highlighted the
moment when Hotspur's wife flatly refuses Hotspur's request that she sing
(sig. F3v). A reader of the Q1 *Lear* (1608) copy, now at the British Library
(c.34.k.17), underlined many passages, beginning with Gloucester's con-
fession that his son Edmund came 'something sawcely into the world' and
that 'there was good sport at his makeing' (sig. B1r). In the same library, a
copy of the 1611 *Hamlet* (c.34.k.4) marks with a cross the moment in the
Pyrrhus speech just before 'reuerent Priam' is killed (sig. F3v), and a Folger
copy of Q3 *Richard II* of 1598 (STC 22309) highlights with a vertical stroke
Richard's sententious words, 'The loue of wicked men conuerts to feare, /
That feare to hate, and hate turnes one or both / To worthy danger and
deserued death' (sig. H2v). In the 1595 octavo of *Richard Duke of York* at the
Bodleian (Arch. G f.1), a line in the margin draws attention to King
Edward's short 'Et tu Brute' speech (sig. E2r), and in the British Library
copy of Q1 *Hamlet* (1603, c.34.k.1), a classically minded reader has

---

[156] See Bartlett and Pollard, *Census*, §41, §226, §258, §785, §812 and §1078.
[157] See Nelson, 'Play Quartos Inscribed by Buc'.   [159] See Bartlett and Pollard, *Census*, §1108.
[158] See Nelson, 'Play Quartos Inscribed by Buc'.
[160] Kiessling, *The Library of Anthony Wood*, 544.
[161] Nelson, 'Shakespeare and the Bibliophiles', 68.
[162] These readers' marks are difficult to date with precision. For a study of manuscript marginalia in early
modern books, see Sherman, *Used Books*.

manicules point to the underlined words, 'Rossios' (i.e. 'Roscius') and 'Plato' (sigs. E3r–v). After a comprehensive survey of early readers' markings, Massai has concluded that they reveal 'the extent to which Shakespeare's early playbooks were increasingly read as literary works'.[163]

Cumulatively, the evidence suggests that many early readers responded to Shakespeare's quarto playbooks in serious, thoughtful ways. Cyndia Susan Clegg has studied how the paratext of playbooks constructs the imagined readers it addresses, arguing that 'The readers we discover in the playwrights' and printers' epistles ... are envisioned as intelligent and discerning. Readers, as co-creators of the literary dramatic text, possessed the capacity to assure the fame of playwrights, and to ensure their perpetuity.'[164] This corresponds quite accurately to the actual readers whose traces we discover in extant copies: they engaged with and annotated the playbooks they were reading and clearly thought of them as more than ephemera.

Readers who marked passages in the margins often did so to copy them into commonplace books, a practice taught in humanist education that had first been applied to classical and Christian authorities and was increasingly applied to vernacular literature as well.[165] Ben Jonson's Sir Politic Would-be, in *Volpone*, collects 'notes / Drawne out of Play-bookes' (sig. M2r), and so, clearly, did a number of Jonson's contemporaries. A series of printed commonplace books emanating from the circle of John Bodenham at the turn of the century constituted a watershed for the use of 'popular, contemporary writers as suitable materials for commonplacing'.[166] Significantly, several of these books contained dramatic excerpts, including by Shakespeare. *England's Parnassus, the Choicest Flowers of Our Modern Poets* (1600), compiled by Robert Allott, brings together numerous literary passages, with author attributions and listed under general subject headings. The majority of Shakespeare extracts derive from *Venus and Adonis* and *The Rape of Lucrece*, but five plays are also represented: *Romeo and Juliet* (with thirteen quotations), *Richard II* (seven), *Richard III* (five), *Love's Labour's Lost* (three) and *1 Henry IV* (two). For instance, in a section on 'Vertue' appears Friar Laurence's sententious admonition, 'Vertue it selfe turnes vice, being misapplied, / And vice sometime by action dignified' (sig. V2r). On the same double page are passages about the same topic by Sir Thomas

---

[163] 'Shakespeare's Early Readers', 151.   [164] 'Renaissance Play-Readers', 34–5.

[165] See Moss, *Printed Commonplace-Books and the Structuring of Renaissance Thought*.

[166] Stallybrass and Chartier, 'Reading and Authorship', 44. See also Lesser and Stallybrass, 'The First Literary *Hamlet*'.

Wyatt, Sir Philip Sidney, Edmund Fairfax (translator of Tasso's *Jerusalem Delivered*), Michael Drayton and others, prestigious company for a Shakespeare play to be in (Figure 5.9).[167] *Belvedere, or the Garden of Muses* (1600), compiled by Bodenham, contains well over four thousand unattributed one- or two-line quotations. More than two hundred of them are by Shakespeare, of which over half are from the narrative poems, forty-seven from *Richard II* and fewer from *Romeo and Juliet*, *Richard III*, *Richard Duke of York*, *Love's Labour's Lost* and *1 Henry IV*. Spenser and Samuel Daniel have about the same number of quotations as Shakespeare, and Drayton is the only poet who is more strongly represented.[168] *England's Helicon* (1600), a literary anthology with entire poems by Sidney, Spenser, Drayton and many others, also collected by Bodenham, includes a song from *Love's Labour's Lost* that had previously appeared in *The Passionate Pilgrim*.[169] 'These volumes', Neil Rhodes has commented, 'start to establish a national literary canon,'[170] and, significantly, lines which Shakespeare had written for plays were considered worthy of inclusion.

Extracts from Shakespeare's quarto playbooks appear not only in printed but also in manuscript commonplace books. One such book, now at the Bodleian Library, combines classical, theological and dramatic material, with sixty passages from plays, including eleven from Shakespeare: *Richard II* (from Q3, 1598), *Hamlet* (Q2, 1604), *Romeo and Juliet* (Q3, 1609) and *Othello* (Q1, 1622). Probably copied in 1622 by a member of Oriel College, Oxford, the dramatic material seems to have been intended for use as sermon material.[171] A manuscript at the British Library (Add. MS 64078) with notes on metaphysics and theology integrates passages from *1 Henry IV* that add up to approximately sixty-two lines (ff. 47r–48r). Dated to *c.* 1598–1603, the excerpts – probably in the hand of Thomas Harriot – are preceded by descriptive headings (e.g. 'of a Temperat ma*n*', f. 47v), and the speeches are recast into the third person, indicating that they were intended for inclusion under topics in a commonplace book.[172] It has been suggested

[167] For the Shakespeare passages in *England's Parnassus*, see Ingleby, ed., *The Shakspeare Allusion-Book*, II.470–9.

[168] See Crawford, '*Belvedere, or The Garden of the Muses*', and 'J. Bodenham's *Belvedere*'.

[169] See Rollins, ed., *England's Helicon 1600, 1614*.   [170] 'Shakespeare's Computer', 253.

[171] Coatalen, 'Shakespeare and Other "Tragicall Discourses" in an Early Seventeenth-Century Commonplace Book from Oriel College, Oxford'.

[172] See Kelliher, 'Contemporary Manuscript Extracts from Shakespeare's *Henry IV, Part I*'. Even earlier are the two stanzas from *Venus and Adonis* copied *c.* 1593–6 by one Henry Collinge along with two other poetic excerpts into a manuscript quarto volume (now at the Cambridge University Library, MS Mm.3.29) with various historical tracts (see Kelliher, 'Unrecorded Extracts from Shakespeare, Sidney and Dyer').

Vertue.

What one art thou thus in torne weede yclad?
Vertue, in price, whom auncient sages had:
Why poorely clad? for fading goods past feare:
Why double fac'd? I marke each fortunes race:
This bridle what? mindes rages to restraine:
VVhy beare you tooles? I loue to take great paine
VVhy wings? I teach aboue the starres to flie:
Why treade you death? I onely cannot die.

S. Th. Wyat.

The path that leades to Vertues Court is narrow,
Thornie, and vp a hill, a bitter iourney:
But being gone through, you find a heauenly soyle,
Th'entrance is all flintie, but at th'end
Two Towres of pearles and cristall you ascend.

Th. Dekker.

Vertue is fayrest in a poore attire.

Idem.

Vertue abhorres too weare a borrowed face.

Idem.

The wisest scholler of the wight most wise,
By Phœbus doome, with sugred sentences,
That vertue if she once insieete with our eyes,
Strange flames of loue it in our soules wouldraise.

S. Ph. Sidney.

That growes apace, that vertue helps t'aspirt.

M. R. nlor.

When vertue riseth, base affections fall.

Ed. Kinfax.

Like as the horse well mand at ides the bit,

And learnes his stoppe by raine in riders hand,
The mountaine colt that is not sadled yet,
Runnes head long on amidst the fallowed land,
Whose fierce resist scarce bends with any band,
So men reclaim'd by vertue tread aright,
When ledde by follies, mischiefes on them light.

Dr. Lodge.

Vertue dab our b affection, and for conscience flieth sin,
T'shun for imperfection, feare or shame no praise doth
                                                (winne.
W. Warner.

Vertue it selfe turnes vice, being misapplyed,
And vice sometime by action dignified.
W. Shakespeare.

Vertue in greatest daunger is most showne,
And though oppress, yet nere is ouerthrowne.
S. Daniell.

Vertue it is said, that men themselues furuiue,

W. W.

How windede, and all things yeeld to death,
(Vertue excepted) which alone suruiues,
And liuing toyleth in an earthlie gaile,
Alast to be extoll'd in heauens high ioyes,   T. Kyd.
All things decay, yet vertue shall not die,
This onely giues vs immortallitie.
M. Drayton.

Whare is it that the flower of the field doth fade,
And lyeth buried long in winters bale,
Yet soon as spring his mantle doth display,
Floweth fresh, as it should neuer faile,
No thing on earth that is of most auaile.

V 2   Releenen

5.9 Double page of *England's Parnassus, the Choicest Flowers of Our Modern Poets* (Q, 1600), sigs. V1v–V2r.

that the Longleat Manuscript, forty lines drawn from *Titus Andronicus* underneath the famous 'Peacham drawing' (probably in 1595), also needs to be understood in the context of commonplacing. 'Like most collectors of commonplaces and quotations of the period', Katherine Duncan-Jones writes, Peacham 'extracted, and in part manufactured, a conventional and blindingly obvious admonitory message'. His treatment of the text, which has puzzled many modern scholars, was in fact 'fairly normal in terms of the practice of individuals in Shakespeare's period who gathered "commonplaces" from contemporary literature'.[173]

Another manuscript commonplace book with Shakespeare extracts is by Edward Pudsey (1573–1613).[174] He compiled most of it in the early 1600s and completed it by 1612. Pudsey's book served him as 'a repository of wisdom and wit gleaned from his reading' and ranges widely from current events and controversies to history, philosophy and drama.[175] It contains passages from plays by Chapman, Heywood, Nashe, Dekker, Lyly, Marston, Jonson, Cyril Tourneur, Webster and, most prominently, Shakespeare, specifically from *The Merchant of Venice*, *Titus Andronicus*, *Romeo and Juliet*, *Richard II*, *Richard III*, *Much Ado about Nothing*, *Hamlet* and *Othello*.[176] Lena Cowen Orlin notes that Pudsey's practice was 'a literary activity': 'Pudsey read published plays as if they were classical texts, studded with bon mots and improving sentiments.'[177]

Conclusion

Early modern playbooks were excerpted on a large scale. Peter Beal's *Index of English Literary Manuscripts* lists more than two hundred manuscripts containing passages from English plays written before 1642.[178] Extracts from

---

[173] *Upstart Crow to Sweet Swan*, 56, 70. The manuscript is at Longleat House, Wiltshire, among the Harley papers, vol. 1, f. 159v. See also Levin, 'The Longleat Manuscript and *Titus Andronicus*'.

[174] The book is now at the Bodleian (MS Eng.poet.d.3), except for four leaves which were taken from the manuscript in the late nineteenth century and are now at the Shakespeare Birthplace Trust Record Office (ER 82/1/21). For Pudsey's book, see Savage, *Shakespearean Extracts from 'Edward Pudsey's Booke'*; Gowan, '"One Man in his Time"'; and Duncan-Jones, *Upstart Crow to Sweet Swan*, 72–83.

[175] See Kathman, 'Edward Pudsey (*bap.* 1573, *d.* 1612/13)'.

[176] *Othello* was not published until nine years after Pudsey's death, and Pudsey's passages correspond loosely to those which were later printed, whereas the quotations from the other plays are very accurate, so it is believed that Pudsey copied the excerpts from *Othello* at a performance.

[177] 'The Private Life of Public Plays', 142.

[178] I owe this count in Beal's *Index* to Estill, 'Proverbial Shakespeare', 36–7. See Beal, comp., *Index of English Literary Manuscripts* (for manuscript extracts from Shakespeare's plays and poems: 1.449–63). See also Estill, 'The Circulation and Recontextualization of Dramatic Excerpts in Seventeenth-Century English Manuscripts'.

Shakespeare's plays appeared alongside not only highly respected poets such as Spenser, Sidney and Wyatt but also classical, philosophical and theological material. Tiffany Stern has argued that 'Shakespeare, always conscious of the people for whom he writes, may even have shaped his plays to the commonplace-book culture. Anticipating sections of his plays being excerpted, some of Shakespeare's punchier quotations . . . may have been intended to be "removable": to appeal to table-books.'[179] Independently of whether Shakespeare did consciously write for commonplace books, by 1600 at the latest, he is likely to have known that his plays were being excerpted, given that two commonplace books and an anthology with lines from his plays were published that year. He may well have realized, in other words, not only that his plays were being published and republished with success and that his name was counted on to sell books, as seen in earlier chapters, but also that his plays and poems were entering the literary canon.

[179] 'Watching as Reading', 144.

The publication of playbooks by Shakespeare and his contemporaries to 1660

(prepared with the assistance of Louise Wilson)

This appendix provides information about the publication of playbooks by Shakespeare and other early modern playwrights up to 1660. The various tables in Chapter 1 are derived from data listed below. Only those plays which were written for the commercial stage are included here. For statistical comparisons between dramatists to be meaningful, a dramatic oeuvre of at least some size is required. I therefore include only playwrights with a corpus of at least five professional plays of which at least twelve editions were printed by 1660 (see summary in Table 7). This means that Greene (13 editions), Ford (13), William Rowley (13) and Webster (13) are included, but William Davenant (11), John Suckling (11), George Wilkins (11) and Thomas Randolph (10) are not. I make an exception for Peele (11) because he is an exact contemporary of, and collaborator with, Shakespeare. On the other hand, I do not include Kyd for whom a very successful play (*The Spanish Tragedy*) but only a very small dramatic corpus has survived.[1] All in all, I provide tables for nineteen playwrights (Tables 8.1–19): Shakespeare and eighteen of his contemporaries and successors.

Columns C and D in Tables 8.1–19 list the number of reprints within twenty-five and ten years of original publication. Like Farmer and Lesser, but unlike Blayney, I include in the count editions published in the tenth or twenty-fifth year after the year of original publication.[2] So a 1608 edition of

---

[1] *The Spanish Tragedy*, *Soliman and Perseda*, and *The First Part of Hieronimo* (which is partly based on Kyd's lost *Don Horatio*) are the only professional plays that have traditionally been associated with Kyd (see Erne, *Beyond 'The Spanish Tragedy'*). Note though that Brian Vickers has argued for an extension of the Kyd canon ('Thomas Kyd, Secret Sharer'). Pending further research, I base my Kyd corpus on my study of 2001.

[2] See Farmer and Lesser, 'The Popularity of Playbooks Revisited', 31; and Blayney, 'The Publication of Playbooks'.

a play originally published in 1598 is considered as having been published inside ten years.

I distinguish between playbooks, which constitute separate publishing ventures, independently of the playbook's size, and play texts, by which I mean any edition of any play. So the Shakespeare First Folio of 1623 is one playbook but contains thirty-six play texts. Certain collections contain as few as two play texts (e.g. the *1590 octavo edition of 1, 2 Tamburlaine*). For easier visibility, collections and their publication dates are printed in italics.

The content of the playbooks needs to be largely identical to count as a reprint. The second Shakespeare Folio of 1632 thus counts as a reprint of the First Folio, but the First Folio does not count as a reprint of a single quarto playbook (e.g. the 1623 First Folio is not a playbook reprint of Q1 *Othello* of 1622 despite the fact that the Folio contains a play text of *Othello*). Reprint rates calculate the success of commercial publishing ventures, and a quarto playbook of a single text is a very different kind of venture from a collection.[3] On the other hand, my reprint count does not distinguish between different versions of a play. I count Q2 *Hamlet* as a reprint of Q1 *Hamlet*, since both are *Hamlet* playbooks, even though the verbal substance of the texts differs. The dates of editions after 1660 are mentioned exclusively (and between brackets) if they occur within twenty-five years of the first edition and therefore have an impact on the number of reprints within a quarter-century of original publication.

I mention the format of playbook editions following the year of publication: '2°' means folio, '8°' octavo and '12°' duodecimo. If the year of publication is not followed by an indication, the playbook appeared in quarto format.

Many plays were written collaboratively. I mention co-authors between brackets and list such plays under each co-author. Accordingly, *Titus Andronicus*, probably a collaborative play by Shakespeare and Peele, appears under both playwrights, and *Eastward Ho* is listed under Chapman, Jonson and Marston. If a play was revised or provided with additions, I usually do not count the author of these revisions or additions as a co-author. For instance, Webster is known to have written additions to *The Malcontent* which were included in Q3 (1604).[4] Nonetheless, I consider *The Malcontent* as a single-authored play by Marston. I acknowledge that the borderlines are

---

[3] I here follow Farmer and Lesser's 'reprint parameters' as explained in 'The Popularity of Playbooks Revisited', 31.

[4] See Gunby, Carnegie and Jackson, eds., *The Works of John Webster*, III.295–356.

fluid and that scholars are likely to disagree about the nature of a playwright's contribution to a play (notably in a case like Massinger).[5]

This brings me to the vexed question of authorship attributions (see also above, p. 40). The authorship of a number of early modern plays, especially of collaborative plays, is still a matter of scholarly debate, and no consensus is likely to be reached any time soon. Inevitably, the inclusion or exclusion of certain plays from certain tables depends on scholarly conjecture. The best I can hope to do in such a situation is to present as transparently as possible the exact authorship attributions to which I adhere. Others may disagree with some of my decisions, but at least they know on what my figures are based.

In the compilation of this appendix, various sources have been drawn upon, including Harbage's *Annals of English Drama, 975–1700*, the *STC*, the *ESTC*, the *DEEP*, Greg's *Bibliography of the English Printed Drama to the Restoration*, Chambers's *The Elizabethan Stage* and Bentley's *The Jacobean and Caroline Stage*. When a recent authoritative edition is available, I have consulted it to determine the boundaries of a playwright's canon.

The thirty-four plays in the 'Beaumont and Fletcher' canon provide some of the thorniest problems in authorship attribution studies: the 1647 Folio appears to contain only a few Beaumont-and-Fletcher collaborations, fewer than a dozen single-authored Fletcher plays and no single-authored Beaumont plays, but a number of Fletcher-and-Massinger collaborations as well as, it seems, collaborations between Fletcher and Nathan Field; Fletcher and Middleton; Fletcher and Rowley; Middleton and Rowley; Fletcher, Massinger and Field; and Fletcher, Massinger, Ford and Webster; and a single-authored play by Ford. Even though the work by Cyrus Hoy has occasionally been criticized, both for specific attributions and on general grounds,[6] it often presents the best available analysis, and his authorship attributions are still adhered to by recent scholars.[7] I occasionally part company with Hoy when more recent scholars have come to different conclusions (as in the case of *The Bloody Brother*), but adopt his findings when no convincing alternatives have been advanced since the mid-twentieth century.

---

[5] The 'Beaumont and Fletcher' Folio of 1647 presents a special case. Given that Massinger's contribution to the thirt-four plays is actually greater than Beaumont's, I count it as a Beaumont, Fletcher and Massinger playbook.

[6] Hoy, 'The Shares of Fletcher and his Collaborators in the Beaumont and Fletcher Canon'. See Vickers *Shakespeare, Co-Author*, 385–8, and Masten, 'Beaumont and/or Fletcher'.

[7] Bowers, ed., *The Dramatic Works in the Beaumont and Fletcher Canon*, is partly built on Hoy's scholarship. See also Gossett, *The Influence of the Jacobean Masque on the Plays of Beaumont and Fletcher*, 35, and Henze, 'Unraveling Beaumont from Fletcher with Music, Misogyny, and Masque'.

Table 7 *Number of playbooks, play texts and reprints by dramatist: a summary*

Name	I	II	III	IV	V	VI	VII	VIII	IX
Shakespeare	24	74	76	38	23	145	147	1.6	0.95
Beaumont	9	26	34	18	5	25	39	2.00	0.55
Brome	8	4	8	2	2	4	16	0.25	0.25
Chapman	14	19	19	3	3	21	21	0.20	0.20
Dekker	21	28	33	9	6	28	33	0.45	0.30
Fletcher	16	34	43	23	6	36	77	1.45	0.40
Ford	11	7	11	1	1	7	13	0.10	0.10
Greene	6	12	13	5	3	12	13	0.85	0.50
Heywood	23	49	51	21	13	55	57	0.90	0.55
Jonson	15	22	22	7	4	41	41	0.45	0.25
Lyly	9	15	15	6	6	20	20	0.65	0.65
Marlowe	8	21	21	11	5	24	24	1.40	0.65
Marston	12	20	20	8	5	25	25	0.65	0.40
Massinger	18	19	25	5	2	19	40	0.30	0.10
Middleton	20	26	32	11	7	28	37	0.55	0.35
Peele	6	9	9	3	2	11	11	0.50	0.35
Rowley	10	6	11	3	2	6	13	0.30	0.20
Shirley	30	30	35	4	3	30	41	0.15	0.10
Webster	7	9	12	6	3	12	13	0.85	0.45

The individual tables, one per dramatist, are preceded by a summary table (Table 7) that brings together all dramatists and certain key figures about the publication of their playbooks. In this table, columns I to IX provide the following information:

I   Total number of playbooks, first editions, up to 1660

II   Total number of playbooks, first and following editions, up to 1642

III   Total number of playbooks, first and following editions, up to 1660

IV   Total number of reprints within twenty-five years of original publication

V   Total number of reprints within ten years of original publication

VI   Total number of play texts, first and following editions, up to 1642

VII   Total number of play texts, first and following editions, up to 1660

VIII   Average rate of reprints within twenty-five years of original publication: number of reprints (IV) divided by number of first editions (I)

IX   Average rate of reprints within ten years of original publication: number of reprints (V) divided by number of first editions (I)

In Tables 8.1–19, columns A to F provide the following information:

A   Number of playbooks, first and following editions, up to 1642
B   Number of playbooks, first and following editions, up to 1660
C   Number of reprints within twenty-five years of original publication
D   Number of reprints within ten years of original publication
E   Number of play texts, first and following editions, up to 1642
F   Number of play texts, first and following editions, up to 1660

Tables 8.1–19   *Number of playbooks, play texts and reprints by dramatist*

Table 8.1   *William Shakespeare*

Title	Dates of editions	A	B	C	D	E	F
Titus Andronicus (with Peele)	1594, 1600, 1611, *1623* (2°), *1632* (2°)	3	3	2	1	5	5
2 Henry VI (*1 Contention*)	1594, 1600, 1619, *1623* (2°), *1632* (2°)	2	2	1	1	5	5
3 Henry VI (*Richard Duke of York*)	1595 (8°), 1600, 1619, *1623* (2°), *1632* (2°)	2	2	1	1	5	5
Edward III	1596, 1599	2	2	1	1	2	2
Richard II	1597, 1598, 1598, 1608, 1615, *1623* (2°), *1632* (2°), 1634	6	6	4	2	8	8
Richard III	1597, 1598, 1602, 1605, 1612, 1622, *1623* (2°), 1629, *1632* (2°), 1634	8	8	5	3	10	10
Romeo and Juliet	1597, 1599, 1609, [1623?], *1623* (2°), *1632* (2°), 1637	5	5	2	1	7	7
Love's Labour's Lost	[1597], 1598, *1623* (2°), 1631, *1632* (2°)	3	3	1	1	5	5
1 Henry IV	[1598], 1598, 1599, 1604, 1608, 1613, 1622, *1623* (2°), *1632* (2°), 1632, 1639	9	9	6	4	11	11
Henry V	1600, 1602, '1608' [i.e. 1619], *1623* (2°), *1632* (2°)	3	3	2	1	5	5
2 Henry IV	1600, *1623* (2°), *1632* (2°)	1	1	0	0	3	3
Much Ado about Nothing	1600, *1623* (2°), *1632* (2°)	1	1	0	0	3	3
A Midsummer Night's Dream	1600, '1600' [i.e. 1619], *1623* (2°), *1632* (2°)	2	2	1	0	4	4
The Merchant of Venice	1600, '1600' [i.e. 1619], *1623* (2°), *1632* (2°), 1637	3	3	1	0	5	5
The Merry Wives of Windsor	1602, 1619, *1623* (2°), 1630, *1632* (2°)	3	3	1	0	5	5
Hamlet	1603, 1604, 1611, [1625?], *1623* (2°), *1632* (2°), 1637	5	5	3	2	7	7
King Lear	1608, '1608' [i.e. 1619], *1623* (2°), *1632* (2°), 1655	2	3	1	0	4	5
Troilus and Cressida	1609, *1623* (2°), *1632* (2°)	1	1	0	0	3	3
Pericles (with Wilkins)	1609, 1609, 1611, 1619, 1630, 1635	6	6	4	3	6	6
The Whole Contention	*1619*	1	1	0	0	–	–

Table 8.1 *(cont.)*

Title	Dates of editions	A	B	C	D	E	F
Othello	1622, *1623* (2°), 1630, *1632* (2°), 1655	2	3	1	1	4	5
The Taming of the Shrew	*1623* (2°), 1631, *1632* (2°)	1	1	0	0	3	3
The Tempest	*1623* (2°), *1632* (2°)	–	–	–	–	2	2
The Two Gentlemen of Verona	*1623* (2°), *1632* (2°)	–	–	–	–	2	2
Measure for Measure	*1623* (2°), *1632* (2°)	–	–	–	–	2	2
The Comedy of Errors	*1623* (2°), *1632* (2°)	–	–	–	–	2	2
As You Like It	*1623* (2°), *1632* (2°)	–	–	–	–	2	2
All's Well That Ends Well	*1623* (2°), *1632* (2°)	–	–	–	–	2	2
Twelfth Night	*1623* (2°), *1632* (2°)	–	–	–	–	2	2
The Winter's Tale	*1623* (2°), *1632* (2°)	–	–	–	–	2	2
King John	*1623* (2°), *1632* (2°)	–	–	–	–	2	2
1 Henry VI	*1623* (2°), *1632* (2°)	–	–	–	–	2	2
Coriolanus	*1623* (2°), *1632* (2°)	–	–	–	–	2	2
Timon of Athens (with Middleton)	*1623* (2°), *1632* (2°)	–	–	–	–	2	2
Julius Caesar	*1623* (2°), *1632* (2°)	–	–	–	–	2	2
Macbeth	*1623* (2°), *1632* (2°)	–	–	–	–	2	2
Antony and Cleopatra	*1623* (2°), *1632* (2°)	–	–	–	–	2	2
Cymbeline	*1623* (2°), *1632* (2°)	–	–	–	–	2	2
Henry VIII (All is True) (with Fletcher)	*1623* (2°), *1632* (2°)	–	–	–	–	2	2
Comedies, Histories, & Tragedies	*1623* (2°), *1632* (2°)	2	2	1	1	–	–
The Two Noble Kinsmen (with Fletcher)	1634	1	1	0	0	1	1

Note
- For the boundaries of the Shakespeare canon and for the conjectural dating of some editions, see above, pp. 11–17.

Table 8.2 *Francis Beaumont*

Title	Dates of editions	A	B	C	D	E	F
The Woman Hater	1607, 1648	1	2	0	0	1	2
The Knight of the Burning Pestle	1613, 1635	2	2	1	0	1	2
Cupid's Revenge (with Fletcher)	1615, 1630, 1635	3	3	2	0	3	3
The Scornful Lady (with Fletcher)	1616, 1625, 1630, 1635, 1639, 1651, '1651' [1657–61?]	5	7	4	1	5	7
A King and No King (with Fletcher)	1619, 1625, 1631, 1639, 1655	4	5	3	1	4	5
The Maid's Tragedy (with Fletcher)	1619, 1622, 1630, 1638, 1641, '1650' [i.e. 1660?]	5	6	4	1	5	6

Table 8.2 (*cont.*)

Title	Dates of editions	A	B	C	D	E	F
Philaster, or Love Lies a-Bleeding (with Fletcher)	1620, 1622, 1628, 1634, 1639, 1652	5	6	4	2	5	6
Thierry and Theodoret (with Fletcher and Massinger)	1621, 1648	1	2	0	0	1	2
The Coxcomb (with Fletcher)	*1647* (2°)	–	–	–	–	0	1
The Captain (with Fletcher)	*1647* (2°)	–	–	–	–	0	1
The Noble Gentleman (with Fletcher)	*1647* (2°)	–	–	–	–	0	1
Beggars' Bush (with Fletcher and Massinger)	*1647* (2°)	–	–	–	–	0	1
Love's Pilgrimage (with Fletcher)	*1647* (2°)	–	–	–	–	0	1
Love's Cure, or The Martial Maid (with Fletcher and Massinger)	*1647* (2°)	–	–	–	–	0	1
Comedies and Tragedies (with Fletcher and Massinger)	*1647* (2°)	0	1	0	0	–	–

Notes

- Two editions of *The Scornful Lady* are misdated 1651. Greg drew on typographical evidence to argue that at least one of these must have been printed considerably later than 1651 (*Bibliography*, 1.478–9). I include one of the two misdated editions in my count (thus assuming that it was printed by 1660) but omit the other on the assumption, shared by Greg, that it was printed after 1660. Note that the 1661 quarto of *Beggars' Bush* has an advertisement on the title page accusing Francis Kirkman of the piracy of several (unidentified) plays, presumably including *The Scornful Lady* (see Bald, 'Francis Kirkman, Bookseller and Author'; and Taylor and Lavagnino, eds., *Thomas Middleton and Early Modern Textual Culture*, 1160).
- The edition of *The Maid's Tragedy* printed *c.* 1660 (Q6) has the date '1650' on the title page but contains advertisements for books printed after this date, one as late as 1660.
- An edition of *Philaster* misdated 1652 is believed by Greg to have been printed in 1661: 'Since Leake is unlikely to have published two editions the same year . . . it may be one of the fraudulent reprints circulated by Kirkman and his associates about 1661 . . . There does not appear to be much doubt on typographical grounds that this edition is some years later than [the 1652 edition]' (*Bibliography*, II.513). This edition is therefore omitted from the present count. For the same reason, the edition of *The Knight of the Burning Pestle*, misdated 1635 but probably of 1661, is similarly excluded (see Greg, *Bibliography*, 1.459).
- Some have attributed *The Noble Gentleman* to Fletcher alone, but others, including Hoy ('The Shares of Fletcher and his Collaborators' (1958), 94–5), consider it a collaboration by Beaumont and Fletcher.

Table 8.3 *Richard Brome*

Title	Dates of editions	A	B	C	D	E	F
The Northern Lass	1632	I	I	O	O	I	I
The Late Lancashire Witches (with Heywood)	1634	I	I	O	O	I	I
The Antipodes	1640	I	I	O	O	I	I
The Sparagus Garden (Tom Hoydon o' Tanton Deane)	1640	I	I	O	O	I	I
A Jovial Crew, or The Merry Beggars	1652, (1661)	O	I	I	I	O	I
The Mad Couple Well Matched	1653 (8°)	–	–	–	–	O	I
The Novella	1653 (8°)	–	–	–	–	O	I
The Court Beggar	1653 (8°)	–	–	–	–	O	I
The City Wit, or The Woman Wears the Breeches	1653 (8°)	–	–	–	–	O	I
The Damoiselle, or The New Ordinary	1653 (8°)	–	–	–	–	O	I
Five New Plays	1653 (8°)	O	I	O	O	–	–
The Queen's Exchange (The Royal Exchange)	1657, (1661)	O	I	I	I	O	I
The English Moor, or The Mock Marriage	1659 (8°)	–	–	–	–	O	I
The Weeding of the Covent Garden	1659 (8°)	–	–	–	–	O	I
The Queen and Concubine	1659 (8°)	–	–	–	–	O	I
The Lovesick Court, or The Ambitious Politic	1659 (8°)	–	–	–	–	O	I
The New Academy, or The New Exchange	1659 (8°)	–	–	–	–	O	I
Five New Plays	1659 (8°)	O	I	O	O	–	–

Notes
- *The Mad Couple Well Matched*, *The Novella*, *The Court Beggar*, *The City Wit* and *The Damoiselle* were published in a volume entitled *Five New Plays* (1653).
- *The English Moor*, *The Weeding of the Covent Garden*, *The Queen and Concubine*, *The Lovesick Court, or The Ambitious Politic* and *The New Academy, or The New Exchange* appeared in a volume entitled *Five New Plays* (1659).

Table 8.4 *George Chapman*

Title	Dates of editions	A	B	C	D	E	F
The Blind Beggar of Alexandria	1598	I	I	O	O	I	I
An Humorous Day's Mirth	1599	I	I	O	O	I	I
Eastward Ho (with Jonson and Marston)	1605, 1605, 1605	3	3	2	2	3	3
All Fools	1605	I	I	O	O	I	I
Monsieur D'Olive	1606	I	I	O	O	I	I
The Gentleman Usher	1606	I	I	O	O	I	I
Sir Giles Goosecap	1606, 1636	2	2	O	O	2	2
Bussy D'Ambois	1607, 1641	2	2	O	O	2	2
The Conspiracy and Tragedy of Charles, Duke of Byron	1608, 1625	2	2	I	I	–	–
The Conspiracy of Charles, Duke of Byron	1608, 1625	–	–	–	–	2	2
The Tragedy of Charles, Duke of Byron	1608, 1625	–	–	–	–	2	2
May Day	1611	I	I	O	O	I	I

Table 8.4 (cont.)

Title	Dates of editions	A	B	C	D	E	F
The Widow's Tears	1612	1	1	0	0	1	1
The Revenge of Bussy D'Ambois	1613	1	1	0	0	1	1
Caesar and Pompey (*The Wars of Caesar and Pompey*)	1631	1	1	0	0	1	1
Chabot, Admiral of France (with Shirley)	1639	1	1	0	0	1	1

Table 8.5 *Thomas Dekker*

Title	Dates of editions	A	B	C	D	E	F
Old Fortunatus	1600	1	1	0	0	1	1
The Shoemaker's Holiday	1600, 1610, 1618, 1624, 1631, 1657	5	6	3	1	5	6
Satiromastix	1602	1	1	0	0	1	1
Blurt Master Constable	1602	1	1	0	0	1	1
Patient Grissel (with Henry Chettle and William Haughton)	1603	1	1	0	0	1	1
The Patient Man and the Honest Whore (with Middleton)	1604, [1604?], 1605, 1615/16, 1635	5	5	3	2	5	5
Westward Ho (with Webster)	1607	1	1	0	0	1	1
The Whore of Babylon	1607	1	1	0	0	1	1
Northward Ho (with Webster)	1607	1	1	0	0	1	1
The Famous History of Sir Thomas Wyatt (with Webster)	1607, 1612	2	2	1	1	2	2
The Roaring Girl (with Middleton)	1611	1	1	0	0	1	1
If It Be Not Good, the Devil Is in It	1612	1	1	0	0	1	1
The Virgin Martyr (with Massinger)	1622, 1631, 1651	2	3	1	1	2	3
2 The Honest Whore	1630	1	1	0	0	1	1
Match Me in London	1631	1	1	0	0	1	1
The Noble Spanish Soldier	1634	1	1	0	0	1	1
The Wonder of a Kingdom	1636	1	1	0	0	1	1
The Bloody Banquet (with Middleton)	1639	1	1	0	0	1	1
The Spanish Gypsy (with Middleton, Ford and W. Rowley)	1653 (1661)	0	1	1	1	0	1
The Sun's Darling (with Dekker)	1656	0	1	0	0	0	1
The Witch of Edmonton (with Ford and W. Rowley)	1658	0	1	0	0	0	1

Notes
- For Dekker's dramatic corpus, see Bowers, ed., *The Dramatic Works of Thomas Dekker*.
- For Dekker's authorship of the anonymously published *Blurt Master Constable* (1602), see Taylor and Lavagnino, eds., *Thomas Middleton and Early Modern Textual Culture*, 444; and Lake, *The Canon of Thomas Middleton's Plays*, 66–90.
- For Dekker's authorship of *The Noble Spanish Soldier*, see the edition by John Price.
- According to Taylor and Lavagnino, eds., *The Collected Works of Thomas Middleton*, *The Spanish Gypsy* is a collaboration by Middleton, William Rowley, Dekker and Ford (see 433–7), despite the fact that the title page only mentions Middleton and Rowley.

Table 8.6 *John Fletcher*

Title	Dates of editions	A	B	C	D	E	F
The Faithful Shepherdess	[1610?], 1629, 1634, 1656	3	4	2	0	3	4
Cupid's Revenge (with Beaumont)	1615, 1630, 1635	3	3	2	0	3	3
The Scornful Lady (with Beaumont)	1616, 1625, 1630, 1635, 1639, 1651	5	6	4	1	5	6
The Maid's Tragedy (with Beaumont)	1619, 1622, 1630, 1638, 1641, '1650' [i.e. 1660?]	5	6	4	1	5	6
A King and No King (with Beaumont)	1619, 1625, 1631, 1639, 1655	4	5	3	1	4	5
Philaster (with Beaumont)	1620, 1622, 1628, 1634, 1639, 1652	5	6	4	2	5	6
Thierry and Theodoret (with Beaumont and Massinger)	1621, 1648	1	2	0	0	1	2
Henry VIII (with Shakespeare)	*1623* (2°), *1632* (2°)	–	–	–	–	2	2
The Two Noble Kinsmen (with Shakespeare)	1634	1	1	0	0	1	1
The Elder Brother (with Massinger)	1637, 1651	1	2	1	0	1	2
Wit Without Money	1639, (1661)	1	1	1	0	1	1
Monsieur Thomas	1639	1	1	0	0	1	1
The Bloody Brother (*Rollo Duke of Normandy*) (with Massinger)	1639, 1640	2	2	1	1	2	2
The Night Walker (with Shirley)	1640, (1661)	1	1	1	0	1	1
Rule a Wife and Have a Wife	1640	1	1	0	0	1	1
The Mad Lover	*1647* (2°)	–	–	–	–	0	1
The Spanish Curate (with Massinger)	*1647* (2°)	–	–	–	–	0	1
The Little French Lawyer (with Massinger)	*1647* (2°)	–	–	–	–	0	1
The Custom of the Country (with Massinger)	*1647* (2°)	–	–	–	–	0	1
The Noble Gentleman (with Beaumont)	*1647* (2°)	–	–	–	–	0	1
The Captain (with Beaumont)	*1647* (2°)	–	–	–	–	0	1
Beggar's Bush	*1647* (2°)	–	–	–	–	0	1
The Coxcomb (with Beaumont)	*1647* (2°)	–	–	–	–	0	1
The False One (with Massinger)	*1647* (2°)	–	–	–	–	0	1
The Chances	*1647* (2°)	–	–	–	–	0	1
The Loyal Subject	*1647* (2°)	–	–	–	–	0	1
The Wandering Lovers (*The Lovers' Progress*) (with Massinger)	*1647* (2°)	–	–	–	–	0	1
The Island Princess	*1647* (2°)	–	–	–	–	0	1
The Humorous Lieutenant	*1647* (2°)	–	–	–	–	0	1
The Nice Valour, or The Passionate Madman (with Middleton)	*1647* (2°)	–	–	–	–	0	1
The Maid in the Mill (with W. Rowley)	*1647* (2°)	–	–	–	–	0	1
The Prophetess (with Massinger)	*1647* (2°)	–	–	–	–	0	1
Bonduca	*1647* (2°)	–	–	–	–	0	1
The Sea Voyage (with Massinger)	*1647* (2°)	–	–	–	–	0	1
The Double Marriage (with Massinger)	*1647* (2°)	–	–	–	–	0	1

Table 8.6 (*cont.*)

Title	Dates of editions	A	B	C	D	E	F
The Pilgrim	*1647* (2°)	–	–	–	–	o	1
The Knight of Malta (with Field and Massinger)	*1647* (2°)	–	–	–	–	o	1
The Woman's Prize, or The Tamer Tamed	*1647* (2°)	–	–	–	–	o	1
Love's Cure, or The Martial Maid (with Beaumont and Massinger)	*1647* (2°)	–	–	–	–	o	1
The Honest Man's Fortune (with Field and Massinger)	*1647* (2°)	–	–	–	–	o	1
The Queen of Corinth (with Field and Massinger)	*1647* (2°)	–	–	–	–	o	1
Women Pleased	*1647* (2°)	–	–	–	–	o	1
A Wife for a Month	*1647* (2°)	–	–	–	–	o	1
Valentinian	*1647* (2°)	–	–	–	–	o	1
The Fair Maid of the Inn (with Ford, Massinger and Webster)	*1647* (2°)	–	–	–	–	o	1
Love's Pilgrimage (with Beaumont)	*1647* (2°)	–	–	–	–	o	1
Four Plays, or Moral Representations, in One (with Field)	*1647* (2°)	–	–	–	–	o	1
Comedies and Tragedies (with Beaumont and Massinger)	*1647* (2°)	o	1	o	o	–	–
The Wild Goose Chase	1652 (2°)	o	1	o	o	o	1
A Very Woman (with Massinger)	1655 (8°)	–	–	–	–	o	1

Notes

- The first quarto of *The Faithful Shepherdess* is undated: 1610 is the date conjectured by the *STC*.
- For Q6 *The Maid's Tragedy*, see the note under Beaumont.
- An edition mistakenly dated 1637 of *The Elder Brother* is conjectured by the *STC* to have been printed in 1661.
- Hoy ('The Shares of Fletcher and his Collaborators' (1961), 56–63) tentatively attributes *The Bloody Brother (Rollo Duke of Normandy)* to Fletcher, Massinger, Chapman and Jonson, but acknowledges that the evidence for Jonson's involvement remains 'pitifully slight' (61) and that for Chapman's 'painfully slight' (63). Bevington, Butler and Donaldson, gen. eds., *The Cambridge Edition of the Works of Ben Jonson*, do not count the play among Jonson's.
- For *The Night Walker or The Little Thief*, see the note under Shirley.
- According to Hoy ('The Shares of Fletcher and his Collaborators' (1960), 100–3), *The Fair Maid of the Inn* is a collaborative work by Fletcher, Ford, Massinger and Webster. See also Vickers, gen. ed., *The Collected Works of John Ford*, Volume II.
- *The Wild Goose Chase*, published in Folio in 1652, was printed separately from the 1647 Folio. In 1647 the play had long been lost and was supposed to be irrecoverable.
- *A Very Woman*, a Fletcher/Massinger collaboration, appeared in a collection of *Three New Plays*, assigned to Massinger, containing *The Guardian, A Very Woman* and *The Bashful Lover*.

Table 8.7 *John Ford*

Title	Dates of editions	A	B	C	D	E	F
The Lover's Melancholy	1629	I	I	O	O	I	I
'Tis Pity She's A Whore	1633	I	I	O	O	I	I
Love's Sacrifice	1633	I	I	O	O	I	I
The Broken Heart	1633	I	I	O	O	I	I
Perkin Warbeck	1634	I	I	O	O	I	I
The Fancies Chaste and Noble	1638	I	I	O	O	I	I
The Lady's Trial	1639	I	I	O	O	I	I
The Laws of Candy	1647 (2°)	–	–	–	–	O	I
The Fair Maid of the Inn (with Fletcher, Massinger and Webster)	1647 (2°)	–	–	–	–	O	I
The Queen, or The Excellency of Her Sex	1653	O	I	O	O	O	I
The Spanish Gypsy (with Middleton, Rowley and Dekker)	1653 (1661)	O	I	I	I	O	I
The Sun's Darling (with Dekker)	1656	O	I	O	O	O	I
The Witch of Edmonton (with Rowley and Dekker)	1658	O	I	O	O	O	I

Notes
- For Ford's dramatic corpus, see Vickers, gen. ed., *The Collected Works of John Ford*, Volumes II and III.
- *The Laws of Candy* and *The Fair Maid of the Inn* were included in the 'Beaumont and Fletcher' Folio.
- For *The Spanish Gypsy*, see the note under Dekker.

Table 8.8 *Robert Greene*

Title	Dates of editions	A	B	C	D	E	F
Orlando Furioso	1594, 1599	2	2	I	I	2	2
Friar Bacon and Friar Bongay	1594, 1630, 1655	2	3	O	O	2	3
A Looking Glass for London and England (with Lodge)	1594, 1598, 1602, [1605?], 1617	5	5	4	2	5	5
The Scottish History of James the Fourth	1598	I	I	O	O	I	I
Alphonsus, King of Aragon	1599	I	I	O	O	I	I
George a Green, the Pinner of Wakefield	1599	I	I	O	O	I	I

Notes
- The only extant copy of Q4 *A Looking Glass for London and England* lacks a title page. For the date 1605, see Maguire, 'The Printer and Date of Q4 *A Looking Glass for London and England*'.
- For the authorship of *Selimus*, see above, p. 31.

Table 8.9 *Thomas Heywood*

Title	Dates of editions	A	B	C	D	E	F
1, 2 Edward IV	*1599, 1600, 1605, 1613, 1619, 1626*	6	6	4	2	–	–
1 Edward IV	*1599, 1600, 1605, 1613, 1619, 1626*	–	–	–	–	6	6
2 Edward IV	*1599, 1600, 1605, 1613, 1619, 1626*	–	–	–	–	6	6
How a Man May Choose a Good Wife from a Bad	1602, 1605, 1608, 1614, 1621, 1630, 1634	7	7	4	2	7	7
1 If You Know Not Me You Know Nobody	1605, 1606, 1608, 1610, 1613, 1623, 1632, 1639	8	8	5	4	8	8
2 If You Know Not Me You Know Nobody	1606, 1609, 1623, 1633	4	4	2	1	4	4
A Woman Killed With Kindness	1607, 1617	2	2	1	1	2	2
The Rape of Lucrece	1608, 1609, 1614, 1630, 1638	5	5	3	2	5	5
The Golden Age	1611	1	1	0	0	1	1
The Brazen Age	1613	1	1	0	0	1	1
The Silver Age	1613	1	1	0	0	1	1
The Four Prentices of London	1615, 1632	2	2	1	0	2	2
1 The Fair Maid of the West	1631	1	1	0	0	1	1
2 The Fair Maid of the West	1631	1	1	0	0	1	1
1 The Iron Age	1632	1	1	0	0	1	1
2 The Iron Age	1632	1	1	0	0	1	1
The English Traveller	1633	1	1	0	0	1	1
The Late Lancashire Witches (with Brome)	1634	1	1	0	0	1	1
A Maidenhead Well Lost	1634	1	1	0	0	1	1
A Challenge for Beauty	1636	1	1	0	0	1	1
The Royal King and the Loyal Subject	1637	1	1	0	0	1	1
The Wise Woman of Hogsdon	1638	1	1	0	0	1	1
Love's Mistress, or The Queen's Masque	1636, 1640	2	2	1	1	2	2
Fortune by Land and Sea (with W. Rowley)	1655	0	1	0	0	0	1
The Old Law (with W. Rowley and Middleton)	1656	0	1	0	0	0	1

Notes

- For Heywood's authorship of the anonymously published *How a Man May Choose a Good Wife from a Bad*, see the edition by Swaen, ed., *How a Man May Choose a Good Wife from a Bad*; Rowland, *Thomas Heywood's Theatre, 1599–1639*, 85–7; and McManus, ed., 'A Critical Edition of *How a Man May Choose a Good Wife from a Bad*'.

Table 8.10 *Ben Jonson*

Title	Dates of editions	A	B	C	D	E	F
Every Man Out of His Humour	1600, 1600, 1600, *1616* (2°), *1640* (2°)	3	3	2	2	5	5
Cynthia's Revels	1601, *1616* (2°), *1640* (2°)	1	1	0	0	3	3
Every Man in His Humour	1601, *1616* (2°), *1640* (2°)	1	1	0	0	3	3
Poetaster, or The Arraignment	1602, *1616* (2°), *1640* (2°)	1	1	0	0	3	3
Eastward Ho (with Chapman and Marston)	1605, 1605, 1605	3	3	2	2	3	3
Sejanus His Fall	1605, *1616* (2°), *1640* (2°)	1	1	0	0	3	3
Volpone, or The Fox	1607, *1616* (2°), *1640* (2°)	1	1	0	0	3	3
The Case is Altered	1609	1	1	0	0	1	1
Catiline His Conspiracy	1611, *1616* (2°), 1635, 1635, *1640* (2°)	3	3	2	0	5	5
The Alchemist	1612, *1616* (2°), *1640* (2°)	1	1	0	0	3	3
Works	*1616* (2°), *1640* (2°)	2	2	1	0	–	–
Epicoene, or The Silent Woman	*1616* (2°), 1620, *1640* (2°)	1	1	0	0	3	3
The New Inn	1631 (8°)	1	1	0	0	1	1
Bartholomew Fair	1631 (2°), *1641* (2°)	1	1	0	0	2	2
The Devil is an Ass	*1641* (2°)	–	–	–	–	1	1
The Staple of News	*1641* (2°)	–	–	–	–	1	1
The Magnetic Lady	*1641* (2°)	–	–	–	–	1	1
Second Volume of Works	*1641* (2°)	1	1	0	0	–	–

Notes
- For Jonson's dramatic corpus, see Bevington, Butler and Donaldson, gen. eds., *The Cambridge Edition of the Works of Ben Jonson.*

Table 8.11 *John Lyly*

Title	Dates of editions	A	B	C	D	E	F
Campaspe	1584, 1584, 1584, 1591, *1632* (12°)	4	4	3	3	5	5
Sappho and Phao	1584, 1584, 1591, *1632* (12°)	3	3	2	2	4	4
Endymion	1591, *1632* (12°)	1	1	0	0	2	2
Gallathea	1592, *1632* (12°)	1	1	0	0	2	2
Midas	1592, *1632* (12°)	1	1	0	0	2	2
Mother Bombie	1594, 1598, *1632* (12°)	2	2	1	1	3	3
The Woman in the Moon	1597	1	1	0	0	1	1
Love's Metamorphosis	1601	1	1	0	0	1	1
Six Court Comedies	*1632* (12°)	1	1	0	0	–	–

Table 8.12 *Christopher Marlowe*

Title	Dates of editions	A	B	C	D	E	F
1, 2 Tamburlaine the Great	*1590* (8°), *1593* (8°), *1597* (8°)	3	3	2	2	–	–
1 Tamburlaine the Great	*1590* (8°), *1593* (8°), *1597* (8°), 1605	1	1	0	0	4	4
2 Tamburlaine the Great	*1590* (8°), *1593* (8°), *1597* (8°), 1606	1	1	0	0	4	4
The Massacre at Paris	[1594?] (8°)	1	1	0	0	1	1
Edward the Second	1594, 1598, 1612, 1622	4	4	2	1	4	4
Dido, Queen of Carthage (with Nashe)	1594	1	1	0	0	1	1
Doctor Faustus	1604, 1609, 1611, 1616, 1619, 1620, 1624, 1628, 1631	9	9	7	2	9	9
The Jew of Malta	1633	1	1	0	0	1	1

Notes

- The two parts of *Tamburlaine* appeared as single octavo playbooks, with continuous signatures, in 1590, 1593 and 1597, but they were published in separate quarto editions in 1605 (*Part I*) and 1606 (*Part II*).
- The title page of the octavo edition of *The Massacre at Paris* mentions no date. For the date of the edition, see Esche, ed., *The Massacre at Paris*, 295.

Table 8.13 *John Marston*

Title	Dates of editions	A	B	C	D	E	F
Jack Drum's Entertainment	1601, 1616	2	2	1	0	2	2
Antonio's Revenge	1602, *1633* (8°)	1	1	0	0	2	2
1 Antonio and Mellida	1602, *1633* (8°)	1	1	0	0	2	2
The Malcontent	1604, 1604, 1604	3	3	2	2	3	3
The Dutch Courtesan	1605, *1633* (8°)	1	1	0	0	2	2
Eastward Ho (with Chapman and Jonson)	1605, 1605, 1605	3	3	2	2	3	3
Sophonisba	1606, *1633* (8°)	1	1	0	0	2	2
Parasitaster	1606, 1606, *1633* (8°)	2	2	1	0	3	3
What You Will	1607, *1633* (8°)	1	1	0	0	2	2
Histriomastix	1610	1	1	0	0	1	1
The Insatiate Countess (with Lewis Machin and William Barkstead)	1613, 1616, 1631	3	3	2	1	3	3
Tragedies and Comedies	*1633* (8°)	1	1	0	0	–	–

Notes

- There are two 1613 issues of *The Insatiate Countess*, one assigning the play to Marston, the other to 'Lewis Machin, and Wiliam Bacster' (the second edition was published anonymously; the third assigns the play to Marston). Melchiori, ed., *The Insatiate Countess*, argues for Marston's co-authorship.
- The 1633 octavo edition of *Tragedies and Comedies* contains the six Marston plays listed in the table.

Table 8.14 *Philip Massinger*

Title	Dates of editions	A	B	C	D	E	F
Thierry and Theodoret (with Beaumont and Fletcher)	1621, 1648	1	2	0	0	1	2
The Virgin Martyr (with Dekker)	1622, 1631, 1651	2	3	1	1	2	3
The Duke of Milan	1623, 1638	2	2	1	0	2	2
The Bondman	1624, 1638	2	2	1	0	2	2
The Roman Actor	1629	1	1	0	0	1	1
The Renegado	1630	1	1	0	0	1	1
The Picture	1630	1	1	0	0	1	1
The Emperor of the East	1632	1	1	0	0	1	1
The Fatal Dowry (with Field)	1632	1	1	0	0	1	1
The Maid of Honour	1632	1	1	0	0	1	1
A New Way to Pay Old Debts	1633	1	1	0	0	1	1
The Great Duke of Florence	1636	1	1	0	0	1	1
The Elder Brother (with Fletcher)	1637, 1651	1	2	1	0	1	2
The Bloody Brother (*Rollo, Duke of Normandy*) (with Fletcher)	1639, 1640	2	2	1	1	2	2
The Unnatural Combat	1639	1	1	0	0	1	1
The Spanish Curate (with Fletcher)	*1647* (2°)	–	–	–	–	0	1
The Little French Lawyer (with Fletcher)	*1647* (2°)	–	–	–	–	0	1
The Custom of the Country (with Fletcher)	*1647* (2°)	–	–	–	–	0	1
The False One (with Fletcher)	*1647* (2°)	–	–	–	–	0	1
The Wandering Lovers (*The Lovers' Progress*) (with Fletcher)	*1647* (2°)	–	–	–	–	0	1
The Prophetess (with Fletcher)	*1647* (2°)	–	–	–	–	0	1
The Sea Voyage (with Fletcher)	*1647* (2°)	–	–	–	–	0	1
The Double Marriage (with Fletcher)	*1647* (2°)	–	–	–	–	0	1
The Knight of Malta (with Field and Fletcher)	*1647* (2°)	–	–	–	–	0	1
The Queen of Corinth (with Field and Fletcher)	*1647* (2°)	–	–	–	–	0	1
The Honest Man's Fortune (with Field and Fletcher)	*1647* (2°)	–	–	–	–	0	1
Love's Cure, or the Martial Maid (with Beaumont and Fletcher)	*1647* (2°)	–	–	–	–	0	1
Beggars' Bush (with Beaumont and Fletcher)	*1647* (2°)	–	–	–	–	0	1
The Fair Maid of the Inn (with Ford, Fletcher and Webster)	*1647* (2°)	–	–	–	–	0	1
Comedies and Tragedies (with Beaumont and Fletcher)	*1647* (2°)	0	1	0	0	–	–
The Guardian	*1655* (8°)	–	–	–	–	0	1
A Very Woman (with Fletcher)	*1655* (8°)	–	–	–	–	0	1
The Bashful Lover	*1655* (8°)	–	–	–	–	0	1
Three New Plays	*1655* (8°)	0	1	0	0	–	–
The City Madam	1658	0	1	0	0	0	1

Notes
- For Massinger's dramatic corpus, see Edwards and Gibson, eds., *The Plays and Poems of John Massinger*.
- All play texts dated 1647 appeared in the 'Beaumont and Fletcher' Folio.
- *The Guardian*, *A Very Woman* and *The Bashful Lover* appeared in an octavo volume entitled *Three New Plays*.

Table 8.15 *Thomas Middleton*

Title	Dates of editions	A	B	C	D	E	F
The Patient Man and the Honest Whore (with Dekker)	1604, [1604?], 1605, 1615/16, 1635	5	5	3	2	5	5
The Puritan	1607	1	1	0	0	1	1
The Phoenix	1607, 1630	2	2	1	0	2	2
Michaelmas Term	1607, 1630	2	2	1	0	2	2
Your Five Gallants	[1608]	1	1	0	0	1	1
A Trick to Catch the Old One	1608, 1616	2	2	1	1	2	2
A Yorkshire Tragedy	1608, 1619	2	2	1	0	2	2
A Mad World, My Masters	1608, 1640	2	2	0	0	2	2
The Revenger's Tragedy	1608	1	1	0	0	1	1
The Roaring Girl, or Moll Cutpurse	1611	1	1	0	0	1	1
A Fair Quarrel (with W. Rowley)	1617, 1622	2	2	1	1	2	2
Timon of Athens (with Shakespeare)	*1623* (2°), *1632* (2°)	–	–	–	–	2	2
A Game at Chess	[1625], [1625], [1625]	3	3	2	2	3	3
A Chaste Maid in Cheapside	1630	1	1	0	0	1	1
The Bloody Banquet: a Tragedy (with Dekker)	1639	1	1	0	0	1	1
The Nice Valour, or The Passionate Madman (with Fletcher)	*1647* (2°)	–	–	–	–	0	1
Wit at Several Weapons (with W. Rowley)	*1647* (2°)	–	–	–	–	0	1
The Widow: a Comedy	1652	0	1	0	0	0	1
The Changeling (with W. Rowley)	1653	0	1	0	0	0	1
The Spanish Gypsy (with W. Rowley, Ford and Dekker)	1653, (1661)	0	1	1	1	0	1
The Old Law, or A New Way to Please You (with Massinger and W. Rowley)	1656	0	1	0	0	0	1
No Wit Like a Woman's (*No Help Like a Woman's*)	*1657* (8°)	0	1	0	0	0	1
More Dissemblers Besides Women	*1657* (8°)	–	–	–	–	0	1
Women Beware Women	*1657* (8°)	–	–	–	–	0	1
Two New Plays	*1657* (8°)	0	1	0	0	–	–

Notes

- For the dramatic corpus of Middleton and questions of authorship attribution, see Taylor and Lavagnino, eds., *Thomas Middleton* and *Thomas Middleton and Early Modern Textual Culture*. My list omits the plays written by Shakespeare in which Middleton probably had a hand as reviser, *Macbeth* and *Measure for Measure*.
- The title page of *Your Five Gallants* is undated, but the edition is likely to have followed soon after the play was entered in the Stationers' Register on 22 March 1608.
- The title pages of the three editions of *A Game at Chess* are undated. For the play's textual history, see Taylor's introduction to the play in Taylor and Lavagnino, eds., *Thomas Middleton and Early Modern Textual Culture*, 712–991.
- *The Nice Valour* and *Wit at Several Weapons* appeared in the 'Beaumont and Fletcher' Folio.
- For *The Spanish Gypsy*, see the note under Dekker.
- *More Dissemblers Besides Women* and *Women Beware Women* appeared in a single octavo volume entitled *Two New Plays*.
- *The Family of Love*, *Blurt Master Constable* and *The Honest Whore, Part Two*, have occasionally been attributed to Middleton. For their rejection from the Middleton canon, see Taylor and Lavagnino, eds., *Thomas Middleton and Early Modern Textual Culture*, 331.

Table 8.16 *George Peele*

Title	Dates of editions	A	B	C	D	E	F
The Arraignment of Paris	1584	I	I	O	O	I	I
Edward I	1593, 1599	2	2	I	I	2	2
Titus Andronicus (with Shakespeare)	1594, 1600, 1611, *1623* (2°), *1632* (2°)	3	3	2	I	5	5
The Battle of Alcazar	1594	I	I	O	O	I	I
The Old Wives Tale	1595	I	I	O	O	I	I
The Love of David and Fair Bathsheba	1599	I	I	O	O	I	I

Table 8.17 *William Rowley*

Title	Dates of editions	A	B	C	D	E	F
The Travels of the Three English Brothers (with John Day and George Wilkins)	1607	I	I	O	O	I	I
A Fair Quarrel (with Middleton)	1617, 1622	2	2	I	I	2	2
A New Wonder, A Woman Never Vexed	1632	I	I	O	O	I	I
All's Lost by Lust	1633	I	I	O	O	I	I
A Shoemaker a Gentleman	1638	I	I	O	O	I	I
Wit at Several Weapons (with Middleton)	*1647* (2°)	–	–	–	–	O	I
The Maid in the Mill (with Fletcher)	*1647* (2°)	–	–	–	–	O	I
The Spanish Gypsy (with Middleton, Ford and Dekker)	1653, (1661)	O	I	I	I	O	I
The Changeling (with Middleton)	1653, (1668)	O	I	I	O	O	I
Fortune by Land and Sea (with Heywood)	1655	O	I	O	O	O	I
The Old Law (with Massinger and Middleton)	1656	O	I	O	O	O	I
The Witch of Edmonton (with Dekker and Ford)	1658	O	I	O	O	O	I

Notes
- *Wit at Several Weapons* and *The Maid in the Mill* appeared in the 'Beaumont and Fletcher' Folio.
- For *The Spanish Gypsy*, see the note under Dekker.
- *A Match at Midnight* was published in quarto in 1633 and attributed to 'W. R.' on the title page. Young, ed., *A Match at Midnight*, argues against Rowley's authorship, and I follow Young by omitting the play from this table. Hoy also had doubts about Rowley's (sole) authorship ('The Shares of Fletcher and his Collaborators' (1960)), whereas Robb, 'The Canon of William Rowley's Plays', attributes the play to Rowley (see, in particular, p. 140).

Table 8.18 *James Shirley*

Title	Dates of editions	A	B	C	D	E	F
The Wedding	1629, 1633, 1660	2	3	1	1	2	3
The Grateful/Faithful Servant	1630, 1637	2	2	1	1	2	2
The School of Compliment (Love Tricks)	1631, 1637	2	2	1	1	2	2
Changes, Or Love in a Maze	1632	1	1	0	0	1	1
The Contention for Honour and Riches	1633	1	1	0	0	1	1
The Witty Fair One	1633	1	1	0	0	1	1
The Bird in a Cage (The Beauties)	1633	1	1	0	0	1	1
The Traitor	1635	1	1	0	0	1	1
The Example	1637	1	1	0	0	1	1
Hyde Park	1637	1	1	0	0	1	1
The Lady of Pleasure	1637	1	1	0	0	1	1
The Gamester	1637	1	1	0	0	1	1
The Young Admiral	1637	1	1	0	0	1	1
The Duke's Mistress	1638	1	1	0	0	1	1
The Royal Master	1638	1	1	0	0	1	1
Chabot, Admiral of France (with Chapman)	1639	1	1	0	0	1	1
The Ball	1639	1	1	0	0	1	1
The Maid's Revenge	1639	1	1	0	0	1	1
The Opportunity	1640	1	1	0	0	1	1
The Constant Maid (Love Will Find Out the Way)	1640, *1657*, (1661)	1	1	1	0	1	2
The Coronation	1640	1	1	0	0	1	1
1 St Patrick for Ireland	1640, *1657*	1	1	0	0	1	2
The Arcadia	1640	1	1	0	0	1	1
Love's Cruelty	1640	1	1	0	0	1	1
The Humorous Courtier (The Duke)	1640	1	1	0	0	1	1
The Night Walker, or The Little Thief (with Fletcher)	1640	1	1	0	0	1	1
The Country Captain (Captain Underwit) (with William Cavendish)	1640	1	1	0	0	1	1
The Sisters	*1652/53* (8°)	—	—	—	—	0	1
The Cardinal	*1652/53* (8°)	—	—	—	—	0	1
The Imposture	*1652/53* (8°)	—	—	—	—	0	1
The Doubtful Heir (Rosania, or Love's Victory)	*1652/53* (8°)	—	—	—	—	0	1
The Brothers (The Politic Father)	*1652/53* (8°)	—	—	—	—	0	1
The Court Secret	*1652/53* (8°)	—	—	—	—	0	1
Six New Plays	*1652/53* (8°)	0	1	0	0	—	—
The Politician	*1655* (4° and 8°)	0	1	0	0	0	1

Table 8.18 *(cont.)*

Title	Dates of editions	A	B	C	D	E	F
The Gentleman of Venice	*1655* (4° and 8°)	o	I	o	o	o	I
Two Plays	1657	o	I	–	–	–	–

Notes
- For the dramatic corpus of Shirley, see Giddens, Grant and Ravelhofer, gen. eds., 'The Complete Works of James Shirley'.
- Giddens, Grant and Ravelhofer, gen. eds., 'The Complete Works of James Shirley', list *The Night Walker or The Little Thief* under 'Doubtful Dramatic Works', but Hoy was confident that Fletcher and Shirley share responsibility for the play as it has come down to us ('The Shares of Fletcher and his Collaborators' (1959), 108–10).
- *The Sisters, The Cardinal, The Imposture, The Doubtful Heir, The Brothers* and *The Court Secret* were published as *Six New Plays* (1652/3).
- The octavo and quarto editions of *The Politician* and *The Gentleman of Venice* are in the same setting of type (see Greg, *Bibliography*, II.856).
- *The Constant Maid* and *1 St Patrick for Ireland* were published in a Shirley collection called *Two Plays*.

Table 8.19 *John Webster*

Title	Dates of editions	A	B	C	D	E	F
Sir Thomas Wyatt (with Dekker)	1607, 1612	2	2	I	I	2	2
Northward Ho (with Dekker)	1607	I	I	o	o	I	I
Westward Ho (with Dekker)	1607	I	I	o	o	I	I
The White Devil	1612, 1631	2	2	I	o	2	2
The Duchess of Malfi	1623, 1640	2	2	I	o	2	2
The Devil's Law Case	1623	I	I	o	o	I	I
The Fair Maid of the Inn (with Ford, Massinger and Webster)	*1647* (2°)	–	–	–	–	o	I
Appius and Virginia	1654, 1655, 1659 (1679)	o	3	3	2	3	3

Notes
- For Webster's dramatic corpus, see Gunby, Carnegie and Jackson, eds., *The Works of John Webster*.
- *The Fair Maid of the Inn* appeared in the 'Beaumont and Fletcher' Folio.

Printed playbooks of professional plays, including reprints, 1583–1622

In the present study, I repeatedly examine Shakespeare playbooks from the late sixteenth and early seventeenth century in the context of the book trade's total output of plays written for the commercial stage. It has therefore seemed necessary to compile the corpus of professional plays in print (see Table 9).[1] My principal authority in doing so is Greg's *Bibliography of the English Printed Drama to the Restoration* (and the numbers and letters in Table 9, e.g. '82a', are those assigned to the respective editions in Greg's *Bibliography*). Greg does not distinguish between plays written for the commercial stage and other dramatic writings (such as closet dramas or translations), so I have eliminated the latter from my corpus. In doing so, most decisions have been straightforward, but others have not. Nor does Greg always include lost editions, even if there is clear evidence that they existed. The following notes thus explain any contentious inclusions and exclusions from Table 9.

The totals at which I arrive are the following: 22 playbooks published in 1583–92; 105 in 1593–1602; 125 in 1603–12; 81 in 1613–22; and 333 in the total forty-year period. My figures differ somewhat from Blayney's: his totals for 1583–1602 and 1603–22 are 117 and 192; mine are 127 and 206.[2]

In Table 9, I underline all Shakespeare playbooks to highlight his share in the print market of professional plays.

---

[1] For what constitutes a 'professional play', see above, p. 37.
[2] See 'The Publication of Playbooks', 384.

Table 9 *Printed playbooks of professional plays, including reprints, 1583–1622*

year																				Number of editions published	Ten-year totals	Total
1583																				0		
1584	82a	82b	83a	84a	84b	84c	85a													7		
1585																				0		
1586																				0		
1587																				0		
1588																				0		
1589	92a																			1		
1590	93a	94/95a																		2		
1591	82c	84d	99a	101a	102a															5		
1592	85b	105a	106a	107a	109a	110aa	110a													7	22	
1593	94/95b	112a	113a																	3		
1594	110b	114a	115a	117a	118a	**119a**	120a	121a	122a	123a	124a	125a	126a	127a	128a	129a	130a	131a	133a	19		
1595	134a	136a	137a	**138a**																4		
1596	120b	139a	**140a**																	3		
1597	94/95c	**141a**	**142a**	**143a**	144a	**150aa**														6		
1598	118b	125b	129b	**141b**	**141c**	**142b**	**145a**	**145b**	146a	148a	149a	**150a**	151a							13		
1599	107b	109b	110c	112b	123b	**140b**	**143b**	**145c**	153/4a	155a	156a	157a	158a	159a	160a	161a	161b			17		

	117b	**119b**	**138b**	**153/4b**	162a	163a	163b	164a	165a	166a	**167a**	**168a**	169a	**170a**	171a	**172a**	173a	174a	175a			
1600	**117b**	119b	138b	153/4b	162a	163a	163b	164a	165a	166a	167a	168a	169a	170a	171a	**172a**	173a	174a	175a		19	
1601	176a	177a	178a	179a	180a	181a	182a														7	
1602	110d	118c	142c	**165b**	184a	18a	186a	**187a**	188a	189a	190a	191a	192a	195a							14	105
1603	110e	**197a**	198a	**197b**																	3	
1604	114b	**145d**	163c?	191b	203a	203b	203c	204a	204b?	205a											10	
1605	94d	**142d**	153/4c	215b	204c	211a	212a	213a	230b	214a	215a	216a	217a	217b	217c	219a	220a	221a	222a		19	
1606	95d	151b	215b	224a	226a	228a	229a	230a	230b	231a	234a	235a	236a								13	
1607	120c	241a	242a	243a	244a	245a	246a	247a	248a	249a	250a	251a	252a	253a	254a	255a	256a	257a	258a	259a	20	
1608	**141d**	**145e**	191c	244a	262a	263a	264a	**265a**	266a	267a	268a	272a	273a	274/5a	276a	277a					16	
1609	**143c**	205b	224b	273b	**279a**	281a	283a	**284a**	**284b**	285a											10	
1610	110f	118d?	151c	175b	215d		286a	287a	290a												9	
1611	101/2b	117c	151d	**197c**	205c	247b	249b	**284c**	290a	292a	293a	294a	296a	297a	298a						15	
1612	129c	142e	256b	264b	299a	300a	301a	303a	305a	306a											10	125
1613	**145f**	151e	153d	154d	189b	212b	215e	307a	313a	315a	316a	317a									12	
1614	191d	234b	273c	321a	323a																5	
1615	110g	141e	151f	204d	255c	327a	328a	329a	333a												9	
1616	151ff	177b	205d	247c	262b	315b	328a	334a	336a	337a											10	
1617	118e	148b	258b	264c	352a					Fr Jonson											5	
1618	110h	151g	171b	175c	356a																5	
1619	151h	153/4e	**165c**	166b	**170b**	**172b**	**187b**	205c	266b	272b	**284d**	357a	360a	**119c/138c**							14	
1620	205f	304c	362a	363a	364a																5	
1621	151i	191e	212c	368a																	4	
1622	101/2c	129d	**142f**	**145g**	323b	352b	357b	363b	379a	380a	382a	384a									12	81

Notes

101 / 102: *1, 2 The Troublesome Reign of John, King of England* was published in 1591 as a two-part play in two bibliographically independent playbooks (like, say, *1 Contention* and *Richard Duke of York* in 1600). In 1611 and 1622, however, the two parts were printed as one playbook, with continuous signatures (like, say, *1, 2 Tamburlaine* in 1590). I thus list the two parts separately under 1591 (101a, 102a) but jointly under 1611 (101/2b) and 1622 (101/2c).

110aa: for the lost 1592 edition of *The Spanish Tragedy*, see Erne, *Beyond 'The Spanish Tragedy'*, 59.

150aa: for the lost 1597 edition of *Love's Labour's Lost*, see above, p. 13.

151ff: the recently discovered *c.* 1615–18 edition of *Mucedorus* is not included in Greg's *Bibliography* (see Proudfoot, "Modernizing" the Printed Play-Text in Jacobean London"). I conjecturally list the edition under the year 1616.

206a: the 1604 quarto of *The Wit of a Woman* does not clearly indicate whether the play was ever performed. A list of 'Interlocutors' (sig. A2r) explains who the characters are (*'Nemo* a Phisitian: and aged'; *'Ferio* a Lawyer: and in yeares'), a feature more suggestive of a closet play than of a professional play. *DEEP*'s 'play type' classification is 'Closet/Unacted (?)', and I agree in not considering the play professional.

223a: Daniel wrote the first three acts of *Philotas* without performance in mind but, as he relates in "The Apology' appended to the play in the 1623 Folio *Works*, he was 'driuen by necessity to make vse of [his] pen, and the Stage to bee the mouth of [his] lines, which before were neuer heard to speake but in silence' (sig. E65v). The play was performed before the King by the Children of the Queen's Revels early in January 1605; a performance which got Daniel into trouble (see Gazzard, '"Those Graue Presentments of Antiquitie"). No performance in front of a paying audience is recorded, and none is likely to have taken place. Despite its one recorded performance, the play can hardly be considered 'professional', and I omit it from my table.

304a: the earliest extant edition of *Epicoene* appears in the 1616 Jonson Folio. William Gifford, in the nineteenth century, mentioned an earlier quarto edition of 1612, and Greg provided the edition with a separate entry. The play's most recent editors have doubted that such an edition existed, however, and I omit it from my table. See Beaurline, ed., *Epicoene, or The Silent Woman*, xx; Dutton, ed., *Epicoene, or, The Silent Woman*, 47; and Bevington, Butler and Donaldson, gen. eds., *The Cambridge Edition of the Works of Ben Jonson*, III.375.

361a: the 1619 title page of *Two Wise Men and All the Rest Fools* claims that it 'hath beene diuerse times acted', but no company or theatre is mentioned, and the claim is likely to be false. Algernon Swinburne called the play a 'wonderful medley' and added: 'it is difficult to believe that this voluminous pamphlet in the form of dialogue on social questions can have been the work of any practised or professional dramatist. It is externally divided into seven acts, and might as reasonably have been divided into twenty-one. A careful and laborious perusal of the bulky tract from prologue to epilogue, which has enabled me in some measure to appreciate the double scientific experiment of Mr Browning on Sibrandus Schafnaburgensis, "emboldens me" also to affirm that it has no vestige of dramatic action, no trace of a story, no phantom of a plot' (*Contemporaries of Shakespeare*, 62–3). I omit the play from my table.

Shakespeare's publishers, 1593–1622

This appendix lists the stationers who published Shakespeare's plays and poems up to 1622, the year preceding the publication of the First Folio. I include the publishers of books that were attributed to Shakespeare on title pages during this period (*The London Prodigal*, *1 Sir John Oldcastle*, *The Troublesome Reign of John, King of England* and *A Yorkshire Tragedy*) or may have been attributed to him by means of initials (*A Funeral Elegy in Memory of the Late Virtuous Master William Peter*, *Locrine*, *The Puritan* and *Thomas Lord Cromwell*), even though they are now not generally believed to be by Shakespeare. I further include publishers of plays which are generally believed to have been authored or co-authored by Shakespeare, even if they were not ascribed to Shakespeare on title pages up to 1622 (*Edward III*, *Titus Andronicus*, *Romeo and Juliet* and *Henry V*). I confine the entries to information regarding the publishing of Shakespeare. For more general biographical sketches, see McKerrow, *A Dictionary of Printers and Booksellers in England, Scotland, and of Foreign Printers of English Books 1557–1640*.

Aspley, William (1573?–1640) entered *Much Ado about Nothing* and *2 Henry IV* on 23 August 1600, with Andrew Wise. The plays were published by him and Wise in quarto format the same year.

Barrett, William (*d.* 1624) had *Venus and Adonis* and twenty-nine other books transferred to him from William Leake on 16 February 1617. He published the poem's tenth edition, in octavo, later that year and transferred the rights in it to John Parker on 8 March 1620.

Blount, Edward (1562–1632) entered *Pericles* and *Antony and Cleopatra* on 20 May 1608. In 1601, he published Robert Chester's *Love's Martyr*, in quarto, to which 'The Phoenix and the Turtle' was appended with a few other poems.

Bonian, Richard and Henry Walley entered *Troilus and Cressida* on 28 January 1609 and published the play in quarto format the same year.

Browne, John (*d.* 1622) had *Thomas Lord Cromwell* transferred to him from William Jones on 16 December 1611. He is likely to have published its second quarto edition in 1613.

Burby, Cuthbert (*d.* 1607) entered *Edward III* on 1 December 1595 and published the play in 1596 (Q1) and 1599 (Q2). The rights in the play were assigned to William Welby by Burby's widow on 16 October 1609. Burby also published Q2 *Love's Labour's Lost* in 1598 and Q2 *Romeo and Juliet* in 1599. He transferred the rights in these two plays to Nicholas Ling on 22 January 1607.

Busby, John (*d.* 1613) and Thomas Millington published Q1 *Henry V* in 1600 before transferring the rights in the play to Thomas Pavier on 14 August of that year. Busby entered *The Merry Wives of Windsor* on 18 January 1602 but transferred the rights in the play to Arthur Johnson on the same day. Busby also entered *King Lear* on 26 November 1607, with Nathaniel Butter, although Butter was the only publisher mentioned in the imprint when the play was published the year after.

Butter, Nathaniel (*bap.* 1583–*d.* 1664) entered *King Lear* on 26 November 1607, with John Busby, and is the only publisher mentioned in the imprint when the play was published in quarto format the year after. Butter probably agreed to and may have financed the publication of the second quarto in 1619 as part of the nonce collection called the 'Pavier Quartos'. He also published *The London Prodigal* – 'By William Shakespeare' according to the title page – in 1605.

Clarke, Sampson published Q1 *The Troublesome Reign of John, King of England* in 1591. No playwright is mentioned on the title page, although the play was ascribed to 'W. Sh.' in Q2 (1611) and to 'William Shakespeare' in Q3 (1622).

Cotton, William (*d.* 1609) entered *Thomas Lord Cromwell* on 11 August 1602 but seems to have sold the rights in the play to William Jones, who published the play – 'Written by W. S.' according to the title page – in quarto format the same year.

Creede, Thomas (*d.* 1619?) entered *Locrine* on 20 July 1594 and published the play – ascribed to 'W. S.' on the title page – in quarto format in 1595.

Danter, John (*d.* 1599) entered *Titus Andronicus* on 6 February 1594 of which a quarto edition appeared later the same year. 'Printed by Iohn Danter' and 'to be sold by Edward White & Thomas Millington', it was probably published not by Danter but by White and Millington (see pp. 139–40). Danter published Q1 *Romeo and Juliet* in 1597.

Dewe, Thomas (*d.* 1625) published Q3 *The Troublesome Reign of John, King of England* – 'Written by W. Shakespeare' according to the title page – in 1622.

Eld, George (*d.* 1624) entered *The Puritan* on 6 August 1607 and published a quarto edition of the play – by 'W. S.' according to the title page – the same year. In 1612 he may have published *A Funeral Elegy in Memory of the Late Virtuous Master William Peter*, in quarto, which is also ascribed to 'W. S.': the poem was entered to Thomas Thorpe on 13 February 1612, but the imprint does not mention Thorpe, stating instead that the poem was 'Imprinted at London by G. Eld'.

Field, Richard (*bap.* 1561–*d.* 1624) entered *Venus and Adonis* on 18 April 1593 and published the poem in quarto in the same year and again the year after. He transferred the rights in the poem to John Harrison on 25 June 1594.

Fisher, Thomas entered *A Midsummer Night's Dream* on 8 October 1600 and published a quarto edition in the same year.

Gosson, Henry (*d.* 1641) published Q1 and Q2 *Pericles*, both in 1609.

Harrison, John (*d.* 1617) entered *The Rape of Lucrece* on 9 May 1594 and published five editions of the poem, in 1594, 1598, 1600 (2x) and 1607, the first in quarto, all the others in octavo. On 25 June 1594, he acquired the rights in *Venus and Adonis*, of which he published the third edition, probably in 1595, and the fourth in 1596, both in octavo. The rights in the poem were transferred to William Leake on 25 June 1596.

Hayes, Thomas (*d.* 1604?), to whom the rights in *The Merchant of Venice* were transferred from James Roberts on 28 October 1600, published its first quarto the same year. Following his death, the play was entered by his son, Lawrence Hayes, on 8 July 1619.

Hayes, Lawrence, entered *The Merchant of Venice* and another title, which 'were the Copies of Thomas Haies his fathers', on 8 July 1619.

Helme, John (*d.* 1616) published Q2 *The Troublesome Reign of John, King of England* – 'Written by W. Sh.' according to the title page – in 1611.

Jackson, Roger (*d.* 1625), to whom the rights in *The Rape of Lucrece* were transferred from John Harrison on 1 March 1614, published the poem's fifth edition, in octavo, in 1616.

Jaggard, William (*c.* 1568–1623) published three editions of *The Passionate Pilgrim*: O1 (1599?), O2 (1599) and O3 (1612).

Johnson, Arthur (*d.* 1631), to whom the rights in *The Merry Wives of Windsor* were transferred from John Busby on 18 January 1602, published the play in quarto that year. He probably agreed to and may have financed the publication of the second quarto in 1619 as part of the nonce collection called the 'Pavier Quartos'.

Jones, William (*d.* 1618) published Q1 *Thomas Lord Cromwell* – 'Written by W. S.' according to the title page – in 1602 and sold the rights in the play to John Brown on 16 December 1611.

Law, Matthew (*d.* 1629) acquired the right to publish *Richard III, Richard II* and *1 Henry IV* on 25 June 1603. He published three editions of *Richard III* (Q4, 1605; Q5, 1612; Q6, 1622), two editions of *Richard II* (Q4, 1608; Q5, 1615) and four editions of *1 Henry IV* (Q3, 1604; Q4, 1608; Q5, 1613; Q6, 1622).

Leake, William (*d.* 1633) acquired the rights to *Venus and Adonis* from John Harrison on 25 June 1596. He published the poem's fifth and sixth editions (1599), the seventh edition, which is conjectured to have appeared in 1602, and two further editions of *c.* 1608/9 and *c.* 1610, which are falsely dated '1602', all in octavo. Another octavo edition dated '1602' and said to have been printed 'for William Leake' in the imprint was surreptitiously published by Robert Raworth, probably in 1607/8.

Ling, Nicholas (*d.* 1607) published Q1 *Hamlet* (1603), with John Trundle, and Q2 alone (1604/5). On 22 January 1607, the rights in *Romeo and Juliet* and *Love's Labour's Lost* were transferred to him by Cuthbert Burby. The rights in these plays and in *Hamlet* were assigned to John Smethwick on 19 November 1607.

Lownes, Matthew (*d.* 1625) reissued in 1611 the remnants of the 1601 *Love's Martyr* edition as *The anuals* [*sic*] *of great Brittaine*.

Millington, Thomas (*d.* 1603) entered *1 Contention* on 12 March 1594 and published the play that year (Q1) and in 1600 (Q2). He further published *Richard Duke of York* in 1595 (in octavo) and in 1600 (in quarto) and, also in 1600, *Henry V* (Q1), with John Busby. *Titus Andronicus*, entered by John Danter on 6 February 1594, appeared that year in an edition 'Printed by Iohn Danter' and 'to be sold by Edward White & Thomas Millington' which was probably published by White and Millington (see pp. 139–40). The rights in *Titus Andronicus, 1 Contention* and *Richard Duke of York* were transferred from Millington to Thomas Pavier on 19 April 1602.

Parker, John (*d.* 1648) to whom the rights in *Venus and Adonis* were transferred on 8 March 1620, published the poem's eleventh edition, in octavo, in the same year.

Pavier, Thomas (*d.* 1625) entered *1 Sir John Oldcastle* on 11 August 1600, *Henry V* on 14 August 1600, *Titus Andronicus*, *1 Contention* and *Richard Duke of York* on 19 April 1602 (by assignment from Thomas Millington) and *A Yorkshire Tragedy* on 2 May 1608. He published Q1 *1 Sir John Oldcastle* in 1600, Q2 *Henry V* in 1602 and Q1 *A Yorkshire Tragedy* in 1608. He was the main publisher of a group of ten plays which appeared in 1619, some with fake imprints, the so-called 'Pavier Quartos', with *The Whole Contention* (i.e. *1 Contention* and *Richard Duke of York*), *Pericles*, *A Yorkshire Tragedy*, *The Merchant of Venice* (misdated 1600), *The Merry Wives of Windsor*, *King Lear* (misdated 1608), *Henry V* (misdated 1608), *1 Sir John Oldcastle* (misdated 1600) and *A Midsummer Night's Dream* (misdated 1600).

Raworth, Robert, surreptitiously published an octavo edition of *Venus and Adonis*, dated '1602' though probably of 1607/8.

Roberts, James (1540?–1618?) entered *The Merchant of Venice* on 22 July 1598 (transferred to Thomas Hayes on 28 October 1600), *Hamlet* on 26 July 1602 and *Troilus and Cressida* on 7 February 1603. He published none of these plays.

Smethwick, John (*d.* 1641) entered *Hamlet*, *Love's Labour's Lost* and *Romeo and Juliet* – all previously owned by Nicholas Ling – on 19 November 1607. He published Q3 *Romeo and Juliet* in 1609 and Q3 *Hamlet* in 1611.

Thorpe, Thomas, to whom the *Sonnets* were entered on 20 May 1609, published them the same year. He may also have published *A Funeral Elegy in Memory of the Late Virtuous Master William Peter*, which he entered on 13 February 1612, although the book, 'Imprinted at London by G. Eld', does not mention his name in the imprint.

Trundle, John (*d.* 1626) published Q1 *Hamlet*, with Nicholas Ling, in 1603.

Walkley, Thomas (*d.* 1641) entered *Othello* on 6 October 1621 and published the play in the following year.

Walley, Henry and Richard Bonian entered *Troilus and Cressida* on 28 January 1609 and published the play in the same year.

White, Edward (*d.* 1613?) published Q2 and Q3 *Titus Andronicus* in 1600 and 1611. 'Printed by Iohn Danter' and 'to be sold by Edward White & Thomas Millington', Q1 was probably published by White and Millington (see pp. 139–40).

Wise, Andrew (*bap.* 1563–1603?) entered *Richard II* on 29 August 1597, *Richard III* on 20 October 1597 and *1 Henry IV* on 25 February 1598, and published Q1–3 *Richard II* (1597, 1597, 1598), Q1–3 *Richard III*

(1597, 1598, 1602) and Q1–3 *1 Henry IV* (1598, 1598, 1599). He transferred the rights in the three plays to Matthew Law on 25 June 1603. Wise, along with William Aspley, also entered *Much Ado about Nothing* and *2 Henry IV* on 23 August 1600. They published both plays in the same year.

Works cited

In this volume, I refer to hundreds of early modern books, including the 106 editions of Shakespeare's plays and poems published up to 1660. It has seemed impracticable to integrate them all below. This list therefore confines itself to modern scholarship. Bibliographical information for early modern texts is included in the main text and footnotes. Unless otherwise stated, the place of publication of early modern printed books is London. The titles of journals which appear repeatedly in the list of 'Works Cited' have been abbreviated (see the list of 'Abbreviations').

Adams, Joseph Quincy, ed. *The Passionate Pilgrim*. New York: Scribner's, 1939.

Allen, Michael J. B., and Kenneth Muir, eds. *Shakespeare's Plays in Quarto: a Facsimile Edition of Copies Primarily from the Henry E. Huntington Library*. Berkeley: University of California Press, 1981.

Anderson, Randall. 'The Rhetoric of Paratext in Early Printed Books'. Eds. Barnard and McKenzie. *The Cambridge History of the Book in Britain, Volume IV*. 636–44.

Arber, Edward, ed. *A Transcript of the Registers of the Company of Stationers 1554–1640 AD*. 5 vols. London, 1875–94.

Atherton, Ian. 'Field, Theophilus (*bap.* 1575, *d.* 1636)'. *ODNB*.

Badcoe, Tamsin, and Lukas Erne. 'The Popularity of Poetry Books in Print, 1583–1622', *The Review of English Studies*, forthcoming.

Baker, David J. *On Demand: Writing for the Market in Early Modern England*. Stanford University Press, 2010.

Bald, R. C. 'Francis Kirkman, Bookseller and Author'. *Modern Philology* 41 (1943): 17–32.

Baldwin, T. W. *Shakespeare's Five-Act Structure*. Urbana: University of Illinois Press, 1947.

　Shakespeare's Small Latine and Lesse Greeke. 2 vols. Urbana: University of Illinois Press, 1944.

Barish, Jonas. *The Anti-Theatrical Prejudice*. Berkeley: University of California Press, 1981.

　'"Soft, Here Follows Prose": Shakespeare's Stage Documents'. Eds. Murray Biggs, Philip Edwards and Inga-Stina Ewbank. *The Arts of Performance in Elizabethan and Early Stuart Drama: Essays for G. K. Hunter*. Edinburgh University Press, 1991. 32–48.

Barkan, Leonard. 'What Did Shakespeare Read?'. Eds. Margreta de Grazia and Stanley Wells. *The Cambridge Companion to Shakespeare*. Cambridge University Press, 2001. 31–47.

Barnard, John. 'The Survival and Loss Rates of Psalms, ABCs, Psalters, and Primers from the Stationers' Stock, 1660–1700'. *The Library* 6th ser. 21 (1999): 148–50.

Barnard, John, and Maureen Bell. 'Appendix 1: Statistical Tables'. Eds. Barnard and McKenzie. *The Cambridge History of the Book in Britain, Volume IV*. 779–93.

The Early Seventeenth-Century York Book Trade and John Foster's Inventory of 1616. Leeds Philosophical and Literary Society, 1994.

Barnard, John, and D. F. McKenzie, eds., assisted by Maureen Bell. *The Cambridge History of the Book in Britain: Volume IV, 1557–1695*. Cambridge University Press, 2002.

Baron, S. A. 'Butter, Nathaniel (*bap.* 1583, *d.* 1664)'. *ODNB*.

Bartlett, Henrietta C. *Mr William Shakespeare: Original and Early Editions of his Quartos and Folios, his Source Books, and Those Containing Contemporary Notices*. New Haven: Yale University Press, 1923.

Bartlett, Henrietta C., and Alfred W. Pollard. *A Census of Shakespeare's Plays in Quarto*. Rev. edn. New Haven: Yale University Press, 1939.

Bate, Jonathan. *Shakespeare and Ovid*. Oxford: Clarendon Press, 1993.

Bate, Jonathan, ed. *Titus Andronicus*. The Arden Shakespeare. London: Routledge, 1995.

Bate, Jonathan, and Eric Rasmussen, gen. eds. *The RSC Shakespeare: William Shakespeare: Complete Works*. New York: Modern Library, 2007.

Batho, G. R. 'The Library of the "Wizard" Earl Henry Percy, Ninth Earl of Northumberland (1564–1632)'. *The Library* 5th ser. 15 (1960): 246–61.

Bawcutt, N. W., ed. *The Control and Censorship of Caroline Drama: the Records of Sir Henry Herbert, Master of the Revels, 1623–73*. Oxford: Clarendon Press, 1996.

Beal, Peter, comp. *Index of English Literary Manuscripts*. 2 vols. London: Mansell, 1980–93.

'John Donne and the Circulation of Manuscripts'. Eds. Barnard and McKenzie. *The Cambridge History of the Book in Britain, Volume IV*. 122–6.

Beaurline, L. A., ed. *Epicoene, or The Silent Woman*. Lincoln, NE: University of Nebraska Press, 1966.

King John. The New Cambridge Shakespeare. Cambridge University Press, 1990.

Beckerman, Bernard. 'The Persons Personated: Character Lists in English Renaissance Play Texts'. Eds. Koshi Nakanori and Yasuo Tamaizumi. *Poetry and Drama in the English Renaissance: In Honour of Professor Jiro Ozu*. Tokyo: Kenkyusha Printing, 1980. 61–9.

Bednarz, James P. 'Canonizing Shakespeare: *The Passionate Pilgrim, England's Helicon*, and the Question of Authenticity'. *ShS* 60 (2007): 252–67.

'*The Passionate Pilgrim* and "The Phoenix and Turtle"'. Ed. Patrick Cheney. *The Cambridge Companion to Shakespeare's Poetry*. Cambridge University Press, 2007. 108–24.

Shakespeare and the Poets' War. New York: Columbia University Press, 2001.

Shakespeare and the Truth of Love: the Mystery of the 'Phoenix and Turtle'. Basingstoke: Palgrave Macmillan, 2012.

Bell, Maureen, and John Barnard. 'Provisional Count of *STC* Titles, 1475–1640'. *Publishing History* 31 (1992): 48–64.

Belsey, Catherine. Review of *Shakespeare, National Poet-Playwright* by Patrick Cheney. *SS* 34 (2006): 170–6.

Bennett, H. S. *English Books and Readers, 1558–1603.* Cambridge University Press, 1965.

Bentley, Gerald Eades. *The Jacobean and Caroline Stage.* 7 vols. Oxford: Clarendon Press, 1941–68.

The Profession of Dramatist in Shakespeare's Time, 1590–1642. Princeton University Press, 1971.

Shakespeare and Jonson: Their Reputations in the Seventeenth Century Compared. 2 vols. University of Chicago Press, 1945.

Berger, Thomas L. 'Shakespeare Writ Small: Early Single Editions of Shakespeare's Plays'. Ed. Andrew Murphy. *A Concise Companion to Shakespeare and the Text.* Oxford: Blackwell, 2007. 57–70.

Berger, Thomas L., and Jesse M. Lander. 'Shakespeare in Print, 1593–1640'. Ed. David Scott Kastan. *A Companion to Shakespeare.* Oxford: Blackwell, 1999. 395–413.

Berger, Thomas L., and George Walton Williams. 'Variants in the Quarto of Shakespeare's *2 Henry IV*'. *The Library* 6th ser. 3 (1981): 109–18.

Bergeron, David M. *Textual Patronage in English Drama, 1570–1640.* Aldershot: Ashgate, 2006.

Bevington, David. *Shakespeare: The Seven Ages of Human Experience.* 2nd edn. Oxford: Blackwell, 2005.

Bevington, David, ed. *Troilus and Cressida.* The Arden Shakespeare. London: Thomas Nelson, 1998.

Bevington, David, Martin Butler and Ian Donaldson, gen. eds. *The Cambridge Edition of the Works of Ben Jonson.* 7 vols. Cambridge University Press, 2012.

Birrell, T. A. 'The Influence of Seventeenth-Century Publishers on the Presentation of English Literature'. Eds. Mary-Jo Arn and Hanneke Wirtjes. *Historical and Editorial Studies in Medieval and Early Modern English.* Groningen: Wolters-Noordhoff, 1985. 163–73.

'Reading as Pastime: the Place of Light Literature in Some Gentlemen's Libraries of the Seventeenth Century'. Eds. Robin Myers and Michael Harris. *Property of a Gentleman: the Formation, Organization, and Dispersal of the Private Library, 1620–1920.* Winchester: St Paul's Bibliographies, 1991. 113–31.

Black, Joseph L., William R. Bowen and Germaine Warkentin, eds. *The Library of the Sidneys of Penshurst Place, ca. 1665.* University of Toronto Press, forthcoming.

Blades, William. *Shakspere and Typography.* London: Trübner, 1872.

Blagden, Cyprian. *The Stationers' Company: a History, 1403–1959.* London: George Allen and Unwin, 1960.

Bland, Mark. 'The Appearance of the Text in Early Modern England'. *Text* 11 (1998): 91–154.

'The London Book-Trade in 1600'. Ed. David Scott Kastan. *A Companion to Shakespeare*. Oxford: Blackwell, 1999. 450–63.

A Guide to Early Printed Books and Manuscripts. Chichester: Wiley-Blackwell, 2010.

Blayney, Peter W. M. 'The Alleged Popularity of Playbooks'. *SQ* 56 (2005): 33–50.

The Bookshops in Paul's Cross Churchyard. London: Bibliographical Society, 1990.

The First Folio of Shakespeare. Washington, DC: Folger Shakespeare Library, 1991.

'Introduction to the Second Edition'. *The Norton Facsimile: the First Folio of Shakespeare*. 2nd edn. 1st edn 1968, ed. Charlton Hinman. New York: Norton, 1996. xxvii–xxxvii.

'The Publication of Playbooks'. Eds. John D. Cox and David Scott Kastan. *A New History of Early English Drama*. New York: Columbia University Press, 1997. 383–422.

'STC Publication Statistics: Some Caveats'. *The Library* 7th ser. 8 (2007): 387–97.

The Texts of King Lear and their Origins: Volume 1, Nicholas Okes and the First Quarto. Cambridge University Press, 1982.

Bohannon, Mary Elizabeth. 'A London Bookseller's Bill: 1635–1639'. *The Library* 4th ser. 18 (1938): 417–46.

Boulton, Jeremy. 'Wage Labour in Seventeenth-Century London'. *Economic History Review* 49 (1996): 268–90.

Bourdieu, Pierre. *The Field of Cultural Production: Essays on Art and Literature*. Ed. Randal Johnson. Cambridge: Polity Press, 1993.

The Rules of Art: Genesis and Structure of the Literary Field. Cambridge: Polity Press, 1996.

Bourus, Terri. 'Shakespeare and the London Publishing Environment: the Publisher and Printers of Q1 and Q2 *Hamlet*'. *Analytical and Enumerative Bibliography* 12 (2001): 206–28.

Bowers, Fredson. 'The Publication of English Renaissance Plays'. Ed. Fredson Bowers. *Elizabethan Dramatists*. Dictionary of National Biography 62. Detroit: Gale, 1987. 406–16.

Bowers, Fredson, ed. *The Dramatic Works in the Beaumont and Fletcher Canon*. 10 vols. Cambridge University Press, 1966–96.

ed. *The Dramatic Works of Thomas Dekker*. 4 vols. Cambridge University Press, 1953–61.

Brennan, Michael. 'William Ponsonby: Elizabethan Stationer'. *Analytical and Enumerative Bibliography* 7 (1983): 91–110.

Brooks, Douglas A. *From Playhouse to Printing House: Drama and Authorship in Early Modern England*. Cambridge University Press, 2000.

'*King Lear* (1608) and the Typography of Literary Ambition'. *RD* 30 (2001): 133–59.

Bruster, Douglas. 'Shakespeare the Stationer'. Ed. Straznicky. *Shakespeare's Stationers*: 112–31.

Bullough, Geoffrey, ed. *Narrative and Dramatic Sources of Shakespeare*. 8 vols. London: Routledge, 1957–75.

Burke, John. *A Genealogical and Heraldic History of the Commoners of Great Britain and Ireland*. 4 vols. London, 1836–8.

Burrow, Colin. 'Life and Work in Shakespeare's Poems'. *Proceedings of the British Academy* 97 (1997): 15–50.

Burrow, Colin, ed. *Complete Sonnets and Poems*. The Oxford Shakespeare. Oxford University Press, 2002.

Burton, Robert. *The Anatomy of Melancholy*. Eds. Thomas C. Faulkner, Nicholas K. Kiessling and Rhonda L. Blair. 3 vols. Oxford: Clarendon Press, 1989–94.

Butt, John, ed. *Imitations of Horace. The Twickenham Edition of the Poems of Alexander Pope*. Volume IV, 2nd edn. New Haven: Yale University Press, 1953.

Calhoun, T. O., and T. L. Gravell. 'Paper and Printing in Ben Jonson's *Sejanus* (1605)'. *PBSA* 87 (1993): 13–64.

Cannan, Paul D. 'Ben Jonson, Authorship, and the Rhetoric of English Dramatic Prefatory Criticism'. *Studies in Philology* 99 (2002): 178–201.

Carey, John, ed. *John Milton: Complete Shorter Poems*. 2nd edn. Longman Annotated English Poets. London: Longman, 1997.

Carnegie, David, and Gary Taylor, eds. *The Quest for Cardenio: Shakespeare, Fletcher, Cervantes and the Lost Play*. Oxford University Press, 2012.

Carr, A. D. 'Mostyn Family (*per*. 1540–1642)'. *ODNB*.

Carroll, D. Allen, ed. *Everard Guilpin: Skialetheia or A Shadowe of Truth, in Certaine Epigrams and Satyres*. Chapel Hill: University of North Carolina Press, 1974.

    Greene's Groatsworth of Wit, Bought with a Million of Repentance (1592). Binghamton, NY: Medieval and Renaissance Texts and Studies, 1994.

Carter, Harry. *A View of Early Typography: Up to about 1600*. Oxford: Clarendon Press, 1969.

Catalogue of the Remains of a Library Partly Collected during the Reign of King James the First. London, 1856.

Cathcart, Charles. '"You Will Crown Him King that Slew Your King": *Lust's Dominion* and Oliver Cromwell'. *MRDE* 11 (1999): 264–74.

Cauchi, Simon. 'The "Setting Foorth" of Harington's Ariosto'. *SB* 36 (1983): 137–68.

Cawley, A. C., and Barry Gaines, eds. *A Yorkshire Tragedy*. The Revels Plays. Manchester University Press, 1986.

Chambers, E. K. *The Elizabethan Stage*. 4 vols. Oxford: Clarendon Press, 1923.

    William Shakespeare: a Study of Facts and Problems. 2 vols. Oxford: Clarendon Press, 1930.

Champion, L. S. 'Dramatic Strategy and Political Ideology in *The Life and Death of Thomas, Lord Cromwell*'. *Studies in English Literature, 1500–1900* 29 (1989): 219–36.

Chartier, Roger. *The Order of Books*. Trans. Lydia Cochrane. Stanford University Press, 1994.

Cheney, Patrick. 'Forum: the Return of the Author'. *SS* 36 (2008): 17–131.
　Shakespeare's Literary Authorship. Cambridge University Press, 2008.
　Shakespeare, National Poet-Playwright. Cambridge University Press, 2004.

Clare, Janet. *Art Made Tongue-Tied by Authority: Elizabethan and Jacobean Dramatic Censorship*. 2nd edn. Manchester University Press, 1999.

Clegg, Cyndia Susan. *Press Censorship in Caroline England*. Cambridge University Press, 2008.
　Press Censorship in Elizabethan England. Cambridge University Press, 1997.
　Press Censorship in Jacobean England. Cambridge University Press, 2001.
　'Renaissance Play-Readers, Ordinary and Extraordinary'. Ed. Marta Straznicky. *The Book of the Play: Playwrights, Stationers, and Readers in Early Modern England*. Amherst: University of Massachusetts Press, 2006. 23–38.
　'"Twill Much Enrich the Company of Stationers": Thomas Middleton and the London Book Trade, 1580–1627'. Eds. Taylor and Lavagnino. *Thomas Middleton and Early Modern Textual Culture*. 247–59.

Coatalen, Guillaume. 'Shakespeare and Other "Tragicall Discourses" in an Early Seventeenth-Century Commonplace Book from Oriel College, Oxford'. *English Manuscript Studies 1100–1700* 13 (2007): 120–64.

Cokayne, George Edward. *The Complete Peerage of England, Scotland, Ireland, Great Britain, and the United Kingdom Extant, Extinct, or Dormant*. 2nd edn. Revised by Vicary Gibbs *et al.* 13 vols. London: St Catherine Press, 1910–59.

Coleridge, Samuel Taylor. *Biographia Literaria*. Ed. James Engell and W. Jackson Bate. Princeton University Press, 1983.
　Lectures 1808–1819: On Literature II. Ed. R. A. Foakes. Princeton University Press, 1987.

Collinson, Patrick. 'Dering, Edward (*c.* 1540–1576)'. *ODNB*.

Corbin, Peter, and Douglas Sedge, eds. *The Oldcastle Controversy: Sir John Oldcastle, Part 1 and The Famous Victories of Henry V*. The Revels Plays Companion Library. Manchester University Press, 1991.

Craig, Hugh. 'The 1602 Additions to *The Spanish Tragedy*'. Eds. Hugh Craig and Arthur F. Kinney. *Shakespeare, Computers, and the Mystery of Authorship*. Cambridge University Press, 2009. 162–80.

Crawford, Charles. 'Appendix D: J. Bodenham's *Belvedere*'. Ed. Ingleby. *Shakspeare Allusion-Book*. II.489–518.
　'Belvedere, or The Garden of the Muses'. *Englische Studien* 43 (1910–11): 198–228.

Cross, K. Gustav. 'The Authorship of *Lust's Dominion*'. *Studies in Philology* 55 (1958): 39–61.

Crummé, Hannah Leah. 'William Scott's Copy of Sidney'. *NQ* 56 (2009): 553–4.

Dane, Joseph A., and Alexandra Gillespie. 'The Myth of the Cheap Quarto'. Ed. John N. King. *Tudor Books and Readers: Materiality and the Construction of Meaning*. Cambridge University Press, 2010. 25–45.

Darnton, Robert. 'Book Production in British India, 1850–1900'. *Book History* 5 (2002): 239–62.

Dawson, G. E. 'An Early List of Elizabethan Plays'. *The Library* 4th ser. 15 (1934–35): 445–56.

Dimmock, Matthew, and Andrew Loukes. 'Plays and Playing at Petworth House (1590–1640)'. http://earlymodern-lit.blogspot.com/2010/05/doctoral-awards.html.

Dobranski, Stephen B. *Milton, Authorship, and the Book Trade*. Cambridge University Press, 1999.

Dobson, Michael. *The Making of the National Poet: Shakespeare, Adaptation and Authorship, 1660–1769*. Oxford University Press, 1992.

Dobson, Michael, and Stanley Wells, eds. *The Oxford Companion to Shakespeare*. Oxford University Press, 2001.

Dominik, Mark. *A Shakespearean Anomaly: Shakespeare's Hand in Sir John Oldcastle*. New York: Philosophical Library, 1985. Rev. edn Beaverton, OR: Alioth Press, 1991.

Duncan-Jones, Katherine. 'Much Ado with Red and White: the Earliest Readers of Shakespeare's *Venus and Adonis* (1593)'. *RES* 44 (1993): 479–501.

Shakespeare: Upstart Crow to Sweet Swan, 1592–1623. London: A. and C. Black, 2011.

Ungentle Shakespeare: Scenes from his Life. London: Thomson Learning, 2001.

'Was the 1609 *Shake-Speares Sonnets* Really Unauthorized?'. *RES* 34 (1983): 151–71.

Duncan-Jones, Katherine, ed. *Shakespeare's Sonnets*. Rev. edn. The Arden Shakespeare. London: Methuen, 2010.

Duncan-Jones, Katherine, and Henry Woudhuysen, eds. *Shakespeare's Poems*. The Arden Shakespeare. London: Thomson Learning, 2007.

Dunn, Kevin. *Pretexts of Authority: the Rhetoric of Authorship in the Renaissance Preface*. Stanford University Press, 1994.

Dutton, Richard, *Licensing, Censorship and Authorship in Early Modern England: Buggeswords*. Basingstoke: Palgrave, 2000.

Mastering the Revels: the Regulation and Censorship of English Renaissance Drama. Basingstoke: Macmillan, 1991.

Dutton, Richard, ed. *Epicoene, or, The Silent Woman*. The Revels Plays. Manchester University Press, 2003.

Edwards, Philip, and Colin Gibson, eds. *The Plays and Poems of John Massinger*. 5 vols. Oxford University Press, 1976.

Egan, Gabriel. '"As it Was, Is, or Will be Played": Title-Pages and the Theatre Industry to 1610'. Eds. Peter Holland and Stephen Orgel. *From Stage to Print in Early Modern England*. London: Palgrave Macmillan, 2006. 92–110.

English Short Title Catalogue. http://estc.bl.uk/.

Erickson, Peter. *Rewriting Shakespeare, Rewriting Ourselves*. Berkeley: University of California Press, 1991.

Erne, Lukas. 'Afterword'. Eds. Meek, Rickard and Wilson. *Shakespeare's Book*. 255–65.

Beyond 'The Spanish Tragedy': a Study of the Works of Thomas Kyd. The Revels Plays Companion Library. Manchester University Press, 2001.

'Print and Manuscript'. Ed. Patrick Cheney. *The Cambridge Companion to Shakespeare's Poetry.* Cambridge University Press, 2007. 54–71.

Shakespeare as Literary Dramatist. Cambridge University Press, 2003 (2nd edn 2013).

Erne, Lukas, ed. *The First Quarto of Romeo and Juliet.* The New Cambridge Shakespeare: the Early Quartos. Cambridge University Press, 2007.

Esche, Edward J., ed. *The Massacre at Paris.* Oxford University Press, 1998.

Esdaile, Arundell. *A List of English Tales and Prose Romances Printed before 1740.* London: Bibliographical Society, 1912.

Estill, Laura. 'The Circulation and Recontextualization of Dramatic Excerpts in Seventeenth-Century English Manuscripts'. Ph.D. diss. Wayne State University, 2010.

'Proverbial Shakespeare: the Print and Manuscript Circulation of Extracts from *Love's Labour's Lost*'. *Shakespeare* 7 (2011): 35–55.

Evans, G. Blakemore, ed. *The Riverside Shakespeare.* 2nd edn. Boston: Houghton Mifflin, 1997.

Falls, C. *Mountjoy: Elizabethan General.* London: Odhams Press, 1955.

Farmer, Alan B. 'Shakespeare, Revision, and the Ephemerality of Playbooks'. Paper presented at the International Shakespeare Conference. Stratford-upon-Avon. 4 August 2008.

Farmer, Alan B., and Zachary Lesser. 'Canons and Classics: Publishing Drama in Caroline England'. Eds. Alan B. Farmer and Adam Zucker. *Localizing Caroline Drama: Politics and Economics of the Early Modern English Stage, 1625–1642.* New York: Palgrave, 2006. 17–41.

DEEP: Database of Early English Playbooks. 2007. http://deep.sas.upenn.edu/.

Plays, Print, and Popularity in Shakespeare's England. Forthcoming.

'The Popularity of Playbooks Revisited'. *SQ* 56 (2005): 1–32.

'Structures of Popularity in the Early Modern Book Trade'. *SQ* 56 (2005): 206–13.

'Vile Arts: the Marketing of English Printed Drama, 1512–1660'. *RORD* 39 (2000): 77–165.

Farr, Harry. 'Notes on Shakespeare's Printers and Publishers with Special Reference to the Poems and *Hamlet*'. *The Library* 4th ser. 3 (1922–3): 225–60.

Feather, John. *A History of British Publishing.* 2nd edn. London: Routledge, 2006.

Fehrenbach, R. J., Michael Poston and Heather Wolfe. 'PLRE.Folger: Private Libraries in Renaissance England'. http://plre.folger.edu/ (accessed 22 October 2012).

Ferguson, W. Craig. *Pica Roman Type in Elizabethan England.* Aldershot: Scolar Press, 1989.

Valentine Simmes. Charlottesville: University of Virginia Press, 1968.

Fiedler, Leslie. 'Shakespeare's Commodity-Comedy: a Meditation on the Preface to the 1609 Quarto of *Troilus and Cressida*'. Eds. Peter Erickson and

Coppélia Kahn. *Shakespeare's 'Rough Magic': Renaissance Essays in Honor of C. L. Barber.* Newark: University of Delaware Press, 1985. 50–60.

Foakes, R. A., ed. *Henslowe's Diary.* 2nd edn. Cambridge University Press, 2002.

'Folger Digital Image Collection'. Folger Shakespeare Library, www.folger.edu/Content/Collection/Digital-Image-Collection.

Foot, Mirjam M. *Studies in the History of Bookbinding.* Aldershot: Scolar Press, 1993.

Forker, Charles R., ed. *King Richard II.* The Arden Shakespeare. London: Thomson Learning, 2002.

ed. *The Troublesome Reign of John, King of England.* The Revels Plays. Manchester University Press, 2011.

Fraser, Russell A. *Shakespeare: a Life in Art.* New Brunswick, NJ: Transaction Publishers, 2008.

Freeman, Arthur, and Janet Ing Freeman. *John Payne Collier: Scholarship and Forgery in the Nineteenth Century.* 2 vols. New Haven: Yale University Press, 2004.

Freeman, Arthur, and Paul Grinke. 'Four New Shakespeare Quartos?'. *TLS* (5 April 2002): 17–18.

'Shakespeare Quartos'. *TLS* (14 June 2002): 17.

Frost, David L. *The School of Shakespeare: the Influence of Shakespeare on English Drama 1600–1642.* Cambridge University Press, 1968.

Furness, Horace Howard, ed. *The Merchant of Venice.* A New Variorum Edition of Shakespeare. Philadelphia: Lippincott, 1888.

Furnivall, F. J. 'Sir John Harington's Shakespeare Quartos'. *NQ* 7th ser. 9 (1890): 382–3.

Galbraith, Steven K. 'English Literary Folios 1593–1623: Studying Shifts in Format'. Ed. John N. King. *Tudor Books and Readers: Materiality and the Construction of Meaning.* Cambridge University Press, 2010. 46–67.

Galloway, David. 'Robert Hayman (1575–1629): Some Materials for the Life of a Colonial Governor and First "Canadian"'. *William and Mary Quarterly.* 3rd ser. 24 (1967): 75–87.

Gants, David L. *Early English Booktrade Database.* http://purl.oclc.org/EEBD.

Garber, Marjorie. *Shakespeare after All.* New York: Pantheon Books, 2004.

Gaskell, Philip. *A New Introduction to Bibliography.* Oxford: Clarendon Press, 1972.

Gazzard, Hugh. '"Those Graue Presentments of Antiquitie": Samuel Daniel's *Philotas* and the Earl of Essex'. *RES* 51 (2000): 423–50.

Genette, Gérard. *Paratexts.* Trans. Jane E. Lewin. Cambridge University Press, 1997.

Gerritsen, Johan. '*Venus* Preserved: Some Notes on Frances Wolfreston'. *English Studies* 45 (Supplement) (1964): 271–4.

Giddens, Eugene, Teresa Grant and Barbara Ravelhofer. 'The Complete Works of James Shirley'. www2.warwick.ac.uk/fac/arts/ren/oupjamesshirley (accessed 22 October 2012).

Gillespie, Alexandra. *Print Culture and the Medieval Author: Chaucer, Lydgate, and their Books 1473–1557.* Oxford University Press, 2006.

Gillespie, Stuart. *Shakespeare's Books: a Dictionary of Shakespeare Sources*. London: Athlone, 2001.

Gillies, John. *Shakespeare and the Geography of Difference*. Cambridge University Press, 1994.

Goldberg, Jonathan. 'The Commodity of Names: "Falstaff" and "Oldcastle" in *1 Henry IV*'. Ed. Jonathan V. Crewe. *Reconfiguring the Renaissance: Essays in Critical Materialism*. Lewisburg, PA: Bucknell University Press, 1992. 76–88.

Gooch, J. L., ed. *The Lamentable Tragedy of Locrine: a Critical Edition*. New York: Garland, 1981.

Gordon, Douglas. 'The Book-Collecting Ishams of Northamptonshire and their Bookish Virginia Cousins'. *Virginia Magazine of History and Biography* 77 (1969): 174–9.

Gossett, Suzanne. *The Influence of the Jacobean Masque on the Plays of Beaumont and Fletcher*. New York: Garland, 1988.

Gowan, Juliet. '"One Man in his Time": the Notebook of Edward Pudsey'. *Bodleian Library Record* 22.1 (April 2009): 94–101.

Grazia, Margreta de. *Shakespeare Verbatim: the Reproduction of Authenticity and the 1790 Apparatus*. Oxford: Clarendon Press, 1991.

Greenblatt, Stephen. *Shakespeare's Freedom*. University of Chicago Press, 2011.

Will in the World: How Shakespeare Became Shakespeare. New York: Norton, 2004.

Greenblatt, Stephen, gen. ed. *The Norton Shakespeare*. 2nd edn. New York: Norton, 2008.

Greg, W. W. 'Act Divisions in Shakespeare'. *RES* 4 (1928): 152–8.

A Bibliography of the English Printed Drama to the Restoration. 4 vols. London: Bibliographical Society, 1939–59.

'On Certain False Dates in Shakespearian Quartos'. *The Library* 2nd ser. 9 (1908): 113–31.

A Companion to Arber. Oxford: Clarendon Press, 1967.

The Shakespeare First Folio. Oxford: Clarendon Press, 1955.

Some Aspects and Problems of London Publishing between 1550 and 1650. Oxford: Clarendon Press, 1956.

Greg, W. W., ed. *The Henslowe Papers*. 2 vols. London: A. H. Bullen, 1907.

ed. *Romeo and Juliet: Second Quarto, 1599*. Shakespeare Quarto Facsimiles 6. Oxford: Clarendon Press, 1949.

Greg, W. W., and E. Boswell, eds. *Records of the Court of the Stationers' Company 1576 to 1602*. London: Bibliographical Society, 1930.

Gregory, Johann. 'Shakespeare's "Sugred Sonnets," *Troilus and Cressida*, and the Odcombian Banquet: an Exploration of Promising Paratexts, Expectations, and Matters of Taste'. *Shakespeare* 6 (2010): 185–208.

Griffin, Robert J. 'Introduction'. Ed. Robert J. Griffin. *The Faces of Anonymity: Anonymous and Pseudonymous Publication from the Sixteenth to the Twentieth Century*. Basingstoke: Palgrave, 2003. 1–17.

Gunby, David, David Carnegie and MacDonald P. Jackson, eds. *The Works of John Webster: an Old-Spelling Critical Edition*. 3 vols. Cambridge University Press, 1995–2007.

Gurr, Andrew. *The Shakespearean Stage, 1574–1642*. 4th edn. Cambridge University Press, 2009.

The Shakespearian Playing Companies. Oxford: Clarendon Press, 1996.

Hackel, Heidi Brayman. 'The Countess of Bridgewater's London Library'. Eds. Jennifer Andersen and Elizabeth Sauer. *Books and Readers in Early Modern England: Material Studies*. (Philadelphia: University of Pennsylvania Press, 2002.) 139–59.

Reading Material in Early Modern England: Print, Gender, and Literacy. Cambridge University Press, 2005.

'"Rowme" of its Own: Printed Drama in Early Libraries'. Eds. John D. Cox and David Scott Kastan. *A New History of Early English Drama*. New York: Columbia University Press, 1997. 113–30.

Hailey, R. Carter. 'The Dating Game: New Evidence for the Dates of Q4 *Romeo and Juliet* and Q4 *Hamlet*'. *SQ* 58 (2007): 367–87.

Hales, J. W. '*The Merchant of Venice* in 1652'. *The Athenaeum* (2 January 1878): n. p.

Halliday, F. E. *A Shakespeare Companion, 1564–1964*. Harmondsworth, Penguin, 1964.

Hammond, Brean, ed. *Double Falsehood*. The Arden Shakespeare. London: Methuen, 2010.

Harbage, Alfred. *Annals of English Drama, 975–1700: an Analytical Record of All Plays, Extant or Lost, Chronologically Arranged and Indexed by Authors, Titles, Dramatic Companies, &c*. 3rd edn rev. by S. S. Wagonheim. London: Routledge, 1989.

Heale, Elizabeth. 'Webbe, William (*fl.* 1566?–1591)'. *ODNB*.

Heawood, E. A. 'Paper Used in England after 1600'. *The Library* 4th ser. 11 (1931): 263–99.

Hebel, J. William. 'Nicholas Ling and *Englands Helicon*'. *The Library* 4th ser. 5 (1924–5): 153–60.

Heltzel, Virgil B. 'The Dedication of Tudor and Stuart Plays'. *Wiener Beiträge zur Englischen Philologie* 65 (1957): 74–86.

Henderson, Diana E. 'From Popular Entertainment to Literature'. Ed. Robert Shaughnessy. *The Cambridge Companion to Shakespeare and Popular Culture*. Cambridge University Press, 2007. 6–25.

Henze, Catherine A. 'Unraveling Beaumont from Fletcher with Music, Misogyny, and Masque'. *Studies in English Literature, 1500–1900* 44 (2004): 379–404.

Hillebrand, H. N. 'William Percy: an Elizabethan Amateur'. *Huntington Library Quarterly* 1 (1937–8): 391–416.

Hingley, Sheila. 'Elham Parish Library'. Eds. Peter Isaac, and Barry McKay. *The Reach of Print*. Winchester: St Paul's Bibliographies, 1998. 175–90.

'Oxinden, Henry (1609–1670)'. *ODNB*.

Hinmann, Charlton. *The Printing and Proof-Reading of the First Folio of Shakespeare*. 2 vols. Oxford: Clarendon Press, 1963.

Hirrell, Michael J. 'The Roberts Memoranda: a Solution'. *RES* 61 (2010): 711–28.

Hobday, C. H. 'Shakespeare's Venus and Adonis Sonnets'. *ShS* 26 (1973): 103–9.

Hoeniger, F. D. 'New Harvey Marginalia on *Hamlet* and *Richard III*'. *SQ* 17 (1966): 151–5.

Hoeniger, F. D., ed. *Pericles*. The Arden Shakespeare. London: Methuen, 1963.

Holdsworth, R. V. 'Middleton's Authorship of *A Yorkshire Tragedy*'. *RES* 45 (1994): 1–25.

Honan, Park. *Shakespeare: a Life*. Oxford University Press, 1998.

Honigmann, E. A. J. *John Weever: a Biography of a Literary Associate of Shakespeare and Jonson, Together with a Photographic Facsimile of Weever's 'Epigrammes' (1599)*. The Revels Plays Companion Library. Manchester University Press, 1987.

Shakespeare's Impact on his Contemporaries. London: Macmillan, 1982.

'Sir John Oldcastle: Shakespeare's Martyr'. Eds. John W. Mahon and Thomas A. Pendleton. *Fanned and Winnowed Opinions: Shakespearean Essays Presented to Harold Jenkins*. London: Methuen, 1987. 118–32.

Honigmann, E. A. J., ed. *King John*. The Arden Shakespeare. London: Methuen, 1954.

ed. *Othello*. The Arden Shakespeare. London: Thomas Nelson, 1997.

Hooks, Adam G. 'Booksellers' Catalogues and the Classification of Printed Drama in Seventeenth-Century England'. *PBSA* 102 (2008): 445–64.

'Book Trade'. Ed. Arthur F. Kinney. *The Oxford Handbook of Shakespeare*. Oxford University Press, 2012. 126–42.

'Shakespeare at the White Greyhound'. *ShS* 64 (2011): 260–75.

'Wise Ventures: Shakespeare and Thomas Playfere at the Sign of the Angel'. Ed. Straznicky. *Shakespeare's Stationers*: 47–62.

Horsman, E. A., ed. *Bartholomew Fair*. The Revels Plays. Manchester University Press, 1960.

Hotson, Leslie. 'The Library of Elizabeth's Embezzling Teller'. *SB* 2 (1949–50): 49–62.

'How Much is That?: Economic History Services'. Economic History Association. www.eh.net/ehresources/howmuch/poundq.php.

Howard-Hill, T. H. 'The Evolution of the Form of Plays in English during the Renaissance'. *Renaissance Quarterly* 43 (1990): 112–45.

Hoy, Cyrus. 'The Shares of Fletcher and his Collaborators in the Beaumont and Fletcher Canon'. *SB* 8 (1956): 129–46. 9 (1957): 143–62. 11 (1958): 85–106. 12 (1959): 91–116. 13 (1960): 77–108. 14 (1961): 45–67. 15 (1962): 71–90.

Hull, Suzanne W. *Chaste, Silent and Obedient: English Books for Women 1475–1640*. San Marino, CA: Huntington Library, 1982.

Hunter, G. K. 'The Marking of Sententiae in Elizabethan Printed Plays, Poems, and Romances'. *The Library* 5th ser. (1951–2): 171–88.

Ingleby, C. M., ed. *The Shakspere Allusion-Book: a Collection of Allusions to Shakspere from 1591 to 1700*. 2 vols. Oxford University Press, 1932.

Isaac, Frank. *English Printers' Types of the Sixteenth Century*. Oxford University Press, 1936.

Jackson, MacDonald P. 'Collaboration'. Ed. Arthur F. Kinney. *The Oxford Handbook of Shakespeare*. Oxford University Press, 2012. 31–52.

'Editions and Textual Studies'. *ShS* 40 (1988): 224–36.

'Francis Meres and the Cultural Contexts of Shakespeare's Rival Poet Sonnets'. *RES* 56 (2005): 224–46.

Review of *Shakespeare, 'A Lover's Complaint', and John Davies of Hereford*. *RES* 58 (2007): 723–5.

'Shakespeare and the Quarrel Scene in *Arden of Faversham*'. *SQ* 57 (2006): 249–93.

'Shakespeare's Sonnet CXI and John Davies of Hereford's *Microcosmos* (1603)'. *Modern Language Review* 102 (2007): 1–10.

Studies in Attribution: Middleton and Shakespeare. Salzburg: Institut für Anglistik und Amerikanistik, 1979.

Jackson, William A. 'Edward Gwynn'. *The Library* 4th ser. 15 (1934): 90–6.

'The Lamport Hall–Britwell Court Books'. Eds. James G. McManaway, Giles E. Dawson and Edwin E. Willoughby. *Joseph Quincy Adams Memorial Studies*. Washington, DC: The Folger Library, 1948. 587–99.

Records of a Bibliographer. Ed. W. H. Bond. Cambridge, MA: Harvard University Press, 1967.

Jackson, W. A., ed. *Records of the Court of the Stationers' Company 1602 to 1640*. London: The Bibliographical Society, 1957.

Jaggard, Captain W. *Shakespeare Once a Printer and a Bookman*. Stratford-upon-Avon: Shakespeare Press, 1933.

Jewkes, Wilfred T. *Act Division in Elizabethan and Jacobean Plays, 1583–1616*. Hamden, CT: Shoe String Press, 1958.

Johns, Adrian. *The Nature of the Book: Print and Knowledge in the Making*. University of Chicago Press, 1998.

Johnson, Francis R. *A Critical Bibliography of the Works of Edmund Spenser Printed before 1700*. Baltimore: Johns Hopkins University Press, 1933.

'Notes on English Retail Book-Prices, 1550–1640'. *The Library* 5th ser. 5 (1950): 83–112.

Johnson, Gerald D. 'John Busby and the Stationers' Trade', *The Library* 6th ser. 7 (1985): 1–15.

'John Trundle and the Book Trade 1603–1626'. *SB* 39 (1986): 177–99.

'Nicholas Ling, Publisher 1580–1607'. *SB* 38 (1985): 203–14.

'The Stationers versus the Drapers: Control of the Press in the Late Sixteenth Century'. *The Library* 6th ser. 10 (1988): 1–17.

'Succeeding as an Elizabethan Publisher: the Example of Cuthbert Burby'. *Journal of the Printing Historical Society* 21 (1992): 71–8.

'Thomas Pavier, Publisher, 1600–1625'. *The Library* 6th ser. 14 (1992): 12–50.

Jones, Emrys. *Scenic Form in Shakespeare*. Oxford: Clarendon Press, 1971.

Jordan, W. K. *The Development of Religious Toleration in England, 1640–1660*. Cambridge, MA: Harvard University Press, 1938.

Joshi, Priya. 'Quantitative Method, Literary History'. *Book History* 5 (2002): 263–74.

Jowett, John. 'For Many of Your Companies: Middleton's Early Readers'. Eds. Taylor and Lavagnino. *Thomas Middleton and Early Modern Textual Culture.* 286–327.

'Johannes Factotum: Henry Chettle and Greene's *Groatsworth of Wit'*. *PBSA* 87 (1993): 453–86.

'Jonson's Authorization of Type in *Sejanus* and Other Early Quartos'. *SB* 44 (1991): 254–65.

'Shakespeare Supplemented'. *Shakespeare Yearbook* 16 (2007): 39–75.

Shakespeare and Text. Oxford Shakespeare Topics. Oxford University Press, 2007.

Jowett, John, ed. *Richard III.* The Oxford Shakespeare. Oxford University Press, 2000.

Jowett, John, and Gary Taylor. 'The Three Texts of *2 Henry IV'*. *SB* 40 (1987): 31–50.

Kahrl, George M., and Dorothy Anderson. *The Garrick Collection of Old English Plays: a Catalogue with an Historical Introduction.* London: British Library, 1992.

Kane, Robert. '"Richard du Champ" in *Cymbeline'*. *SQ* 4 (1953): 206.

Kastan, David Scott. 'Humphrey Moseley and the Invention of English Literature'. Eds. Sabrina Alcorn Baron, Eric N. Lindquist and Eleanor F. Shevlin. *Agent of Change: Print Culture Studies after Elizabeth L. Eisenstein.* Amherst: University of Massachusetts Press, 2007. 105–24.

'Plays into Print: Shakespeare to his Earliest Readers'. Eds. Jennifer Lotte Andersen and Elizabeth Sauer. *Books and Readers in Early Modern England: Material Studies.* Philadelphia: University of Pennsylvania Press, 2002. 23–41.

Shakespeare after Theory. London: Routledge, 1999.

Shakespeare and the Book. Cambridge University Press, 2001.

'"To Think these Trifles Some-thing": Shakespearean Playbooks and the Claims of Authorship'. *SS* 36 (2008): 37–48.

Kathman, David. 'Edward Pudsey (*bap.* 1573, *d.* 1612/13)'. *ODNB.*

'Field, Richard (*bap.* 1561, *d.* 1624)'. *ODNB.*

'Roberts, James (*b.* in or before 1540, *d.* 1618?)'. *ODNB.*

'Smith, Wentworth (*bap.* 1571)'. *ODNB.*

'Thorpe, Thomas (1571/2–1625?)'. *ODNB.*

Katz, David S. *The Jews in the History of England, 1485–1850.* Oxford: Clarendon Press, 1994.

Kelliher, Hilton. 'Contemporary Manuscript Extracts from Shakespeare's *Henry IV, Part I'*. *English Manuscript Studies* 1 (1989): 133–81.

'Unrecorded Extracts from Shakespeare, Sidney and Dyer'. *English Manuscript Studies* 2 (1991): 163–87.

Kesson, Andy, and Emma Smith, eds. *The Elizabethan Top Ten: Defining Print Popularity in Early Modern England.* Aldershot: Ashgate, 2013.

Kewes, Paulina. 'Between the "Triumvirate of Wit" and the Bard: the English Dramatic Canon, 1660–1720'. Eds. Cedric C. Brown and Arthur F. Marotti.

Texts and Cultural Change in Early Modern England. Basingstoke: Macmillan, 1997. 200–24.

Kiernan, Michael, ed. *Sir Francis Bacon: the Essayes or Counsels, Civill and Morall*. Oxford: Clarendon Press, 1985.

Kiessling, Nicholas K. *The Library of Anthony Wood*. Oxford Bibliographical Society, 2002.

The Library of Robert Burton. Oxford Bibliographical Society, 1988.

Kincaid, Arthur. 'Buck, Sir George (*bap.* 1560, *d.* 1622).' *ODNB*.

Kirschbaum, Leo. *Shakespeare and the Stationers*. Columbus: Ohio State University Press, 1955.

Kirwan, Peter. 'The First Collected "Shakespeare Apocrypha"'. *SQ* 62 (2011): 594–601.

Kirwood, A. E. M. 'Richard Field, Printer, 1589–1624'. *The Library* 4th ser. 12 (1931): 1–39.

Klotz, Edith L. 'A Subject Analysis of English Imprints for Every Tenth Year from 1480 to 1640'. *Huntington Library Quarterly* 1 (1937–8): 417–19.

Knafla, Laris A. 'Egerton, John, First Earl of Bridgewater (1579–1649)'. *ODNB*.

Knapp, Jeffrey. 'What Is a Co-Author'. *Representations* 89 (2005): 1–29.

Knight, Jeffrey Todd. 'Making Shakespeare's Books: Assembly and Intertextuality in the Archives'. *SQ* 60 (2009): 304–40.

Knowles, James. 'Conway, Edward, Second Viscount Conway and Second Viscount Killultagh (*bap.* 1594, *d.* 1655)'. *ODNB*.

Knutson, Roslyn, L. *The Repertory of Shakespeare's Company, 1594–1613*. Fayetteville: University of Arkansas Press, 1991.

Knutson, Roslyn L. 'Shakespeare's Repertory'. Ed. David Scott Kastan. *A Companion to Shakespeare*. Oxford: Blackwell, 1999. 346–61.

Konkola, Kari. '"People of the Book": The Production of Theological Texts in Early Modern England'. *PBSA* 94 (2000): 5–31.

Krivatsy, Nati H., and Laetitia Yeandle. 'Sir Edward Dering'. Eds. R. J. Fehrenbach and E. S. Leedham-Green. *Private Libraries in Renaissance England: A Collection and Catalogue of Tudor and Early Stuart Book-Lists*. New York: Medieval and Renaissance Texts and Studies, 1992. 137–269.

Laing David, ed. *Auctarium Bibliothecae Edinburgenae sive Catalogus Librorum quos Guilielmus Drummondus ab Hawthornden DDQ Anno 1627*. Edinburgh, 1815.

ed. *Extracts from the Hawthornden Manuscripts*. Edinburgh, 1831–2.

Lake, David, J. *The Canon of Thomas Middleton's Plays: Internal Evidence for the Major Problems of Authorship*. Cambridge University Press, 1975.

Lancashire, Anne, and Jill Levenson. 'Anonymous Plays'. Eds. Terence P. Logan, and Denzell S. Smith. *The Predecessors of Shakespeare: a Survey and Bibliography of Recent Studies in English Renaissance Drama*. Lincoln, NE: University of Nebraska Press, 1973. 161–311.

'Anonymous Plays'. Eds. Terence P. Logan, and Denzell S. Smith. *The Popular School: a Survey and Bibliography of Recent Studies in English Renaissance Drama*. Lincoln, NE: University of Nebraska Press, 1975. 148–249.

Lancaster, Henry Carrington. *A History of French Dramatic Literature in the Seventeenth Century.* 2 vols. Baltimore: Johns Hopkins University Press, 1929.

Lapides, Fred, ed. *The Raigne of King Edward the Third: a Critical, Old-Spelling Edition.* New York: Garland, 1980.

Larsen, Kenneth J., ed. *Edmund Spenser's Amoretti and Epithalamion: a Critical Edition.* Tempe, AZ: Medieval and Renaissance Texts and Studies, 1997.

Lecercle, Anne. 'Ombres et nombres: Le *parergon* dans *Venus and Adonis*'. Eds. Jean-Marie Maguin and Charles Whitworth. *William Shakespeare, Venus and Adonis: Nouvelles perspectives critiques.* Montpellier: Centre d'Etudes et de Recherches sur la Renaissance Anglaise, Université Paul-Valéry-Montpellier III, 1999. 57–83.

Lee, Sir Sidney. *A Life of William Shakespeare.* London: Smith, Elder and Co., 1898.

Lee, Sir Sidney, ed. *'Pericles': Being a Reproduction in Facsimile of the First Edition, 1609, from the Copy in the Malone Collection in the Bodleian Library.* Oxford: Clarendon Press, 1905.

Leggatt, Alexander. 'The Presence of the Playwright'. Eds. P. B. Parker and Sheldon P. Zitner. *Elizabethan Theater: Essays in Honor of S. Schoenbaum.* Newark: University of Delaware Press, 1996. 130–46.

Lennam, T. N. S. 'Sir Edward Dering's Collection of Playbooks, 1619–1624'. *SQ* 16 (1965): 145–53.

Lesser, Zachary. 'Playbooks'. Ed. Joad Raymond. *The Oxford History of Popular Print Culture.* Oxford University Press, 2011. 520–34.

   Renaissance Drama and the Politics of Publication: Readings in the English Book Trade. Cambridge University Press, 2004.

   'Typographic Nostalgia: Play-Reading, Popularity, and the Meanings of Black Letter'. Ed. Marta Straznicky. *The Book of the Play: Playwrights, Stationers, and Readers in Early Modern England.* Amherst: University of Massachusetts Press, 2006. 99–126.

   'Walter Burre's *The Knight of the Burning Pestle*'. *ELR* 29 (1999): 22–43.

Lesser, Zachary, and Peter Stallybrass. 'The First Literary *Hamlet* and the Commonplacing of Professional Plays'. *SQ* 59 (2008): 371–420.

Levin, Richard. 'The Longleat Manuscript and *Titus Andronicus*'. *SQ* 53 (2002): 323–40.

Levith, Murray J. *Shakespeare's Italian Settings and Plays.* Basingstoke: Macmillan, 1989.

Lindenbaum, Peter. 'Publishers' Booklists in Late Seventeenth-Century London'. *The Library* 7th ser. 11 (2010): 381–404.

Loewenstein, Joseph. *Ben Jonson and Possessive Authorship.* Cambridge University Press, 2002.

   'Idem: Italics and the Genetics of Authorship'. *Journal of Medieval and Renaissance Studies* 20 (1990): 205–24.

Loxley, James. *The Complete Critical Guide to Ben Jonson.* London: Routledge, 2002.

Lyly, John. *'Euphues: The Anatomy of Wit' and 'Euphues and His England':* an *Annotated Modern-Spelling Edition.* Ed. Leah Scragg. The Revels Plays Companion Library. Manchester University Press, 2003.

MacDonald, R. H. *The Library of Drummond of Hawthornden.* Edinburgh University Press, 1971.

McDonald, Russ. 'Shakespeare's Plays in Print'. *The Bedford Companion to Shakespeare: an Introduction with Documents.* Boston: Bedford/St Martin's Press, 2001. 201–6.

McElligott, Jason. 'Wolfreston, Frances (*bap.* 1607, *d.* 1677)'. *ODNB.*

McGann, Jerome. *The Textual Condition.* Princeton University Press, 1991.

McJannet, Linda. *The Voice of Elizabethan Stage Directions.* Newark: University of Delaware Press, 1999.

McKenzie, D. F. *Bibliography and the Sociology of Texts.* Cambridge University Press, 1999.

'Printers of the Mind: Some Notes on Bibliographical Theories and Printing-House Practices'. *Making Meaning: 'Printers of the Mind' and Other Essays.* Eds. Peter D. McDonald and Michael F. Suarez, SJ. Amherst: University of Massachusetts Press, 2002. 13–85.

'Printing and Publishing 1557–1700: Constraints on the London Book Trades'. Eds. Barnard and McKenzie. *The Cambridge History of the Book in Britain, Vol. IV.* 553–67.

'Stationers' Company Liber A: an Apologia'. Eds. Robin Myers and Michael Harris. *The Stationers' Company and the Book Trade 1550–1990.* New Castle, DE: Oak Knoll Press, 1997. 35–63.

'Typography and Meaning: the Case of William Congreve'. Eds. Giles Barber and Bernhard Fabian. *Buch und Buchhandel in Europa im achtzehnten Jahrhundert: The Book and the Book Trade in Eighteenth-Century Europe.* Hamburg: Ernst Hauswedell, 1977. 81–123.

McKerrow, R. B. 'Booksellers, Printers, and the Stationers' Trade'. Ed. John Phillip Immroth. *Ronald Brunlees McKerrow: a Selection of his Essays.* Metuchen, NJ: Scarecrow Press, 1974. 45–68.

A Dictionary of Printers and Booksellers in England, Scotland, and Ireland, and of Foreign Printers of English Books 1557–1640. London: Bibliographical Society, 1910.

An Introduction to Bibliography for Literary Students. Oxford: Clarendon Press, 1927.

Printers' and Publishers' Devices in England and Scotland, 1485–1640. London: Bibliographical Society, 1913.

McKitterick, David. '"Ovid with a Littleton": the Cost of English Books in the Early Seventeenth Century'. *Transactions of the Cambridge Bibliographical Society* 9.2 (1997): 184–234.

McManaway, James G. 'Latin Title-Page Mottoes as a Clue to Dramatic Authorship'. *The Library* 4th ser. 26 (1945): 28–36.

McManus, Emer, ed. 'A Critical Edition of *How a Man May Choose a Good Wife from a Bad* '. Ph.D. diss. University College, Dublin. 2008.

Maguire, Laurie E. 'The Craft of Printing (1600)'. Ed. David Scott Kastan. *A Companion to Shakespeare*. Oxford: Blackwell, 1999. 434–48.

'The Printer and Date of Q4 *A Looking Glass for London and England*'. *SB* 52 (1999): 155–60.

'Shakespeare Published'. Eds. Stanley Wells and Lena Cowen Orlin. *Shakespeare: an Oxford Guide*. Oxford University Press, 2003. 582–94.

Manley, Lawrence. 'Shakespeare and the Countess of Bridgewater: Playing, Patronage, and the Biography of Books'. Paper presented at the Shakespeare Association of America Conference. San Diego. April 2007.

Marder, Louis. *His Exits and his Entrances: the Story of Shakespeare's Reputation*. Philadelphia: Lippincott, 1963.

Marino, James J. *Owning William Shakespeare: the King's Men and their Intellectual Property*. Philadelphia: University of Pennsylvania Press, 2011.

Marotti, Arthur F. *Manuscript, Print, and the English Renaissance Lyric*. Ithaca: Cornell University Press, 1995.

'Shakespeare's Sonnets as Literary Property'. Eds. Elizabeth D. Harvey and Katharine Eisaman Maus. *Soliciting Interpretation: Literary Theory and Seventeenth-Century English Poetry*. University of Chicago Press, 1990. 143–73.

Marotti, Arthur F., and Laura Estill. 'Manuscript Circulation'. Ed. Arthur F. Kinney. *The Oxford Handbook of Shakespeare*. Oxford University Press, 2012. 53–70.

Martin, Patrick H., and John Finnis. 'Thomas Thorpe, "W. S.", and the Catholic Intelligencers'. *ELR* 33 (2003): 3–43.

Massai, Sonia. 'Editorial Pledges in Early Modern Dramatic Paratexts'. Eds. Smith and Wilson. *Renaissance Paratexts*. 91–106.

'Edward Blount, the Herberts, and the First Folio'. Ed. Straznicky. *Shakespeare's Stationers*: 132–46.

'Shakespeare's Early Readers'. Ed. Arthur F. Kinney. *The Oxford Handbook of Shakespeare*. Oxford University Press, 2011. 143–64.

Shakespeare and the Rise of the Editor. Cambridge University Press, 2007.

'Shakespeare, Text and Paratext'. *ShS* 62 (2010): 1–11.

Massai, Sonia and Thomas L. Berger, eds. *The Paratext in English Printed Drama to the Restoration*. Cambridge University Press, Forthcoming.

Masten, Jeffrey. 'Beaumont and/or Fletcher: Collaboration and the Interpretation of Renaissance Drama'. *English Literary History* 59 (1992): 337–56.

Textual Intercourse: Collaboration, Authorship, and Sexualities in Renaissance Drama. Cambridge University Press, 1997.

Maxwell, Baldwin. *Studies in the Shakespeare Apocrypha*. New York: King's Crown Press, 1956.

Meek, Richard, Jane Rickard and Richard Wilson, eds. *Shakespeare's Book: Essays in Reading, Writing, and Reception*. Manchester University Press, 2008.

Melchiori, Giorgio, ed. *The Insatiate Countess*. The Revels Plays. Manchester University Press, 1984.

ed. *King Edward III*. The New Cambridge Shakespeare. Cambridge University Press, 1998.

Melnikoff, Kirk. 'Jones, Richard (*fl.* 1564–1613)'. *ODNB.*

'Nicholas Ling's Republican *Hamlet* (1603)'. Ed. Straznicky. *Shakespeare's Stationers*: 95–111.

Melnikoff, Kirk, and Edward Gieskes, eds. *Writing Robert Greene: Essays on England's First Notorious Professional Writer.* Aldershot: Ashgate, 2008.

Mentz, Steve. *Romance for Sale in Early Modern England: the Rise of Prose Fiction.* Aldershot: Ashgate, 2006.

Metz, G. Harold. 'How Many Copies of *Titus Andronicus* Q3 are Extant?'. *The Library* 6th ser. 3 (1981): 336–40.

Miller, Edward. 'A Collection of Elizabethan and Jacobean Plays at Petworth'. *The National Trust Year Book 1975–76.* London: The National Trust, 1975. 62–4.

Miller, Stephen Roy, ed. *The Taming of a Shrew: the 1594 Quarto.* The New Cambridge Shakespeare: the Early Quartos. Cambridge University Press, 1998.

Miola, Robert S. 'Creating the Author: Jonson's Latin Epigraphs'. *Ben Jonson Journal* 6 (1999): 35–48.

Shakespeare's Reading. Oxford Shakespeare Topics. Oxford University Press, 2000.

Mish, Charles C. 'Black Letter as a Social Discriminant in the Seventeenth Century'. *PMLA* 68 (1953): 627–30.

'Comparative Popularity of Early Fiction and Drama'. *NQ* 197 (1952): 269–70.

Miskimin, Alice S. *The Renaissance Chaucer.* New Haven: Yale University Press, 1975.

Montgomery, William, ed. 'The Contention of York and Lancaster: a Critical Edition'. 2 vols. D. Phil. diss. University of Oxford. 1985.

  ed. *The First Part of the Contention 1594.* Malone Society Reprints. Oxford University Press, 1985.

Moore Smith, G. C., ed. *Gabriel Harvey's Marginalia.* Stratford-upon-Avon: Shakespeare Head Press, 1913.

Morgan, Paul. 'Frances Wolfreston and "Hor Bouks": a Seventeenth-Century Woman Book-Collector'. *The Library* 6th ser. 2 (1989): 197–219.

Morrish, P. S. *Bibliotheca Higgsiana: a Catalogue of the Books of Dr Griffin Higgs (1589–1659).* Oxford Bibliographical Society, 1990.

Moss, Ann. *Printed Commonplace-Books and the Structuring of Renaissance Thought.* Oxford: Clarendon Press, 1996.

Murphy, Andrew. *Shakespeare in Print: a History and Chronology of Shakespeare Publishing.* Cambridge University Press, 2004.

Myers, Robin. *The Stationers' Company Archive 1554–1984.* Winchester: St Paul's Bibliographies, 1990.

Myers, Robin, and Michael Harris, eds. *The Stationers' Company and the Book Trade 1550–1990.* Winchester: St Paul's Bibliographies, 1997.

Nashe, Thomas. *The Works of Thomas Nashe.* Ed. R. B. McKerrow. Rev. by F. P. Wilson. 5 vols. Oxford University Press, 1958.

Neidig, William. 'The Shakespeare Quartos of 1619'. *Modern Philology* 8 (1910): 145–63.

Neill, Michael, ed. *Othello*. The Oxford Shakespeare. Oxford University Press, 2006.

Nelson, Alan H. 'George Buc, William Shakespeare, and the Folger *George a Greene*'. *SQ* 49 (1998): 74–83.

Nelson, Alan H. 'Play Quartos Inscribed by Buc'. http://socrates.berkeley.edu/~ahnelson/BUC/quartos.html (accessed 22 October 2012).

'Shakespeare and the Bibliophiles: From the Earliest Years to 1616'. Eds. Robin Myers, Michael Harris and Giles Mandelbrote. *Owners, Annotators, and the Signs of Reading*. London: Oak Knoll Press, 2005. 49–73.

Newcomb, Lori Humphrey. *Reading Popular Romance in Early Modern England*. New York: Columbia University Press, 2002.

Nicolson, Marjorie Hope, ed. *The Conway Letters: the Correspondence of Anne, Viscountess Conway, Henry More, and their Friends, 1642–1684*. Rev. edn. Ed. Sarah Hutton. Oxford: Clarendon Press, 1992.

North, Marcy L. *The Anonymous Renaissance: Cultures of Discretion in Tudor–Stuart England*. University of Chicago Press, 2003.

'Rehearsing the Absent Name: Reading Shakespeare's Sonnets through Anonymity'. Ed. Robert J. Griffin. *The Faces of Anonymity: Anonymous and Pseudonymous Publication from the Sixteenth to the Twentieth Century*. Basingstoke: Palgrave, 2003. 19–38.

'Notes on Sales'. *TLS* (26 February 1920): 144.

'Notes on Sales: the Mostyn Plays'. *TLS* (13 February 1919): 88.

O'Dell, Sterg. *A Chronological List of Prose Fiction in English Printed in England, and Other Countries, 1475–1640*. Cambridge, MA: Technology Press of MIT, 1954.

O'Donnell, Mary Ann. 'Egerton, Frances, Countess of Bridgewater (1583–1636)'. *ODNB*.

Orgel, Stephen. *Imagining Shakespeare: a History of Texts and Visions*. Basingstoke: Palgrave Macmillan, 2003.

Orlin, Lena Cowen. 'The Private Life of Public Plays'. Eds. Richard Fotheringham, Christa Jansohn and R. S. White. *Shakespeare's World / World Shakespeares*. Newark: University of Delaware Press, 2008. 140–52.

Osterman, Nathan. 'The Controversy over the Proposed Readmission of the Jews to England (1655)'. *Jewish Social Studies* 3 (1941): 301–28.

Parker, William Riley. *Milton: a Biography*. 2 vols. Oxford: Clarendon Press, 1968.

Parrott, Thomas Marc, ed. *The Plays and Poems of George Chapman: the Comedies*. London: Routledge, 1914.

Pask, Kevin. *The Emergence of the English Author: Scripting the Life of the Poet in Early Modern England*. Cambridge University Press, 1996.

Patinkin, Don. 'Mercantilism and the Readmission of the Jews to England'. *Jewish Social Studies* 8 (1946): 161–78.

Peters, Julie Stone. *Theatre of the Book 1480–1880: Print, Text, and Performance in Europe*. Oxford University Press, 2000.

Petrucci, Armando. 'Alle origini del libro moderno: Libri da banco, libri da bisaccia, libretti da mano'. *Italia medioevale e umanistica* 12 (1969): 295–313.

Phelps, Wayne H. 'The Leakes of St Dunstan's in the West: a Family of Seventeenth-Century Stationers'. *PBSA* 73 (1979): 86–9.

Pickwoad, Nicholas. 'Onward and Downward: How Binders Coped with the Printing Press before 1800'. Eds. Robin Myers and Michael Harris. *A Millennium of the Book: Production, Design and Illustration in Manuscript and Print, 900–1900.* Winchester: St Paul's Bibliographies, 1994. 61–106.

Piggott, J. R. 'Edward Alleyn's Books'. Eds. Aileen Reid and Robert Maniura. *Edward Alleyn: Elizabethan Actor, Jacobean Gentleman.* Dulwich Picture Gallery, 1994. 63–5.

Pitcher, John. 'Literature, the Playhouse, and the Public'. Eds. Barnard and McKenzie. *The Cambridge History of the Book in Britain, Volume IV.* 351–75.

Plant, Marjorie. *The English Book Trade: an Economic History of the Making and Sale of Books.* 2nd edn. London: George Allen and Unwin, 1965.

Pollard, Alfred W. *Shakespeare Folios and Quartos: a Study in the Bibliography of Shakespeare's Plays 1594–1685.* London: Methuen, 1909.

Pollard, A. W., and G. R. Redgrave, comp. *Short-Title Catalogue of Books Printed in England, Scotland, and Ireland, 1475–1640 and of English Books Printed Abroad.* 2nd edn. Rev. by W. A. Jackson, F. S. Ferguson and Katherine Panzer. 3 vols. London: Bibliographical Society, 1976–91.

Price, John, ed. *Thomas Dekker: 'The Noble Spanish Soldier'.* www.pricejb.pwp. blueyonder.co.uk (accessed 22 October 2012).

Prothero, G. W. 'A Seventeenth-Century Account Book'. *English Historical Review* 7 (1892): 88–102.

Proudfoot, Richard. 'Is There, and Should There Be, a Shakespeare Apocrypha?'. Ed. Christa Jansohn. *In the Footsteps of William Shakespeare.* Münster: LIT Verlag, 2005. 49–71.

'"Modernizing" the Printed Play-Text in Jacobean London: Some Early Reprints of *Mucedorus'.* Eds. Linda Anderson and Janis Lull. *'A Certain Text': Close Readings and Textual Studies on Shakespeare and Others in Honor of Thomas Clayton.* Newark: University of Delaware Press, 2002. 18–28.

'Shakespeare's Most Neglected Play'. Eds. Laurie E. Maguire and Thomas L. Berger. *Textual Formations and Reformations.* Newark: University of Delaware Press, 1998. 149–57.

Proudfoot, Richard, and Eric Rasmussen, eds. *The Two Noble Kinsmen.* Malone Society Reprints. Oxford University Press, 2005.

Proudfoot, Richard, Ann Thompson and David Scott Kastan, eds. *The Arden Shakespeare: Complete Works.* London: Thomson Learning, 2001.

Rasmussen, Eric. *The Shakespeare Thefts: In Search of the First Folios.* New York: Palgrave Macmillan, 2011.

Rasmussen, Eric, and Anthony James West. *The Shakespeare First Folios: a Descriptive Catalogue.* Basingstoke: Palgrave Macmillan, 2012.

Raven, James. *The Business of Books: Booksellers and the English Book Trade.* New Haven: Yale University Press, 2007.

The Records of the Stationers' Company 1554–1920. Cambridge: Chadwyck-Healey, 1987. 115 reels of microfilm.

Reid, Lindsay Ann. "'Certaine Amorous Sonnets, Betweene Venus and Adonis": Fictive Acts of Writing in *The Passionate Pilgrime* of 1612', *Études Épistémè* 21 (2012). revue.etudes-episteme.org/?certaine-amorous-sonnets-betweene (accessed 22 October 2012).

Rhodes, Neil. 'Shakespeare's Computer: Commonplaces/Databases'. *The Shakespearean International Yearbook: Where Are We Now in Shakespearean Studies?* 3 (2003): 249–67.

Ricci, Seymour de. *English Collectors of Books and Manuscripts (1530–1930) and their Marks of Ownership*. Cambridge University Press, 1930.

Ricci, Seymour de, ed. *Fulgens and Lucres*. New York: George D. Smith, 1920.

Rickard, Jane. 'The "First" Folio in Context: the Folio Collections of Shakespeare, Jonson and King James'. Eds. Meek, Rickard and Wilson. *Shakespeare's Book*. 207–32.

Ringler, Jr, William A., ed. *The Poems of Sir Philip Sidney*. Oxford University Press, 1962.

Robb, Dewar M. 'The Canon of William Rowley's Plays'. *Modern Language Review* 45 (1950): 129–41.

Roberts, Sasha. 'Reading the Shakespearean Text in Early Modern England'. *Critical Survey* 7 (1995): 299–306.

    Reading Shakespeare's Poems in Early Modern England. Basingstoke: Palgrave Macmillan, 2003.

Robertson, J. M. *An Introduction to the Study of the Shakespeare Canon, Proceeding on the Problem of 'Titus Andronicus'*. London: Routledge, 1924.

Roe, John, ed. *William Shakespeare: the Poems*. The New Cambridge Shakespeare. Cambridge University Press, 1992.

Rollins, Hyder Edward, ed. *England's Helicon 1600, 1614*. 2 vols. Cambridge, MA: Harvard University Press, 1935.

    ed. *The Poems*. A New Variorum Edition of Shakespeare. Philadelphia: Lippincott, 1938.

Rose, Mark. *Authors and Owners: the Invention of Copyright*. Cambridge, MA: Harvard University Press, 1993.

Rostenberg, Leona. *Literary, Political, Scientific, Religious and Legal Publishing, Printing and Bookselling in England, 1551–1700: Twelve Studies*. 2 vols. New York: Burt Franklin, 1965.

    'Thomas Thorpe, Publisher of "Shake-speares Sonnets"'. *PBSA* 54 (1960): 16–37.

Rowland, Richard. *Thomas Heywood's Theatre, 1599–1639: Locations, Translations, and Conflict*. Aldershot: Ashgate, 2010.

Roy, Ian. 'The Libraries of Edward, 2nd Viscount Conway, and Others: an Inventory and Valuation of 1643'. *Bulletin of the Institute of Historical Research* (May 1968): 35–46.

Saeger, James P., and Christopher J. Fassler. 'The London Professional Theater, 1576–1642: a Catalogue and Analysis of the Extant Printed Plays'. *RORD* 34 (1995): 63–109.

Saenger, Michael. *The Commodification of Textual Engagements in the English Renaissance*. London: Ashgate, 2006.

St Clair, William. *The Reading Nation in the Romantic Period*. Cambridge University Press, 2004.

Salt, S. P. 'Dering, Sir Edward, First Baronet (1598–1644)'. *ODNB*.

Savage, Richard. *Shakespearean Extracts from 'Edward Pudsey's Booke'*. Stratford-upon-Avon: Simpkin and Marshall, 1888.

Schoenbaum, S. *William Shakespeare: a Compact Documentary Life*. Rev. edn. Oxford University Press, 1987.

William Shakespeare: a Documentary Life. Oxford: Clarendon Press, 1975.

William Shakespeare: Records and Images. London: Scolar Press, 1981.

Schoenfeldt, Michael. *The Cambridge Introduction to Shakespeare's Poetry*. Cambridge University Press, 2010.

Schurink, Fred. 'An Unnoticed Early Reference to Shakespeare'. *NQ* 53 (2006): 72–5.

Scott, Charlotte. *Shakespeare and the Idea of the Book*. Oxford University Press, 2007.

Scott-Warren, Jason. 'Books in the Bedchamber: Religion, Accounting, and the Library of Richard Stonley'. Ed. John N. King. *Tudor Books and Readers: Materiality and the Construction of Meaning*. Cambridge University Press, 2010. 232–52.

'Harington, Sir John (*bap.* 1560, *d.* 1612)'. *ODNB*.

Sir John Harington and the Book as Gift. Oxford University Press, 2001.

Shaaber, M. A. 'The Meaning of the Imprint in Early Printed Books'. *The Library* 4th ser. 24 (1944): 120–41.

'Shakespeare in Quarto'. www.bl.uk/treasures/shakespeare/homepage.html (accessed 22 October 2012).

'The Shakespeare Quartos Archive'. www.quartos.org (accessed 22 October 2012).

Shapiro, Fred R., and Joseph Epstein. *The Yale Book of Quotations*. New Haven: Yale University Press, 2006.

Shapiro, James. *A Year in the Life of William Shakespeare: 1599*. London: Faber and Faber, 2005.

Sherlock, Peter. 'Bysshe, Sir Edward (*c.* 1610–1679)'. *ODNB*.

Sherman, William H. *John Dee: the Politics of Reading and Writing in the English Renaissance*. Amherst: University of Massachusetts Press, 1995.

'On the Threshold: Architecture, Paratext, and Early Print Culture'. Eds. Sabrina Alcorn Baron, Eric N. Lindquist and Eleanor F. Shevlin. *Agent of Change: Print Culture Studies after Elizabeth L. Eisenstein*. Amherst: University of Massachusetts Press, 2007. 67–81.

Used Books: Marking Readers in Renaissance England. Philadelphia: University of Pennsylvania Press, 2008.

Sider, J. W., ed. *The Troublesome Reign of John, King of England*. New York: Garland, 1979.

Sidney, Sir Philip. *Miscellaneous Prose of Sir Philip Sidney*. Eds. Katherine Duncan-Jones and Jan van Dorsten. Oxford: Clarendon Press, 1973.

Simpson, James. *The Oxford English Literary History: Volume II, 1350–1547: Reform and Cultural Revolution*. Oxford University Press, 2002.

Simpson, Percy. 'King Charles the First as Dramatic Critic'. *Bodleian Quarterly Record* 8 (1935–7): 257–62.

Smallwood, R. L., ed. *King John*. New Penguin Shakespeare. Harmondsworth: Penguin, 1974.

Smith, Denzell S. 'Francis Beaumont and John Fletcher'. Eds. Terence P. Logan and Denzell S. Smith. *The Later Jacobean and Caroline Dramatists: a Survey and Bibliography of Recent Studies in English Renaissance Drama*. Lincoln, NE: University of Nebraska Press, 1978. 3–89.

Smith, Helen. '"Imprinted by Simeon Such a Signe": Reading Early Modern Imprints'. Eds. Smith and Wilson. *Renaissance Paratexts*. 17–33.

Smith, Helen, and Louise Wilson, eds. *Renaissance Paratexts*. Cambridge University Press, 2011.

Smith, Robert M. 'Why a First Folio Shakespeare Remained in England'. *RES* 15 (1939): 257–64.

Spiller, Michael R. G. 'Drummond, William, of Hawthornden (1585–1649)'. *ODNB*.

Stallybrass, Peter, and Roger Chartier. 'Reading and Authorship: the Circulation of Shakespeare 1590–1619'. Ed. Andrew Murphy. *A Concise Companion to Shakespeare and the Text*. Oxford: Blackwell, 2007. 35–56.

Starner, Janet Wright, and Barbara Howard Traister, eds. *Anonymity in Early Modern England: 'What's in a Name?'*. Farnham: Ashgate, 2011.

Starza-Smith, Daniel. '"La Conquest du Sang Real": Edward, Second Viscount Conway's Quest for Books'. Eds. John Hinks and Matthew Day. *From Compositors to Collectors: Essays on Book-Trade History*. London: British Library, 2012. 191–208.

Steele, R. L. 'Humphrey Dyson'. *The Library* 3rd ser. 1 (1910): 144–51.

Stern, Tiffany. *Documents of Performance in Early Modern England*. Cambridge University Press, 2009.

   '"The Forgery of Some Modern Author"?: Theobald's Shakespeare and Cardenio's *Double Falsehood*'. *SQ* 62 (2011): 555–93.

   '"On Each Wall and Corner Poast": Playbills, Title-pages, and Advertising in Early Modern London'. *ELR* 36 (2006): 57–89.

   'Watching as Reading: the Audience and Written Text in Shakespeare's Playhouse'. Ed. Laurie Maguire. *How to Do Things with Shakespeare: New Approaches, New Essays*. Oxford: Blackwell, 2008. 136–59.

Stern, Virginia. *Gabriel Harvey: His Life, Marginalia and Library*. Oxford: Clarendon Press, 1979.

Stevenson, Allan H. 'Shirley's Publishers: the Partnership of Crooke and Cooke'. *The Library* 4th ser. 25 (1944): 140–61.

Stoddard, Roger E. 'Morphology and the Book from an American Perspective'. *Printing History* 17 (1987): 2–14.

Straznicky, Marta, ed. *Shakespeare's Stationers: Studies in Cultural Bibliography*. Philadelphia: University of Pennsylvania Press, 2013.

Suarez, Michael F., SJ. 'Historiographical Problems and Possibilities in Book History and National Histories of the Book'. *SB* 56 (2003–4): 141–70.

Swaen, A. E. H., ed. *How a Man May Choose a Good Wife from a Bad*. Louvain: A. Uystpruyst, 1912.

Swart, Felix. 'Chaucer and the English Reformation'. *Neophilologus* 62 (1978): 616–19.

Swift, Jonathan. *Poems*. Ed. Harold Williams. 3 vols. Oxford: Clarendon Press, 1958.

Swinburne, Algernon. *Contemporaries of Shakespeare*. London: Heinemann, 1919.

Tanselle, G. T. 'The Concept of Format'. *SB* 53 (2000): 67–115.

Taylor, Archer, and Frederic J. Mosher. *The Bibliographical History of Anonyma and Pseudonyma*. University of Chicago Press, 1951.

Taylor, F. 'The Books and Manuscripts of Scipio le Squyer, Deputy Chamberlain of the Exchequer, 1620–1659'. *Bulletin of the John Rylands Library* 25 (1941): 137–64.

Taylor, Gary. 'Blount, Edward (*bap*. 1562, *d*. in or before 1632)'. *ODNB*.

'The Canon and Chronology of Shakespeare's Plays'. Stanley W. Wells and Gary Taylor with William Montgomery and John Jowett. *William Shakespeare: a Textual Companion*. Oxford University Press, 1987. 69–144.

'The Fortunes of Oldcastle'. *ShS* 38 (1985): 85–100.

'Making Meaning Marketing Shakespeare 1623'. Eds. Peter Holland and Stephen Orgel. *From Performance to Print in Shakespeare's England*. Basingstoke: Palgrave, 2006. 55–72.

Reinventing Shakespeare: a Cultural History from the Restoration to the Present. London: Vintage, 1989.

'Some Manuscripts of Shakespeare's Sonnets'. *Bulletin of the John Rylands Library* 68 (1985–6): 210–46.

'The Structure of Performance: Act-Intervals in the London Theatres, 1576–1642'. Taylor and Jowett. *Shakespeare Reshaped*. 3–50.

'William Shakespeare, Richard James, and the House of Cobham'. *RES* 38 (1987): 334–54.

'Works Included in This Edition: Canon and Chronology: *The Widow*'. Gen. eds. Taylor and Lavagnino. *Thomas Middleton and Early Modern Textual Culture*. 379–82.

Taylor, Gary, assisted by Celia R. Daileader and Alexandra G. Bennett. 'The Order of Persons'. Eds. Taylor and Lavagnino. *Thomas Middleton and Early Modern Textual Culture*. 31–79.

Taylor, Gary, and John Jowett. *Shakespeare Reshaped, 1606–1623*. Oxford: Clarendon Press, 1993.

Taylor, Gary, and John Lavagnino, gen. eds. *Thomas Middleton: the Collected Works*. Oxford: Clarendon Press, 2007.

gen. eds. *Thomas Middleton and Early Modern Textual Culture: a Companion to the Collected Works*. Oxford: Clarendon Press, 2007.

Thomas, Keith. 'The Meaning of Literacy in Early Modern England'. Ed. Gerd Baumann. *The Written Word: Literacy in Transition*. Oxford: Clarendon Press, 1986. 97–131.

Travers, James. 'Aspley, William (*b*. in or before 1573, *d*. 1640)'. *ODNB*.

Veylit, Alain. 'Some Statistics on the Number of Surviving Printed Titles for Great Britain and Dependencies from the Beginnings of Print in England to the year 1800'. http://estc.ucr.edu/ESTCStatistics.html (accessed 22 October 2012).

Vickers, Brian. *'Counterfeiting' Shakespeare: Evidence, Authorship and John Ford's Funerall Elegye*. Cambridge University Press, 2002.

   Shakespeare, Co-Author: a Historical Study of Five Collaborative Plays. Oxford University Press, 2002.

   Shakespeare, 'A Lover's Complaint', and John Davies of Hereford. Cambridge University Press, 2007.

   'Thomas Kyd, Secret Sharer'. *TLS* (11 April 2008): 17–18.

   '*The Troublesome Raigne*, George Peele, and the Date of *King John*'. Ed. Brian Boyd. *Words That Count: Essays on Early Modern Authorship in Honor of MacDonald P. Jackson*. Newark: University of Delaware Press, 2004. 78–116.

Vickers, Sir Brian, gen. ed. *The Collected Works of John Ford*. 3 vols. Oxford University Press, 2011–.

Vitkus, Daniel, ed. *Three Turk Plays from Early Modern England*. New York: Columbia University Press, 2000.

Voss, Paul J. 'Books for Sale: Advertising and Patronage in Late Elizabethan England'. *Sixteenth Century Journal* 29 (1998): 733–56.

   'Printing Conventions and the Early Modern Play'. *MRDE* 15 (2002): 98–115.

Walker, Greg. *The Politics of Performance in Early Renaissance Drama*. Cambridge University Press, 1998.

Wall, Wendy. *The Imprint of Gender: Authorship and Publication in the English Renaissance*. Ithaca: Cornell University Press, 1993.

Walter, J. H. '*Revenge for Honour*: Date, Authorship and Sources'. *RES* 13 (1937): 425–37.

Warkentin, Germaine. 'The World and the Book at Penshurst: the Second Earl of Leicester (1595–1677) and his Library'. *The Library* 6th ser. 20 (1998): 325–46.

Watt, Tessa. *Cheap Print and Popular Piety, 1550–1640*. Cambridge University Press, 1991.

Weiss, Adrian. 'Casting Compositors, Foul Cases, and Skeletons: Printing in Middleton's Age'. Eds. Taylor and Lavagnino. *Thomas Middleton and Early Modern Textual Culture*. 195–225.

Wells, Stanley. 'General Introduction'. Gen. eds. Stanley Wells and Gary Taylor. *William Shakespeare: the Complete Works*. 2nd edn. Oxford: Clarendon Press, 2005. xv–xlii.

   'A New Early Reader of Shakespeare'. Eds. Meek, Rickard and Wilson. *Shakespeare's Book*. 233–40.

   'Works Included in This Edition: Canon and Chronology: *A Yorkshire Tragedy*'. Gen. eds. Taylor and Lavagnino. *Thomas Middleton and Early Modern Textual Culture*. 355–6.

Werstine, Paul. 'The Hickmott–Dartmouth Copy of *Love's Labour's Lost* Q1 (1598)'. *NQ* 32 (1985): 473.

West, Anthony James. *The Shakespeare First Folio: The History of the Book: Volume I, An Account of the First Folio Based on its Sales and Prices, 1623–2000.* Oxford University Press, 2001.

The Shakespeare First Folio: The History of the Book: Volume II, A New Worldwide Census of First Folios. Oxford University Press, 2003.

Wheeler, G. W., ed. *Letters of Sir Thomas Bodley to Thomas James, First Keeper of the Bodleian Library.* Oxford: Clarendon Press, 1926.

White, Paul Whitfield. 'Shakespeare, the Cobhams, and the Dynamics of Theatrical Patronage'. Eds. Paul Whitfield White and Suzanne R. Westfall. *Shakespeare and Theatrical Patronage in Early Modern England.* Cambridge University Press, 2002. 64–89.

Williams, Franklin B. 'Commendatory Verses: the Rise of the Art of Puffing'. *SB* 19 (1966): 1–14.

Index of Dedications and Commendatory Verses in English Books before 1641. London: Bibliographical Society, 1962.

'An Initiation into Initials'. *SB* 9 (1957): 163–78.

Williams, George Walton, and G. Blakemore Evans, eds. *The Dering Manuscript: William Shakespeare's History of King Henry the Fourth, as Revised by Sir Edward Dering, Bart.* Charlottesville: University Press of Virginia, 1978.

Williams, Kathleen. *Jonathan Swift: the Critical Heritage.* London: Routledge, 1996.

Williams, W. P. 'Paper as Evidence: the Utility of the Study of Paper for Seventeenth Century English Literary Scholarship'. Ed. Stephen Spector. *Essays in Paper Analysis.* Washington, DC: Folger Shakespeare Library, 1987. 191–9.

Willoughby, E. E. *A Printer of Shakespeare: the Books and Times of William Jaggard.* London: Allan and Co., 1934.

Wilson, Richard, Jane Rickard and Richard Meek. 'Introduction: "Th'World's Volume": Printer, Page and the Literary Field'. Eds. Meek, Rickard and Wilson. *Shakespeare's Book.* 1–26.

Woods, Susanne. *Lanyer: a Renaissance Woman Poet.* Oxford University Press, 1999.

Woudhuysen, H. R. 'Early Play Texts: Forms and Formes'. Eds. Ann Thompson and Gordon McMullan. *In Arden: Editing Shakespeare.* The Arden Shakespeare. London: Thomson Learning, 2003. 48–61.

'The Foundations of Shakespeare's Text'. *Proceedings of the British Academy* 125 (2004). 69–100.

Wright, Louis B. 'The Reading of Plays during the Puritan Revolution'. *Huntington Library Bulletin* 6 (1934): 73–108.

Yamada, Akihiro. *Thomas Creede: Printer to Shakespeare and his Contemporaries.* Tokyo: Meisei University Press, 1994.

Yeandle, Laetitia. 'The Dating of Sir Edward Dering's Copy of "The History of King Henry the Fourth"'. *SQ* 37 (1986): 224–6.

Young, Stephen Blase, ed. *A Critical Old-Spelling Edition of 'A Match at Midnight'.* New York: Garland, 1980.

Index